Inventing Human Science

Inventing Human Science

Eighteenth-Century Domains

EDITED BY

Christopher Fox, Roy Porter, and Robert Wokler

UNIVERSITY OF CALIFORNIA PRESS

Berkeley   Los Angeles   London

The publisher gratefully acknowledges the contribution
provided by the General Endowment Fund of the
Associates of the University of California Press
and the Institute for Scholarship in the Liberal
Arts, College of Arts and Letters, University
of Notre Dame

University of California Press
Berkeley and Los Angeles, California

University of California Press
London, England

Copyright © 1995 by
The Regents of the University of California

Library of Congress Cataloging-in-Publication Data
Inventing human science: eighteenth-century domains / edited by
Christopher Fox, Roy Porter, and Robert Wokler.
    p.   cm.
Includes bibliographical references and index.
ISBN 0–520–20010–1 (alk. paper)
    1. Social sciences—History—18th century.   2. Enlightenment.
I. Fox, Christopher, 1948–   . II. Porter, Roy, 1946–   .
III. Wokler, Robert, 1942–   .
H51.I58   1995
300'.9'034—dc20   95–6242
                                                              CIP

Printed in the United States of America

1 2 3 4 5 6 7 8 9

For John W. Yolton and
Robert M. Young

CONTENTS

vii

ILLUSTRATIONS

CONTRIBUTORS

David W. Carrithers is Adolph Ochs Professor of Government and Chair of the Department of Political Science at the University of Tennessee at Chattanooga. He is the editor of Montesquieu's *De l'esprit des lois* (1977) and the author of articles on such subjects as Montesquieu's philosophy of history, his republican theory, and his influence on Thomas Jefferson. An active member of the American Society for Eighteenth-Century Studies, he has served on that association's executive board and as Review Editor for *Eighteenth-Century Studies*.

Gloria Flaherty was Professor of German at the University of Illinois at Chicago. She had previously taught at Johns Hopkins, Northwestern, and Bryn Mawr College, where she also served as chair. A former president of the American Society for Eighteenth-Century Studies, she published articles on wide-ranging subjects and also wrote several books, including *Opera in the Development of German Critical Thought* (1978) and *Shamanism and the Eighteenth Century* (1992). Before her untimely death, she was nearing completion of a new book, *The Other Enlightenment: European Confrontations with the World and Its Peoples*.

Christopher Fox chairs the Department of English at the University of Notre Dame and also teaches in the Graduate Program in the History and Philosophy of Science. He is the author of *Locke and the Scriblerians: Identity and Consciousness in Early Eighteenth-Century Britain* (1988) and has edited and contributed to several books, including *Psychology and Literature in the Eighteenth Century* (1987), *Teaching Eighteenth-Century Poetry* (1990), *Walking Naboth's Vineyard: New Studies of Swift* (1995), and *Gulliver's Travels: Case*

Studies in Contemporary Criticism (1995). He is currently writing a book on Swift and science.

Gary Hatfield is Professor of Philosophy at the University of Pennsylvania. He has written *The Natural and the Normative: Theories of Spatial Perception from Kant to Helmholtz* (1990), which examines the historical interaction between psychological and philosophical theories of mind—and hence the origin of distinct philosophical and psychological conceptions of mind—focusing on the case of spatial perception. He has published several articles in the history and philosophy of psychology, including "The Sensory Core and the Medieval Foundations of Early Modern Perceptual Theory," which appeared in *Isis* in 1979, and articles on psychology in the works of Descartes and Kant, in the recent *Cambridge Companion* to each author.

Ludmilla Jordanova is Professor of History at the University of York. Her training has been in the Natural Sciences, History and Philosophy of Science, and Art History. She is the author of *Lamarck* (1984) and *Sexual Visions* (1989) and has edited and contributed to *Images of the Earth* (1979), *Women in Society* (1981), *Languages of Nature* (1986), and *The Enlightenment and Its Shadows* (1990). Currently, she is undertaking research on the cultural history of the family in eighteenth-century Britain and France and on the biomedical sciences in those countries between 1780 and 1820.

Roy Porter is Professor of Social History of Medicine at the Wellcome Institute for the History of Medicine. Recent books include *Mind Forg'd Manacles: Madness in England from the Restoration to the Regency* (1987), *A Social History of Madness* (1987), *In Sickness and in Health: The British Experience, 1650–1850* (1988), *Patient's Progress* (1989)—these last two co-authored with Dorothy Porter—and *Health for Sale: Quackery in England, 1660–1850* (1989).

Phillip Sloan is a Professor in the Program of Liberal Studies at the University of Notre Dame and also chairs the Graduate Program in the History and Philosophy of Science. His specialized work is in the history of life science in the eighteenth and nineteenth centuries. Recent publications include his *Richard Owen's Hunterian Lectures: May–June 1837* (1992), two articles in *Buffon 88: Colloque internationale* (1992), and the chapter titled "Natural History" for the *Companion of the History of Modern Science*, ed. J. Christie et al., (1991). He has coedited and translated (with John Lyon) *From Natural History to the History of Nature: Readings from Buffon and His Critics* (1981) and is currently working on the history of German life science in early Victorian Britain.

Roger Smith is a Senior Lecturer in History of Science, Department of History, Lancaster University. From 1987 to 1992 he was president of Cheiron:

The European Society for the History of Behavioural and Social Sciences, and he is the author of *Trial by Medicine: Insanity and Responsibility in Victorian Trials* (1981) and *Inhibition: History and Meaning in the Sciences of Mind and Brain* (1992).

Sylvana Tomaselli is an intellectual historian working predominantly on the seventeenth and eighteenth centuries. She was a Research Fellow of Newnham College, Cambridge (1985–88). Her publications include a translation of Jacques Lacan's *Seminar II: The Ego in Freud's Theory and in Psychoanalytic Technique* (1988). She edited with Roy Porter *Rape: An Historical and Social Enquiry* (1986) and *The Dialectics of Friendship* (1989). She has contributed to a number of reference works on the Enlightenment and other subjects. Her book *Seduction and Civilization: An Enlightenment Perspective on the History of Woman* will soon be published, as will her Cambridge edition of Mary Wollstonecraft's *Vindication of the Rights of Woman*.

Robert Wokler, Reader in the History of Political Thought at the University of Manchester, is joint editor of *Diderot's Political Writings*, a three-volume revised edition of John Plamenatz's *Man and Society* and *Rousseau and the Eighteenth Century* (all 1992), and the forthcoming *Cambridge History of Eighteenth-Century Political Thought*. His numerous publications in Rousseau, Enlightenment, and anthropological studies include *Rousseau on Society, Politics, Music, and Language* (1987), "Apes and Races in the Scottish Enlightenment," in *Science and Philosophy in the Scottish Enlightenment* (1987), *Rousseau* (1995), and *Rousseau's Enlightenment* (forthcoming 1996).

ACKNOWLEDGMENTS

For their help with this project, the editors especially thank T. Christopher Bond, Angela Brant, James G. Buickerood, Joseph Buttigieg, Julia Douthwaite, Greg Kucich, Laura Sue Fuderer, Nila Gerhold, Edward Manier, Philip Mirowski, David G. Schappert, and Margaret Stein. At the University of Notre Dame, Nathan O. Hatch has generously supported the project through the Graduate School, as has Dean Jennifer Warlick of the College of Arts and Letters, through the Institute for the Scholarship in the Liberal Arts. At the University of California Press, Elizabeth Knoll, Rebecca Frazier, Linda Benefield, and the editorial staff have also been a great source of support.

Everyone who ventures into these waters does so with the help and work of the scholars to whom this book is dedicated.

ONE

Introduction

How to Prepare a Noble Savage: The Spectacle of Human Science

Christopher Fox

Central to the intellectual revolution of the Enlightenment was the ambition of creating a science of man. Though it is difficult to speak with certainty about the precise birth of a given discipline, that "the human and the social sciences, or at least a certain number of them, were born during the eighteenth century" is a largely accepted view.[1] This birth was also proclaimed in the eighteenth century itself, in a flood of announcements and bold new titles such as Ernst Platner's *New Anthropology* (1771–72) or P. J. Barthez's *New Elements of the Science of Man* (1778). It is "a grand and beautiful sight," said Jean-Jacques Rousseau in 1750, "to see man . . . dissipate, by the light of his reason, the darkness in which nature had enveloped him." After soaring intellectually into the heavens, he has in recent generations done something "even grander and more difficult—come back to himself to study man and know his nature, his duties, and his end."[2] Several decades after that, Lord Kames would affirm that "Natural history, that of man especially, is of late years much ripened."[3] It "is but lately," Destutt Tracy would add, "that we have begun to occupy ourselves with some success on social economy." Progress was simply impossible, he says, "before the birth of the true study of the human understanding."[4] Adam Smith's work, claimed another contemporary, is "a specimen of a particular sort of inquiry . . . entirely of modern origin." It was only "reserved for modern times," he argued elsewhere, "to investigate those universal principles of justice and of expediency" that should "regulate the social order."[5] On opposite ends of the political spectrum, Edmund Burke condemned the brave new world of sophists, economists, and calculators; and the Marquis de Condorcet celebrated "those sciences, almost created in our own day, the object of which is man himself."[6]

Perhaps the best-known statement concerning the new "science of man"

1

appears in David Hume's *Treatise of Human Nature* (1739–40), where the attempt to describe the full extent of human cognitive and affective nature is portrayed as a radical departure. "Human Nature," writes Hume, "is the only science of man; and yet has been hitherto the most neglected. 'Twill be sufficient for me, if I can bring it a little more into fashion." Since there "is no question of importance, whose decision is not compriz'd in the science of man," he adds, in explaining "the principles of human nature, we in effect propose a compleat system of the sciences, built on a foundation almost entirely new." The second volume of his *Treatise*, he says later, contains "opinions, that are altogether as new and extraordinary" as those in the first.[7]

We should not mistake the rhetoric of discovery for discovery itself. Hume's own claim to novelty, for instance, might be qualified on several counts. For one, the term "science of man" is never fully defined by Hume; nor was it by earlier writers, like the late-seventeenth-century thinker Nicolas Malebranche, who also used it.[8] There also appear to be parallels between Hume's *Treatise* and the earlier work of the British philosopher Thomas Hobbes, especially his *Elements of Law* (1650).[9] The extent to which Hume, instead of breaking with tradition, was continuing the study of natural law pursued by Hobbes, Hugo Grotius, Samuel Pufendorf, and the Scots remains a question.[10] So does Hume's relation to "Newtonianism," which has turned out to be very difficult to trace.[11] This is not to reduce the genuine novelty of Hume's project or to say that science was unimportant to his concerns. Judging by his recently discovered membership in the Edinburgh University "Physiological Library," it appears that Hume had firsthand experience of experimental science, as a student in Robert Steuart's natural philosophy course in 1724–25. As Michael Barfoot shows, Steuart's brand of experimental philosophy—a "particular version of the mechanical philosophy, international in scope but exemplified in Britain by Boyle"—seems to have offered a special model for Hume's approach to human science, his attempt to "introduce the 'experimental' method of reasoning into moral philosophy."[12]

Important here are the broader connections between human science and natural science, which turn out to be more than rhetorical. In his project, Hume shares with contemporaries a new-felt need to "account for moral as for natural things."[13] In his own words, he wants to determine whether "the science of *man* will not admit of the same accuracy which several parts of natural philosophy are found susceptible of."[14] Paradoxically, what is most new is the desire to complete unfinished business. The "progress of the physical sciences," another writer would say, cannot be contemplated without "wishing to make the other sciences follow the same path."[15] Hume historicizes his own project, in arguing that the recent redefinition of the cosmos called for a corresponding redefinition of man in the cosmos. "[M]oral philosophy is in the same condition" now, he asserts, as astronomy was "before the time of *Copernicus.*" In an age following the scientific revolution, thinkers have nevertheless begun "to put the science of man on a new footing, and have engaged the attention, and excited the curiosity of the public."[16]

The distinctive feature of the eighteenth century—so Peter Gay argued in his classic study, *The Enlightenment, an Interpretation* (1966–69)—lay partly in the rediscovery of classical values, but above all in the impetus created by the scientific revolution, with its critical, progressive, and practical program. Natural philosophers from Copernicus to Newton had forged a science of nature. Eighteenth-century thinkers sought to cap this with a science of human nature. This point is also emphasized in more recent major histories, including Georges Gusdorf's massive survey of human science (1966–78)[17] and more specialized studies such as Michèle Duchet's *Anthropologie et histoire au siècle des lumières* (1971), Sergio Moravia's *Science and Philosophy in France, 1780–1815* (1974) and Keith Baker's *Condorcet: From Natural Philosophy to Social Mathematics* (1975).

These works were written at a time when intellectuals generally endorsed the aims and values of science. Since then, science itself has been the subject of vast scrutiny, both as a system of inquiry and in respect to its global impact. In the ensuing turmoil, we have heard much about the evils and mystifications of Enlightenment scientific rationality, notably through the writings of Michel Foucault. Though scholars have found much to correct in Foucault's history (or archaeology) of the human sciences, there is a growing sense that he brought to the study a certain self-consciousness that was needed. Baker, for instance, characterized Foucault's contention that a "human science was simply unthinkable" in the eighteenth century as "sheer intellectual provocation." Nonetheless, Foucault's contention (said Baker) "underlines the lack of definition" implied "in the characterizations of the idea of social science" in Gay and Gusdorf, and "it prompts a more critical consideration of the terms in which the history of the idea during this period should be written."[18]

A point Foucault brought to the fore was the significance of preconditions underlying categories of thought. Here, silence on a given subject is often as expressive as talk. In the present volume, Roger Smith, for example, examines the term *human nature,* which remained largely undefined, while providing a key organizing principle for eighteenth-century thought. Another question Foucault (and his mentor, Georges Canguilhem) raised was whether a given human science shares an unbroken continuity over time. That assumption, implied in earlier histories, tends to ignore ruptures, discontinuities, sometimes even history itself.[19] This critique underlies the more recent disciplinary history of Wolf Lepenies and others.[20]

From such work, we are learning that we cannot visit the eighteenth

century with a modern campus map. The human sciences did not have
the formal and conceptual structures of modern academic disciplines,
or the same institutional support. Even when the support was there—as
in the short-lived French Institute Class of Moral and Political Sciences
(1795–1803)—eighteenth-century disciplines such as "Human Geography"
do not always look or feel like ours.[21] As Gloria Flaherty's chapter in this
volume shows, sciences such as Franz Gall's "organology" or Johann Lavater's "physiognomy" are often crucial to our understanding of eighteenth-
century concerns. In fields with more familiar names, discontinuity is also
sometimes disconcertingly present. Even here, we cannot always assume
that nominal identity implies conceptual identity, that "psychology," for
example, meant the same thing to eighteenth-century thinkers it means to
us.[22]

Along with the new disciplinary history, the era since Gay and Gusdorf
has witnessed a major revisionist critique of the Enlightenment project
and the very idea of human science. To some extent, this has been fueled
by earlier critiques by anarchists like Theodor Adorno *and* by conserva-
tives like Lester Crocker, who have found the Enlightenment drive toward
a human science to be deeply perverse, counterproductive, and sinister.[23]

Two prominent figures in the more recent discussion are Jürgen Habermas and Foucault (though their promising debate over Kant's question
"What is Enlightenment?" was sadly cut short by Foucault's death).[24] Foucault found the human sciences to be a form of "insidiously operating disciplinary power"[25] generating "programs for a new man"[26] that would become twentieth-century nightmares. Habermas recognized the ill effects
of what he took to be Enlightenment developments but found the human
sciences still recoverable, through a new approach to reason and commu-
nicative action.[27] Important here, in either case, is the question of the uses
of "rationality" and so-called ends of enlightenment. As Roy Porter notes
elsewhere, "it is not good enough simply to applaud enlightened intellectuals for attempting to tackle social problems; we must also assess the
practical implications of their policies."[28] This issue is important to other
recent criticism that argues that dominant twentieth-century views of humans as accountable, knowing beings are the direct result of Enlightenment human sciences, and that those views are flawed. To this argument,
advanced by Alasdair MacIntyre and others, we could add the important
critiques of Richard Rorty of Enlightenment theories of cognition, and
Charles Taylor of mistaken models in the social sciences.[29]

A danger in such critiques is "the presumption"—as J. G. A. Pocock
puts it—that the Enlightenment itself is "a single unitary process, displaying a uniform set of characteristics."[30] The age itself, however, was
marked by extraordinary diversity, which made for many different self-
interpretations, often divided along ideological and national lines.[31] Even

today, the Enlightenment looks different in North America than it does (say) in Europe, where it is often believed to have taken a darker path.[32] In approaching Enlightenment human science, we must keep that larger diversity in view and remember that there were many competing conceptions at work.[33] Eighteenth-century writers were not always clear themselves about the specific status of the "science of man." A glance at its place in the map of knowledge in the *Encyclopédie* makes one appreciate Jean d'Alembert's comment that the "general system of the sciences and the arts is a sort of labyrinth, a tortuous road which the intellect enters without quite knowing what direction to take."[34] The "real universe and the way of ideas," his fellow Encyclopedist Diderot would add, "have an infinite number of aspects by which they may be made comprehensible, and the number of possible 'systems of human knowledge' is as large as the number of these points of view."[35] Such statements give us pause in any attempt to place early human science or the Enlightenment itself in a simple definitional frame.

The recent critique of the Enlightenment project has nevertheless enriched our understanding of the place of human science in eighteenth-century thought. Along with this work, the last several decades have also seen an explosion in eighteenth-century studies, as well as the opening up of feminist and other new techniques of inquiry—poststructuralist literary theories, for example, which have insisted that we should not take Enlightenment rhetoric, including scientific rhetoric, at face value.[36]

The result has been a refreshing widening of horizons; new light has been shed on old figures and problems. But the cost has been a certain fragmentation. Our perception of the eighteenth-century quest to make the human being an object of science has fallen out of focus. In spite of the recent stress on interdisciplinary approaches, the study has suffered from the divisions in the modern academic community. Historians of medicine, historians of science, historians of philosophy, intellectual historians, and literary historians have all approached Enlightenment human science from their own disciplinary points of view, which are unavoidably narrower than those held by eighteenth-century thinkers themselves. Given the current diffusion, it is our belief that the time is ripe for a critical but coherent reexamination of Enlightenment ideas of the subject. That is what the present volume attempts to do. In pursuing that end, this book takes a path that cuts across modern disciplinary boundaries. It also assumes a need to examine the wider public reaction to the scientific ideal.

Consider the domains of literature, entertainment, and spectacle, and what they might tell us about human science. One work that brings these together is Jonathan Swift's *Gulliver's Travels* (1726). In Part 2 (The Voyage to Brobdingnag) we find the sailor and hero, Lemuel Gulliver, stranded in a land populated by giants, and eventually brought to their king. Educated in natural philosophy and "particularly Mathematicks," the giant king (Gulliver notes) "observed my Shape exactly," and seeing "me walk erect, before I began to speak, conceived I might be a piece of Clock-work . . . contrived by some ingenious Artist." But after Gulliver speaks in a "regular and rational" way, the king is astonished. He asks Gulliver several questions (which receive "rational Answers, no otherwise defective than by a Foreign Accent") and then calls in the scholars. After the scholars "had a while examined my Shape with much Nicety," Gulliver tells us, they

> were of different Opinions concerning me. They all agreed that I could not be produced according to the regular Laws of Nature; because I was not framed with a Capacity of preserving my Life, either by Swiftness, or climbing of Trees, or digging Holes in the Earth. They observed by my Teeth, which they viewed with great Exactness, that I was a carnivorous Animal; yet . . . they could not imagine how I should be able to support my self, . . . which they offered by many learned Arguments to evince that I could not possibly do. One of them seemed to think that I might be an Embrio, or abortive Birth. But this Opinion was rejected by the other two, who observed my Limbs to be perfect and finished; and that I had lived several Years, as it was manifested from my Beard; the stumps whereof they plainly discovered through a Magnifying-Glass. They would not allow me to be a Dwarf, because my Littleness was beyond all Degrees of Comparison; for the Queen's favourite Dwarf, the smallest ever known in that Kingdom, was nearly thirty Foot high.

Finally, after much debate, the scholars declare him to be a "Lusus Naturae," a sport of nature.[37]

In Swift's satire, this scene and the events surrounding it evoke all kinds of eighteenth-century questions about what it means to turn a human creature (or a creature resembling a human) into an object of science. How does this creature stand, walk, talk, think, eat, survive? Where does he fit into a known order of nature, a *scala naturae*? How does he compare to other known creatures? Is he subject to natural law? If not, how is this creature to be categorized? How did he get to be this way: by design or by accident? Portraying Gulliver as a little speaking animal also brings up a question raised by Locke's example of the "rational parrot" in *An Essay concerning Human Understanding*.[38] To what extent is language a constituent of human identity? This would be explored throughout the eighteenth century by such figures as Giambattista Vico, Rousseau, Lord Monboddo, and Adam Smith. The larger question of language itself propels numerous eighteenth-century attempts to construct a science of man.

The scene in Swift also suggests ways in which the language of science—and of human science—penetrates the language of literature. The word "Clock-work," for example, in the question of how Gulliver moves, immediately evokes those "automatical men" and mechanical toys that had fascinated Descartes,[39] as well as subsequent debates over human motility and iatromechanical medicine satirized elsewhere by Swift and his friends John Arbuthnot and Alexander Pope in their *Memoirs of the Extraordinary Life, Works, and Discoveries of Martinus Scriblerus* (1741). There, we learn about a "great Virtuoso at Nuremberg" who has been employed

> to make a sort of an Hydraulic Engine, in which a chemical liquor resembling Blood, is driven through elastic chanels resembling arteries and veins, by the force of an Embolus like the heart, and wrought by a pneumatic Machine of the nature of the lungs, with ropes and pullies, like the nerves, tendons and muscles: And we are persuaded that this our artificial Man will not only walk, and speak, and perform most of the outward actions of the animal life, but (being wound up once a week) will perhaps reason as well as most of your Country Parsons.[40]

The question of whether Gulliver is an "Embrio, or abortive Birth" similarly evokes scientific talk about teratology and embryology (through perhaps a more famous literary preformationist figure would be Laurence Sterne's "little gentleman," Tristram Shandy's *homunculus*[41]). Embryology had occupied such scientists as William Harvey and Marcello Malphigi in the seventeenth century; in the eighteenth it would be vigorously pursued by John Needham, Lazzaro Spallanzani, Charles Bonnet, and Albrecht von Haller, among others.[42] Johann Friedrich Blumenbach, for instance, would rely on the study to deflate the belief that the Ethiopian's depressed nose comes from the mother's method of carrying the child. (That this results from nature and not art is shown, he says, by "the two Ethiopian foetuses preserved in the Royal Museum."[43]) From the time of Ambroise Paré, teratology or "the study of monstrous living forms"[44] had increasingly interested such medicos as Fortunio Liceti, whose *Of Monsters* (1616) would be translated and updated by the French physician Jean Palfyn in 1708. In the *New Organon*, Francis Bacon had called for the need to collect natural histories of "all monsters and prodigious births of nature"; by the eighteenth century, such investigations had become part of the normal study of anatomy and embryology, and viewed as the "key to understanding more regular phenomena."[45] The *Philosophical Transactions* of the Royal Society are filled with reports of anomalies like the Norfolk pigmy, John Coan, scrupulously weighed and measured by William Arderon on April 3, 1750.[46] Such pursuits did not escape satirists of the time. In *Tom Jones* (1749), Henry Fielding would complain that natural philosophy knows "nothing of Nature, except her monsters and imperfections" (XIII.v). In search of "the Curiosities of Nature," Swift's fictional scholar Dr. Martinus Scriblerus becomes obsessed with and marries a set of beautiful Siamese twins, described as "a Master-piece . . . for none but a Philosopher."[47]

Not unlike those fantastic Others who populated the pages of classical natural history and Renaissance cosmography[48] or the margins of maps, Gulliver fits no known Brobdingnagian category. It was as a sport of nature, a *homo monstrosus*, that he first attracted the court's attention. Before he was scrutinized by the scientists, Gulliver had been discovered and exhibited by an enterprising farmer turned monster-monger. Being "carried about" and "exposed for Money as a public Spectacle" ruined Gulliver's health. In a few short weeks the numerous performances (he says) nearly reduced him "to a Skeleton."[49] Having Gulliver transported in a box—much the way the German "Dwarf of the World" was in eighteenth-century London—plays off the popular rage for human oddities.[50] In Swift's century, argued one historian, the "taste for Monsters became a disease."[51] Whether or not this is true, the eighteenth century was certainly a time when man made a spectacle of himself. In early eighteenth-century London alone, along with the Dwarf of the World who arrived by request "in a little box," one could see the Painted Prince, in whom "the whole Mystery of Painting or Staining upon Human Bodies seem[s] to be comprised in one stately piece"; or, for more limited engagements during the weeks of Bartholomew Fair, that "Admirable Work of Nature, a Woman having Three Breasts; and each of them affording Milk at one time, or differently, . . . as they are made use of."[52]

Interesting here in Gulliver's story is the movement from the spectacle of the sideshow to the spectacle of science—a pattern often repeated by actual eighteenth-century figures, such as the Norfolk pigmy discovered on display in Norwich, or Hopkin Hopkins, the thirty-one-inch fifteen-year-old found on exhibition near Bristol in 1751 and reported in volume 47 of the *Philosophical Transactions* to be "*wonderful in the sight of all beholders.*"[53] A later and more dramatic case was that of the Irishman Charles Byrne, who suffered from acromegaly, or uncontrollable growth. After arriving in London in April 1782, he was advertised as the

> *Irish Giant.* To be seen this, and every day this week, in his large elegant room, at the cane shop, next door to late Cox's Museum, Spring Gardens. Mr. Byrne, the surprising Irish Giant, who is allowed to be the tallest man in the world; only 21 years of age. His stay will not be long in London, as he proposes shortly to visit the Continent. . . . Hours of admittance every day, Sundays excepted, from 11 till 3; and from 5 till 8, at half-a-crown each person.[54]

Despite Byrne's precautions to avoid such a fate, on his untimely death the hungry surgeons (so a report ran) "surrounded his house just as Greenland harpooners would an enormous whale."[55] Ironically, his performing days in London were not over. Byrne reappears in a nineteenth-century catalogue of the Hunterian Museum, as "No. 1. The skeleton of Charles Byrne or O'Brian. . . . 'the famous Irish Giant, whose death is said to have been precipitated by excessive drinking. In August 1780 he measured eight feet. . . .' This skeleton measures eight feet in height."[56] Gulliver's complaint about being reduced to a skeleton was close to actual truth for some eighteenth-century "monsters."

Gulliver in Brobdingnag is not only strange because of his size; he also speaks with a "Foreign Accent"[57] and comes from parts unknown. This suggests a related point about the eighteenth-century presentation of human spectacles. Freaks and exotics often shared the same stage. At Bartholomew Fair, for example, one could see "A Prodigious Monster . . . a Man with one Head and two distinct Bodies, both Masculine," and "with him his Brother, who is a Priest of the Mahometan Religion."[58] The "discoveries that have been made by European navigators upon distant oceans and along distant coasts," Schiller would later say, "afford us a spectacle as instructive as it is entertaining."[59] Many exotics, from American Indians to South Sea islanders, literally entertained audiences of the time.

William Dampier would bring the islander Jeoly from the southern Philippines to England in 1691. With his body painted in ornamental fashion "all down the breasts," on "his thighs," and in "several broad rings, or bracelets round his arms and legs," Jeoly would be shown in various sideshows before he died of smallpox at Oxford.[60] Years later, in the summer of 1762, three Cherokee chiefs from the Carolina-Tennessee mountains would be shipped to London by the Indian fighters Henry Timberlake and Thomas Sumter, and subsequently shown in a pub that advertised, "*Walk in, Gentlemen, see 'em alive!*" The *London Chronicle* lamented the Cherokees' reception at Vauxhall, asking:

> What . . . can apologize for people running in such shoals to all public places, at the hazard of health, life, or disappointment, to see the savage chiefs that are come among us? . . . These poor creatures make no more than theatrical figures, and can be seen with no satisfaction from the pressure of a throng: why then are people mad in their avidity to behold them? . . . to read in the papers, how these poor wild hunters were surrounded by as [many] wild gazers on them at Vauxhall, and that three hundred eager crouders were made happy by shaking hands with them. . . . I should like to read a letter (if they could write one) on that subject, to their friends at home, in order to learn what they think of the mad savages of Great Britain.[61]

The stage metaphor implied in these examples is now new, of course. The connection between theater and display of the body had roots in the elaborate ritual attending medieval and Renaissance dissections, which seem to have been understood as a form of performance or entertainment. This element was heightened by the virtuosity of Andreas Vesalius[62] and, later, by such developments as the construction of the spectacular anatomy theater at Leiden (1591)[63] and the appearance of various *kunstkammern,* or cabinets of curiosities, like that in the Great Chamber at Delft. Here, the Surgeons' Guild displayed such marvels as "a baby's body preserved in alcohol," "hermaphrodites, bearded women, strange tumours and diseases," along with the skeleton of a murderer who served as a mannequin for American Indian feather work.[64] In Oxford in the seventeenth century, there was also an exhibit of anatomical specimens on the first floor of the south side of the Bodleian.[65]

Much of this carried over into the eighteenth century, including the interest in the drama of public dissection, still vivid in William Hogarth's "The Reward of Cruelty," exposing executed Tom Nero's end under the knife at Surgeon's Hall. But there were also significant shifts of emphasis. Among these was the appearance of new exhibits that put more attention on the human place in nature, and on what Comte de Buffon came to call "the natural history of man."[66] The great seventeenth-century "collectors," said Blumenbach, had "embraced the history of all the three animal kingdoms; everything in fact, with the single and solitary exception of the natural history of man." It has been left to the eighteenth century to learn "that man also is a natural product."[67] That "MAN" is, as Adam Ferguson states, "an animal in the full extent of that designation"[68] was dramatically demonstrated by the growing inclusion of human artifacts and remains in various natural history collections, the best known of which perhaps were those of Blumenbach and Petrus Camper on the Continent and John Hunter in Britain. Like the British Museum (founded in 1753) and the later Louvre (1793),[69] such collections were stocked by colonial expansion and the great voyages of discovery, especially into the eighteenth century's "new world," the Pacific.[70] With the improved navigational equipment of such instrument makers as John Hadley (1682–1744) and Jesse Ramsden (1735–1800),[71] explorers visited and revisited exotic lands, returning with riches and rarities and "ever-increasing numbers of ethnographic specimens." As one recent commentator notes, "in the eighteenth century the *Kunstkammer*" in a sense "exploded so that instead of a collection including one or two amber bottles," a whole room would be filled with them.[72]

The collecting of human remains also picked up considerably in the latter part of the century, especially in the wake of the voyages of Captain James Cook (1768–1779). According to Georges Cuvier at the end of the century, however, this important work still lagged behind. In a memoir prepared for the Baudin Australian expedition (1800–1804), Cuvier would call for a search for savage skeletons. Every opportunity should be taken, he said, to bring the bones home. Once obtained, through (or by observing) battles with native peoples or by visiting "the places where the dead are deposited," preparing specimens for a trip to Europe would be easy. "To boil the bones in a solution of caustic potash and rid them of their flesh is a matter of several hours." It would also be advisable to save some heads with flesh intact. One had only to dip them in a solution of corrosive sublimate, and hang them out to dry.[73] Such headhunting had gone on for some time. In a collection he liked to call his "Golgotha,"[74] Blumenbach displayed in the late eighteenth century "the head of a Carib chief, who died at St. Vincent eight years ago, and whose bones, at the request of [Sir Joseph] Banks, were dug up there" during a voyage of Cook. In a prefatory letter to the third edition of *On the Natural Variety of Mankind* (1795) Blumenbach would tell Banks: "For many years past you have spared neither pains nor expense to enrich my collection of the skulls of different nations with those specimens I was so anxious above all to obtain."[75]

One wonders about the natives' response to such activities. A gauge might be the reaction of Eskimos who came from Labrador to London in the 1770s. Rattled by the sight of skeletons in Dr. John Hunter's Museum, one asked: "Are these the bones of Esquimaux whom Mr. Hunter has killed and eaten?" "Are we to be killed?" "Will he eat us, and put our bones there?"[76] Though such fears were laid to rest, they were in some sense justified. Blumenbach would later speak of those "wonderfully worn teeth in two Esquimaux skulls which have lately come to me," and list, among his ethnological rarities, "Ettuiack, an Esquimaux magician; brought to London in 1773 from the coast of Labrador."[77]

For the European scientists, such collecting was, of course, a prerequisite for systematic comparison and classification. An eighteenth-century Englishman would speak admiringly of Hunter's heads, which were

> placed upon a table in a regular series, first shewing the human skull, with its varieties, in the European, the Asiatic, the American, the African; then proceeding to the skull of a monkey, and so on to that of a dog; in order to demonstrate the gradation both in the skulls, and in the upper and lower jaws. On viewing this range, the steps were so exceedingly gradual and regular that it could not be said that the first differed from the second more than the second from the third, and so on to the end.[78]

Before John Hunter's museum, William Blizard would say in 1823, such collections had been simple "Gazing Stocks, for Admiration." After, Thomas Chevalier would add, the natural history exhibit was no longer "a mere cabinet of rarities" but "a systematic and illuminated record of the operations and products of life."[79]

This does not downplay the performative aspect of such displays. John Hunter began his collection in 1770s in his Jermyn Street residence and, when it outgrew his house, moved the exhibit to 28 Leicester Square. Shown periodically to visiting scientists and distinguished guests, the exhibit would end up on permanent view in the Royal College of Surgeons, where it would attract a reported 32,208 visitors between 1800 and 1833.[80] Blumenbach, whose own collection of skulls in his estimate surpassed those of Petrus Camper (the father of the facial angle) and of John Hunter, spoke of the spectacular force of human rarities. A "most beautiful skull of a Georgian female" seems to have been a prized possession. Fair even in death, this "beautiful typical head of a young Georgian female," Blumenbach said, "always of itself attracts every eye, however little observant."[81] Along with these exhibits, smaller ones proliferated, like that of Charles White of Manchester, the author of *An Account of the Regular Gradation In Man* (1799). "Mr. White's museum," said Thomas De Quincey, "furnished attractions to an unusually large variety of tastes." De Quincey, who visited White's exhibit as a child, would later regret that "nothing except the *humanities* of the collection" survived—one a skeleton, the other a modern mummy of a former patient of White's who reportedly left him £25,000. She did so on the condition that he would embalm her "as perfectly as the resources in that art of London and Paris could accomplish" and that, annually in front of witnesses, he would lift the veil from her face. "The lady," said De Quincey, "was placed in a common English clock-case, having the usual glass face: but a veil of white velvet obscured from all profane eyes the silent features behind. The clock I had myself seen, when a child, and had gazed upon it with inexpressible awe."[82]

When Volney called in the 1790s for the establishment of a museum that would truly represent the "science of man,"[83] his suggestion had been prepared for by a series of eighteenth-century exhibits. The involvement of the spectator connects these eighteenth-century productions to the larger "practice of public display" Simon Schaffer has found to mark natural philosophy of the time.[84]

Other spectacles were available to more exclusive audiences. Among these were the live specimens shown in "the laboratory of polite society"[85] or to more specialized individuals and groups, such as the Société des Observateurs de l'Homme. The first category would include the parade of feral children who marched in and out of attention—Wild Peter of Hanover, sent to Dr. John Arbuthnot for study, the Wild Girl of Champagne, the Wild Boy of Aveyron entrusted to Dr. Jean-Marc-Gaspard Itard, and others.[86] This group would also take in the long line of exotics—Louis Antoine de Bougainville's Ahutoru, Tobias Furneaux's Omai, Joseph Banks's Tupia—brought back for European view. When Banks left Tahiti with his very own Tahitian, the plan was to keep him as a curiosity, the way (said Banks) "some of my neighbors do lions and tygers," though "at greater expense than he will probably ever put me to."[87] When Duke Frederick I built an oriental village (with gardens and pagodas) in Germany, he planned a grander display, to be completed by the insertion of live Chinese. None could be found, however, so he settled a group of Africans there instead, to study "their customs and anatomy." Most died, at least one committing suicide. The anatomist Samuel Thomas von Sömmerring dissected several and wrote a basic book on African physique.[88] In France, L.-F. Jauffret's Observateurs de l'Homme (founded in late 1799) had better luck locating an actual Chinese when the Cantonese Tchong-A-Sam was taken off an English ship and brought to Paris. Tchong-A-Sam was examined by Cuvier to ascertain race and nationality. His skull was measured to Blumenbach's classifications. His face was sketched for J.-J. Virey's *Histoire naturelle du genre humain.* His reactions were monitored as he was handed various objects and instructed to put on (what were believed to be) Chinese clothes. He was studied intensely by Roche-Ambroise Cucurron Sicard, the director of the Institute for the Deaf-Mute. Tchong-A-Sam also managed to escape.[89]

If Tchong-A-Sam's experience highlights the eighteenth-century interest in human spectacle, it also returns us to our originating scene in Swift, and points to some larger issues underlying the present book. Not the least of these pertains to the so-called birth of the observer. The Brobdingnagians, we recall, do not simply look at Gulliver; they stare at him.[90] Even after being removed from the public eye, Gulliver is "observed" by the king, then handed over to the scholars who "examined" his shape "with much Nicety," "observed" his teeth (which are "viewed with great Exactness"), "observed" his limbs, and finally put him under "a Magnifying-Glass."[91] The operative verb here is obvious. Gulliver is under the gaze.

But it is not that simple, for Gulliver is gazing back. In his minute view of such objects as Brobdingnagian breasts, Gulliver indeed becomes a kind of human microscope, detailing the coarseness and dark patches of skin in graphic ways that parody descriptions in such works as Robert Hooke's *Micrographia* and the *Philosophical Transactions.*[92] Like any scientifically literate sailor, Gulliver also manages to return from Brobdingnag with his own "Collection of Rarities" (mostly anatomical).[93] And he later publishes an account of the Brobdingnagian land and people as part of his larger book subtitled *Travels Into Several Remote Regions of the World.* (As one scholar quips, "No fellow of the Royal Society could do more."[94]) Gulliver celebrates modern ways of knowing—including the modern love of quantification—and criticizes the Brodingnagians for "not having hitherto reduced *Politicks* into a *Science,* as the more acute Wits of Europe have done."[95] Along with being observed, Gulliver then is also an observer, in a self-consciously scientific sense.[96]

The complications of this relation are captured nicely in a nineteenth-century illustration by J. J. Grandville,[97] which shows Gulliver observing and simultaneously being observed by a great Brobdingnagian eye. In this illustration (fig. 1.1), both spectators are so close that it is hard to see how either can get a clear view of the other. Gulliver's position, resting an elbow on a rounded ledge, makes him almost appear to be *inside* the giant eye. Gulliver cannot remove himself from what he sees. Though what he sees—that sharp "M" in the gigantic lens—appears to be clear and distinct, what it means is far from clear and distinct. What we have here is the illusion of clarity, the fiction of some objective truth. The "loss of the detached spectator 'out there'"[98] has been a recent theme in the history of the human sciences (especially since Foucault's analysis of Diego Velázquez's "Las Meninas" in *The Order of Things*), as has the question of how one "can be both an object in the world and a subject constituting that world."[99] In Swift's satire we find a similar questioning of the very possibility of a detached point of view. As a number of essays here suggest, "observation" is a central problem in eighteenth-century human science and in our constructions of it.

The Brobdingnagians' view of Gulliver raises other issues, among these, questions about the uses of comparison. Comparison, of course, is central to *Gulliver's Travels*. (As Samuel Johnson would comment, one only had to imagine the big people and the little people, and the rest of Swift's work would follow.[100]) Yet, it is the failure to find such grounds that frustrates the Brobdingnagian scientists. Gulliver's littleness is "beyond all Degrees of Comparison."[101] Establishing clear criteria for comparison was a key question in human science. "Not until the late seventeenth and early eighteenth centuries," we learn, for instance, "did comparison become, instead of an . . . accessory to anatomy, the primary aim of the science."[102] The comparison of humans with other primates in such works as Edward Tyson's *Anatomie of a Pygmie* (1699) and Petrus Camper's *Account of the Organs of Speech in the Orang-Outang* (1779)[103] was increasingly matched by comparisons *within* the human group itself—between different races, cultures, and sexes.

The last is suggested by the title alone of E.-T. Moreau's *A Medical Question: Whether Apart from Genitalia There Is a Difference Between the Sexes?* (1750). Moreau and others—including the French physician Pierre Roussel and the German anatomist Jakob Ackermann—sparked a movement in the second half of the century to establish comparative differences between men and women that go well beyond their respective modes of reproduction.[104] Sexual difference also played a part in eighteenth-century discussions of cultural difference, if we judge by such writings as J.-F. Lafitau's *Customs of the American Indians* (1724), with its comments on gynocracy and the occupations of Iroquois women,[105] or Francis Moore's *Travels Into the Inland Parts of Africa* (1736), with its account of an evening

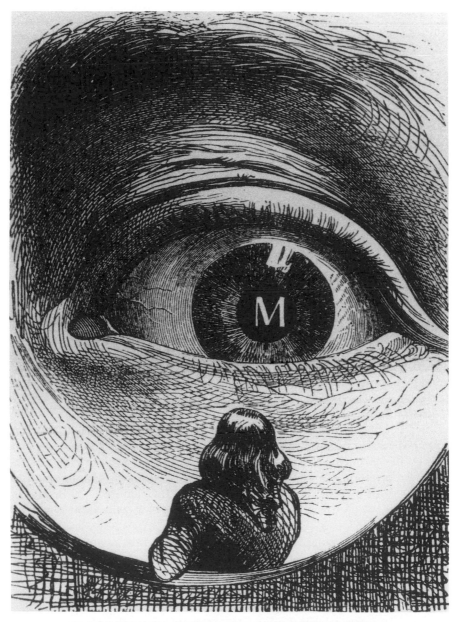

Fig. 1.1. From Jean Ignace Isidore Gerard (J.J.) Grandville's
Gulliver's Travels (1838; reprint, Arlington, Va., 1980).
Courtesy of the University of Notre Dame Library.

encounter with a "*Mumbo Jumbo.*" This figure, "a kind of cunning Mystery" among "the *Mundigoes*" is, Moore says,

> dressed in a long Coat made of the Bark of Trees, with a Tuff of fine Straw on the Top of it, and when the Person wears it, it is about eight or nine Foot high. This is a Thing invented by the Men to keep their Wives in awe, who are so ignorant (or at least are obliged to pretend to be so) as to take it for a Wild Man; and indeed no one but what knows it, would take it to be a Man, by reason of the dismall Noise it makes, and which but few of the Natives can manage. It never comes abroad but in the Night-time, which makes it have the better Effect. Whenever the Men have Dispute with the Women, this *Mumbo Jumbo* is sent for to determine it; which is, I may say, always in Favor of the Men.[106]

Cross-cultural comparison was also important to various attempts to construct stadial theories of progess[107] and conjectural histories of man, explored here in Robert Wokler's chapter on the subject (chapter 2). In "the beginning all the World was *America*," said Locke.[108] Eighteenth-century Europeans believed that traveling in space also meant traveling in time; the Others they encountered were earlier versions of themselves. It is in the Indians' "present condition, that we are to behold, as in a mirrour, the features of our own progenitors," claimed Adam Ferguson.[109] We "possess at this time very great advantages towards the knowledge of human nature," wrote Edmund Burke, for "now the great map of mankind is unrolld at once; and there is no state or gradation of barbarism, and no mode of refinement which we have not at the same instant under our view."[110]

It was understandable, then, to identify North American Indians with earlier peoples in the Bible or with the German tribes in Tacitus. It was also a measure of how far Europeans had come, especially in an age that coined the term *civilization* and embraced the idea of progress. This raises a related question. To what extent did cultural hegemony and nationalism shape various human sciences—anthropology, for example—by inventing a "past" by which the progress of present European civilization might be judged?[111]

In any case, in comparing European and non-European peoples, sex and gender again play significant roles. In *Observations of Savage Peoples* (1800), Joseph-Marie Degérando remarks, "it seems that consideration for the female sex is an effect of civilization."[112] The "subjection of the weaker sex," Turgot had argued earlier, is "always bound up with barbarism."[113] Savages, said Buffon, are "tyrannical to their women"[114]—a point also affirmed in Richard Payne Knight's *The Progress of Civil Society* (1796).[115] In the accounts we have of "savage nations," reports Thomas Robert Malthus in his *Essay on Population*, "the women are represented as much more completely in a state of slavery than the poor are to the rich in civilized countries."[116] J. R. Forster, who sailed with Captain Cook, agreed. "The rank assigned to women in domestic society, among the various nations, has," he says, "so great an influence on their civilization and morality, that I cannot leave this subject, without adding a few remarks. The more debased the situation of a nation is, and of course the more remote from civilization, the more harshly we found the women treated."[117]

It is not surprising then to find John Millar beginning his work *The Origin of the Distinction of Ranks* (third edition, 1781) with a long chapter titled "The Rank and Condition of Women In Different Ages." For Millar and other social theorists, the treatment of women is the central comparative mark by which a group's relative degree of "civilization" can be judged.[118] Such accounts rarely question whether this might also be a problem in "civilized" Europe. That critique is nonetheless suggested in the representations of exotic women[119] made by such writers as Mme de Graffigny and Diderot. As Ludmilla Jordanova shows in chapter 6, it is also implied in the cross-cultural comparisons in works like Montesquieu's *Lettres persanes* (1721). Defining the ends and limits of comparative thinking is an issue that cuts across many eighteenth-century concerns.

As *Gulliver's Travels* suggests, cultural productions like literature can tell us much about constructions of human science. The use of Swift's satire, however, should not obscure the fact that the aim of this volume is investigative rather than polemical. Our study neither repudiates nor uncritically endorses the concept of human science. Instead, it explores various meanings this project held for eighteenth-century thinkers and activists when they spoke about the human place in nature, about medicine and mind and language and human origins, about human nature and natural law, about man as a social and legal being or as a member of a family group, about racial and sexual difference, about getting and spending, or about population and politics. Our analysis of these and other eighteenth-century domains is set both against a longer chronological perspective and in the context of the real social, economic, political, and cultural milieux of the ancien régime. The contributors discuss debates within their fields, but their chapters are not primarily historiographical. Instead, each has been asked to present an interpretation in an original and challenging manner.

In exploring the human place in nature, Phillip Sloan, for instance, studies the development of two competing conceptions of the "natural history of man," those of Carolus Linnaeus (1707–1778) and Georges-Louis Leclerc, Comte de Buffon (1707–1788) (chapter 5). It was in the context of this rivalry, Sloan shows, that Buffon's revolutionary views of physical truth and species, and his application of these principles to human beings, took shape. One major implication is that man is an animal among animals, a species subject to "zoogeographical" analysis. Another is a long-standing physiological basis for a concept of "race" as distinguished from geographical "variety."

The stress on geophysical determinants (evident in such writers as Buffon and John Arbuthnot) was not in itself unique. Climate had occupied Western medical thinking at least since Hippocrates' classic tract, "Airs, Waters, and Places."[120] As Roy Porter argues (chapter 3), such determinants nonetheless took on new importance in eighteenth-century medical attempts to study man as an embodied being, and to extrapolate human destiny from anatomy. Eighteenth-century medicine embraced a positive environmentalism in searching for larger relations between health and disease and modes of life. Why, for example, did sickness levels vary from society to society, and from group to group? In exploring such questions, medical reformers sought to forge a science of man based on observation and experience, a study of biomedical regularities, and a new stress on education and public health.

Education itself took on added significance in the eighteenth century, especially in light of the natural history of the understanding set forth by John Locke (1632–1704). The Lockean child came into the world intellectually as well as physically naked—a blank slate (or tabula rasa) open to inscriptions of experience. That child would in fact learn about the world *only* through experience. This had enormous implications for human science of the time. Children were not just born into their worlds; they were *made* by their worlds. Theoretically, if one could change the surroundings—be they familial, social, economic, political, or institutional—one could change the child. This new sense of human possibility shaped much Enlightenment thought.

This sense of human malleability was certainly prominent, as Ludmilla Jordanova shows (chapter 6), in eighteenth-century views of the family, sex, and gender. Here, a child's mind and body were believed to be molded by continual interaction with the setting. For the French hygienists or for a *philosophe* like Claude-Adrien Helvétius, environment was everything. As David Carrithers argues (chapter 8), the same can be said with some modifications about the thought of a social theorist like Montesquieu, who gave real attention to environmental influences, both moral and physical, on human behavior. The physical influence on human behavior plays a role, as well, in eighteenth-century political thought, examined here by Robert Wokler (chapter 11).

If a child develops consciousness through time in a given environment, so (it was believed) does an entire people. "Not only the individual advances from infancy to manhood," Adam Ferguson went so far to assert, "but the species itself from rudeness to civilization."[121] In a somewhat different formulation, Giambattista Vico (1668–1744) argued for what Roger Smith (chapter 4) calls "a new understanding of man as a cultural being constituted through a historical process." As Wokler also shows, this idea undergirds the new social anthropology and Enlightenment attempts to construct conjectural history. A key concern here is the study of language, which accelerated with the work of Locke and Etienne Bonnot de Condillac (1714–1780). Through the study of language itself, Lord Monboddo and others believed, one could trace the history of human progress and even "enter into the thoughts that guided earlier peoples."[122]

Interacting with their worlds, humans are also very much what their needs make them. This point is investigated by Sylvana Tomaselli in her chapter on eighteenth-century economic thought, which extended the work of such earlier figures as Sir William Petty (1623–1687). Tomaselli's examination of demographic thinking (chapter 10) touches on an important factor raised by Roy Porter and several other contributors—the "quantifying spirit in the 18th century"[123] and its special application to a science of man. The new faith in numbers was also evident in several non-normal sciences, examined here by Gloria Flaherty (chapter 9).

This is not to equate progress in human science with progress in quantitative description of phenomena. As Gary Hatfield points out in his chapter on psychology as a natural science, the "eighteenth century was replete with novel observations of sensory phenomena, including after-images and color blindness, that were not quantitative" (chapter 7). Even if we decide to limit (or reduce) our exploration to quantitative or so-called empirical approaches, we will discover no one "single disciplinary matrix" at work. The question is more complicated than that.

In exploring such subjects, this book is meant finally to be suggestive rather than exhaustive. Granting that there were diverse views of human science in the eighteenth century, one scholar spoke some years ago of a need to "characterize these approaches more clearly, analyze their nature and development, and clarify their relationship to the more general evolution of Enlightenment thought."[124] This book pursues those larger goals, in light of scholarship of the last decade. In the process, we hope to chart some key directions for future work.

ACKNOWLEDGMENTS

I wish to thank T. Christopher Bond, Thomas Bonnell, Julia V. Douthwaite, Roy Porter, and Phillip Sloan for comments on an earlier draft of this chapter, and the American Council of Learned Societies for generous support while I worked on this and other projects.

NOTES

1. Sergio Moravia, "The Enlightenment and the Sciences of Man," *History of Science* 18 (1980): 247–268, especially 247. Also see *The History of the Human Sciences* 6 (1993), which is devoted to the origins of the human sciences, and see Richard Olson, *The Emergence of the Social Sciences, 1642–1792* (New York: Twayne Publishers, 1993).

2. Jean-Jacques Rousseau, *Discourse which won the Prize of the Academy of Dijon in the Year 1750*, in *The First and Second Discourses*, trans. Roger D. and Judith R. Masters (New York: St. Martin's Press, 1964), 35.

3. Henry Home, Lord Kames, *Sketches of the History of Man*, 3 vols. (Edinburgh: W. Creech, 1813), 1:55.

4. Destutt Tracy, *A Treatise On Political Economy To Which is Prefixed A Supplement to a Proceeding Work On the Understanding or, Elements of Ideology*, trans. Thomas Jefferson (1817; reprint, New York: Augustus M. Kelley, 1970), 69, 135.

5. Dugald Stewart, "Account of the Life and Writings of Adam Smith, L.L.D.," in Adam Smith's *The Theory of Moral Sentiments . . . To Which is added, A Dissertation on the Origin of Languages . . . With A Biographical And Critical Memoir of the Author* (London: Henry G. Bohn, 1853), xlix, xxxiv.

6. Edmund Burke, *Works of the Right Honourable Edmund Burke*, 16 vols. (London, 1815), vol. 2: *Reflections on the Revolution in France*, 149. Also see Condorcet's comments to the French Academy in February 1782, quoted in Keith Michael Baker, *Condorcet: From Natural Philosophy to Social Mathematics* (Chicago and London: University of Chicago Press, 1975), 86.

7. David Hume, *A Treatise of Human Nature*, ed. L. A. Selby-Bigge, rev. P. H. Nidditch, 2d ed. (Oxford: Clarendon Press, 1978), 273, xvi, 659.

8. Peter Jones, introduction to *The 'Science of Man' in the Scottish Enlightenment: Hume, Reid, and Their Contemporaries*, ed. P. Jones (Edinburgh: Edinburgh University Press, 1989), 1.

9. See Paul Russell, "Hume's *Treatise* and Hobbes's *The Elements of Law*," *Journal of the History of Ideas* 46 (1985): 51–63.

10. For Hume's connections with natural law, see Duncan Forbes, *Hume's Philosophical Politics* (Cambridge: Cambridge University Press, 1975), especially 3–90. Forbes would also add to my discussion that "what was really and radically new, apart from the attempt to apply the principle of association consistently, was what set Hume apart from the Newtonians: the discovery that a genuine experimental philosophy ruled out final causes and involved a conscious separation or bracketing off of the natural from the supernatural" (53). Elsewhere, more generally, Donald R. Kelley argues that "what has been regarded as the birth of social science, in fact, can also be seen as the fulfillment" of directions in the legal tradition. See "The Prehistory of Sociology: Montesquieu, Vico, and the Legal Tradition," *Journal of the History of the Behavioral Sciences* 16 (1980): 133–144; also Kelley's more recent work, *The Human Measure: Social Thought in the Western Legal Tradition* (Cambridge, Mass.: Harvard University Press, 1990).

11. On this question, see John P. Wright, *The Sceptical Realism of David Hume* (Minneapolis: University of Minnesota Press, 1983), especially chap. 5, "Hume's Science of Human Nature," 187–246; also Michael Barfoot, "Hume and the

Culture of Science in the Early Eighteenth Century," in *Studies in the Philosophy of the Scottish Enlightenment,* ed. M. A. Stewart (Oxford: Clarendon Press, 1990), 151–190, especially 160–161.

12. Barfoot, "Hume and the Culture of Science," 167.

13. Alexander Pope, *The Twickenham Edition of the Works of Alexander Pope,* ed. John Butt, 11 vols. (New Haven, Conn.: Yale University Press, 1939–69), vol. 3, part 1: *An Essay on Man,* ed. Maynard Mack (1950), 35.

14. Hume, *Treatise,* 645. As John Christie has recently argued, "the methodological history of the human sciences before 1800 was not one of attempts to design methods which would exclusively differentiate a human topic from the study of objective, external nature. Rather, it was a history of attempts to appropriate, transfer and apply natural science methodological canons to the human world." See John Christie, "The Human Sciences: Origins and Histories," *History of the Human Sciences* 6 (1993): 1–12, especially 3, 9–11.

15. Marie Jean Antoine-Nicolas Marquis de Condorcet, *Sketch For A Historical Picture of the Progress of the Human Mind* (1797), trans. June Barraclough (London: Weidenfeld and Nicolson, 1955), 164.

16. Hume, *Treatise,* 282, xvii.

17. For a recent review of Gusdorf's massive project, see Donald R. Kelley, "Gusdorfiad," *History of the Human Sciences* 3 (1990): 123–140.

18. Baker, *Condorcet,* viii.

19. For this critique, see, e.g., Roger Smith, "Does the History of Psychology Have a Subject?" *History of the Human Sciences* 1 (1988): 147–177, especially 147–148.

20. It should also be said that there is a sense (contra Foucault) among some that, with a healthy skepticism, one can write narrative histories of the early human sciences "without relapsing into an unexamined continuism." See Christie, "Human Sciences," 10, and *Functions and Uses of Disciplinary Histories,* ed. Loren Graham, Wolf Lepenies, and Peter Weingart (Dordrecht: D. Reidel, 1983), xii. Also: Wolf Lepenies, *Between Literature and Science: The Rise of Sociology,* trans. R. J. Hollingdale (Cambridge: Cambridge University Press, 1988).

21. Martin S. Staum, "Human Geography in the French Institute: New Discipline or Missed Opportunity?" *Journal of the History of the Behavioral Sciences* 23 (1987): 332–340. Also see Staum's excellent *Cabanis: Enlightenment and Medical Philosophy in the French Revolution* (Princeton, N.J.: Princeton University Press, 1980).

22. On this point, see Christopher Fox, "Defining Eighteenth-Century Psychology: Some Problems and Perspectives," in *Psychology and Literature in the Eighteenth Century,* ed. C. Fox (New York: AMS Studies in the Eighteenth Century, 1987), 1–22; Christopher Fox, "Crawford, Willis, and *Anthropologie Abstracted:* Some Early English Uses of Psychology," *Journal of the History of the Behavorial Sciences* 24 (1988): 378–380; and Fernando Vidal, "Psychology in the Eighteenth Century: A View from Encyclopaedias," *History of the Human Sciences* 6 (1993): 89–120. I thank Dr. Vidal for sending an early version of this paper.

23. See Theodor W. Adorno and Max Horkheimer, *Dialectic of Enlightenment,* trans. John Cumming (1944; reprint, New York: Herder and Herder, 1972), which argues that the "enlightenment is as totalitarian as any system" (24); and Lester

Crocker, *Nature and Culture: Ethical Thought in the French Enlightenment* (Baltimore: Johns Hopkins University Press, 1963). Also see Crocker's introduction to *The Blackwell Companion to the Enlightenment,* ed. John W. Yolton, Roy Porter, Pat Rogers, and Barbara Maria Stafford (Oxford: Basil Blackwell Publisher 1991), 1–10, which emphasizes the antithetical legacy of the Enlightenment, as a source of both liberal *and* totalitarian tenets.

24. On the Habermas-Foucault exchange, see especially David R. Hiley, "Foucault and the Question of Enlightenment," *Philosophy and Social Criticism* 11 (1985–86): 63–83. Foucault's "What Is Enlightenment?" is in *The Foucault Reader,* ed. Paul Rabinow (New York: Pantheon Books, 1984), 32–50. He takes as his title and starting point Kant's famous essay in Johann Erich Biester's *Berlinische Monatsschrift* in November 1784. Jürgen Habermas's "Taking Aim at the Heart of the Present" is available in *Foucault: A Critical Reader,* ed. David Couzens Hoy (Oxford: Basil Blackwell Publisher, 1986), 103–108.

25. See Habermas, "Taking Aim," 106.

26. Foucault, "What Is Enlightenment?" 47. The literature on Foucault is immense. Among works of help to us are the special issue devoted to him in *History of the Human Sciences* 3 (February 1990) and Gary Gutting's discussion of Foucault among the historians: "Michel Foucault's *Phänomenologie des Krankengeistes,*" in *Discovering the History of Psychiatry,* ed. Roy Porter and Mark Micale (New York and Oxford: Oxford University Press, 1994), 331–347. I thank Gary Gutting for showing me an early draft of his chapter.

27. Also see here Jürgen Habermas, "The Entwinement of Myth and Enlightenment: Re-Reading *Dialectic of Enlightenment,*" *New German Critique* 26 (1982): 13–30.

28. Roy Porter, *The Enlightenment* (Atlantic Highlands, N.J.: Humanities Press International, 1990), 9. On this point, also see Isaac Kramnick, "Eighteenth-Century Science and Radical Social Theory: The Case of Joseph Priestley's Scientific Liberalism," *Journal of British Studies* 25 (1986): 1–30.

29. From Gusdorf on, we have also seen a recovery of interest in Wilhelm Dilthey and the hermeneutics of human science. Charles Taylor also argues the need for connecting human science with hermeneutics. See his "Interpretation and the Sciences of Man," *The Review of Metaphysics* 25 (1971): 3–51; also Taylor's *Philosophy and the Human Sciences* (Cambridge: Cambridge University Press, 1985). For a critique of the larger attempt to see social sciences as hermeneutical, see Richard Rorty, "Method, Social Science, and Social Hope," in *Consequences of Pragmatism: Essays: 1972–1980* (Minneapolis: University of Minnesota Press, 1982), 191–210. Also see Gerald Bruns, "The Weakness of Language in the Human Sciences," in *The Rhetoric of the Human Sciences: Language and Argument in Scholarship and Public Affairs,* ed. Allan Megill, Donald McCloskey, and John Nelson (Madison: University of Wisconsin Press, 1987), 239–262. For Alasdair MacIntyre's critique, see *After Virtue: A Study in Moral Theory,* 2d ed. (Notre Dame, Ind.: University of Notre Dame Press, 1984), especially 62–78; and Robert Wokler's "Projecting the Enlightenment," in *After MacIntyre,* ed. John Horton and Susan Mendus (Notre Dame, Ind.: University of Notre Dame Press, 1994), 108–126.

30. J. G. A. Pocock, "Enlightenment and the Revolution: The Case of English-

speaking North America," in *Seventh International Congress on the Enlightenment: Introductory Papers* (Oxford: Voltaire Foundation, 1987), 45–57, especially 48.

31. See Roy S. Porter and Mikuláš Teich, eds., *The Enlightenment in National Context* (Cambridge: Cambridge University Press, 1981).

32. "Americans, in a more unadulterated way than Europeans, are heirs of the Enlightenment" and see it differently, argues Lester Crocker. See his "Interpreting the Enlightenment: A Political Approach," *Journal of the History of Ideas* 46 (1985): 211–230, especially 228. On problems of defining "enlightenment" in the eighteenth century itself, see James Schmidt, "The Question of Enlightenment: Kant, Mendelssohn, and the *Mittwochsgesellschaft*," *Journal of the History of Ideas* 50 (1989): 269–291. "The words enlightenment, culture and cultivation," said Moses Mendelssohn, "are still newcomers to our language. The crowd hardly understands them." On his and others' difficulties with this "recently changed vocabulary," see E. J. Hundert, "A Cognitive Ideal and Its Myth: Knowledge as Power in the Lexicon of the Enlightenment," *Social Research* 53 (1986): 133-157, especially 132–133.

33. On the diverse views of human science in the eighteenth century, see Porter, *Enlightenment*, 12.

34. Jean Le Rond d'Alembert, *Preliminary Discourse to the Encyclopedia of Diderot*, trans. Richard N. Schwab and Walter Rex (Indianapolis: Bobbs-Merrill Co., 1963), 46. On the "Division of the *Science of Man*," see p. 162. "The very attempt to impose a new order on the world made the Encyclopedists conscious of the arbitrariness in all ordering," argues Robert Darnton. See his "Philosophers Trim the Tree of Knowledge," in *The Great Cat Massacre and Other Episodes in French Cultural History* (New York: Basic Books, 1984), 195.

35. Denis Diderot, "Encyclopedia" [1755], in *Rameau's Nephew and Other Works*, trans. Jacques Barzun and Ralph H. Bowen (New York: Bobbs-Merrill Co., 1964), 306. Like Ephraim Chambers, Diderot (it has been argued) "was less concerned with schemes of rational classification than with the imperative of collecting human knowledge in some manageable form." See Richard Yeo, "Reading Encyclopedias: Science and the Organization of Knowledge in British Dictionaries of Arts and Sciences, 1730–1850," *Isis* 82 (1991): 24–49, especially 25.

36. For recent work here, see Peter Dear's introduction to *The Literary Structure of Scientific Argument: Historical Studies*, ed. P. Dear (Philadelphia: University of Pennsylvania Press, 1991), 1–9. For applications of this new methodology to eighteenth-century concerns, see for instance Ludmilla J. Jordanova, ed., *Languages of Nature: Critical Essays on Science and Literature* (London: Free Association Books, 1986).

37. Jonathan Swift, *Gulliver's Travels*, ed. Herbert Davis (1726; reprint, Oxford: Basil Blackwell Publisher, 1959), 103–104. On the general notion of *lusus naturae*, see Paula Findlen, "Jokes of Nature and Jokes of Knowledge: The Playfulness of Scientific Discourse in Early Modern Europe," *Renaissance Quarterly* 43 (1990): 292–331.

38. For Locke's parrot who "spoke, and asked, and answered common Questions like a reasonable Creature," see book 2, chap. 27, section 8 of *An Essay concerning Human Understanding*, ed. Peter H. Nidditch (Oxford: Clarendon Press, 1975), 332–333. Locke found this example in Sir William Temple's *Memoirs*, transcribed by young Jonathan Swift for press. On the larger discussion of human

identity, see Christopher Fox, *Locke and the Scriblerians: Identity and Consciousness in Early Eighteenth-Century Britain* (Berkeley, Los Angeles, London: University of California Press, 1988).

39. Descartes speaks of those "clocks, artificial fountains, mills and similar machines which, though made entirely of man, lack not the power to move, of themselves, in various ways"; later, of the water in the king's gardens that "is able of itself to move diverse machines and even to make them play certain instruments or pronounce certain words." See René Descartes, *Treatise of Man*, trans. T. S. Hall (Leyden, 1662; reprint, Cambridge, Mass.: Harvard University Press, 1972), 4, 21. For eighteenth-century discussion on this point, see especially John W. Yolton's "The Automatical Man," in *Thinking Matter: Materialism in Eighteenth-Century Britain* (Minneapolis: University of Minnesota Press, 1983), 29–48. Elsewhere, Douglas Patey has called attention to possible connections of this passage to physico-theology in "Swift's Satire on 'Science' and the Structure of *Gulliver's Travels*," *English Literary History* 58 (1991): 809–833, especially 828.

40. Jonathan Swift, John Arbuthnot, Alexander Pope et al., *Memoirs of the Extraordinary Life, Works, and Discoveries of Martinus Scriblerus*, ed. Charles Kerby-Miller (New Haven, Conn.: Yale University Press, 1950), 141. The Nuremberg virtuoso may be a reference to the medical authority Friedrich Hoffman (1700–1743).

41. Laurence Sterne, *The Life and Opinions of Tristram Shandy, Gentleman* (1759; ed. Graham Petrie, London: Penguin Books, 1987), Vol. I, chap. 2, p. 36.

42. On embryology, see especially Shirley A. Roe, *Matter, Life, and Generation: Eighteenth-Century Embryology and the Haller-Wolff Debate* (Cambridge, Mass.: Harvard University Press, 1981), and Jacques Roger, *Les Sciences de la vie dans la pensée française du XVIIIᵉ siècle*, 2d ed. (Paris: Armand Colin, 1971).

43. Johann Friedrich Blumenbach, *On the Natural Variety of Mankind* (1775 ed.), in *The Anthropological Treatises of Johann Friedrich Blumenbach*, trans. Thomas Bendyshe (London: Longman, Green, Longman, Roberts, and Green, 1865), 123.

44. Annemarie de Waal Malefijt, "Homo Monstrosus," *Scientific American* 219 (1968): 112–118, especially 118. Ambroise Paré's 1573 work on the subject was titled *Des Monstres et prodiges*.

45. Francis Bacon, *New Organon*, 3 vols. (London, 1620), 2:29; and Katherine Park and Lorraine J. Daston, "Unnatural Conceptions: The Study of Monsters in Sixteenth- and Seventeenth-Century France and England," *Past and Present* 92 (1981): 20–54, especially 25.

46. At twenty-two years of age, Coan stood 36 inches tall and weighed 27 ½ pounds. See David Erskine Baker, "*Extract of Letter from Mr. William Arderon, F.R.S. to Mr. Henry Baker, F.R.S. containing an Account of a Dwarf; together with a Comparison of his Dimensions with those of a Child under four years old*," *Philosophical Transactions* 46 (1749–1750): 467–470.

47. Swift, Arbuthnot, and Pope, *Martinus Scriblerus*, 144, 149.

48. Margaret T. Hodgen, *Early Anthropology in the Sixteenth and Seventeenth Centuries* (Philadelphia: University of Pennsylvania Press, 1964), 127–128.

49. Swift, *Gulliver's Travels*, 96, 97, 101. For Swift's connection to such shows, see especially Aline MacKenzie Taylor, "Sights and Monsters and Gulliver's Voyage to Brobdingnag," *Tulane Studies in English* 7 (1957): 29–82; also Dennis Todd, "The

Hairy Maid at the Harpsichord: Some Speculations on the Meaning of *Gulliver's Travels*," *Texas Studies in Literature and Language* 34 (1992): 239–283.

50. Another famous midget, John Wormberg, drowned in such a box in 1695. See Taylor, "Sights and Monsters," 56. For a more recent exploration of the eighteenth-century fascination with "monsters," see Barbara Maria Stafford, *Body Criticism: Imagining the Unseen in Enlightenment Art and Medicine* (Cambridge, Mass.: M.I.T. Press, 1991), especially 38.

51. Henry Morley, *Memoirs of Bartholomew Fair* (London: Frederick Warne and Co., 1874), 246.

52. Ibid., 251, 249, 255.

53. "*Extract of a Letter from* John Browning Esq. of Barton-Hill *near* Bristol, *to Mr.* Henry Baker, F.R.S. *concerning A Dwarf*," *Philosophical Transactions* 47 (1751–52): 278–281. The same volume of the *Philosophical Transactions* contains "*An Account of a* double Child, *communicated to the Rights Honourable the Lord* Willoughby, *of* Parham, F.R.S. *by* Thomas Percival *Esquire*"; see 360–362.

54. Jessie Dobson, *John Hunter* (Edinburgh and London: E. & S. Livingstone, 1969), 263.

55. Colin Clair, *Human Curiosities* (London: Abelard-Schuman, 1968), 32.

56. *Synopsis of the Arrangement of the Preparations in the Museum of the Royal College of Surgeons of England* (London: J. E. Taylor, 1845), 17.

57. Swift, *Gulliver's Travels*, 103.

58. Morley, *Bartholomew Fair*, 254.

59. Johann Christoph Friedrich von Schiller, quoted in *Readings in Early Anthropology*, ed. J. S. Slotkin (Chicago: Aldine Publishing Co., 1965), 384.

60. P. J. Marshall and Glyndwr Williams, *The Great Map of Mankind: Perceptions of New Worlds in the Age of Enlightenment* (Cambridge, Mass.: Harvard University Press, 1982), 39.

61. Richard D. Altick, *The Shows of London* (Cambridge, Mass., and London: Harvard University Press, 1978), 47.

62. "In the 1530s and 1540s," writes Luke Wilson, "Vesalius began a trend in which the anatomist seems to have become a central performer on the stage of the theater." The "dissection was understood as an entertainment or performance, an enactment whose significance went beyond the medical and forensic contexts from which it had evolved." See "William Harvey's *Prelectiones:* The Performance of the Body in the Renaissance Theater of Anatomy," *Representations* 17 (1987): 62–95, especially 69.

63. On the extraordinary *Kabinet van Anatomie en Rariteiten* at Leiden, see Arthur MacGregor, "Collectors and Collections of Rarities in the Sixteenth and Seventeenth Centuries," in *Tradescant's Rarities: Essays on the Foundation of the Ashmolean Museum, 1683, with a Catalogue of the Surviving Early Collections*, ed. A. MacGregor (Oxford: Clarendon Press, 1983), 78–79.

64. See William Schupbach, "Some Cabinets of Curiosities in European Academic Institutions," in *The Origins of Museums: The Cabinet of Curiosities in Sixteenth- and Seventeenth-Century Europe*, ed. Oliver Impey and Arthur MacGregor (Oxford: Clarendon Press, 1985), 172–173.

65. Hodgen, *Early Anthropology*, 114–115.

66. See Comte de Buffon, "The Natural History of Man," in *Natural History*,

General and Particular, By the Count De Buffon, trans. William Smellie, 20 vols. (London, 1812), vol. 3: *The History of Man and Quadrupeds,* 95–446. For a recent excellent exposition of the term, see P. B. Wood, "The Natural History of Man in the Scottish Enlightenment," *History of Science* 28 (1990): 89–123. Also see Phillip Sloan, chap. 5, below.

67. Blumenbach, *Contributions to Natural History, Part I,* in *Anthropological Treatises,* 298, 299.

68. Adam Ferguson, *An Essay on the History of Civil Society* (Edinburgh, 1767), 69.

69. Amy Boesky argues more strongly for a real continuity between the earlier wonder cabinets and eighteenth-century museums. See her "'Outlandish Fruits': Commissioning Nature for the Museum of Man," *English Literary History* 56 (1991): 305–330, especially 307.

70. See especially Alan Frost, "The Pacific Ocean: The Eighteenth Century's New World," *Studies on Voltaire and the Eighteenth Century* 152 (1976): 779–822.

71. J. C. Beaglehole, "Eighteenth-Century Science and Voyages of Discovery," *New Zealand Journal of History* 3 (1969): 107–123, especially 115.

72. J. C. H. King, "North American Ethnography in the Collection of Sir Hans Sloane," in Impey and MacGregor, *Origins of Museums,* 236 (note 64 above).

73. See George W. Stocking, *Race, Culture, and Evolution: Essays in the History of Anthropology* (New York: Free Press, 1968), 30.

74. Karl Marx, *Life of Blumenbach,* trans. Thomas Bendysche, in *Anthropological Treatises of Johann Friedrich Blumenbach,* 8: "Blumenbach used to call it his 'Golgotha,' and though they do not often go to a place of skulls, still the curious and inquisitive of both sexes came there to wonder and reflect."

75. Blumenbach, *On the Natural Variety of Mankind* (3d ed., 1795), in *Anthropological Treatises,* 149, 162.

76. Altick, *Shows of London,* 48.

77. Blumenbach, *On the Natural Variety of Mankind* (3d ed., 1795), in *Anthropological Treatises,* 161, 245.

78. Charles White, *An Account of the Regular Gradation In Man, And In Different Animals And Vegetables And From The Former to the Latter* (London, 1799), 41.

79. See William Blizard, *The Hunterian Oration* (London, 1823), 13–14; and Thomas Chevalier, *The Hunterian Oration Delivered before the Royal College of Surgeons* (London, 1823), 34. Also see L. S. Jacyna, "Images of John Hunter in the Nineteenth Century," *History of Science* 21 (1983): 85–108, especially 93.

80. See Altick, *Shows of London,* 28; and George Qvist, *John Hunter, 1728–1793* (London: William Heinemann Medical Books, 1981), 72.

81. Blumenbach, *Anthropological Treatises,* 155, 237, 300.

82. Thomas De Quincey, *The Collected Writings,* ed. David Masson, 14 vols. (London: Black, 1896–97), vol. 1: *Autobiography from 1785 to 1803,* 388.

83. Constantin François Volney, *A New Translation of Volney's Ruins,* 2 vols. (1802; reprint, New York and London: Garland Publishing, 1979), 1: 171–172.

84. Simon Schaffer, "Natural Philosophy and Public Spectacle in the Eighteenth Century," *History of Science,* 21 (1983): 1–43, especially 1.

85. Porter, *Enlightenment,* 18.

86. For connections between the "wild child" and the history of human science in the eighteenth century, see especially David E. Leary, "Nature, Art, and Imitation: The Wild Boy of Aveyron as a Pivotal Case in the History of Psychology," in *Studies in Eighteenth Century Culture: Volume 13*, ed. O M Brack, Jr. (Madison: University of Wisconsin Press, 1984), 155–172. Also see Roger Shattuck, *The Forbidden Experiment: The Story of the Wild Boy of Aveyron* (New York: Farrar, Straus and Giroux, 1980), and Harlan Lane, *The Wild Boy of Aveyron* (Cambridge, Mass.: Harvard University Press, 1976). On Wild Peter of Hanover, seen by Swift in April 1726: Maximillian E. Novak, "The Wild Man Comes to Tea," in *The Wild Man Within: An Image in Western Thought from the Renaissance to Romanticism*, ed. M. E. Novak and Edward Dudley (Pittsburgh: University of Pittsburgh Press, 1972), 183–221. On the Wild Girl of Champagne, see the fascinating study by Julia Douthwaite, "Rewriting the Savage: The Extraordinary Fictions of the 'Wild Girl of Champagne,'" *Eighteenth-Century Studies* 28 (1994–95): 163–192.

87. Sir Joseph Banks, *The Endeavour Journal of Joseph Banks, 1768–1771* (Sydney: Angus and Robertson, 1962), 312–313.

88. Londa Schiebinger, "The Anatomy of Difference: Race and Sex in Eighteenth-Century France," *Eighteenth-Century Studies* 23 (1990): 387–405, especially 387. Also see her *Nature's Body: Gender in the Making of Modern Science* (Boston: Beacon Press, 1993), 115–142.

89. On Tchong-A-Sam, see Sergio Moravia, *La scienza dell'uomo nel Settecento* (Bari: Laterza, 1970), 112–117. For other comments, also see George W. Stocking, "French Anthropology in 1800," *Isis* 55 (1964): 134–150, especially 134.

90. On this point, see John F. Sena, "*Gulliver's Travels* and the Genre of the Illustrated Book," in *The Genres of Gulliver's Travels*, ed. Frederik N. Smith (Newark: University of Delaware Press, 1990), 101–138, especially 109–110.

91. Swift, *Gulliver's Travels*, 103–104.

92. See Frederik N. Smith, "Scientific Discourse: *Gulliver's Travels* and *The Philosophical Transactions*," in *Genres of Gulliver's Travels*, 139–162, especially 141–142.

93. Swift, *Gulliver's Travels*, 146. Still helpful here are the chapters on "the traveller and the scientific approach" in R. W. Frantz's *The English Traveller and the Movement of Ideas, 1660–1732* (1930; reprint, New York: Octagon Books, 1960), 15–71.

94. David Oakleaf, "*Trompe l'Oeil*: Gulliver and the Distortions of the Observing Eye," *University of Toronto Quarterly* 53 (1983–84): 166–180, especially 166.

95. Swift, *Gulliver's Travels*, 135. Gulliver's emphasis on "first hand experience" and "the production of knowledge acquired in a rigorously empirical way" points to a distinctly "modern" sensibility, parodied by Swift. On such attributes of the enlightened traveler, see the introduction to *The Enlightenment and its Shadows*, ed. Peter Hulme and Ludmilla Jordanova (London and New York: Routledge, 1990), 12. The ancients guess, the moderns count, argued Samuel Johnson. Like another Swift figure, the modest proposer, Gulliver likes to count. For a recent exploration of eighteenth-century social science in light of the new stress on quantification, see Karin Johannisson, "Society in Numbers: The Debate over Quantification in 18th-Century Political Economy," in *The Quantifying Spirit in the 18th Century*, ed. Tore Frängsmyr, J. L. Heibron, and Robin E. Rider (Berkeley, Los Angeles, Oxford:

University of California Press, 1990), 343–361. Johannisson reminds us (p. 344, n. 4) that the word *statistics* was used for the first time in England in the 1770s. Also see Sylvana Tomaselli, chap. 10 in this volume, and Peter Buck, "People Who Counted: Political Arithmetic in the Eighteenth-Century," *Isis* 73 (1982): 28–45.

96. The word *observation* (in various forms) occurs 140 times in *Gulliver's Travels*. On this point, see Pat Rogers, "Gulliver's Glasses," in *The Art of Jonathan Swift*, ed. Clive T. Probyn (London: Vision Press, 1978), 179–188, especially 184.

97. The illustrations of J. J. Grandville (1838) are discussed by David Lenfest, "Grandville's Gulliver," *Satire Newsletter* 10 (1973): 12–24, and by Sena (note 90 above).

98. The language is from Gilian Beer's "Science and Literature," in *Companion to the History of Modern Science*, ed. R. C. Olby, G. N. Cantor, J. R. R. Christie, and M. J. S. Hodge (New York and London: Routledge, 1990), 785.

99. See Gary Gutting, *Michel Foucault's Archaeology of Scientific Reason* (Cambridge: Cambridge University Press, 1989), 212.

100. See James Boswell, *Life of Johnson*, ed. G. B. Hill, rev. L. F. Powell, 6 vols. (Oxford: Clarendon Press, 1971), 2:319.

101. Swift, *Gulliver's Travels*, 104.

102. William Coleman, *Georges Cuvier, Zoologist: A Study in the History of Evolution Theory* (Cambridge, Mass.: Harvard University Press, 1964), 61.

103. See Robert Wokler, chap. 2 in this volume, and also his "Tyson and Buffon on the Orang-utan," *Studies on Voltaire and the Eighteenth Century*, vol. 165, ed. Theodore Besterman (Oxford: Voltaire Foundation, 1976), 2301–2319.

104. See Londa Schiebinger, "Skeletons in the Closet: The First Illustrations of the Female Skeleton in Eighteenth-Century Anatomy," in *The Making of the Modern Body: Sexuality and Society in the Nineteenth Century*, ed. Catherine Gallagher and Thomas Laqueur (Berkeley, Los Angeles, London: University of California Press, 1987), 42–82, especially 51. Also see Schiebinger's *The Mind Has No Sex? Women in the Origins of Modern Science* (Cambridge, Mass.: Harvard University Press, 1989) and Thomas Laqueur, *Making Sex: Body and Gender from the Greeks to Freud* (Cambridge, Mass.: Harvard University Press, 1990), especially 149–192. Sylvana Tomaselli has discussed the emergence in the later eighteenth century of a "science of woman" to parallel the new science of man; see "Reflections on the History of the Science of Woman," *History of Science* 29 (1991): 185–205.

105. Joseph François Lafitau, *Customs of the American Indians Compared with the Customs of Primitive Times*, trans. William H. Fenton and Elizabeth L. Moore, 2 vols. (Toronto: Champlain Society, 1974), 1:71–74, 2:47–97.

106. Francis Moore, *Travels Into the Inland Parts of Africa: Containing A Description of the Several Nations for the Space of Six Hundred Miles up the River Gambia . . . To which is added Capt. Stibb's Voyage up the Gambia in the Year 1723, to make Discoveries* (London, 1736), 116; also see 122.

107. For the most popular of these views, the "four stages theory" of progress from hunting, pasturage, agriculture, to commerce, see especially Ronald L. Meek, *Social Science and the Ignoble Savage* (Cambridge and New York: Cambridge University Press, 1976).

108. John Locke, *The Second Treatise,* in *Two Treatises of Government,* rev. ed., ed. Peter Laslett (New York: New American Library, 1965), section 49, p. 343.

109. Ferguson, *Essay on the History of Civil Society,* 122.

110. Edmund Burke, quoted in Marshall and Williams, *Great Map of Mankind,* 93.

111. The earliest known use of the word *civilization* was ca. 1756. See Jean Starobinski, "Le mot civilization," *Temps de la réflexion* 4 (1983): 13–51; Anthony Pagden, "The 'Defence of Civilization' in Eighteenth-Century Social Theory," *History of the Human Sciences* 1 (1988): 33–45; and Lucien Febvre, "Civilization: Evolution of a Word and a Group of Ideas," in *A New Kind of History,* ed. Peter Burke (New York: Harper and Row, 1973), 217–257. On the attempt to invent the present by constructing a place called "the past," see Johannes Fabian, *Time and the Other: How Anthropology Makes Its Object* (New York: Columbia University Press, 1983). I thank my colleague Kathleen Biddick for bringing Fabian to my attention. See her consideration of the same question in "Decolonizing the English Past: Readings in Medieval Archeology and History," *Journal of British Studies* 32 (1993): 1–23, especially 3–4.

112. Joseph-Marie Degérando, *The Observation of Savage Peoples,* trans. F. C. T. Moore (Berkeley and Los Angeles: University of California Press, 1969), 89.

113. See *Turgot on Progress, Sociology, and Economics,* trans. Ronald L. Meek (Cambridge: Cambridge University Press, 1973), 69.

114. Buffon, *Natural History,* 3:202.

115. See Richard Payne Knight, *The Progress of Civil Society: In Six Books* (London, 1796), 21–22:

> long inured to rapine, waste and spoil,
> The listless savage shrunk from care and toil;
> And, on the humble partner of his bed,
> Devolved the labour that his leisure fed.

116. Thomas Robert Malthus, *An Essay on the Principle of Population,* ed. Philip Appleman (New York: W. W. Norton and Co., 1976), 27.

117. John Reinold Forster, *Observations Made During A Voyage Round the World* (London, 1778), 418.

118. John Millar, *The Origin of the Distinction of Ranks; or, An Inquiry Into the Circumstances which Give Rise to Influence and Authority,* in *John Millar of Glasgow, 1735–1801,* by William C. Lehmann (New York: Arno Press, 1979), 183–228.

119. On such eighteenth-century cultural criticism, see Julia V. Douthwaite, *Exotic Women: Literary Heroines and Cultural Strategies in Ancien Régime France* (Philadelphia: University of Pennsylvania Press, 1992), especially 140–183.

120. A still helpful study here is Clarence J. Glacken's *Traces on the Rhodian Shore: Nature and Culture in Western Thought from Ancient Times to the End of the Eighteenth Century* (Berkeley and Los Angeles: University of California Press, 1967). See especially his chapters "Airs, Waters, and Places" (80–115) and "Climate, the Moeurs, Religion, and Government" in the eighteenth century (551–622). I thank my colleague Chris Hamlin for calling this to my attention.

121. Ferguson, *Essay on the History of Civil Society,* 1.

122. Hans Aarsleff points this out in an unpublished paper, quoted with the author's permission. For more on this question, see, e.g., Aarsleff's *From Locke to Saussure: Essays on the Study of Language and Intellectual History* (Minneapolis: University of Minnesota Press, 1982) and his *Study of Language in England, 1780–1860* (Minneapolis: University of Minnesota Press, 1983).

123. See the fine recent volume edited by Tore Frängsmyr and his colleagues, *The Quantifying Spirit in the 18th Century* (note 95 above), which tends to view quantification as a post-1760 development. For Sir William Petty, also see Alessandro Roncaglia, *Petty: The Origins of Political Economy* (Armonk, N.Y.: M. E. Sharpe, 1985).

124. Baker, *Condorcet*, viii.

TWO

Anthropology and Conjectural History in the Enlightenment

Robert Wokler

The discovery of the New World and the need to devise appropriate colonial policies in the sixteenth and seventeenth centuries inspired much Christian speculation about the moral condition and treatment of savages and slaves. In 1550, Emperor Charles V convened a Council of the Indies to assess the justice of his own conquest of the Mexican and Inca empires, and the great debate on the nature and moral status of American Indians thus initiated between Juan Ginés de Sepúlveda and Bartolomé de Las Casas was to give rise to many of the central questions of the modern discipline of anthropology. But the leading thinkers who addressed the subject in this period were characteristically concerned only with the apparent attributes and capacities of primitive man and woman. They turned to ancient and medieval authorities such as Aristotle, Saint Augustine, and Thomas Aquinas to show that savages merited the treatment they had received because of their sinful nature or their lack of sufficient reason to rule themselves; or, alternatively, they argued that savage cultures were merely youthful and undisciplined, in need not of forceful subjection but rather of a gospel of peaceful persuasion. Even the most progressive and compassionate figures among them, including Francisco de Vitoria and José de Acosta, addressed the customs and achievements of savage peoples—their cannibalism and bestiality, on the one hand, or their artifacts and languages, on the other—only in order to locate their proper place among peoples the Greeks had already classified as barbarian.[1] Not until the late seventeenth century was it widely perceived that the behavior of primitive peoples might shed light upon the early history of civilization; not until the eighteenth century did it come to be accepted that the study of human nature in general, and empirical investigations of savage societies in particular, form precisely the same field. Anthropology now means that above all else, and the presuppositions upon which its current professional practice is based were first conceived—that is to say, the contemporary science of anthropology was invented—in the Enlightenment.

Few professional anthropologists would be disposed to agree with this claim. Most—when they reflect upon such matters—are more likely to locate the origins of their subject in the early or mid–nineteenth century, when social anthropology became the down-to-earth investigation of primitive cultures just insofar as its practitioners abandoned what they judged to be the abstract approaches to human nature pursued in the Enlightenment. They might even add that a similar attachment to scientific exactitude as against conjectural imprecision gave rise, again around the turn of the nineteenth century, to the subject of physical anthropology, which has come to have an independent, and—to social anthropologists—largely unintelligible, history of its own. But in discrediting the claims of those who speculated about mankind's nature and development before anthropology became professionalized, its practitioners risk adopting a view of their own past which is more shallow and ill-informed than the doctrines about human nature they have all too ignorantly relegated to the prehistory of a contemporary science. No age of European intellectual history was more fascinated by ideas of human nature—by its biological and moral dimension, and its physical and spiritual attributes—than the Enlightenment. The two, now separate, fields embraced by the term *anthropology* were in the eighteenth century often characteristically perceived as one, whose dual aspects—the study of mind and culture, on the one hand, and of bodily form and structure, on the other—were believed to stand in need of a comprehensive and systematic explanation. The study of *la pensée sauvage,* in its various articulations, was judged to be a central part, but only a part, of a general theory of human nature which had to embrace the history of civilization and a grasp of mankind's place among the animals as well.[2]

Within such a theory a number of recurrent themes—to do with the origin of language, for instance, the invention of ideas, the genesis of sexuality, the treatment of the insane, or the comparative anatomy of apes or races—were all thought essential to a proper development of the *science of man,* itself an expression, together with the term *anthropology* (which of course is of ancient Greek derivation), invented or substantially redefined in the course of the Enlightenment.[3] From eighteenth-century speculation about such matters arose the disciplines of both social and physical anthropology in their modern forms, along lines of which current practitioners are all too often unaware, though they help to explain the genesis of today's anthropologists' own past, and hence some central, if forgotten, features of their collective identity. My remarks here are intended to shed just a few glimmers of light upon that past. With the broadest possible strokes, I mean to concentrate upon a central and, indeed, overarching framework of eighteenth-century anthropological studies—that is, the physical and moral dimensions of human nature, of which the successive transformations of one into the other were thought to mark what later came to be described, although by then it was perceived quite differently, as savage mankind's passage from nature to culture.[4] Conjectural history, as I understand it, was designed to reconstruct that dynamic relation along the presumed path it must or might have taken to generate the institutions and attributes of civilized men and women. The hypothetical history of the human race, as postulated in the eighteenth century, was meant to explain, in effect, how our nature would have undergone change and become what it is.

I begin with a commonplace as true of the human sciences as of much else besides in the Enlightenment—indeed one reason why the human sciences are so prominent among the sciences of nature in this period—which is that God came to be transported from the proscenium to the wings of scientific explanation, His voice muted, rendered as "noises off." In the seventeenth century, one consequence of the revolution of the physical sciences was that mechanical laws came to be invoked to explain the nature of animal behavior no less than the motion of particles, and, in the Cartesian tradition of discourse, the pipes and vessels of animals regarded as natural machines were held to be just forms of extended matter, as was the case equally of human matter—which raised the additional problem, of course, of how such matter might have come to think.[5]

Now this sense of a mechanical universe gave rise, perhaps paradoxically, to what may be termed the spiritualization of humanity. For man and woman came increasingly to be judged by scientists and philosophers to be their own artificers, because uniquely among creatures in the world of extended matter, we possess a soul. Most seventeenth-century mechanists, as distinct from a number of their followers among French materialists of the late eighteenth century, did not subscribe to monistic explanations of human behavior. By and large, they were dualists, and, with the notable exception of Thomas Hobbes, they believed in the incorporeal essence of the soul; if they perceived *le corps* to be extended matter, they judged *l'âme* the animating, immaterial principle of our nature, an incorporeal essence that gave purpose and direction to the physical properties of the human body. Nowhere is this dualism more evident than in the seventeenth- and eighteenth-century perspectives of a fundamental break in the great chain of being, separating man and woman from all other creatures below them. Claude Perrault in his *Histoire des animaux* of 1676, or Edward Tyson in his *Orang-Outang* of 1699, or the Comte de Buffon in 1766 in his *Histoire naturelle,* all contended that apes were distinct from humans because, though they possessed bodies much like those of men and women, these bodies were not animated by the spiritual principle that shaped our nature.

Today, if we compare the genetic material of apes with that of our own species, we are likely to be so impressed with the similarities that we judge our unfortunate fellow creatures to be worthy medical specimens for the treatment of human diseases, or, like the deaf, as fit for the teaching of sign languages. Chimpanzees are akin to us; hence we may infer matters useful to mankind from the study of their bodies and behavior. In the seventeenth and eighteenth centuries, however, for mechanists who subscribed to a dualist perspective of the world, it was otherwise. Apes were judged fundamentally distinct from man and woman, just because they did not possess the necessary attributes of human behavior. They bore a physical resemblance to us, of course, but lacked all the traits associated with human morality. What greater proof could there be of the uniqueness of mankind, it was argued, than that nearly perfect copies of the human body, having a similar brain, larynx, and the other organs of speech, were incapable of giving these physical properties the moral animation that only the human soul can inspire? The more perfect the physical likeness of apes to ourselves, the more plain was this manifest truth about the spiritual essence with which our species alone had been endowed.[6]

God's growing superfluousness also gave greater prominence to men's and women's earthly passage—that is, to human history, than had ever been the case before. In a desanctified world our nature came increasingly to be understood as manufactured by mankind itself, with the history of civilization standing to human nature as the Creation itself stands to God. Notwithstanding the biblical chronologies of Bishop James Ussher and his followers in the seventeenth century, and, in the eighteenth century, even of Newton himself, the human race came to be recognized as the author of its own world, as creator and demiurge, and man the promulgator of his own persona, no longer shaped in the image of God but rather according to his own design. Unlike all other animals, mankind, it was claimed, can change, improve, and perfect its nature. Freed from the tyranny of passions, it can establish the rule of reason, and this passage from the domination of passions to the fulfillment of reason—from barbarism to civility, from a rude state of nature to a polite and refined state of culture—is what is here described as the transformation of physical man and woman into moral man and woman, whose successive metamorphoses constitute the conjectural history of our species which anthropologists of the Enlightenment sought to retrace.

There are countless expressions of that dichotomy in Enlightenment thought—in Montesquieu, Rousseau, Buffon, La Mettrie, Diderot, or Cabanis, not to mention Adam Smith, whose hypothetical reconstruction of the origins of mankind's moral sentiments within the context of a wider theory of natural jurisprudence, embracing the development of economic and social institutions and the emergence of government, prompted Dugald Stewart to coin the expression "conjectural history" as one description of his project. The point to be stressed as the beginning of this treatment of eighteenth-century anthropology is that such terminology of physicality and morality or, in French, *le physique* and *le moral*, can also be found throughout seventeenth-century natural philosophy, jurisprudence, and even theology. As far as I know it originates with Nicolas Malebranche's *Méditations chrétiennes et métaphysiques* of 1683, in a passage in which he speaks of the combination within mankind of *le physique* and *le moral*,[7] terms that might at first look interchangeable with *l'âme* and *corps*—except that, unlike *l'âme* and *corps*, they have an evolutionary connection in that one may give rise to and become transformed into the other. The shifting terminology from *corps* and *l'âme* to *physique* and *moral* is one of the principal expressions of what Arthur Lovejoy called the temporalizing of the "chain of being" in the Enlightenment.[8] Together, the spiritualization of mankind in a mechanical universe, and the temporalization of human nature once the Celestial City has almost entirely vanished, inform what I take to be a central paradigm of both physical and social anthropology in the Enlightenment. Elaboration of these themes lies at the heart of Enlightenment human science, and it was also this paradigm which in the eighteenth century was to become the focus of criticism of those who sought to construct a theory of human nature on alternative foundations.

With regard to physical anthropology, much the best illustration of that thesis I can offer comes from Buffon. No one in the eighteenth century made the distinction between *le physique* and *le moral* in human nature more central to the whole of his or her philosophy, nor did anyone achieve greater distinction in the Enlightenment as a true conjectural historian at once of the development of the human race and of the formation of the world itself. Whereas Carolus Linnaeus, in his profoundly significant *Systema naturae* (dating from 1735), had already classified mankind's zoological place in nature within the context of other animal species, Buffon, in his essay devoted to the "Histoire naturelle de l'homme" of 1752, addressed himself to the developmental and degenerative characteristics of human nature, through the flux and variations modulating all created matter.[9] Buffon sought to reconstruct both the earth's past and mankind's own metamorphoses, in the unavoidable absence of surviving testimony, along lines that must have been the case. In his *Histoire naturelle*, he remarks that "Just as civil history records the epochs of the revolutions of human affairs, and the occurrences of *moral* events, so does natural history record the physical development and transformations of the world."[10] In His creation of heaven and earth, God made only the matter of the universe. In the beginning it was without form, and its consolidation, followed by the appearance of water, the birth of volcanoes, the generation of animals, the separation of continents, and the emergence of the human race, all constitute what Buffon termed "les époques de la Nature." Within natural history, moreover, every species, he observed, passes through stages of development as well. Nature is in continual vicissitude, and all species are either undergoing perfection or degradation—a point Buffon emphasized especially with regard to animal species in the New World, which he claimed were degenerative forms of their counterparts in the Old.[11]

As a monogenist, Buffon viewed the whole of humanity as forming only one species—tinged with the color of climate, as he put it. There could perhaps be other physical determinants of race, he thought (such as bile or blood), but in general he supposed that skin color was an acquired characteristic, shaped essentially by climate, much as the Baron de Montesquieu had believed that climate gives rise to diverse human dispositions and temperaments;[12] he consequently ignored alternative, and especially polygenist, explanations of the origins of race such as those put forward by Isaac de La Peyrère in the seventeenth century and by Henry Home, Lord Kames, in the eighteenth, which aspired to greater compatibility with scripture. Since the human race must originally have been white, as Buffon conjectured, black populations were—rather like llamas in comparison to camels, or pumas in relation to tigers—merely deformations of the archetype of humanity. This proposition, it should be noted, excludes the evolution of mankind from ape, since the white archetype could scarcely have arisen from a black animal without a soul, although it did permit a proposition which others would later pursue to a racist conclusion—that apes might just be degenerate blacks.[13] As a rule, Buffon adopted the Cartesian perspective of an unbridgeable gulf between humanity and animals. They occupy nothing more than the physical world of extended matter. We fill a spiritual world—the world of civil history—in which our nature is manufactured by us. The history of mankind does not follow the life history of each individual person; for the human race alone, we might remark, phylogeny does not reproduce ontogeny. In transforming our nature, in our passage from the *sociétés naturelles* of our forebears to the *sociétés policées* of a civil association, we overcome the fixity of animal nature and make ourselves subject to the variable rules of morality which we establish for ourselves.

About the civil or moral history of mankind, Buffon has relatively little to say: his is, after all, a natural, that is, a physical, history of the development of the world and of human nature. Yet that civil history lies precisely at the heart of what I call the social anthropology of the Enlightenment. Samuel Pufendorf, in his *De jure naturae et gentium* of 1672, provided the quintessential account of man's and woman's passage from barbarism to civilization, upon which so many thinkers of the Enlightenment, especially French, Scottish, and German, were to construct their own philosophies of human nature. Before the publication of Montesquieu's *De l'esprit des lois* in 1748, Pufendorf's text—not least because of its remarkable annotation and cross-references with the classics by its translator, Jean Barbeyrac—was to prove the most important work, the handbook, even, of Enlightenment anthropology. Pufendorf accepted a Hobbesian conception of human nature as selfish, but added to the Hobbesian perspective what might be termed the social dimension of selfishness. He sought to explain how humanity might have advanced from a savage state, in which each person's needs were few and easily satisfied, into a world of interdependent relations, in which men's and women's more complex and sophisticated wants required the continual assistance of others for their fulfillment. The feebleness of individuals in isolation would have required their cooperation so that each might survive, he claimed. This was the theory of natural sociability or *socialitas,* which excluded any notion of primitive benevolence such as had been postulated by Hugo Grotius, and which Immanuel Kant would later describe as the doctrine of "unsocial sociability."[14] According to Pufendorf, the selfish needs that must have driven our ancestors into society would have given rise to forms of cooperative life which in turn must have led to the formation of new desires. And since every person's perception of his or her needs is limitless, those needs themselves therefore become infinite, so that the patterns of cooperation which men and women established must in turn have generated new desires and thereby stimulated the emergence of ever more richly and densely organized forms of the selfishly motivated structure of communal life. Thus was generated the history of civil society, as Pufendorf conceived it—a history in which our species progressively parts company from other animals because, unlike them, mankind is capable of fruitful culture and useful improvement. This is a history of which humanity itself and not God is the author. As Pufendorf puts it, the original way of producing *natural* (or physical) entities is by creation; that of producing *moral* entities is by imposition.[15]

We here note again the passage from our species' physical to its moral state, in the sense in which morality pertains to what humans do, rather than to how they are made—that is, insofar as members of the human race are responsible for the institutional arrangements with which they therefore bind themselves. Their civil history, as the Cardinal de Retz, Adam Ferguson, and, later, Karl Marx contended, may not proceed along the paths they choose, but it is the outcome or expression of human design, "the world of civil society," having been, as Giambattista Vico observed, shaped by its own subjects.[16] The most characteristic idiom in which this institutional establishment of the moral life of mankind was articulated in the Enlightenment was probably that of the social contract, as devised by the philosophers of natural law in the tradition of Grotius, Pufendorf, and their disciples. According to this conception of the human manufacture of society, the gulf between nature and culture was bridged by an artifice that made it possible for persons to will what they should become collectively, to subject themselves by common consent—that is, to authorize—a moral authority by which they would be freely bound, in a manner quite unlike the force exercised upon them by their physical appetites. By and large, the social contract was a political metaphor designed to explain the way that individuals' moral obligations might be self-imposed. Some of its eighteenth-century proponents allowed that it was difficult to conceive how human society might have originated from any primordial contract, since the parties to it would have had initially to possess already the moral qualities which it alone could engender, while Enlightenment critics of the doctrine, including the third Earl of Shaftesbury, David Hume, Adam Smith, and Edmund Burke, found fault with its assumption that primordial men and women might once have lived in a presocietal state of nature, since society itself was natural. Proponents and critics alike, however, contended that individuals' social ties shaped their moral beliefs and that these beliefs at once informed and reflected changes in the institutions of society.

The correspondence between persons' moral ideas and their social relations, indeed, forms a central feature of conjectural history in the Enlightenment, and Pufendorf's version of that doctrine, and his model of the stadial development of society, came to form one of the principal threads of anthropological speculation in the period, particularly in what later proved a four-stages model, in the various formulations propounded by Montesquieu, A. R. J. Turgot, Smith, Adam Ferguson, John Millar, and many other—mainly French and Scottish—thinkers of the second half of the eighteenth century.[17] According to this theory, societies were shaped by the prevailing mode of sustenance or economic activity. In the savage or primeval state, the only form of sustenance was hunting, and following the growth of such societies, and the progressive inadequacy of hunting as a mode of life which could maintain that growth, they would have become increasingly transformed, it was argued, into pastoral economies, which in turn would have become agrarian and subsequently commercial societies, which—because they provided for the satisfaction of ever more luxurious wants—were the most advanced and refined communities the world had ever known.

These propositions were elaborated in treatises and philosophical dictionaries, including the *Encyclopédie*, by a whole host of both leading and minor social philosophers and conjectural historians of the day throughout enlightened Europe. Some commentators were unpersuaded by them and instead preferred to remark upon the diversity and multiplicity of cultures throughout the world, such as had been reported by explorers and missionaries to Africa, China, the Americas, and Polynesia. Richly documented expeditionary surveys and travelers' tales, like those assembled in the abbé Prévost's *Histoire générale des voyages* of 1746–89 and similar great collections, might appear to confirm ancient and medieval observations on other civilizations and perhaps belie a unidimensional perspective of barbarism's passage into modernity.[18] But as often as not, those who sought a scientific understanding of human nature subscribed, with Montesquieu and Denis Diderot, both to the moral significance and attractions of a plurality of social systems (and hence decried colonialism and slavery) and equally to a developmental and evolutionary perspective of human history as a whole. J.-F. Lafitau's much appreciated *Moeurs des sauvages ameriquains, comparées aux moeurs des premiers temps* of 1724 makes plain this juxtaposition of two perspectives in its very title. The elaboration and refinement of the propositions put forward by Pufendorf and his disciples, as well as the reservations expressed about them by equally notable figures such as Lord Monboddo and J. G. von Herder, form perhaps the most substantial and coherent theme of speculation about the development of human nature in this period.

I stress the notion of the refinement of polite society—the *politesse* that accompanies the development of *les sociétés policées*—which in the eighteenth century took a variety of forms. One striking expression of the thesis appears in Smith's *Theory of Moral Sentiments* of 1759, where he claims that it is distasteful to express in any strong degree those passions which arise from certain dispositions of the body. About sex, which he describes as "naturally the most furious of all the passions," he says that any striking display of it is indecent—even between husband and wife; "such is our aversion to all the appetites which take their origin from the body." "All strong expressions of it," he claims, "are loathsome and disagreeable." "It is quite otherwise," however, "with those passions which take their origin from the imagination."[19] Buffon had made much the same point in his *Histoire naturelle*. With regard to the relations between male and female of the human species, the history of civilization is the history of the refinement of attraction into affection, of sex (*le physique*) into love (*le moral*). In perversely inverted form, we find this thesis also in the Marquis de Sade, in his remarks, which figure more than once in his novels, upon the fascination of sexually aroused women in cretinous males, who, while they may not have been uplifted by civilization, possess in their disproportionately large penises a more materially uplifting trait that civilized men too often lack.[20] Imbeciles, that is, make up in *le physique* what they lack in *le moral*.

Now it should be noted that this developmental history is not at all teleological. It is described in terms of the original sources that prompt it, not backward from its conclusion. It issues from the springs of human action, whose impetus is undirected by the supposed destiny of mankind's moral development. Perhaps the best and most familiar illustration of that thesis can be found in Montesquieu, particularly in his early "Essai sur les causes qui peuvent affecter les esprits et les caractères," most likely drafted between 1736 and 1743. In an argument that may have been drawn from the Neapolitan scholar Paolo Mattia Doria, Montesquieu contends that these causes are of two kinds—*physical* and *moral*. Some operate on the human body, providing spring to its muscle fibers or relaxing them, while others, like customs or education, generally achieve their effects upon our minds. Montesquieu makes the same claim in his *Considérations sur le grandeur des romains* and in his *Défense de l''Esprit des lois'*. The point he emphasizes most of all is that moral causes actually contribute more than do physical causes to the general character of a nation and to the quality of mind of a population, and to establish the truth of that proposition he gives the example of Jews, who, whatever their physical circumstances and however they live, scattered all over the world, always show a lack of common sense.[21] Much the same stress upon the predominance of moral causes can be found in Hume's "Essay of National Characters."[22]

With respect to physical causes, and particularly climate, Montesquieu's argument is quite familiar. Much inspired by John Arbuthnot's *Essay concerning the effects of air on human bodies* of 1733, it has two main elements that address nerve fibers, on the one hand, and the productivity of the soil, on the other. A hot climate, claimed Montesquieu, expands nerve fibers, and because nature is bountiful it renders men and women plentifully supplied with the fruits of the earth, making them indolent, more passive, more inclined to despotism, and thus to Catholicism. A cold climate constricts nerve fibers, and because in cold regions the fruits of the earth are more scarce, individuals are forced to be more self-reliant, more inclined to freedom, more drawn to republicanism, and also to Protestantism.[23] Rousseau, it should be noted, took exactly the opposite line in his *Essai sur l'origine des langues,* which dates mainly from the 1760s but was published posthumously, claiming that the spirit of liberty came from the south and from the classical republicanism of Rome, while that of despotism, he remarked, came from the Gothic north.[24] But the point to be stressed here is the sense of the physical determination of men's and women's moral attributes.

Beyond the determination of morality from below, as it were—rather than from above in a teleological sense—this argument points to another and related principle: that it is morality which determines politics, and not, as Aristotle, or in the Enlightenment, Rousseau, supposed, politics which determines morality.[25] For Montesquieu, moreover, there is a major difference between the manner and operation of moral and physical causes, since while physical causes make certain consequences occur, moral causes tend instead to act as limits upon what may be legislated. They are not so much agents of change as barriers to it—underlying forces that arrest superficial reforms and at once sustain and constrain our national patterns of political life.

In addition to claims about the physical and moral causes that shape human nature everywhere and in all epochs, we find in the Enlightenment a number of arguments about the physical determination of mankind's passage from one stage of its civil history to the next. A frequently reiterated thesis, proffered somewhat in anticipation of Sigmund Freud, might be termed that of the genital determination of culture or the sexual prompting of civilization. Kames puts it thus: Americans, he claims, have feeble organs of generation, that is, small penises, little used. From this shortcoming stems the consequence that American savage males display insufficient ardor for the female sex, so that matings are infrequent, and children scarce, keeping the population low, thus retarding the pressure of numbers which had forced the savages of the Old World to find more ample sustenance, first through livestock and then agriculture, thereby ensuring the advance of human culture and society.[26]

A second argument is that mankind's passage from the brutish and natural world to the moral domain is made possible, not by any physical impulsion, but by the absence among us of internal physical impediments or instincts. According to this perspective, we are not bound to become civilized, but are enabled to do so because we are by our nature "let loose from the trammels of instinct," as Ferguson puts it, malleable, flexible, in continually regenerative transformations, such as are discussed by Herder.[27] *Socialitas* is here rendered not as a propensity but as a capacity. Defined as the human race's self-development because of this potentiality for change, our history is thus perceived as different from animal history—a species history of advance from brute sensibility to the attainment of reason and language. So whereas population growth drives mankind to civilization, the human qualities of liberty and adaptability are negative in their effects, pointing in no particular direction but merely removing natural obstructions to a possible history of change. They operate in the opposite way from sexual impulsion; instead of prompting, they merely do not arrest, the course of human development.

The main point to be emphasized about both arguments is that they explain the development of civilization as natural to mankind—as made possible by human nature—either negatively or positively. Ferguson in his *Essay on the History of Civil Society* of 1767 puts that proposition as follows, in a passage which was to catch the attention of Herder and would inform his own philosophy of history as well: Art, says Ferguson, is not to be distinguished from nature. "Art itself is natural to man," who is "in some measure the artificer" of his own nature. "He is perpetually busied in reformations." There is no human state of repose. Like a coiled spring, our nature expands and grows.[28] Civilization, Ferguson might have added, is just the measure of that growth—the passage from the physical to the moral world. The history of the self-directed evolution of morality is thus the history of the refinement of human nature.

Some central criticisms of this scenario, it should be remarked, were already elaborated in the Enlightenment, in particular, and most notably, by Jean-Jacques Rousseau, who took issue with both the cultural and physical anthropology of his day—with both Pufendorf and his disciples, on the one hand, that is, and with Buffon, on the other. With respect to cultural anthropology Rousseau offered a direct challenge to the proposition that art and civilization, as Ferguson conceived them, are natural to man. There is no link at all, claims Rousseau, between our physical and moral attributes. Moral inequalities do not arise from natural differences, but are established by consent, by artifice, indeed by deception and fraud. Mankind, he thought, was through art made not *Homo sapiens* but *Homo deceptus* or *Homo traductus*. Physical differences are mere variations of bodily traits; moral distinctions are of ranking and preference; the first are *lexical*, the second *cardinal*. The history of civilization, according to Rousseau, is not the history of the refinement of human nature but of its deformation.[29] It relates the perfection of the individual, but at the same time the corruption of the species. Moral man, he claimed, is not naturally fulfilled, but denatured, living *hors de soi*—outside himself—drawing his identity from others, finding his self-esteem only through his reputation.

Rousseau put forward at least two versions of his philosophy of history, according to which the passage from *le physique* to *le moral* is rendered as a measure of mankind's unnatural depravity, rather than its natural ascent. In one, the *Essai sur l'origine des langues,* he adopts the same four-stages model that Turgot and the Scots had done, along the lines already anticipated by Pufendorf and others, but only to show how steep has been our fall. Men and women, he claims, were once moved by physical passions—unaffected, unreflective, unadorned, largely exuberant and childlike. They cried out "Aimez-moi" as they embraced each other, expressing the fundamental joy of their physical attraction. As their nature was slowly transformed and they became more social, they began to cooperate in more calculated ways and eventually, he states, called out "Aidez-moi" to one another. Now, in contemporary society, they do not even cooperate but only make use of one another. "Aimez-moi," superseded by "aidez-moi," has finally been supplanted by "Donnez de l'argent." This is the prevailing ethos of the moral world we inhabit; it is the secular history of mankind's fall, in its passage from the savage state of nature to the selfish vices of commercial society.[30]

Rousseau's second account of our corruption, actually produced earlier but which I address in reverse order because I wish to invoke it to criticize the mainstream tradition of physical anthropology in the Enlightenment, is developed in his *Discours sur l'inégalité* or second *Discours* of 1755. This whole work is built round the imagery of mankind's passage from natural appetites to factitious duties, largely in terms of the incompatibility of two kinds of inequality. His argument here is principally designed to show that physical inequality—indeed the realm of human nature as a whole—is not responsible for moral inequality, that is, the realm of artifice, consent, and corruption generally, and his text was clearly read in this way by its critics, of whom one, Louis-Bertrand Castel, entitled his reply of 1756 *L'Homme moral opposé à l'homme physique*.[31] Our species was made in the image of God, Castel exclaimed; hence brute animal nature must not be preferred over a divinely inspired order of morally righteous conduct to which we ought to aspire. Rousseau's distinction between *le physique* and *le moral* in human affairs—it should, moreover, be noted—informs not just his anthropology but his social, moral, and political philosophy in general. It accounts for the difference between sex and love, again in the second *Discours,* and between natural liberty, on the one hand, and moral liberty, on the other, and even between force and right—that is, between government and sovereignty—in his *Contrat social*.[32]

But it is the contrast between these terms in the *Discours* that I wish to emphasize here, and particularly that opposition between animality and morality in human nature which was, correctly, the focus of Castel's attention. For if culture is not natural to mankind, then the signs of human culture—such as justice, property, virtue, reason, and language—are similarly not natural. These are acquired attributes and institutions, Rousseau claimed. By nature, we are indeed very much like animals—more flexible, more malleable, no doubt, and uniquely capable of change—but, at bottom, moved by the same impulses of *amour de soi* and *pitié*. It follows, therefore, that the great gulf between us and the rest of animal creation which had been postulated by Perrault, Tyson, Buffon, and others, simply did not exist. There was, for Rousseau, no break in the *scala naturae,* no missing rung in nature's ladder. From such claims, which effectively animalize human nature (or at least bridge the gulf between our own species and those of the great apes), he concluded that the creature commonly called an *orangutan,* meaning "man of the woods" in Malay, might indeed be a progenitor of mankind. The *Discours sur l'inégalité,* although a conjectural history of the human race which seeks to abstract our nature from the social forces that have corrupted it, in fact turns out to be a very good piece of empirical primatology, since Rousseau's portrayal of the solitary, frugivorous, indolent, and itinerant creature described in that text actually accords rather well with the true orangutan of Southeast Asia, and indeed forms one of the best such descriptions available in the West until the fieldwork undertaken since the late 1960s by Biruté Galdikas, John MacKinnon, and Peter Rodman. Although inadvertent, Rousseau's generally accurate contribution to empirical primatology by way of a hypothetical deconstruction of mankind provides as striking a justification for conjectural history as any I know.[33]

In the early 1770s the debate was pursued by Monboddo, who followed Rousseau's contention that language is not natural to our species and therefore agreed that these creatures, which apparently possess bodies— that is, *physical* attributes—much like our own, must not be denied membership of the human race simply because, as he put it, they have not "come the length of language."[34] If persons who silently play chess, or dine alone, are not thereby excluded from the status of mankind, why then, asked Monboddo, should orangutans be denied it? For Rousseau, their being apparently mute might indeed be proof of their higher rationality rather than their inferiority to the human race—a pretence of stupidity so as to avoid enslavement. At any rate, whether they were human or not, Rousseau thought, depended—according to Buffon's own definition of a viable species—on the fecundity of the offspring of matings between orangutans and humans. This was a matter, he claimed, which could only be settled by experiment[35]—a physical definition of a species, I might add, and not a moral one.

Monboddo's main contribution to the history of anthropology, however, was more by way of criticism of Buffon than in terms of his debt to Rousseau. What are the orangutan's vocal organs for, he asked in the second edition of the first volume of his *Origin and Progress of Language* (1773– 92), if not to be employed for speech and rendered active through use? Everywhere in nature, he claimed, a creature that has the outward form of another creature is, on that evidence alone, a member of the same species. Why should it not be so for mankind as well? Is it not more fitting to describe language as a skill acquired and perfected through use, than to portray it as a mysterious incorporeal divide between man and beast? Why should God have encumbered orangutans with speech organs they cannot use? Was He so uneconomical as to engage in redundant design? Orangutans are speechless, Monboddo contended, not because of their lack of a spiritual faculty, but because they have not yet had occasion to exercise their vocal organs and put them to the use which God intended for them in the course of their own social development.[36]

These propositions excited much interest among comparative anatomists and other scientific authorities in the late eighteenth century, most of whom decried both the hypotheses about the mental capacities of apes and the conjectural history of mankind which had informed them. J. F. Blumenbach, in *De generis humani varietate nativa* of 1775, Petrus Camper in his roughly contemporary anatomy of the orangutan, S. T. Sömmerring, Herder, and many other interested commentators all claimed that the true distinction between mankind and ape lies in their different physical constitutions—in the (human) intermaxillary bone, for instance; in the (orangutan) laryngial pouch; or in the (human) upright posture—all of these variations pointing to a divide between ourselves and apes which was not based on language or any other attribute of an incorporeal soul.[37] With the orangutan now cast out of the human race on account of physical or material divergences only, the attention of anthropologists came to be refocused on the apparent boundaries within the human race, rather than upon the animal limits of humanity. Thereafter physical anthropology came to be addressed to the origins and significance, if any, of races.

It is around this new approach to the study of races under the influence of Blumenbach,[38] especially, that modern physical anthropology and the professional associations and university chairs devoted to its study were established in the early nineteenth century. Blumenbach's comparative anatomy of racial differences was judged altogether more reliable than the earlier speculative and even fabulous classifications of the varieties of man propounded by Linnaeus, and it soon came to be much preferred, as well, to the genetic and evolutionary perspective—on the racial deformations of a single human archetype—adopted by Buffon and his followers. Modern physical anthropology, in effect, may be said to have arisen in response to the hypothetical taxonomies and conjectural natural histories of the Enlightenment. In challenging the framework of those eighteenth-century philosophies of history which plotted the metamorphosis of savagery into citizenship, this new discipline disregarded its precursors' explanations of the rise of *l'homme moral* and concentrated instead upon *l'homme physique* or, rather, *les physiques de l'homme*, in all their empirically distinguishable traits.

By the mid–nineteenth century, moreover, modern social anthropology had also begun to assume some of its current forms—that is, in terms of the empirical investigation of languages, ritual, and the cultural patterns of kinship, diet, and exchange of primitive peoples. Whether their perspectives have been comparative or evolutionary, social anthropologists have addressed only the moral dimension and functions of savage practices and institutions. They have sometimes, often unwittingly, been inspired by Enlightenment doctrines—by Herder's pluralist conception of the mysterious *Kräfte* or dynamic forces that come to be realized in communal life, for instance; or by Vico's reflections on the mythology of the natural symbols of divinity around which he supposed that the earliest civilizations had been shaped; or—a debt they more frequently recognized— by Montesquieu's strictures on the study of governments and cultures by alien commentators able to fathom their apparently skewed logic because uncontrolled by their values. No less than physical anthropologists today, social anthropologists characteristically reject the genetic continuities postulated in the Enlightenment between *l'homme physique* and *l'homme moral*—with this difference, of course: that their concern lies with the manifestations of morality alone. In place of the dynamic and evolutionary perspectives of the Enlightenment, modern physical and social anthropology have, indeed, reverted—albeit on different sides—to the seventeenth-century dichotomy between *corps* and *l'âme*. The prospect of a unified human science embracing both the biological and cultural attributes of mankind, must, therefore, appear more remote, more implausible, now than in the eighteenth century.

In fact, Enlightenment anthropologists themselves, and not only their critics, came progressively to challenge the supposition of speculative historians that the moral ideas we have adopted could be traced to the successive refinements of at least some of our physical impulses. Even contemporaneously with the great age of conjectural history from about 1750 to 1800 other anthropological commentators came to reject the idea of a passage from *le physique* to *le moral*—indeed, came to reject the very distinction between those terms—in favor of one dimension, *le physique*, alone. Diderot, in *Jacques le fataliste*, first published posthumously in 1796, claims that the dichotomy of the moral world from the physical world appears without foundation—"vide de sens"[39]—thereby adopting a claim he draws from the materialists, J. J. O. de La Mettrie and especially the Baron d'Holbach, who in his *Système de la nature* had argued that men and women are purely physical beings. The same point—that the physicality of human nature explains all—appears in a central passage of the *Histoire des Deux Indes*, dating from 1772, which we now know to have been drafted by Diderot himself rather than by the abbé Raynal, and indeed it can be found as an important theme in many of Diderot's writings.[40] His interest in physical explanations of human nature was inspired in part by his appreciation of the Montpellier School of Medicine—Dr. Théophile Bordeu and others—and it led him to make the claim that morality must always accord with human physiology and natural passions. Hence his critique of Christianity, a religion of celibacy, abstinence, and self-restraint, in contrast to the sexual license, or the pure reign of physical impulsions, which marks the natural morality of the people of Tahiti, as he recounts in the *Supplément au Voyage de Bougainville* (posthumously published for the first time also in 1796). In Tahiti we find a society of utter physicality—not the hypocritical suppression of physical appetites which Smith thought was the measure of civilization—but a society where sexuality prevails: a society in which morality is thus more healthy, freed of the torments of celibacy. A society without population decline—a society whose sexuality promotes the growth of numbers—is therefore utilitarian. Sex both makes the people happy and the population increase, at the same time.[41]

From Montesquieu, Diderot, and the mid–eighteenth-century materialists we thus derive what I should like to term some deep structural explanations of human nature and behavior: the idea that physicality determines morality, that morality (*les moeurs* and *les manières*) determines politics, rather than the reverse, as we have seen, in the tradition of classical Greek thought. With the *idéologues* in the course of the French Revolution, many of them members of the *Classe des sciences morales et politiques* at the *Institut,* these ideas were developed into general propositions about the physiological sources of morality—the shaping of human nature, not out of metaphysical abstractions, but from springs within the matter of the human body itself,[42] as P. J. G. Cabanis argued in his *Rapports du physique et du moral de l'homme,* whose first collected edition dates from 1802. Just as that human body came to be perceived as determined by its physical constitution, so, moreover, did the body politic. With Claude Henri de Saint-Simon—a disciple of Xavier Bichat, Cabanis, and the *idéologues* in general—there arose a science of society which looked below the surface of political life, to inner forces and mechanisms, rather than to legislation and government, as giving human affairs their natural direction. With Saint-Simon Enlightenment political theory yields to post-Enlightenment administration. The hygiene of the body politic, and its internal structure and arrangements, are seen to supplant any principles of superimposed authority or organization from above. *Le physique* replaces *le moral* as the determinant of human nature, and, for those who took these principles to heart and sought to understand the regulative forces and metabolic principles that gave social life its form, it was not anthropology but rather the new discipline of *sociology* which was to become the preeminent human science of the next age.[43]

NOTES

1. On this subject, see especially Lewis Hanke, *Aristotle and the American Indians* (London: Hollis and Carter, 1959); Margaret Hodgen, *Early Anthropology in the Sixteenth and Seventeenth Centuries* (Philadelphia: University of Pennsylvania Press, 1964); and Anthony Pagden, *The Fall of Natural Man: The American Indian and the Origins of Comparative Ethnology* (Cambridge: Cambridge University Press, 1982).

2. The best treatment of Enlightenment anthropology, albeit with a predominantly French focus, remains Michèle Duchet's *Anthropologie et histoire au siècle des lumières* (Paris: F. Maspero, 1971). See also Carminella Biondi, *Mon frère, tu es mon esclave* (Pisa: Libreria Goliardica, 1973); Clarence Glacken, *Traces on the Rhodian Shore* (Berkeley and Los Angeles: University of California Press, 1967); John Greene, *The Death of Adam* (Ames: Iowa State University Press, 1959); Georges Gusdorf, *Dieu, la nature et l'homme au siècle des lumières,* Vol. V of *Les sciences humaines et la pensée occidentale* (Paris: Payot, 1972); Marvin Harris, *The Rise of Anthropological Theory* (New York: Crowell, 1968), chap. 2; P. J. Marshall and G. Williams, *The Great Map of Mankind: Perceptions of New Worlds in the Age of Enlightenment* (London: Dent, 1982); Sergio Moravia, *La scienza dell'uomo nel Settecento* (Bari: Laterza, 1970); Roy Pearce, *Savagism and Civilization,* revised ed. (Baltimore: Johns Hopkins University

Press, 1967); G. S. Rousseau, ed., *The Languages of Psyche, Mind, and Body in Enlightenment Thought* (Berkeley, Los Angeles, Oxford: University of California Press, 1990); Franck Tinland, *L'Homme sauvage* (Paris: Payot, 1968); and Herbert Wendt, *I Looked for Adam* (London: Weidenfeld and Nicolson, 1955), chaps. 1–5. On nineteenth-century anthropology, see especially George W. Stocking, Jr., *Race, Culture, and Evolution* (New York: Free Press, 1968), and *Victorian Anthropology* (New York: Free Press, 1987). On the history of physical anthropology, see F. J. C. Cole, *The History of Comparative Anatomy* (London: Macmillan, 1944), and Frank Spencer, ed., *History of Physical Anthropology: An Encyclopedia* (forthcoming).

3. On the early history of the term, which figured even in the titles of medical or physiological tracts from the early sixteenth century, see Georges Gusdorf, *Introduction aux sciences humaines* (Paris: Payot, 1974), 155–156, and, especially for its French language usages, Claude Blanckaert, "L'Anthropologie en France: Le mot et l'histoire (XVIe–XIXe siècle)," *Bulletin et mémoires de la Société d'Anthropologie de Paris* 1 (1989): 13–44. As Phillip Sloan contends in chap. 5 in this volume, the medical senses of the term came gradually to be supplanted with natural historical meanings by the late eighteenth century. On the putative invention of the science of man at the end of the eighteenth century, see Michel Foucault, *Les Mots et les choses* (Paris: Gallimard, 1966), chaps. 8 and 10.

4. The study of *la pensée sauvage*, and of savage man's passage from nature to culture, are, of course, in modern anthropological theory associated above all with the work of Claude Lévi-Strauss, who, in his *Totémisme aujourd'hui* (Paris: Presses Universitaires de France, 1962), 145, and elsewhere, traces this view of the discipline to Rousseau. For a brief introduction to the place of *l'homme physique* and *l'homme moral* in the history of ideas, see Sergio Moravia, "'Moral'—'physique': Genesis and evolution of a 'rapport,'" in *Enlightenment Studies in Honour of Lester G. Crocker*, ed. Alfred Bingham and Virgil Topazio (Oxford: Voltaire Foundation, 1979), 163–174.

5. On mechanistic doctrines of animal and human behavior in the Enlightenment, see especially Jacques Roger, *Les sciences de la vie dans la pensée française du XVIIIe siècle*, 2d ed. (Paris: Armand Colin, 1971); Aram Vartanian, *Diderot and Descartes: A Study of Scientific Naturalism in the Enlightenment* (Princeton, N.J.: Princeton University Press, 1953); Robert Schofield, *Mechanism and Materialism: British Natural Philosophy in an Age of Reason* (Princeton, N.J.: Princeton University Press, 1970); and John Yolton, *Thinking Matter: Materialism in Eighteenth-Century Britain* (Minneapolis: University of Minnesota Press, 1983).

6. See my "Tyson and Buffon on the Orang-utan," *Studies on Voltaire and the Eighteenth Century* 151–155 (1976): 2301–2319.

7. See Nicolas Malebranche, *Méditations chrétiennes et métaphysiques*, VII.22, in his *Oeuvres complètes*, ed. Henri Gouhier and André Robinet (Paris: J. Vrin, 1959), X.79.

8. See Arthur Lovejoy, *The Great Chain of Being*, first published in 1936 (Cambridge, Mass.: Harvard University Press), chap. 9.

9. On Linnaeus's anthropology, see especially Gunnar Broberg, *Homo sapiens Linn*, in Swedish with an English summary (Uppsala and Stockholm: Almqvist and Wiksell, 1975), and Broberg, "Homo Sapiens: Linnaeus's Classification of Man," in *Linnaeus: The Man and His Work*, ed. T. Frängsmyr (Berkeley and Los Angeles:

University of California Press, 1983), 156–194. On Buffon's anthropology, see the introduction and collection of texts assembled by Michèle Duchet, *Buffon: De l'homme* (Paris: Maspero, 1971), and Claude Blanckaert, "Buffon and the Natural History of Man," *History of the Human Sciences* 6, no. 1 (1993): 13–50.

10. Buffon, "Des époques de la Nature," in his *Histoire naturelle,* supplement, vol. 5 (1778), in *Oeuvres philosophiques de Buffon,* ed. Jean Piveteau (Paris: Presses Universitaires de France, 1954), 117.

11. Above all vol. 14 of Buffon's *Histoire naturelle* (1766), titled "De la dégénération des animaux," in the *Oeuvres philosophiques,* 408–413. For an extraordinary and particularly critical treatment of this subject in the work of Buffon and his disciples, see Antonello Gerbi, *The Dispute of the New World* (1955, in Italian; English translation, Pittsburgh: University of Pittsburgh Press, 1973).

12. See especially Montesquieu's *De l'esprit des lois,* Livre XIV, chaps. 2–3, and Buffon's *Histoire naturelle,* vol. 3: "Variétés dans l'espèce humaine," in the *Oeuvres philosophiques,* 312–313.

13. See Buffon, *Oeuvres philosophiques,* 354–355, and Sloan, "The Idea of Racial Degeneracy in Buffon's *Histoire naturelle,*" in *Studies in Eighteenth-Century Culture,* vol. 3, ed. Harold Pagliaro (Cleveland: Case Western Reserve University Press, 1973), 293–321.

14. On Pufendorf's negative theory of human nature and sociability in connection with the doctrines of Hobbes, see especially his *De jure naturae et gentium,* II.i.6, II.iii.15, II.iii.20, and IV.iv.2; Istvan Hont, "The Language of Sociability and Commerce," in *The Languages of Political Theory in Early-Modern Europe,* ed. Anthony Pagden (Cambridge: Cambridge University Press, 1987), 253–276; Fiammetta Palladini, *Discussioni seicentesche su Samuel Pufendorf: Scritti latini (1663–1700)* (Bologna: Il Mulino, 1978), and idem, *Samuel Pufendorf discepolo di Hobbes* (Bologna: Il Mulino, 1990).

15. Pufendorf, *De jure naturae et gentium,* I.i.4, in a discussion, "On the Origin and Variety of Moral Entities."

16. In the context of Enlightenment thought, see especially Adam Ferguson's formulation of this principle, in his *Essay on the History of Civil Society,* Part III, section 1, in the Duncan Forbes edition (Edinburgh: Edinburgh University Press, 1966), 122: "Nations stumble upon establishments, which are indeed the result of human action, but not the execution of any human design." Vico's remark appears in his *Scienza nuova,* in the 3d (1744) ed., I.iii.331. See also Leon Pompa, *Vico: A Study of the "New Science"* (Cambridge: Cambridge University Press, 1975), 15–41.

17. See Ronald Meek, *Social Science and the Ignoble Savage* (Cambridge: Cambridge University Press, 1976).

18. On the contribution to anthropology of eighteenth-century voyages of discovery and exploration, see especially Gilbert Chinard, *L'Amérique et le rêve exotique dans la littérature française au XVIIe et au XVIIIe siècle* (Paris: Hachette, 1913); Alan Frost, "The Pacific Ocean: The Eighteenth Century's 'New World,'" *Studies on Voltaire and the Eighteenth Century* 152 (1976): 779–822; and Marshall and Williams, *The Great Map of Mankind.*

19. Adam Smith, *Theory of Moral Sentiments,* ed. D. D. Raphael and A. L. Macfie (Oxford: Clarendon Press, 1976), I.ii.1.1–6, 27–29.

20. In the *Histoire de Juliette* (Paris: Union générale d'éditions, 1966 ed.), 2:63,

for instance, the Marquis de Sade describes the member of the imbecile friar Claude as "semblable à celui d'un mulet . . . neuf pouces six lignes de tour sur treize pouces de long . . . le plus beau champignon . . . qu'il soit possible d'imaginer."

21. See Montesquieu, *Oeuvres complètes*, ed. Roger Caillois (Paris: Gallimard, 1949–51), II.60, 173 and 1145, and Robert Shackleton, *Montesquieu: A Critical Biography* (London: Oxford University Press, 1961), 313–319.

22. Like Montesquieu, Hume there distinguishes physical from moral causes, and, while doubting the operation of the former upon traits of national character, claims that the latter determine the character not only of nations but also of different professions.

23. See especially Montesquieu, *De l'esprit des lois*, Livres XIV–XVII; Robert Shackleton, "The Evolution of Montesquieu's Theory of Climate," *Revue internationale de philosophie* 33–34 (1955): 318–329; and Shackleton, *Montesquieu*, chap. 14.

24. See Rousseau, *Essai sur l'origine des langues*, chaps. 9, 10, 19.

25. See the *Confessions*, Livre IX, in Rousseau's *Oeuvres complètes*, ed. Bernard Gagnebin, Marcel Raymond et al. (Paris: Gallimard, 1959–), 1:404–405.

26. See Lord Kames, *Sketches of the History of Man* (Edinburgh 1774), I.i.1 and II.ii.12, 24–25 and 75–84, and my "Apes and Races in the Scottish Enlightenment: Monboddo and Kames on the Nature of Man," in *Philosophy and Science in the Scottish Enlightenment*, ed. Peter Jones (Edinburgh: John Donald, 1988), 152–156.

27. Adam Ferguson, *Principles of Moral and Political Science*, 2 vols. (Edinburgh 1792), I.ii.10, 120, and J. G. Herder, *Auch eine Philosophie der Geschichte zur Bildung der Menschheit*, section 1, in his *Sämmtliche Werke* (Berlin: Weidmannsche Buchh., 1877–1913), 5: 503. See also Gladys Bryson, *Man and Society: The Scottish Inquiry of the Eighteenth Century* (Princeton, N.J.: Princeton University Press, 1945), 114–147, and F. M. Barnard, ed., *J. G. Herder on Social and Political Culture* (Cambridge: Cambridge University Press, 1969), 33–60.

28. Ferguson, *Essay on the History of Civil Society*, Part I, section 1, 6–7.

29. For a notable treatment of this subject, see Michèle Ansart-Dourlen, *Dénaturation et violence dans la pensée de Rousseau* (Paris: Klincksieck, 1975).

30. See Rousseau's *Essai sur l'origine des langues*, chaps. 9–11; his *Contrat social*, III.15; my "Rousseau on Rameau and Revolution," in *Studies in the Eighteenth Century*, Vol. IV, ed. R. F. Brissenden and J. C. Eade (Canberra: Australian National University Press, 1979), 272–282; and my "Rousseau's Pufendorf: Natural Law and the Foundations of Commercial Society," in *History of Political Thought* 15 (1994): 391–393.

31. François Louis Claude Marin adopted a similar title, *Lettre de l'homme civil à l'homme sauvage* (Amsterdam 1763), for his own critique of Rousseau, not intended, however, as a rejoinder to the *Discours sur l'inégalité*.

32. See especially Rousseau's *Discours sur l'inégalité*, part 1, and *Contrat social*, I.iii and III.i (*Oeuvres complètes*, III.157, 354 and 395).

33. For a fuller treatment of the subject of this paragraph, and of Rousseau's speculative anthropology in general, see my "Perfectible Apes in Decadent Cultures: Rousseau's Anthropology Revisited," in *Daedalus* (summer 1978): 107–134, and Victor Goldschmidt, *Anthropologie et politique: Les principes du système de Rousseau* (Paris: J. Vrin, 1974).

34. See Monboddo, *Of the Origin and Progress of Language* (Edinburgh 1773–92), I.i.14, 177–182.

35. See Rousseau's *Discours sur l'inégalité*, n. 10 (*Oeuvres complètes*, 211 and 1371–1372).

36. On Monboddo's contribution to Enlightenment anthropology, see my "Apes and Races," 147–152, and "The Orangutan as Speechless Man: Monboddo as Critic of Buffon," *Journal of the History of the Behavioral Sciences* (forthcoming).

37. For commentaries on the orangutan and its subhumanity in the period immediately following the publication of Monboddo's work, see especially J. G. Herder's *Abhandlung über den Ursprung der Sprache* (1772) and his foreword to *Des Lord Monboddos Werk von dem Ursprung der Sprache* (1784), in his *Sämmtliche Werke*, 5: 44–45 and 15: 185–186; J. F. Blumenbach's *De generis humani varietate nativa* (Göttingen 1775), 35–39; Arnout Vosmaer's "Description de l'orang-outang" (Amsterdam 1778), 12–13; Petrus Camper's "Account of the Organs of Speech of the Orang Outang, in a Letter to Sir John Pringle," *Philosophical Transactions of the Royal Society* (1779), LXIX.i.139–159, and his "De l'orang-outang, et de quelques autres espèces de singes," in his *Oeuvres* (Paris 1803), i.5–196; Buffon's "Addition à l'article des Orangs-outangs," *Histoire naturelle*, supplement, vol. 7 (1789): 15–16; William Smellie's *Philosophy of Natural History* (Edinburgh 1790–99), i.521; and Jean-Baptiste Audebert's *Histoire naturelle des singes et des makis* (Paris 1799–1800), 12–13.

38. On this subject, see especially the memoirs and accounts from several sources edited by Thomas Bendyshe, in *The Anthropological Treatises of Blumenbach* (London: Longman, Green, Longman, Roberts and Green, 1865). See also Hans Plischke, *Johann Friedrich Blumenbachs Einfluss auf die Entdeckungsreisenden seiner Zeit* (Göttingen: Philol.-hist. Klasse,1937).

39. See *Jacques le fataliste* in *Diderot: Oeuvres romanesques*, ed. H. Bénac (Paris: Garnier, 1959), 670.

40. See John Hope Mason and Robert Wokler, eds., *Diderot: Political Writings* (Cambridge: Cambridge University Press, 1992), introduction and "Extracts from the *Histoire des Deux Indes*," xxxiii–xxxiv and 206.

41. Ibid., xix–xxi and 63–64.

42. On the *idéologues'* conception of anthropology, see especially Sergio Moravia's *Il pensiero degli idéologues: Scienza e filosofia in Francia (1780–1815)* (Florence: La Nuova Italia, 1974); his "The Enlightenment and the Sciences of Man," *History of Science* 18 (1989): 247–268; and Martin Staum's *Cabanis: Enlightenment and Medical Philosophy in the French Revolution* (Princeton, N.J.: Princeton University Press, 1980).

43. On that path toward social science in the late Enlightenment, see especially Keith Baker, "The Early History of the Term 'Social Science,'" *Annals of Science* 20 (1964): 211–226; Georges Gusdorf, *La conscience révolutionnaire: Les idéologues*, vol. 8 of *Les sciences humaines et la pensée occidentale* (Paris: Payot, 1978), 392–406; Brian W. Head, "The origins of 'La science sociale' in France, 1770–1800," *Australian Journal of French Studies* 19 (1982): 115–132; Moravia, *Il pensiero degli idéologues*, 743–753; and my "Saint-Simon and the Passage from Political to Social Science," in *The Languages of Political Theory in Early-Modern Europe*, 325–338. A section of this paper was presented at the 1991 Bristol Congress of the Enlightenment. A

differently conceived and shorter version was prepared for a 1990 conference at the University of Lancaster on the human sciences in the seventeenth and eighteenth centuries, now published as "From *L'Homme Physique* to *L'Homme Moral* and Back," *History of the Human Sciences* 6, no. 1 (1993): 121–138. I am grateful to participants in each case for their comments, and especially to Christopher Fox for some trenchant observations that I have tried to accommodate without abandoning my thesis or producing a wholly different paper.

THREE

Medical Science and Human Science in the Enlightenment

Roy Porter

This chapter is in two halves, because it tackles two questions. How far, and in what ways, did eighteenth-century medicine seek to become "scientific"? How was eighteenth-century medicine involved in Enlightenment ambitions to create a science of man? In addressing both, my concern is rather to uncover the ideologies of the past than to write the history of the present. I shall neither judge the contribution of the premoderns to medical progress,[1] nor appraise the epistemologies and methodologies of social science today.[2] Questions will be raised, however, regarding the roots of our notions of the affinities between medicine and science, between natural and social science, between biology and culture.

HISTORIOGRAPHY

Eighteenth-century medicine has been subject to radically diverse readings. Standard postwar histories of the rise of modern science—by Herbert Butterfield, A. R. Hall, C. C. Gillispie, and so forth—find little to say.[3] Why? It is tacitly assumed that medicine doesn't fall within the sphere of science at all, being an art or applied knowledge, and so more appropriately treated as part of the history of technology (not that medicine achieves much space in histories of technology either).[4] But it is also presumed that medicine—indeed, life science in general—was eclipsed by the revolutionary breakthroughs in natural philosophy, mathematics, and experimental physics in the seventeenth century.[5] This impression is confirmed by the synoptic histories of medicine that became canonical in the first half of this century—notably, those of Fielding Garrison, Charles Singer, Arturo Castiglioni—which typically dismiss the Enlightenment period as a wasteland of speculative theorizing and arid rationalism; "the lost half-century in English medicine," William Lefanu has called the post-1700 era.[6] There was no medical Newton, nor even Franklin; no transformation was wrought in the understanding of the laws of life, of health and disease, until the nineteenth century, with Xavier Bichat, Karl Ernst von Baer, Theodor Schwann, Karl Ludwig, Claude Bernard, Pasteur, and others—in other words, with pathoanatomy, histology, cell biology, and the advent of bacteriology. Charles Rosenberg further argues that there was no "therapeutic revolution" till the nineteenth century (the date might be set even later).[7] And, discussing the "birth of the clinic," Michel Foucault contends that medicine did not achieve a "scientific gaze" till the reform of the Paris Hospital in 1794—whereafter the sick were seen, not as objects of charitable care, but as specimens of disease:[8] medicine's delayed-action response to the Boylean invention of the experimental laboratory a full century and a half earlier. Indeed, Bruno Latour has hinted that medicine came of scientific age only with the Pasteurization of the laboratory from the 1870s.[9]

Thus medicine got left behind. A revisionist historiography is, however, emerging. The title of a recent volume of essays, *The Medical Revolution of the Seventeenth Century*, proclaims a transformation, its editors argue, stimulated in part by the ferment of science itself.[10] This reading is not unproblematic—indeed, one of the editorial pair, in his solo contribution, is at pains to emphasize continuities rather than ruptures[11]—but it is becoming widely accepted in today's scholarship that, at least from the mid–seventeenth century, the stream of medical theorizing became confluent with the rapids of the scientific revolution.[12]

Indeed, the Enlightenment historian Peter Gay has suggested that medicine was in the van of progress in the age of the *philosophes*. In his "The Enlightenment as Medicine and as Cure" (1967), an essay substantially incorporated into the second volume of his *The Enlightenment: An Interpretation*, Book Three: "The Pursuit of Modernity," chapter 1, "The Recovery of Nerve," Section 2, under the heading, "Enlightenment: Medicine and Cure,"[13]—the titles tell the story—Gay pictured medical progress as the boosting of general optimism.

On the eve of Enlightenment, humoralism was still in the saddle, and practice hidebound. "It is safe to speculate," argues Gay, "that in the eighteenth century a sick man who did not consult a physician had a better chance of surviving than one who did."[14] But things were changing fast. Inspired by Bacon, Descartes, Locke, and above all Newton, eighteenth-century medicine pulled its weight in the scientific team. "By the time of Locke . . . [m]edicine, it seemed, was transforming itself from a medieval mystery . . . into a thoroughly philosophical science," through casting off tradition, authority, and metaphysics, and pioneering observation and cognitive pluralism.[15] In developments owing much to Herman Boerhaave, "all this stress on experience, on clinical study and experimentation, revolutionized medicine."[16]

The progress of medicine in turn reinforced Enlightenment confidence. If, as Gay admits, "the most powerful agent in the recovery of nerve was obviously the scientific revolution,"[17] medical improvements also played their part, for in many fields of clinical practice, "the results remained impressive."[18] In particular, thanks to the success of smallpox inoculation, "the recovery of nerve was visible on men's very faces"—thereby making medicine "the most highly visible and the most heartening index of general improvement."[19] In sum, Gay concludes, "for observant men in the eighteenth century, philosophes as well as others, the most tangible cause for confidence lay in medicine."[20]

Gay's enthusiasm is perhaps excessive. It is questionable whether Boerhaavian "scientific medicine" truly advanced understanding of disease or improved clinical practice.[21] His belief that medicine contributed to the population explosion would be queried by today's demographers, who tend to see birthrate, not death rate, fluctuations determining the premodern demographic curve.[22]

Nevertheless, Gay offers a valuable starting point, because he engages with the self-image of eighteenth-century medicine. Whiggish judgments aside, there is abundant evidence to show that leading medical thinkers aimed to assimilate and capitalize upon the paradigms of scientificity rendered so prestigious by Bacon, Descartes, the Royal Society, the Académie Royale des Sciences, and, above, all, by Newton—aimed, in short, to bring themselves within force field of natural philosophy.[23]

MEDICINE, HISTORY, AND PROGRESS

Medical luminaries drew on the triumphs of the "new philosophy" and the rhetoric of "the party of humanity"[24] to create progressive profiles for medicine itself. For their part, the *philosophes* forged mythic histories of the arts and sciences, of morals and politics, chronicling battles down the centuries between the forces of good and evil, reform and reaction;[25] paralleling these, medical authors too dramatized the former struggles of reason against superstition, open-mindedness against dogmatism, experience against blinkered book learning, to illustrate the adage that truth was great and would prevail.[26] If the noble advances of the Hippocratics (supposedly the founding fathers of philosophical medicine) had been stifled throughout the Middle Ages by bigoted reverence for blind authority, the advent of printing, the genius of Leonardo, and the daring of Vesalius had rekindled the investigative spirit.[27] William Harvey was the ideal icon: his connections with Padua, his friendships spanning the generation between Bacon and the founders of the Royal Society, his impeccable experimentalism—all bespoke the happy marriage of medicine and science, enshrined above all in the emblem of heart as a pump, perfect proof that knowledge advanced when medicine and the mechanical philosophy pulled together. Harvey's links with the Court told further exemplary tales of the place of patronage in the advancement of learning.[28] At a later stage, homage could be paid, in another exemplary biography, to John Hunter, whose fame was recruited as an object lesson in the Baconian union of hand and head, manual and mental labor, thanks to which surgery had supposedly become a science.[29]

Eighteenth-century medical propagandists harped on standard Enlightenment chords—the glories of Greece, revived by the Renaissance, the importance in later times of freedom, patronage, and public support—to evoke a medical past that rationalized the present and forecast a glorious future. The strains became very familiar indeed. In its article "Medicine," Chambers's *Cyclopaedia* traced the birth of medicine with Hippocrates and its corruption with the idolators of Galen:

> At length, however, they [Galen's errors] were purged out and exploded by two different means; principally indeed by the restoration of the pure discipline of Hippocrates in France; and then also by the experiments and discoveries of chymists and anatomists; till at length the immortal Harvey overturning, by his demonstrations, the whole theory of the antients, laid a new and certain basis of the science. Since his time, Medicine is become free from the tyranny of any sect, and is improved by sure discoveries in anatomy, chymistry, physics, botany, mechanics &c. See MECHANICAL.

In short, concluded the historical part of this article, "it appears, that the art originally consisted in the faithful collecting of observations; and that a long time after, they began to enquire and dispute, and form theories; the first part has ever continued the same; but the latter always mutable. See HYPOTHESES &c."[30]

Above all, Enlightenment historiography named for medicine a noble mission. In North America, Benjamin Rush, physician and signatory to the Declaration of Independence, and in Britain, William Buchan, author of the best-selling *Domestic Medicine* (1769),[31] represented the improvement of health as essential to human emancipation—from fear, from want, from suffering. If, heretofore, the medical profession had, alas, all too often taken a leaf out of the church's book, pursuing a closed shop and cynically keeping the people in the dark, this "dark age" was about to end: physic would be laid open to the people, health and humanity would march forward together.[32]

IATROMECHANISM, THE MEDICAL MODEL, MEDICAL MATERIALISM

Eighteenth-century medical thinkers sought to render their study truly scientific—or, in contemporary idiom, "philosophical"—in various ways. Observation and experiment became the watchwords of many. Giorgio Baglivi, Bernard Mandeville, and other early eighteenth-century polemicists advocated the bedside over the library, and experience over a priori rationalism, while being careful to elevate "philosophical" empiricism above the "vulgar" empiricism of "empirics" or quacks.[33]

The line between blind empiricism and vain rationalism was difficult to trace and tread. The jargon of traditional rational medicine, and such supposed entities as "animal spirits" or "black bile," also formed easy targets: were they not the relics of scholasticism, mere words, much bruited, never seen by the anatomist?[34] And Mandeville mocked Thomas Willis's attempts to explicate the internal workings of the body by means of mechanico-chemical analogies with stoves, stills, and circuits of pipes and wires—what were these but the fancies of an idle brain?[35] Yet critics of rationalism themselves adopted a broadly mechanical approach to the animal economy, concentrating upon the gross anatomy of the major organs, and the motions, pressures, and velocities of the fluids. Baglivi valued a mathematical approach, arguing in his *De Praxi Medica* (1699) that "the human body in its structure, and equally in the effects depending on this structure, operates by number, weight, and measure," and that herein lay the essence of science, for "it operates thus by the wish of God, the highest Creator of all things, who, so that the framework of the human body should be accommodated more suitably to the capacity of the mind, seems to have sketched the most ordered series of proportions in the human body by the pen of Mathematics alone."[36]

Among iatro-mathematicians such as Archibald Pitcairn, sickness was resolved into quantifiable hydraulic problems, health apparently depending upon the unobstructed passage of life-sustaining fluids throughout the physical system. The belief of late-seventeenth-century iatro-chemists, -mathematicians, and -mechanists that the human being could be represented as a machine that broke down when sick was increasingly dismissed as crude and simplistic: doctors were not plumbers. All the same, Boerhaave's mechanical conceptualization of the body proved easily the most influential medical schema of the first half of the eighteenth century.[37]

It was, of course, superseded after around 1750, but the shifting of the accent from the vascular to the nervous system (irritability, sensibility, excitability, reflex action) in the work of Albrecht von Haller in Göttingen;[38] William Cullen,[39] John Brown,[40] and others in Scotland; and among the Montpellier "material vitalists"[41]—indicates that the next generation was

no less committed to the conviction that understanding the organic economy demanded systematic investigation of corporeal fibers, tissues, vessels,
and membranes. The pioneering by Giambattista Morgagni of the theory
and practice of morbid anatomy—the belief that postmortem dissections
would reveal the lesions that constituted disease—followed naturally from
the confidence in structural/functional correlations created by the mechanical outlook.[42]

Medicine was never monolithic. In Halle, Georg Ernst Stahl repudi-
ated the materialist reductionism implied in mechanistic theorizings, es-
pousing an "animism" that postulated a superadded nonmechanical soul
("anima"), acting purposively at various planes of consciousness, as the
sine qua non of living beings.[43] The Stahlian view saw disease conditions
less as structural/functional breakdowns than as the attempt of the soul
to counter threats from morbific matter. In stressing the limits of mechanism, Stahl was not alone; his doubts were echoed by François Boissier de
Sauvages's insistence that life required a central organizing principle.[44] And
in their different ways, Théophile Bordeu in Montpellier,[45] Robert Whytt
in Edinburgh,[46] and John Hunter in London[47] equally denied the suffi-
ciency of statics, hydraulics, and mechanics for explaining animation and
the animal economy, postulating instead some form of vital force and/or
structured nervous organization that transcended the merely mechanistic.

Only a very few radical polemicists, of whom J. O. de La Mettrie is of
course the most notorious, truly sought to reduce *l'homme* to *une machine.*[48]
Even so, it is clear that eighteenth-century biomedical theory had substantially taken on board the terms and tenets posited and popularized by the
new Newtonian natural philosophy. To some degree this shows the weath-
ercock of intellectual fashion at work. But weightier matters were at stake.
Confronted by the more bizarre, irrational manifestations of human behavior—coma, convulsions, malformations, delirium, and the like—traditional opinion had commonly looked beyond, seeking explanation in
divine will or demoniacal possession, in astrological influences, or in imagination. Medical mechanists, by contrast, insisted that such phenomena
could and should be comprehensively accounted for in terms of the internal organs and local operations of the body itself. The mechanistic program
thus promised to enlarge medicine's exclusive explanatory authority.[49]

MEDICINE AND MATHEMATICS

Medicine sought in other ways to subject the mysteries of the organism
to rational inquiry. Doctors participated in the wider quantifying quest.
Seventeenth-century scientific metaphysics claimed that the real was what
could be measured.[50] And, as has recently been emphasized by Ian Hack-

ing, Lorraine Daston, Theodore Porter, and others, the extension of the empire of science was furthered by the systematic reduction to intelligibility of the marvelous, mysterious, and miraculous through fact collection and processing, through *l'esprit géometrique*, through application of the law of large numbers, and through the routine digestion of data in tables, formulae, equations, and ratios.[51] What could be enumerated could be formulated as natural laws, albeit only laws of probability. The empire of chance—so-called acts of God—could thereby be tamed.

Falling sick had traditionally epitomized the arbitrariness of existence, or rather the essentially providential meaning of things. When mortal affliction struck ("out of the blue"), eyes had looked upward.[52] From the mid–seventeenth century, physicians strove to extend their control over frail mortal existence by plotting biomedical regularities. From the balancing chair of Santorio Sanctorius to the hemostatic experiments of Stephen Hales, the physiological operations of the body were weighed, measured, and numbered. Collection of vital statistics led to life tables and the calculation of differential life expectations, essential for insurance, annuities, and other actuarial computations. Bills of Mortality were published, upon which morbidity profiles could be based, and plotted against season, environment, and other variables. As Ulrich Troehler has demonstrated, epidemic mortality ("mortality crises") became the object of investigation by army, navy, and civilian doctors, especially after 1750, in the expectation that if periodicities in outbreaks of epidemic disorders such as smallpox and putrid and gaol fevers could be established, such infections might be predicted, controlled, and even prevented.[53] It is no accident that it was James Jurin, secretary of the Royal Society as well as a prominent physician, who led the attempt to state the superior benefits of smallpox inoculation in numerical terms.[54] By the close of the eighteenth century, birth and death, once those great mysterious ministers of Providence, had been reduced to a formula in the larger Malthusian ecobiology.[55]

The statistical worldview tended toward secularization:[56] a human destiny was implied whose key was not, it seemed, the decrees of Calvinist soteriology but the balance of possibilities. Numerical laws, even probabilistic laws, also entail a certain determinism: trends do not tarry for personal free will. Attention to the mass as well as the individual thus beckoned medicine away from the bedside to the wider panorama of life chances in context of the animal economy and the human comedy.[57]

MEDICINE AND TAXONOMY

Another initiative lay in classification. John Ray, Joseph Pitton de Tournefort, and, most systematically, Linnaeus, sought to enhance the power and glory of natural history by establishing a rational coherent, and organized inventory of creation, be it "natural" or "artificial." It was obviously attractive for medicine to follow suit. In France, Boissier de Sauvages in his *Nouvelles classes des maladies* (1731), and in Scotland, William Cullen, devised particularly influential taxonomies.[58]

The rationales of such schemes partly lay in pedagogic needs: nosological charts of discrete diseases presented from the podium were easily assimilated by students and readily applied on call. But, more significantly, and in line with Thomas Sydenham's advocacy of a "natural history of disease,"[59] such taxonomies reinforced a growing conviction (itself marked in the shift from humoral fluidism to structural/functional solidism) that diseases truly were distinct entities, possibly localizable, possessing an ontological status perhaps analogous to chemical elements. Even more ambitiously, in his *Zoonomia*, Erasmus Darwin advanced a disease taxonomy—supposedly not just heuristic but natural, because grounded in physiology—predicated upon the organization of the nervous system: diseases were to be pigeonholed as disorders of irritability, sensation, volition, and association, according to the tier in the psychophysiological hierarchy they affected.[60]

No consensus clinched the objective truth or usefulness of such disease grids. Cullen's variegated disease-distribution map was challenged by John Brown's counter-insistence upon the unitary nature of disease. Yet Brunonian medicine drew no less, in its own way, upon contemporary scientific idiom. Brown devised a disease barometer, calibrated upon a single arithmetic scale, running from zero (asthenic disorders: the *ultima thule* of under-stimulus) to eighty degrees (lethal over-stimulus), in which the midpoint represented a healthy equilibrium. The image of a single axis thus translated illness into an objective, quantifiable entity, and, in turn, made for a therapeutics that boiled down entirely into a matter of dosage size.[61]

THE IDEOLOGICAL THRUST

Thus medical authors attempted to set their discipline upon more "scientific" footings. The advances of the "new philosophy" afforded many attractions. But "scientific medicine" was also a highly contentious shibboleth, a pawn in intraprofessional rivalries, an ideological shuttlecock. After all, the relations between medical reality and medical philosophy were exceptionally problematic—large claims might be being staked for medicine's potential, precisely because its actual state seemed the very reverse: an intellectual backwater, a sordid scandal. "Scientific medicine" might thus be less a proud boast than a dream, even a compensatory wish fulfillment. For what vexed many practitioners was that, in truth, medicine never had caught up with chemistry, or experimental physics, or even botany: high time it did. To examine the politics of "scientific medicine," I wish briefly to discuss one such writer, whose decrial of medical backwardness went hand-in-hand with an almost millennialist vision of scientific medicine's potential: Thomas Beddoes.[62]

Chemist, physician, researcher, educator, poet, political radical, Beddoes was a paladin of the late Enlightenment.[63] A middle-class lad of parts, Beddoes rose through talent, taking his B.A. at Oxford, and then studying medicine, first in London and then at Edinburgh University, before returning to Oxford in the early 1790s as reader in chemistry. An energetic experimentalist,[64] he was a fervent publicist for the French Revolution in chemistry.[65]

And for the French Revolution in politics, at least before the Terror. Outspoken radicalism[66] made him enemies in high places, spurring his decision in 1793 to quit Oxford and remove to Bristol, where he engaged in private practice while nursing his brainchild, the Pneumatic Institution, born in 1799.[67]

Modern chemistry, Beddoes insisted, was a triumph; medicine, by contrast, a disgrace. Surveying health beliefs held among even the well educated, he reflected, drawing upon the archetypal Enlightenment image:[68]

> So much is there to unlearn on the present subject, that to reduce the mind to that *blank* state in which, according to Locke, it originally exists, would be no mean advantage to four out of five among those, who may take up these essays. The author is certainly accustomed to see invalids, for whom it would be happy if their whole mass of ideas . . . could be abolished.

Clinical medicine was a swamp of ignorance, folly, and deception.[69] Why? Society, judged the Enlightenment humanitarian, had its priorities all wrong. Pursuit of higher things had deflected the human race from the relief of suffering: "an infinitely small portion of genius has hitherto been exerted in attempts to diminish the sum of our painful sensations; and the force of society has been exclusively at the disposal of Despots and Juntos, the great artificers of human evil."[70] Swords should be beaten into scalpels: "there is no improvement in the condition of the World, for which we might not hope from the bloodless rivalship of nations."[71]

But, worse, medicine itself was corrupt. Clinical practice—history taking, diagnosis, prognosis, therapeutics—ought to be scientific and objective. The reverse was the case. In Britain's booming commercial economy, medicine had been seduced from rational ends by the cash nexus: rich patients and grasping, servile doctors were equally to blame.[72] For money talked in medicine no less than politics. High society clients, though generally oozing "the most profound ignorance," pretended to a wondrous wisdom of their own,[73] all too frequently, Beddoes lamented, picked up from conversations with doctors or culled from tomes like William Buchan's

Domestic Medicine. They demanded deference from doctors, and, alas, top doctors colluded in this charade. For they had sold their souls to "the sick trade,"[74] toadying shamelessly to their patients' prejudices, needlessly multiplying visits and worthless medicaments: medicine, Beddoes grumbled, "is become an art of administering drams."[75]

So while chemistry was a freeway of scientific progress, medicine was a cul-de-sac of quackery. Radical change was imperative,[76] but what was to be done? Beddoes pinned his faith on science. He cultivated close contacts with the Midlands Lunar Society group, especially Erasmus Darwin and James Watt.[77] He devoured scientific and philosophical literature in all the major languages. And he pondered, like a good *philosophe,* the dialectics of science and society.[78]

Beddoes saw history as broadly progressive. He was equivocal about the Ancients, being apt to chide Plato for his "mystic passages,"[79] and the Christian Middle Ages were a slough of superstition.[80] But the breakthroughs of the sixteenth and seventeenth century were beyond praise. Indeed, Beddoes wanted, as it were, to cancel the intervening century, and retrace medicine's steps to the zesty youth of the Royal Society, when the cross-fertilization of science and medicine had yielded so much. Preoccupied with pulmonary diseases, Beddoes republished the pioneer gas researches of the Restoration natural philosopher John Mayow. This great inquirer had not only "discovered several elastic fluids, and the essential properties of the most active of them all," but he had also "aspired to change the whole face of medicine and physiology, by the application of his wonderful discoveries to the appearances of animal nature."[81] Beddoes's tribute clearly carved out a niche for the eulogist.[82]

For Beddoes believed that by rerunning Mayow's program, stupendous breakthroughs in scientific medicine would follow. Touting the applicability of gases to respiratory disorders, he predicted in 1793 that "from chemistry, which is daily unfolding the profoundest secrets of nature," we can hope for "a safe and efficacious remedy for one of the most frequent painful and hopeless of diseases," that is, consumption.[83] The physical sciences proffered the model for the biomedical. In his *Chemical Experiments and Opinions* (1790), he forecast that, "however remote medicine may at present be from such perfection," there was no reason to doubt that:[84]

> by taking advantage of various and continual accessions as they accrue to science, the same power will be acquired over living, as is at present exercised over some inanimate bodies, and that not only the cure and prevention of diseases, but the art of protracting the fairest season of life and rendering health more vigorous will one day half realise half the dream of Alchemy.

Chemistry thus portended a medical millennium.[85] "In a future letter," he announced to Erasmus Darwin in 1793,[86]

I hope to present you with a catalogue of diseases in which I have effected a cure. The power of the various elastic fluids, and of a diet and medicines calculated according to the theory, which prescribes a particular mixture of airs in any given case, will I hope soon be determined. . . . Many circumstances indeed seem to indicate that a great revolution in this art is at hand. . . . And if you do not, as I am almost sure you do not, think it absurd to suppose the organization of man equally susceptible of improvement from culture with that of various animals and vegetables, you will agree with me in entertaining hopes not only of a beneficial change in the practice of medicine, but in the constitution of human nature itself.

As is clear, Beddoes's Promethean expectations of science's revolutionizing life were underpinned by an Enlightenment vision of *homo* as a creature of infinite possibility. Human attributes were not fixed, the mind not straitjacketed by original sin or innate ideas. A champion of Locke's philosophical empiricism, Hartley's physiological psychology, and the learn-by-doing educational theories of Rousseau and Richard Edgeworth, Beddoes set no limits to improvement under the stimulus of sense experience, and to progress through dynamic interaction with the environment, natural and social.[87] Convinced that nature was truth, and lay open to the senses, Beddoes regarded education as necessarily, in the widest sense, experimental.

Thus experimental sciences such as chemistry were miniatures of the wider panorama of human progress. Chemistry had found its true locus: the laboratory, the scientific society. Medicine still lacked its own milieu and methods. What should they be? It is an interesting comment on the times that, in his plans for progress, Beddoes ascribed no role to medical colleges or universities. Nor did he expect much from hospitals, since these were typically run by cabals of those very noblemen and sycophantic physicians responsible for medicine's stagnation.[88] "I could name a variety of hospitals," he growled, "which in a long course of years have furnished nothing or next to nothing to medical philosophy."[89]

Beddoes urged a mental revolution in the medical profession, accompanied by a measure of state aid. Trapped in the ethos of private practice, medicine was jealous and even secretive. Knowledge was rarely pooled, and often lost. Such "waste of facts"[90] was shocking, for the "the grand expedient for rendering physiology popular and medicine certain, is to enlarge our stock of observations on animal nature."[91] Data must standardly enter the public domain.

Beddoes proposed two solutions. The first was personal: more energetic medical publication. A copious author himself, he also edited *Contributions to Physical and Medical Knowledge* (1799), a compendium of scientific papers written largely by his friends, and published widely in the new medical press.[92] Looking back, he saw it as no accident that Gutenberg had soon been followed by Vesalius—it was the printing press that had guaranteed the superiority of the medical Moderns over the Ancients.[93]

The second was institutional: he urged agencies for systematic collection and storage of medical facts in some convenient archive.[94] "Why should not reports be transmitted at fixed periods from all the hospitals and medical charities in the kingdom to a central board?"[95] Physicians at large should also be encouraged to submit information. A salaried clerical staff of data processors working at such "register offices" should make findings freely available.

Without proper information storage and retrieval, medicine would never become a progressive science or an effective art.[96] The desideratum was the founding of "a national bank of medical wealth, where each individual practitioner may deposit his gains of knowledge, and draw out, in return, the stock, accumulated by all his brethren."[97] Pathological laboratories should also provide greater information to stock such data "banks."[98] "An institution for the minute examination of dead bodies and for inventing superior methods of examination might be so conducted in the metropolis as possibly to double the number of facts, useful to medicine, in twenty years."[99] How absurd that superstitions about corpses should be allowed to stymie beneficial medical research![100]

Dissection rooms provided ready-made data. Something more active was needed too: an investigation center. In this regard, Beddoes's ideal seems to have been his custom-built Pneumatic Institution in Clifton. Small, privately owned, and under his personal direction, it conducted primary research (above all, into gases and respiration) with in- and out-patients as guinea pigs.[101] Beddoes worked at the Institution with hand-picked helpers, including the young Humphry Davy, while also drawing on the support of far-flung fellow workers via a postal network.

The Institution's strength, Beddoes believed, lay in the opportunities it afforded for integrating laboratory inquiry with clinical research. One had to know the sick, not just their diseases. Such sites would kindle the vital spirit of experiment. Conventional doctors stooped to the prejudices of the present: experiment would create the agenda of the future.

But in picturing the good physician as the experimentalist, Beddoes knew he was skating on thin ice. For experimentalism smacked of quackery, and the public was anxious lest hospitals become theaters for uncontrolled experimentation. Not least, in the counterrevolutionary atmosphere after 1793, innovation in speculative theorizing, and, above all, anything hinting at a French connection, had fallen under grave suspicion.[102] In short, "the protective feeling of indignation against men supposed capable of sporting with life and suffering . . . has set the public against experiments, as they are called, in physic."[103]

Replying to such "antagonists of research,"[104] Beddoes lauded experiment as the soul of science, and called upon history as his witness. "Since the reign of James I experimenters have prodigiously thriven in this country . . . Boyle and Newton are names as familiar to every one as his A, B, C"; "the immortal Sydenham" was their medical peer.[105] Such "experimentalists . . . take the utmost pains to inform themselves of the previously discovered qualities of the objects to which they direct their attention. They apply their faculties coolly that they may not impose upon themselves, and report scrupulously that they may not impose upon others."[106] In short, experimenters "are in earnest to discover truth,"[107] and modern medicine's leading lights were all of their colors: "Our Potts and Hunters" have "made all their improvements in defiance of routine," and "the improvements in medicine which at this moment occupy the attention of civilized society"—Beddoes gave vaccination as an example—"are due to experimenting."[108] "Who but must shudder," he inquired, with heavy irony, "at the idea of the havoc that would ensue, if a tribe of Bergmans, Lavoisiers, Bertollets, and Cavendishes, were to break in among us under the guise of physician."[109]

In short, Beddoes promoted the medical experimentalist as the analogue of the chemist; open minds who "believe in cool dedication": "When one mode of investigation does not succeed, they lose no time in recruiting their thoughts and returning to the charge."[110] Setting medicine thus on an experimental basis would change clinical relations. Under the benevolent care of experimentalists, patients should no longer meddle in doctors' decisions. But if the laity must not mess with medicine, they too, for their health's sake, should cultivate science. What better than to encourage every girl and boy to take up chemistry?[111]—not merely as a schooling of the mind, but as a prophylactic against disease itself. "I should not be surprised," ventured the never-say-die *philosophe*, "if, in a few years, it should become as common for persons to go about to instruct private families in chemistry, mechanics, in tangible geometry and various sorts of manufactures, as it now is in music and drawing."[112]

In short, rendering medicine scientific carried implications for its social relations. To these issues I shall return.

MEDICINE AND THE SCIENCES OF MANKIND

As needs no emphasis, the moral and political thinkers of the Enlightenment, seeking to understand and change society, looked to science for their model. Science was a matchless engine of analysis: objective, critical, progressive. Natural order promised models of social order, in particular (for many *philosophes*) a vision of free individual activity in systems governed by natural law.

If humanists were looking to science, medical men were, as it were, returning the gaze, and looking out at society. The spirit of inquiry encouraged medicine away from individual cases in search of the laws of health and sickness in wider contexts, examining climate, environment, the rhythms of epidemics over the historical *longue durée*. As Ludmilla Jordanova has emphasized, the Enlightenment was marked by energetic medical environmentalism.[113] Certain eighteenth-century physicians developed an enlarged social awareness, confronting the interplay of medicine, sickness, and society. What determined the patterns and pathways of illness in the community? Why did sickness levels vary from group to group, society to society, region to region? Confronting such wider variables, many eighteenth-century physicians felt obliged to be more than bedside healers: they had to become anatomists, and doctors, of society.[114]

In some ways, this was nothing new. The Hippocratic "airs, waters, and places" tradition had, centuries earlier, alerted medicine to environmental hazards, underpinning the rise of "miasmatist" thinking.[115] Occupational disorders had long been studied;[116] and bubonic plague had focused a medical politics of contagion and quarantine.[117] Even so, eighteenth-century physicians felt driven to develop a richer understanding of sickness as a function of time, place, and society.

A mark of this may be the coining by the ultra-Newtonian, Scottish-born physician George Cheyne of the phrase the "English malady"—the title of his book of 1733.[118] A malaise of anxiety and depression, the English malady bore a formal resemblance to traditional "melancholia."[119] But there were also subtle differences. The melancholiac had customarily been asocial, the solitary, the outsider. The sufferer from the English malady was, according to Cheyne, par excellence a creature of society: it was the prospects and the pressures of a mobile, open, affluent, urban, polite society that precipitated this quintessentially "nervous" disorder.

Cheyne denied the English malady was merely an imaginary disease of fashion—physiologically speaking, it was all too real, arising from that destruction of the digestive and nervous system all too often produced by modern lifestyles, with their gourmandizing and toping, lack of exercise, tight lacing, late hours, and stuffy rooms. It was nothing if not serious, commonly leading to derangement, madness, and even suicide. But central to Cheyne's analysis was a fascination with the malady's specific socio-cultural etiology. It was unknown in simpler, primitive societies or among the rustic and laboring classes (too impoverished in nervous sensibility, so to speak, to be capable of falling victim). One of the triumphs of Enlightenment medicine's social awareness lay in its formulation of the notion of diseases of civilization.[120]

It is also telling that, two generations later, Thomas Trotter argued, in his *A View of the Nervous Temperament* (1807), that the kind of nervous breakdowns identified by Cheyne had grown dramatically more prevalent.[121] The English malady had trickled down the social scale, to afflict the middle classes and even prosperous working men, and women above all.

Trotter extended Cheyne's account of the sociocultural nature of the sickness in yet a further way, analyzing the intimate interpenetration of *mœurs*, maladies, and medicine. A high-pressure, mobile, competitive society made its citizens live on their nerves. They took to stimulants: hot beverages, tobacco, alcohol, narcotics. Excitements were subject to the law of diminishing returns. Powerful and habit-forming stimulants were consumed in ever greater quantities. The result? Deleterious physiological consequences (pain, insomnia, hypochondria), which in turn compelled the consumption of ever-increasing quantities of medicaments, some of which, opium above all, produced devastating side effects and were themselves habit-forming. Driven by morbid cravings for stimulus and by artificially induced compulsions, where would the spiral end? The consumer society was becoming an addicted society.[122]

Trotter thus offered—in a manner presaging analysis of "degenerationism" a century later—a powerful account of the irresistible interdependency of sickness, medicine, and lifestyle in the self-glamorizing world of modernity.[123] He further grounded his account upon a vision of human potential. Citing Locke, Trotter argued that human nature was not fixed, being rather the inherited product of self-fashioning and habituation down the centuries. Man thus made his own nature, all too frequently his own pathological habits and morbid tendencies, his own susceptibility to sickness. Trotter thus presented a dramatic medicalization of the promise and pitfalls of human destiny.[124]

Trotter was not alone. As the fusion point between the physiological and the cultural, "nervous disorders" provided the focal point for a stream of works by (among others) the Swiss physician Tissot, examining the psychomedical, and, not least, psychosexual, ailments of modern society.[125] Tissot's lurid denunciation of masturbation dramatized the pathological consequences of what had once been handled as a rather venial sin, and thereby underscored the essential role of the physician as social monitor, for only the doctor could truly foresee the power of personal vice and harmful habits to ravage and scar the body.[126] In an age when intellectuals were charting the sociohistorical determinants of language, morals, legal codes, taste, and faith, medical men were not merely proposing that disease had its cultural history, but were suggesting, in turn, that physiology and pathology were, in a sense, sedimented social history and hence essential for a wider grasp of the dynamics of culture.

This helps define the wider question. A central aim of the Enlightenment was to establish analysis of society on the same footing as that upon which the natural sciences had been emplaced in the previous century.[127] It was a widespread ambition: it was not only Hume who sought to be the

Newton of the moral sciences. The motives were manifold. A more secular age wanted to understand mankind in relation not merely to God and the scriptures but to nature, history, and society.[128] An era of rapid sociohistorical change needed a philosophy of man that could embrace difference and relativism, yet simultaneously posit a framework of social laws governing difference and change. For some, a science of society offered legitimations for the present order. For most, social science would provide tools for criticism, reform, even revolution, and blueprints for the future.[129] In any case, a science of man would serve the cause of emancipation from ignorance, would promote the mission of *sapere aude*, furthering man's escape from self-imposed tutelage. Montesquieu, Voltaire, Diderot, Rousseau, Condillac, Helvétius, Bentham, Cesare Beccaria, Turgot, Adam Smith, d'Holbach, Ferguson, Millar, Herder, Erasmus Darwin, Condorcet—the list could be extended *ad libitum*—no end of Enlightenment luminaries applied themselves to forging scientific accounts of man's mind, speech, imagination, emotions, psyche, gender relations, family structures, social organization, relations with nature, economic activities, legal systems, political development, and so forth, laying bare the hidden chains interlinking man and milieu, individual with group, and past, present, and future. As has been documented by such leading Enlightenment historians as Peter Gay, Georges Gusdorf, and Keith Baker, putative sciences of society sprang up like mushrooms, in all shapes and sizes.[130]

Many prominent Enlightenment spokesmen were medics: Locke, Mandeville, David Hartley, J. O. de La Mettrie, the chevalier de Jaucourt, François Quesnay, Erasmus Darwin, and P. J. G. Cabanis, to mention a few. In the light of this fact, and of Gay's claims, discussed earlier, that medicine spurred the Enlightenment "recovery of nerve," surely medicine (or, more broadly, the biomedical sciences) played a crucial part in supplying the intellectual foundations, the images and idioms, of Enlightenment sciences of man? It is easy to find instances to substantiate this view.

Did not Montesquieu ground his theory of the determination of temperament by climate upon a physiological experiment?—showing, by putting ice on an animal's tongue, that cold produced sluggishness and diminution of sensations?[131] Anatomy and physiology provided critical evidence (or, perhaps, ideological reinforcement) in other fields of human science. The new differentiation of gender roles widely touted in the eighteenth century was accompanied by shifts in biomedical teachings, accentuating the dimorphism between male and female skeletons, pointing to differential cranial capacity, and newly insisting upon radical differences in reproductive apparatus—in short, the switch, as Thomas Laqueur has put it, from a one-sex to a two-sex model.[132] Women, it was further argued, had been proven by neurology to possess finer, that is to say, weaker, nervous organization.[133]

Furthermore, study of physical anthropology and comparative anatomy from Camper to Blumenbach gave legitimacy to a notion of the natural hierarchy of the races, perhaps within the grander framework of the Great Chain of Being, on the strength of scrutiny of anatomical form, cranial angles, and skin pigmentation:[134] blackness, it was suggested, might even be a disease.[135] Not least, as documented by Ludmilla Jordanova, the fierce debate in the 1790s regarding the supposed superior humanity of the guillotine—did the severed head experience painful sensations?—hinged upon the rival testimonies of a gaggle of medicos, not least, Dr. Guillotin himself.[136]

Acute observers of the affinities between knowledge and self-interest, *philosophes* would hardly have been surprised to find that various *médecin-philosophes* argued, as a matter of first principles, that there could be no scientific understanding of man without the firm foundation of a biomedical substrate. It was central to the program of the *idéologues*, that group of thinkers clustering in Auteuil in the salon of Mme. Helvétius, that a true knowledge of man demanded a *science* of ideas, which in turn presupposed analysis of the physiological basis of consciousness.[137] The leading *idéologue*, Cabanis, himself prominent in medical circles, spent many years and much ink explicating the nervous roots of mind, above all in his *Rapports du Physique et du moral de l'homme* (1802): mind was not a separate, superadded principle but a function of higher nervous organization. So distasteful, so threatening, were such teachings, on account of their materialist overtones, that Napoleon responded in 1803 by closing down the section of the Institut devoted to the moral sciences.[138]

In Britain, Cabanis's somewhat older contemporary, the Midlands practitioner Erasmus Darwin, evolved a rather comparable biomedical theory of the material basis of human powers and human progress, expounded within a bold philosophy of cosmic evolution. Drawing on both Hartley and Haller, Darwin delineated the gradual, progressive series of neurologically based phenomena (irritability, sensation, volition, and association) that marked the rise, simultaneously hierarchical and evolutionary, from the lowest molecule right up to mighty man. There were no sharp divides separating beings endowed with mere life from those possessing will and those finally blessed with consciousness. Nor was human nature fixed. Man, argued Darwin, possessed an unlimited capacity further to develop his faculties through learning, for acquired ideas and characteristics could be passed down to posterity through inheritance. Hence, as argued in his evolutionary poem *The Temple of Nature*, medical materialism offered the grounds and the guarantee of the perfectibility—social, moral, intellectual, and scientific—of the human race.[139]

Moreover, with Darwin, as with Cabanis, biomedical beliefs were more than *engagé* rhetoric. They shaped an agenda of social action—for instance, his insistence upon the primacy of practical education under conditions of intellectual freedom.[140] They suggested other distinctive views that he advanced, such as his theory of taste. Contemporary aesthetics was fascinated by the fact that curved forms (Hogarth's "line of beauty") seemed to please. Why so? Purely geometrical or psychological explanations were generally offered. Darwin looked to corporeal causes: our pleasure in curves derived from the infant's experience of the "good breast."[141]

With Cabanis and Erasmus Darwin, the stipulation of a biomedical bedrock for a philosophy of social man, the assertion of the indissoluble and two-way association between the *physique* and the *morale*, was expressed with some subtlety and should not be viewed as a crude expression of professional prejudice or radical polemic. Rather more naked in his political program was La Mettrie. In his *L'Homme Machine* (1747), and, to a lesser degree, his *Histoire naturelle de l'âme* and his *Discourse préliminaire*, this sometime student of Herman Boerhaave and long-practicing physician advanced an uncompromisingly reductionist vision of man as a predetermined being, whose consciousness was a function of his material-organic needs. La Mettrie's writings were militantly targeted against the tribe of metaphysicians—be they Sorbonne theologians or Cartesian metaphysicians—who postulated dualistic accounts of human nature, privileging Soul or Mind as separate from and superior to body.

Such views, La Mettrie contended, were false, unscientific, mystifying, and subservient to the vested interests of ecclesiastical and secular authority. La Mettrie's intervention offers a foretaste of the protracted French struggle, still being waged during the Third Republic, between the medical and the clerical profession for the right to pronounce upon human nature (material or spiritual?).[142]

Less easy to place is Diderot. In a stream of provocative works—such as the *Lettre sur les aveugles* (1749), the *Rêve de d'Alembert* (written in 1769; it significantly uses the Montpellier vitalist, Théophile Bordeu, as fictive interlocutor), and the *Elémens de physiologie* (written around 1774); the last two works remained unpublished in the author's lifetime—Diderot posed and reposed, earnestly, teasingly, and certainly without resolution, the issues, already dealt with to his own satisfaction by La Mettrie (doctors "ont éclairé le labyrinthe de l'homme"),[143] of the relationship between man the material, and man the moral being. If man is a product of his biomedical makeup, does he have free will? Can he be held responsible for his actions? Is consciousness the captain of the soul? (Is there anything resembling a soul?) Or is consciousness just a by-product of the brain, as bile is a secretion of the liver? Is there, not least, any true difference between *homo rationalis* healthy and sick, sane and lunatic, man and beast?[144]

Diderot brilliantly reinstates and restates the old humanist topos: what a piece of work is a man! Rabelais, Montaigne, Shakespeare, Sir Thomas Browne, and the neo-Stoic tradition had, of course, as Herschel Baker long ago showed,[145] engaged with the peculiarities, the paradox, and the "great amphibium," man, in all his dignity, the bizarre amalgam of body and soul, angel and animal, spiritual and corporeal being, immaterial and material, immortal and mortal, that "glory, jest, and riddle and the world." Diderot put the questions once again, from the viewpoint of Enlightenment monist naturalism. How far he thought they were soluble is another question.

The Renaissance and neo-Classical Humanists had opted in favor of broadly Platonic, Stoic, and Christian propositions. Man was compounded of a dual nature; an immortal essence remained after one had shuffled off this mortal coil. Such a model of man, challenged by a few of the "moderns," such as Hobbes and, perhaps, Spinoza, had in the end been bolstered by the metaphysics of the "new philosophy," with its natural theological insistence upon the Divine Mind behind the Divine Machine, or Nature.[146] It was Descartes who had, most daringly and influentially, shored up dualism, by postulating a model of man as a corporeal mechanism presided over by a nonmaterial consciousness almost free—save for the pineal gland!—of any limiting connection with organic materiality.

Descartes had thereby mapped attractive intellectual territories with defensible metaphysical boundaries. There was a legitimate, if ultimately subordinate, role for a (natural) science of man as a physical being: there lay the charter of anatomy, physiology, medicine, and so forth. But, as commentators insisted, such studies could not be expected—for therein would lie an elementary category error—to offer significant accounts of mind, will, soul, inner states, behavior, values, morals, language, the achievements of art or intellect. These were the provinces of theology or philosophy, of the humanities, and, maybe, of the moral sciences.[147] Cartesianism took these propositions as self-evident: the beasts of the field (those "bêtes machines"), who manifestly lacked consciousness or a soul, even if they were superbly physiologically endowed, clearly lacked such uniquely human characteristics.[148]

The role of Descartes's thought in the fabrication, and then the fall, of philosophical dualism is complex and much contested. It is, nevertheless, beyond dispute that, to a very large degree, Enlightenment endeavors to formulate sciences of man—"philosophical" or "natural" histories of man—operated overtly or tacitly within "Cartesian" guidelines. They engaged in analysis—often intentionally radical and subversive—of man as a social, moral, rational, historical being, not as a primarily material entity who happened to be endowed with a potential for psychological, social, and cultural developments. Or, as recent social-scientific jargon would put it, the bias, or error, of eighteenth-century social inquiry was chiefly "psycho-logistic" or "sociologistic," not "biologistic": the study of human nature was, in actuality, chiefly a study of nurture.[149]

This point perhaps needs underlining with examples. Locke was, both by training and to some degree by practice, a physician.[150] It might be ex-pected, therefore, that he would have projected a fundamentally physio-logical account of man. Not so. The state of nature envisaged in his politi-cal writings is one in which the salient matters are man's duties under God and his rights vis-à-vis his fellow men. Locke's *Essay on Humane Under-standing* (1690), that cornerstone of Enlightenment empiricist epistemol-ogy, is essentially a philosophical inquiry into the coherence of conscious-ness. The physical basis or apparatus of perception is barely discussed: Locke's interest lies in mind, not brain.[151] Locke celebratedly raises the possibility that matter might think, but far, say, from suggesting physiologi-cal experiments, translates the issue into theology (it would not be impos-sible for God to create thinking matter).[152]

Post-Lockean empiricism and sensationalism drove still further Locke's repudiation of a priori ideas and other modes of innatism. Reason, will, and the passions were not "given"—innate, immutable, beyond analysis and alteration. They were the products of conditioning; they were amen-able to change; they were open to investigation. Such was the radical pro-gram of Enlightenment thinkers like Condillac and Helvétius.[153] But it by no means automatically followed that such inquirers needed or wanted to translate understanding of mental operations into the language of bio-medicine. Far from it. Condillac analyzed the role of sensation; Hume undermined the reliability of sense knowledge and proposed a dramatic reworking of the relations between reason and the passions;[154] Helvétius exhaustively examined the process of motivation; but they did so without feeling obliged to enter into substantial discussion of physical correlates. The same applies to many other departments of, and debates within, En-lightenment ideas. For instance, after Shaftesbury the basis for aesthet-ics shifted from metaphysical geometry to empiricist psychology, but the method of such analyses was largely introspection.[155]

In so many of the classic strategies of Enlightenment sciences of man, the postulates and parameters had little need to give prominence to the physical dimension. Many theorists—from Vico, through Boulanger, Tur-got, and Ferguson, finally to Herder and Millar—used history as the key to a "naturalistic" understanding of man: human nature was revealed as a product of human history.[156] The truth of phenomena such as taste, morals, or language could be understood through imaginatively reenact-ing the unfolding of consciousness, from rudeness to refinement, from the savage to the Scotsman, or, analogically, in the course of the develop-ment from infancy to adulthood. Or, more radically, "fictions" such as, perhaps, religion could be demystified by probing the processes whereby they had been impressed upon suggestible and primitive psyches.[157]

Not all *philosophes* approached human understanding through history. Utilitarianism, surely the most powerful engine of social-scientific thinking in the late Enlightenment, began by positing a "scientific" psychology (man as a selfish, hedonic ego) and a numerical calculus (pleasures and pains could be weighed and measured). Retrospectively, one might expect that utilitarian political, legal, or economic premises would have launched programs for investigating actual psychophysiological processes. In all the vast corpus of Bentham's plans, there is little sign of this. Bentham was more impressed by chemistry than by medicine. Science meant precision analysis. The Panopticon would be a great laboratory, but the felicific calculus was a matter for the control of minds.[158]

All this may be perfectly self-evident, and I do not wish to invent puzzles where none exist. It is entirely unremarkable that the "party of humanity" should have believed that the proper study of mankind was anthropology, prehistory, history, the structure of emotions, the classification of political institutions and the distribution of wealth. Some points may, however, be worth emphasis. For one thing, many influential Enlightenment polemics were specifically targeted to refute what they took to be vulgar reductionist and mechanistic readings of man. Kant challenged materialism, in the name of human dignity. Scottish Common Sense philosophy fiercely attacked Hartley and Joseph Priestley for suggesting that mind was a function of brain.[159]

Furthermore, it became axiomatic within Enlightenment thinking that some of the more intractable, bizarre, or irrational facets of human behavior could be understood—and, by extension, rectified—only by novel apprehension of their mental, or psychological, aspects.[160] Take drunkenness. Late-eighteenth-century analyses contended that the phenomenon of habitual drinking could not be explained in terms of the material properties of liquor and the digestive system. Enslavement to the demon drink must be reinterpreted as a psychological disorder, a mental disease, or what would soon be called alcoholism.[161] Similarly with sexual excess. Traditionally, excessive venery had been put down to exorbitant irritation of the genitals. Increasingly, nymphomania, satyriasis, and onanism were newly attributed to overstimulus of the imagination.[162] In earlier traditions, malaises such as "hysteria" and "hypochondria" had been interpreted as essentially physical conditions; increasingly, they too were seen as mental aberrations.[163]

In a parallel move, prominent penologists, including Beccaria and Bentham, argued that age-old corporal punishments for criminals—the wheel, lash, or gibbet—were ineffective. Efficient punishment must target not the body but the mind or spirit. Torture must be abolished, capital punishment minimized, for the only true corrective agent was the mental anguish of solitary confinement during protracted prison terms. In these and other respects, Enlightenment activists prided themselves that they were developing a more refined and more *humane* grasp of the subtleties of motivation and behavior, and so a more effective therapeutics. Hume notably argued that politics was henceforth to be understood not in terms of force but of the gravitational field of "opinion." Sociopolitical ills, and their remedies, seemed increasingly to lie in the realm of "mind": on the one hand, ignorance, prejudice, and propaganda; on the other, the remedies of education, enlightenment, and opinion. The Enlightenment began the march of mind.[164]

For such developments, sociology of knowledge suggests a plausible, if somewhat simplistic, explanation. "The party of humanity" preoccupied itself with the criticism of opinions and the psychological determinants of social behavior, because consciousness is the natural engine of a rising intelligentsia, flexing its muscles.[165] To such critics, wielding their pens and hoping to change the world through education, medicomaterialist strains of analysis would have had a limited applicability: they wished not to diminish the empire of consciousness, but to rectify it, establishing its true mission and authority. And other reasons may have operated too.

For one thing, despite Gay's emphasis upon the symbiosis between medicine and the *philosophe* movement, it is far from clear that Enlightenment intellectuals held the medical profession in specially high esteem or were bowled over by advances in medicine itself. *Philosophes* often castigated medicine, in the manner of Molière, for its oafishness, mercenariness, and precious pomposities; surgeons were seen as butchers, physicians as quacks—and *philosophes* prided themselves upon battling the hydra, intellectual quackery. The standard Enlightenment joke, visualized by Gillray and Rowlandson, was that the sick died not of disease but of the doctors. Under such circumstances, medicine was a rather equivocal role model to Enlightenment. It is not surprising that the medical profession became an early target of the French Revolution. Monopolistic professional structures were dismantled, and Jacobins sought to replace organized medicine with do-it-yourself citizen health.[166]

Medicine further suffered from the ambiguity of having for its object the sick body. It was a discipline oriented on defects, on pathology. In some respects, this epitomized the Enlightenment mission: dissection of the ills of society, a certain amount of bloodletting, discriminating social surgery. But the medical model also had pronounced limitations for progressives. Enlightenment propagandists needed eligible representations of a natural, harmonious, flourishing socioeconomic and political order, to serve to criticize, and then to reform, the ancien régime. Though one must avoid oversimplifying the *philosophes'* sociopolitical outlooks, it is clear that values such as individuality, freedom, and self-improvement were widely commended. These were often translated into visions of political liberalism and the free-market economy. It was expected that, thanks to the operation of the natural laws of supply and demand, and with a little help from the hidden hand, self-love and social would prove the same; allowed their free play, diverse interests would, in the end, prove identical. Did medicine provide useful analogies for such social blueprints? On the whole, not. Rather authors such as David Hume, Adam Smith, and Condorcet drew, time and time again, upon the authority of high-prestige Newtonian physics, with its image of matter perpetually in motion, governed by laws of force in a permanent system. The symbolism of the body had less to offer liberal individualists.[167]

It is true, as Anne Marcovich has argued, that medicine's concern with "circulation" could serve as an attractive political-economic metaphor.[168] But ever since Aristotle, physiological images had lent themselves most readily to the support of hierarchical and conservative models of a corporate, organic society, guaranteeing a fixed place and role for each member, within a system in which the whole was prior to, and greater than, the part.[169] And so it should come as no surprise that biomedical models figured prominently in Romantic, anti-Enlightenment political ideologies—in Burke, Coleridge, or Joseph de Maistre—in the postrevolutionary age.[170] If, as Rudolf Virchow's career suggests, the development of cell biology, with its decentralized and "democratic" potential, made physiological models available once again to liberals, the resurgence in the twentieth century of conservative sociological structural-functionalism in the Parsonian mold has reestablished the ready affinity between organic metaphors and style of conservative thought.[171]

Of course, models are multiple and metaphors are labile. There was at least a further potential attraction in medical models for the *philosophes*. The physician's vocation is to heal the sick, and ever since Plato, the doctor and the statesman have been doubles.[172] Thus the image of the *médecin-philosophe*, doctor of a sick society, was ready to hand. And it was utilized, particularly in the programs of centralized public health advanced by such physicians as Johann Peter Frank, working within the framework of Central European *Cameralwissenschaft*. Certain *philosophes* found attractions in enlightened absolutism, orchestrated by wise ministers: it opened a role for them as physicians to society, administering a new sociotherapeutics.[173]

Yet this was a far-from-universal vision. Centrally administered systems of medical police did not have many advocates beyond the German-speaking territories. The use of compulsion—for example, quarantine in case of contagious diseases—fell from favor.[174] Such physicians chiming with Enlightenment ideals as Tissot, Rush, and Buchan, and health reformers like Charles Volney, sought to promote public health and hygiene more through education and enlightened self-interest than through medical bureaucracies endowed with police powers.[175] A latter-day child of the Enlightenment, René Louis Villermé, the leading public health publicist in post-Restoration France, deemed that public hygiene must operate within the immutable laws of classical economics.[176]

CONCLUSION

I have been trying to plot the complex intertwining of medical men and biomedical ideas with the Enlightenment endeavor. The signs are that, insofar as capital was made of science to provide working models of natural order, physics came first (and, of course, as noted above, proved a serviceable model for medical thinking too). In their attempts to formulate fully naturalistic accounts of the human economy within a law-governed universe, radicals such as d'Holbach looked primarily to the physical sciences. The egalitarianism of atomism agreed with the liberal commitments of most *philosophes.* Condorcet conceived a social *mathematics,* a social *mechanics.*[177]

Some social analysts found medical materialism valuable for dissecting metaphysics and idealism, but most prominent Enlightenment critiques of theology, corrupt *mœurs,* and political obscurantism drew on *philosophy* for the tasks of intellectual deconstruction and ideological demystification—reason, history, criticism, fiction. As an activist movement, the Enlightenment was principally interested in culture criticism, in formulating psychologies, learning theories, in the workings of publicity and propaganda.

Biomedical inputs had a role. Doctors could deal, literally or metaphorically, with individual sickness and psychopathology, and with specific, if in the end limited, fields of social pathology—witchcraft, religious enthusiasm, demogogy.[178] And, of course, the biomedical sciences have had an enduring role within the Cartesian carving up of the human sciences, wherein, for instance, physical anthropology operates alongside cultural anthropology. Yet my argument has been that the medical model did not become hegemonic for the human sciences; it could equally be argued, that, for its part, "social medicine" made but slow inroads into the domain of "scientific medicine."[179] It is noteworthy that medicalized visions of man were widely invoked—under the rubric of stern reality—specifically to knock Enlightenment aspirations on the head, as in particular with Malthus's reactionary biosexual claim that nature set drastic limits to social options.[180]

It would, of course, be possible to claim that the whole of the foregoing analysis is utterly misguided. For Foucault has maintained that the Enlightenment did not formulate a science of man. Eighteenth-century discourse, argues *Les mots et les choses* (that "archaeology of the human sciences"), was about the analysis and classification of representations of nature. Man did not—*could* not—exist, as a discursive object ("there was no epistemological consciousness of man as such").[181] Man, Foucault claims, was the product of the new constellation of disciplines arriving, after a radical rupture, with Cuvier, Franz Bopp, and David Ricardo in the nineteenth century; man as subject and object of discourse was born with life, language, and labor, permitting the great age of speculative "anthropocentric" anthropologies (Hegel, Feuerbach, Marx), before Nietzsche and Freud, not before time, killed him off again.[182] Others have elaborated Foucault's point; Andrew Cunningham has contended that we have no business to be speaking of "science" before the close of the eighteenth century, for, till then, there was only "natural philosophy," whose ultimate object was God. By implication there can have been no science of man, only theology.[183]

I am not, however, convinced by these attempts to postulate a drastic intellectual rupture around 1800. Condorcet was himself quite happily talking about the "social sciences," and, for what it is worth, many nineteenth-century social scientists unproblematically viewed themselves as the natural heirs to the *philosophes*.[184] But Foucault has established one valuable point. The scientific medicine that emerged with the "birth of the clinic"—the emphasis in nineteenth-century hospital medicine upon pathological anatomy, scrutiny of diseases rather than sick people, mass observation, and the collection of statistics (Pierre Louis's "méthode numerique")—led, in the work of François Broussais and later in Bernard, to the continuum of physiology and pathology.[185] Disease was part of body processes. Hence health and sickness became redefined as analysis of the normal and the pathological. And these concepts in turn, especially through Durkheim, became central analytical tools of modern social science, used as normalizing, medicalizing, value judgments. If, *pace* Foucault, one does not insist on the revolutionary birth of clinical medicine, but acknowledges its continuities with eighteenth-century developments—in the political arithmetic of Bills of Mortality, in biopolitics, and in vital statistics—it may be suggested that medicine was implicated in the Enlightenment formulation of the positivistic human sciences.[186]

NOTES

1. For the efficacy of medicine, see T. McKeown, *The Modern Rise of Population* (London: Edward Arnold, 1976); for the social history approach, see J. Woodward, "Towards a Social History of Medicine," in *Health Care and Popular Medicine in Nineteenth-Century England,* ed. J. Woodward and D. Richards (London: Croom Helm, 1977), 15–55.

2. See Karl M. Figlio, "The Historiography of Scientific Medicine: An Invitation to the Human Sciences," *Comparative Studies in Society and History* 19 (1977): 262–286.

3. Herbert Butterfield, *The Origins of Modern Science, 1300–1800* (London: Bell, 1949); A. R. Hall, *The Scientific Revolution, 1500–1800* (London: Longman, 1954); C. C. Gillispie, *The Edge of Objectivity: An Essay in the History of Scientific Ideas* (Princeton, N.J.: Princeton University Press, 1960).

4. Ian McNeil, ed., *An Encyclopedia of the History of Technology* (London: Routledge, 1990), makes virtually no mention of medicine.

5. The view that medicine did not work is nicely summed up in the titles of two books by Guy Williams: *The Age of Agony: The Art of Healing c. 1700–1800* (London: Constable, 1975) and *The Age of Miracles: Medicine and Surgery in the Nineteenth Century* (London: Constable, 1981).

6. Fielding H. Garrison, *An Introduction to the History of Medicine* (Philadelphia and London: Saunders, 1917), 303, speaks of the eighteenth century as the "age of theories and systems" with a "mania for sterile, dry-as-dust classifications of everything in nature." See also Charles Singer, *A Short History of Medicine* (Oxford: Clarendon Press, 1928); A. Castiglioni, *History of Medicine* (New York: Alfred A. Knopf, 1941); W. R. LeFanu, "The Lost Half Century in English Medicine, 1700–1750," *Bulletin of the History of Medicine* 46 (1972): 319–348. For the best modern corrective, see W. F. Bynum, "Health, Disease, and Medical Care," in *The Ferment of Knowledge,* ed. G. S. Rousseau and R. Porter (Cambridge: Cambridge University Press, 1980), 211–254.

7. C. Rosenberg, "The Therapeutic Revolution," in *The Therapeutic Revolution,* ed. M. Vogel and C. Rosenberg (Philadelphia: University of Pennsylvania Press, 1979), 3–25.

8. M. Foucault, *The Birth of the Clinic,* trans. A. M. Sheridan Smith (London: Tavistock Publications, 1973).

9. Bruno Latour, *The Pasteurization of France* (Cambridge, Mass.: Harvard University Press, 1988).

10. Roger French and Andrew Wear, eds., *The Medical Revolution of the Seventeenth Century* (Cambridge: Cambridge University Press, 1989).

11. Andrew Wear, "Medical Practice in Late Seventeenth- and Early Eighteenth-Century England: Continuity and Union," in *Medical Revolution of the Seventeenth Century,* ed. Roger French and Andrew Wear, 294–320.

12. See Lester S. King, *The Medical World of the Eighteenth Century* (Chicago: University of Chicago Press, 1958).

13. P. Gay, "The Enlightenment as Medicine and as Cure," in *The Age of the Enlightenment: Studies Presented to Theodore Besterman,* ed. W. H. Barber (Edinburgh: St. Andrews University Publications, 1967), 375–386; idem, *The Enlightenment,* 2 vols. (New York: Alfred A. Knopf, 1967–69).

14. Gay, *Enlightenment,* 2:19. I cite the version as printed in the book, since its situation at the outset of the second volume (*The Science of Freedom*) signals its centrality to Gay's interpretation.

15. Ibid., 2: 18.

16. Ibid., 2: 19.

17. Ibid., 2: 12.

18. Ibid., 2: 22.

19. Ibid., 2: 23.

20. Ibid., 2: 12.

21. Rosenberg, "Therapeutic Revolution."

22. E. A. Wrigley, "No Death without Birth: The Implications of English Mortality in the Early Modern Period," in *Problems and Methods in the History of Medicine, 1750–1850*, ed. Roy Porter and A. Wear (London: Croom Helm, 1987), 133–150.

23. For the Royal Society, see Roy Porter, "The Early Royal Society and the Spread of Medical Knowledge," in *Medical Revolution of the Seventeenth Century*, ed. French and Wear, 272–293. On Newton worship, see Julian Martin, "Sauvages's Nosology: Medical Enlightenment in Montpellier," in *The Medical Enlightenment of the Eighteenth Century*, ed. Andrew Cunningham and Roger French (Cambridge: Cambridge University Press, 1990), 111–137.

24. Peter Gay, *The Party of Humanity: Essays in the French Enlightenment* (New York: W. W. Norton and Co., 1971).

25. F. Manuel, *The Eighteenth Century Confronts the Gods* (Cambridge, Mass.: Harvard University Press, 1959).

26. For polemical histories of medicine created by medics, see Julian Martin, "Explaining John Freind's *History of Physick*," *Studies in the History and Philosophy of Science* 19 (1988): 399–418; R. N. Schwab, "The History of Medicine in Diderot's *Encyclopédie*," *Bulletin of the History of Medicine* 32 (1958): 216–223.

27. See Andrew Cunningham, "Medicine to Calm the Mind: Boerhaave's Medical System, and Why It Was Adopted in Edinburgh," in *Medical Enlightenment*, ed. Cunningham and French, 40–66.

28. Robert G. Frank, *Harvey and the Oxford Physiologists: Scientific Ideas and Social Interaction* (Berkeley, Los Angeles, London: University of California Press, 1980).

29. L. S. Jacyna, "Images of John Hunter in the Nineteenth Century," *History of Science* 22 (1983): 85–108.

30. E. Chambers, *Cyclopaedia, Or an Universal Dictionary of Arts and Sciences*, 2d ed., 2 vols. (London: Midwinter, 1738), vol. 2, unpaginated.

31. C. Lawrence, "William Buchan: Medicine Laid Open," *Medical History* 19 (1975): 20–35; Charles Rosenberg, "Medical Text and Medical Context: Explaining William Buchan's *Domestic Medicine*," *Bulletin of the History of Medicine* 57 (1983): 22–24; Lamar Riley Murphy, *Enter the Physician: The Transformation of Domestic Medicine, 1760–1860* (Tuscaloosa and London: University of Alabama Press, 1991).

32. Roy Porter, ed., *The Popularization of Medicine, 1650–1850* (London: Routledge, 1992), 215–231.

33. G. Baglivi, *De Praxi Medica* (Rome: Typis D. A. Herculis, 1696); B. Mandeville, *A Treatise of the Hypochondriack and Hysterick Diseases*, 2d ed. (London: Tonson, 1730; reprint, Hildesheim: George Olms Verlag, 1981).

34. See V. G. Myer, "Tristram and the Animal Spirits," in *Laurence Sterne: Riddles and Mysteries*, ed. Valerie Grosvenor Myer (London: Vision Press, 1984).

35. K. Dewhurst, *Thomas Willis as a Physician* (Berkeley and Los Angeles: University of California Press, 1964).

36. Baglivi, *De Praxi Medica*, quoted in Martin, "Sauvages's Nosology," 115.

37. G. A. Lindeboom, *Hermann Boerhaave: The Man and His Work* (London: Methuen, 1968).

38. Karl M. Figlio, "Theories of Perception and the Physiology of the Mind in the Late Eighteenth Century," *History of Science* 13 (1975): 177–212.

39. C. Lawrence, "The Nervous System and Society in the Scottish Enlighten-

ment," in *Natural Order,* ed. B. Barnes and S. Shapin (Beverly Hills and London: Sage Publications, 1980), 19–40.

40. W. F. Bynum and Roy Porter, eds., *Brunonianism in Britain and Europe* (London: *Medical History,* Supplement 8, 1989).

41. F. Duchesneau, "Vitalism in Late Eighteenth-Century Physiology: The Cases of Barthez, Blumenbach, and John Hunter," in *William Hunter and the Eighteenth-Century Medical World,* ed. W. F. Bynum and Roy Porter (Cambridge: Cambridge University Press, 1985), 259–295.

42. Saul Jarcho, trans. and ed., *The Clinical Consultations of Giambattista Morgagni* (Boston: Countway Library of Medicine, 1984).

43. Johanna Geyer-Kordesch, "Passions and the Ghost in the Machine: Or What Not to Ask about Science in Seventeenth- and Eighteenth-Century Germany," in *Medical Revolution of the Seventeenth Century,* ed. French and Wear, 145–163; idem, "Georg Ernst Stahl's Radical Pietist Medicine and Its Influence in the German Enlightenment," in *Medical Enlightenment,* ed. Cunningham and French, 67–88.

44. Roger French, "Sickness and the Soul: Stahl, Hoffman, and Sauvages on Pathology," in *Medical Enlightenment,* ed. Cunningham and French, 88–110.

45. Elizabeth Haigh, "Vitalism, the Soul and Sensibility: The Physiology of Theophile Bordeu," *Journal of the History of Medicine* 31 (1976): 30–41; idem, "The Vital Principle of Paul Joseph Barthez: The Clash between Monism and Dualism," *Medical History,* 21 (1977): 1–14.

46. R. French, *Robert Whytt, the Soul and Medicine* (London: Wellcome Institute for the History of Medicine, 1969).

47. S. Cross, "John Hunter, the Animal Oeconomy, and Late Eighteenth Century Physiological Discourse," *Studies in the History of Biology,* 5 (1981): 1–110.

48. Ann Thomson, *Materialism and Society in the Mid–Eighteenth Century: La Mettrie's Discours Préliminaire* (Geneva: Librairie Droz, 1981); Kathleen Wellman, *La Mettrie: Medicine, Philosophy, and Enlightenment* (Durham, N.C.: Duke University Press, 1992).

49. See K. Park and L. Daston, "Unnatural Conceptions: The Study of Monsters in Sixteenth-Century France and England," *Past and Present* 92 (1981): 20–54; Simon Schaffer, "Natural Philosophy," in *Ferment of Knowledge,* ed. Rousseau and Porter, 55–91.

50. E. A. Burtt, *The Metaphysical Foundations of Modern Science* (London: Kegan Paul, Trench, 1925).

51. And through the technology that allowed measuring: see Simon Schaffer, "Measuring Virtue: Eudiometry, Enlightenment, and Pneumatic Medicine," in *Medical Enlightenment,* ed. Cunningham and French, 281–318.

52. Andrew Wear, "Puritan Perceptions of Illness in Seventeenth-Century England," in *Patients and Practitioners,* ed. R. Porter (Cambridge: Cambridge University Press, 1985), 55–99.

53. For Hales, see D. G. C. Allan and R. E. Schofield, *Stephen Hales: Scientist and Philanthropist* (London: Scolar Press, 1980); Ulrich Tröhler, "Quantification in British Medicine and Surgery, 1750–1830, with Special Reference to Its Introduction into Therapeutics" (Ph.D. thesis, University of London, 1978).

54. G. Miller, *The Adoption of Inoculation for Smallpox in England and France* (London: Oxford University Press, 1957).

55. Catherine Gallagher, "The Body Versus the Social Body in the Works of Thomas Malthus and Henry Mayhew," in *The Making of the Modern Body: Sexuality and Society in the Nineteenth Century,* ed. C. Gallagher and T. Laqueur (Berkeley: University of California Press, 1987), 83–106.

56. The case for secularization of medicine is forcibly made in the introduction to Cunningham and French, eds., *Medical Enlightenment.*

57. James C. Riley, *Sickness, Recovery, and Death: A History and Forecast of Ill Health* (London: Macmillan Publishers, 1989).

58. Knud Faber, *Nosography: A History of Clinical Medicine* (New York: Hoeber, 1930).

59. K. Dewhurst, *Dr. Sydenham, 1624–1689* (Berkeley and Los Angeles: University of California Press, 1966).

60. Roy Porter, "Erasmus Darwin: Doctor of Evolution?" in *History, Humanity, and Evolution,* ed. James R. Moore (Cambridge: Cambridge University Press, 1989), 39–69.

61. Bynum and Porter, eds., *Brunonianism.*

62. D. A. Stansfield, *Thomas Beddoes, M.D., 1760–1808, Chemist, Physician, Democrat* (Lancaster: D. Reidel, 1984).

63. Roy Porter, *Doctor of Society: Thomas Beddoes and the Sick Trade in Late Enlightenment England* (London: Routledge, 1992).

64. See T. H. Levere, "Dr. Thomas Beddoes and the Establishment of His Pneumatic Institution: A Tale of the Three Presidents," *Notes and Records of the Royal Society of London* 32 (1977): 41–49.

65. M. P. Crosland, *Historical Studies in the Language of Chemistry* (New York: Dover Publications, 1962).

66. See T. Beddoes, *Where would be Harm of a Speedy Peace?* (Bristol: N. Biggs, 1795).

67. T. H. Levere, "Thomas Beddoes: The Interaction of Pneumatic and Preventative Medicine with Chemistry," *ISR: Interdisciplinary Science Reviews* 7 (1982): 137–147.

68. Thomas Beddoes, *Hygëia: or Essays Moral and Medical, on the Causes Affecting the Personal State of our Middling and Affluent Classes,* 3 vols. (Bristol: J. Mills, 1802), 1.i.53.

69. See Roy Porter, "Reforming the Patient: Thomas Beddoes and Medical Practice," in *Medicine in the Age of Reform,* ed. Roger French and Andrew Wear (London: Routledge and Kegan Paul, 1991), 9–44.

70. Thomas Beddoes, *Observations on the Nature and Cure of Calculus, Sea Scurvy, Consumption, Catarrh, and Fever: together with conjectures upon several other subjects of physiology and pathology* (London: J. Murray, 1793), iv.

71. Beddoes, *Observations,* iv.

72. See Roy Porter, "Plutus or Hygeia? Thomas Beddoes and Medical Ethics," in *The Codification of Medical Morality: Historical and Philosophical Studies of the Formalization of Western Medical Morality in the Eighteenth and Nineteenth Centuries,* ed. Robert Baker, Dorothy Porter, and Roy Porter, vol. 1 (Dordrecht: Kluwer, 1993), 73–92.

73. Beddoes, *Hygëia,* 1.i.45, 48.

74. Ibid., 1.i.46.

75. Beddoes, *Observations,* viii.

76. Ibid., *Observations,* viii.

77. R. E. Schofield, *The Lunar Society of Birmingham* (London: Oxford University Press, 1963).

78. D. King-Hele, *Doctor of Revolution: The Life and Genius of Erasmus Darwin* (London: Faber and Faber, 1977).

79. Beddoes, *Hygëia,* 1.iv.45.

80. Ibid., 1.iv.7.

81. T. Beddoes, ed., *Chemical Experiments and Opinions; extracted from a work published in the last century* (Oxford: Clarendon Press, 1790).

82. Beddoes, *Observations,* 42.

83. Ibid., 13.

84. Beddoes, *Chemical Experiments,* 60.

85. Beddoes, *A Letter to Erasmus Darwin,* 58.

86. Ibid., 60.

87. For the psychological background, see J. Yolton, *John Locke and the Way of Ideas* (Oxford: Oxford University Press, 1956).

88. Thomas Beddoes, *Contributions to Physical and Medical Knowledge, Principally from the West of England* (London: T. N. Longman and O. Rees, 1799), 11.

89. Ibid., 13.

90. Thomas Beddoes, *A Letter to the Right Honourable Sir Joseph Banks . . . on the Causes and Removal of the Prevailing Discontents, Imperfections, and Abuses, in Medicine* (London: Richard Phillips, 1808), 85.

91. Beddoes, *Contributions,* 6.

92. Roy Porter, "The Rise of Medical Journalism in Britain to 1800," in *Medical Journals and Medical Knowledge,* ed. W. F. Bynum, Stephen Lock, and Roy Porter (London: Routledge and Kegan Paul, 1992), 6–28.

93. Beddoes, *Contributions,* introduction.

94. Beddoes, *Letter to . . . Banks,* 82.

95. Ibid., 83.

96. Ibid.

97. Ibid., 85.

98. Ibid., 86.

99. Thomas Beddoes, *Researches Anatomical and Practical concerning Fever, as Connected with Inflammation* (London: Longman, Hurst, Rees, and Orme, 1807).

100. Ruth Richardson, *Death, Destitution, and Dissection* (London: Routledge and Kegan Paul, 1987).

101. Beddoes, *Contributions,* 11.

102. Seamus Deane, *The French Revolution and Enlightenment in England, 1789–1832* (Cambridge, Mass.: Harvard University Press, 1989).

103. T. Beddoes, *A Manual of Health: or, the Invalid Conducted Safely Through the Seasons* (London: Johnson, 1806), 416.

104. Beddoes, *Manual of Health,* 413.

105. T. Beddoes, *A Lecture Introductory to a Course of Popular Instruction on the Constitution and Management of the Human Body* (Bristol: Joseph Cottle, 1797), 56.

106. Beddoes, *Manual of Health,* 412.

107. Ibid., 411.

108. Ibid., 417.

109. Ibid., 419.

110. Ibid., 413.

111. Beddoes, *Hygëia*, 3.ix.108.

112. Ibid.

113. L. J. Jordanova, "Earth Science and Environmental Medicine: The Synthesis of the Late Enlightenment," in *Images of the Earth: Essays in the History of the Environmental Sciences,* ed. L. J. Jordanova and Roy Porter (Chalfont St. Giles: British Society for the History of Science Monographs, 1979), 119–146. James C. Riley, *The Eighteenth Century Campaign to Avoid Disease* (Basingstoke: Macmillan, 1987).

114. See Roy Porter, *Doctor of Society: Thomas Beddoes and Medicine in the Age of Revolution* (London: Routledge and Kegan Paul, 1992).

115. G. Miller, "Airs, Waters, and Places in History," *Journal of the History of Medicine* 17 (1962): 129–138; R. Cooter, "Anticontagionism and History's Medical Record," in *The Problem of Medical Knowledge,* ed. P. Wright and A. Treacher (Edinburgh: Edinburgh University Press, 1982), 87–108.

116. Paul Weindling, ed., *The Social History of Occupational Health* (London: Croom Helm, 1985).

117. C. F. Mullett, "A Century of English Quarantine (1709–1825)," *Bulletin of the History of Medicine* 23 (1949): 527-545.

118. See the introduction by Roy Porter to George Cheyne's *The English Malady* (1733; reprint, London: Routledge and Kegan Paul, 1990).

119. Roy Porter, *Mind Forg'd Manacles: Madness and Psychiatry in England from Restoration to Regency* (London: Athlone Press, 1987; paperback ed., London: Penguin Books, 1990).

120. B. Inglis, *The Diseases of Civilisation* (London: Hodder and Stoughton, 1981).

121. Thomas Trotter, *An Essay, Medical, Philosophical and Chemical on Drunkenness* (London: Longman, 1804); idem, *A View of the Nervous Temperament* (London: Longman, Hurst, Rees, and Owen, 1807); Roy Porter, "Addicted to Modernity: Nervousness in the Early Consumer Society," in *Culture in History,* ed. J. Melling and J. Barry (Exeter: Exeter Studies in History, 1992), 180–194.

122. Roy Porter, "Consumption: Disease of the Consumer Society?" in *Consumption and the World of Goods,* ed. John Brewer and Roy Porter (London: Routledge and Kegan Paul, 1993), 58–84.

123. J. E. Chamberlin and S. L. Gilman, eds., *Degeneration: The Dark Side of Progress* (New York: Columbia University Press, 1985).

124. John Passmore, *The Perfectibility of Man* (London: Gerald Duckworth and Co., 1972).

125. A. Emch-Dériaz, "Towards a Social Conception of Health in the Second Half of the Eighteenth Century: Tissot (1728–1797) and the New Preoccupation with Health and Well-Being," Ph.D. dissertation, University of Rochester, 1984.

126. Ludmilla J. Jordanova, "The Popularisation of Medicine: Tissot on Onanism," *Textual Practice* 1 (1987): 68–80.

127. Gay, *Party of Humanity*; G. Gusdorf, *Les Sciences Humaines et la Pensée Occidentale*, vol. 5, *Dieu, la nature et l'homme au siècle des Lumières* (Paris: St. Armand, 1972).

128. F. Manuel, *The Eighteenth Century Confronts the Gods* (Cambridge, Mass.: Harvard University Press, 1959).

129. P. Vereker, *Eighteenth-Century Optimism* (Liverpool: Liverpool University Press, 1967); D. Spadafora, *The Idea of Progress in Eighteenth-Century Britain* (New Haven, Conn.: Yale University Press, 1990).

130. K. M. Baker, *Condorcet: From Natural Philosophy to Social Mathematics* (Chicago: University of Chicago Press, 1975).

131. Thomas L. Hankins, *Science and the Enlightenment* (Cambridge: Cambridge University Press, 1985), 160.

132. Thomas Laqueur, *Making Sex* (Cambridge, Mass.: Harvard University Press, 1990); Sylvana Tomaselli, "The Enlightenment Debate on Women," *History Workshop Journal* 20 (1985): 101–124.

133. Paul Hoffmann, *La Femme dans la Pensée des Lumières* (Paris: Ophrys, 1977).

134. John Greene, *The Death of Adam* (Ames: Iowa State University Press, 1959).

135. Benjamin Rush, "Observations Intended to Favour a Supposition that the Black Color (as it is called) of the Negroes is Derived from the Leprosy," *Transactions of the American Philosophical Society* 4 (1799): 289–297.

136. Ludmilla Jordanova, "Medical Mediations: Mind, Body, and the Guillotine," *History Workshop* 28 (1989): 39–52; Dorinda Outram, *The Body and the French Revolution: Sex, Class, and Political Culture* (New Haven, Conn.: Yale University Press, 1989).

137. S. Moravia, "The Enlightenment and the Sciences of Man," *History of Science* 18 (1980): 247–268.

138. Martin S. Staum, *Cabanis: Enlightenment and Medical Philosophy in the French Revolution* (Princeton, N.J.: Princeton University Press, 1980).

139. Maureen MacNeil, *Under the Banner of Science: Erasmus Darwin and His Age* (Manchester: Manchester University Press, 1987).

140. Erasmus Darwin, *A Plan for the Conduct of Female Education in Boarding Schools* (Derby: J. Johnson, 1797).

141. S. Hipple, *The Beautiful, the Sublime, and the Picturesque in Eighteenth Century British Aesthetic Theory* (Carbondale: Southern Illinois University Press, 1957).

142. Thomson, *Materialism and Society*; Aram Vartanian, *Diderot and Descartes: A Study of Scientific Naturalism in the Enlightenment* (Princeton, N.J.: Princeton University Press, 1953).

143. La Mettrie, *L'Homme Machine*, ed. A. Vartanian (Princeton, N.J.: Princeton University Press, 1960), 151.

144. Arthur Wilson, *Diderot: The Testing Years, 1713–1759* (New York: Oxford University Press, 1969); Jacques Proust, *Diderot et l'Encyclopédie* (Paris: Colin, 1962).

145. H. Baker, *The Dignity of Man: Studies in the Persistence of an Idea* (Cambridge, Mass.: Harvard University Press, 1947).

146. The relative conservatism of Newtonianism is stressed in M. C. Jacob, *The Newtonians and the English Revolution* (Ithaca, N.Y.: Cornell University Press, 1976). See also Simon Schaffer, "Natural Philosophy," in *Ferment of Knowledge*, ed. Rousseau and Porter, 55–91; idem, "States of Mind: Enlightenment and Natural Phi-

losophy," in *The Languages of Psyche: Mind and Body in Enlightenment Thought*, ed. G. S. Rousseau (Berkeley, Los Angeles, Oxford: University of California Press, 1990), 233–290.

147. R. B. Carter, *Descartes's Medical Philosophy: The Organic Solution to the Mind-Body Problem* (Baltimore: Johns Hopkins University Press, 1983).

148. L. W. B. Brockliss, "The Medico-Religious Universe of an Early Eighteenth Century Parisian Doctor: The Case of Philippe Hecquet," in *Medical Revolution of the Seventeenth Century*, ed. French and Wear, 191–221; L. C. Rosenfield, *From Beast-machine to Man-machine: The Theme of Animal Soul in French Letters from Descartes to La Mettrie* (New York: Oxford University Press, 1941).

149. Paul Hirst and Penny Woolley, *Social Relations and Human Attributes* (London: Tavistock Publications, 1982).

150. K. Dewhurst, *John Locke (1632–1704), Physician and Philosopher* (London: Wellcome Historical Medical Library, 1963).

151. John Yolton, *John Locke and the Way of Ideas* (Oxford: Oxford University Press, 1956).

152. John Yolton, *Thinking Matter: Materialism in Eighteenth-Century Britain* (Minneapolis: University of Minnesota Press, 1983).

153. Isabel Knight, *The Geometric Spirit: The Abbe de Condillac and the French Enlightenment* (New Haven, Conn.: Yale University Press, 1968); D. W. Smith, *Helvétius: A Study in Persecution* (Oxford: Clarendon Press, 1965).

154. John P. Wright, *The Sceptical Realism of David Hume* (Manchester: Manchester University Press, 1983).

155. Hipple, *The Beautiful, the Sublime, and the Picturesque.*

156. P. Rossi, *The Dark Abyss of Time: The History of the Earth and the History of Nations from Hooke to Vico* (Chicago: University of Chicago Press, 1984); Henry Vyverberg, *Historical Pessimism in the French Enlightenment* (Cambridge, Mass.: Harvard University Press, 1958).

157. Manuel, *Eighteenth Century Confronts the Gods.*

158. Elie Halévy, *The Growth of Philosophic Radicalism* (London: Faber and Faber, 1928).

159. Anand Chitnis, *The Scottish Enlightenment and Early Victorian Society* (London: Croom Helm, 1986).

160. Roy Porter, "Barely Touching," in *Languages of Psyche*, ed. Rousseau, 45–80; see the introduction to the same volume. G. S. Rousseau, "Science and the Discovery of the Imagination in Enlightenment England," *Eighteenth-Century Studies* 3 (1969–70): 108–135.

161. Roy Porter, "The Drinking Man's Disease: The 'Pre-History' of Alcoholism in Georgian Britain," *British Journal of Addiction* 80 (1985): 385–396.

162. Roy Porter, "Love, Sex, and Madness in Eighteenth-Century England," *Social Research* 53 (1986): 211–242; George S. Rousseau, "Nymphomania, Bienville, and the Rise of Erotic Sensibility," in *Sexuality in Eighteenth Century Britain*, ed. P. G. Boucé (Manchester: Manchester University Press, 1982), 95–119.

163. See Sander Gilman, Helen King, Roy Porter, George Rousseau, and Elaine Showalter, *Hysteria Beyond Freud* (Berkeley, Los Angeles, Oxford: University of California Press, 1993).

164. M. Foucault, *Discipline and Punish: The Birth of the Prison* (London:

Harmondsworth, 1979): Michael Ignatieff, *A Just Measure of Pain: The Penitentiary in the Industrial Revolution, 1750–1850* (London: Macmillan Publishers, 1978); Duncan Forbes, *Hume's Philosophical Politics* (Cambridge: Cambridge University Press, 1975).

165. Raymond Williams, *The Long Revolution* (London: Chatto and Windus, 1961); Wolf Lepenies, *Between Literature and Science: The Rise of Sociology* (Cambridge: Cambridge University Press, 1988); B. Barnes, *Interests and the Growth of Knowledge* (London: Routledge and Kegan Paul, 1977).

166. For Britain, see Dorothy Porter and Roy Porter, *Patient's Progress: Doctors and Doctoring in Eighteenth-Century England* (Cambridge: Polity Press, 1989); for France, see Matthew Ramsey, *Professional and Popular Medicine in France, 1770–1830* (New York: Cambridge University Press, 1988). For changing self-images of the physician and scientist, see Dorinda Outram, "The Language of Natural Power: The 'Eloges' of Georges Cuvier and the Public Language of Nineteenth-Century Science," *History of Science* 16 (1978): 153–178.

167. C. B. Macpherson, *The Political Theory of Possessive Individualism* (Oxford: Oxford University Press, 1983); W. Letwin, *The Origins of Scientific Economics* (London: Methuen, 1963); A. O. Hirschman, *The Passions and the Interests: Political Arguments for Capitalism before Its Triumph* (Princeton, N.J.: Princeton University Press, 1977). A similar point is made by Sylvana Tomaselli in chap. 10 of this volume.

168. A Marcovich, "Concerning the Continuity between the Image of Society and the Image of the Human Body: An Examination of the Work of the English Physician J. C. Lettsom (1746–1815)," in *Problem of Medical Knowledge,* ed. Wright and Treacher, 69–87.

169. L. Barkan, *Nature's Work of Art: The Human Body as Image of the World* (New Haven, Conn.: Yale University Press, 1975).

170. R. White, *Political Thought of Samuel Taylor Coleridge* (London: Jonathan Cape, 1938); J. V. Pickstone, "Bureaucracy, Liberalism, and the Body in Post-Revolutionary France: Bichat's Physiology and the Paris School of Medicine," *History of Science* 19 (1981): 115–142.

171. Karl Figlio and Paul Weindling, "Was Social Medicine Revolutionary? Rudolf Virchow and the Revolutions of 1848," *Bulletin of the Society for the Social History of Medicine* 34 (1984): 10–18.

172. Plato, *The Republic,* ed. James Adam (Cambridge: Cambridge University Press, 1905–07).

173. J. P. Frank, *A System of Complete Medical Police,* trans. Erna Lesky (Baltimore: Johns Hopkins University Press, 1976).

174. C. F. Mullett, "A Century of English Quarantine (1709–1825)," *Bulletin of the History of Medicine* 23 (1949): 527–545.

175. Antoinette Emch-Dériaz, "Towards a Social Conception of Health in the Second Half of the Eighteenth Century: Tissot (1728–1797) and the New Preoccupation with Health and Well-Being" (Ph.D. dissertation, University of Rochester, and Ann Arbor, Mich.: University Microfilms International, 1984); J. Jordanova, "Guarding the Body Politic: Volney's Catechism of 1793," in *1789: Reading, Writing, Revolution: Proceedings of the Essex Conference on the Sociology of Literature,* ed. Francis Barker, Jay Bernstein, Peter Hulme, Margaret Iverson, and Jennifer Stone (Colchester: University of Essex, 1982), 12–21; W. Coleman, "Health

and Hygiene in the *Encyclopédie*: A Medical Doctrine for the Bourgeoisie," *Journal of the History of Medicine and Allied Sciences* 29 (1974): 399–421.

176. W. Coleman, *Death Is a Social Disease: Public Health and Political Economy* (Madison: University of Wisconsin Press, 1982).

177. A. C. Kors, *D'Holbach's Circle: An Enlightenment in Paris* (Princeton, N.J.: Princeton University Press, 1977); M. Norton Wise, with the collaboration of Crosbie Smith, "Work and Waste: Political Economy and Natural Philosophy in Nineteenth Century Britain," *History of Science* 27 (1989): 263–301, 391–449; 28 (1990): 221–261.

178. Porter, *Mind Forg'd Manacles.*

179. George Rosen, "What Is Social Medicine? A Genetic Analysis of the Concept," *Bulletin of the History of Medicine* 21 (1947): 674–733.

180. See Catherine Gallagher, "The Body versus the Social Body in the Works of Thomas Malthus and Henry Mayhew," in *Making of the Modern Body*, ed. Gallagher and Laqueur, 83–106.

181. M. Foucault, *The Order of Things: An Archaeology of the Human Sciences* (London: Tavistock Publications, 1970), 309.

182. Ibid. It is worth stressing that Foucault equally denies the existence of "psychology" in the eighteenth century. He does however argue that health became a prime value at this time: Michel Foucault, *Histoire de la sexualité*, vol. 1, *La volonté de savoir* (Paris: Gallimard, 1976) (trans. Robert Hurley: *The History of Sexuality: Introduction* [London: Allen Lane, 1978]).

183. Andrew Cunningham, "Getting the Game Right: Some Plain Words on the Identity and Invention of Science," *Studies in History and Philosophy of Science* 19 (1988): 365–389.

184. Raymond Aron, *Main Currents in Sociological Thought* (London: Penguin Books, 1968); Frank Manuel, *The Prophets of Paris* (Cambridge, Mass.: Harvard University Press, 1962); K. Baker, "The Early History of the Term 'Social Science'," *Annals of Science* 20 (1964): 211–226.

185. Foucault, *Birth of the Clinic*; G. Canguilhem, *On the Normal and the Pathological* (Dordrecht: Reidel, 1978).

186. Dorinda Outram, "Science and Political Ideology, 1790–1848," in *Companion to the History of Modern Science*, ed. R. C. Olby, G. N. Cantor, J. R. R. Christie, and M. J. S. Hodge (London: Routledge, 1990), 1008–1023; Theodore M. Porter, "Natural Science and Social Theory," in *Companion to the History of Modern Science*, 1024–1043; B. Haines, "The Inter-relations between Social, Biological, and Medical Thought, 1750–1850: Saint-Simon and Comte," *The British Journal for the History of Science* 11 (1978): 19–35; J. V. Pickstone, "Bureaucracy, Liberalism, and the Body in Post-Revolutionary France: Bichat's Physiology and the Paris School of Medicine," *History of Science* 19 (1981): 115–142; Adrian Desmond, *Radical Science in London* (Chicago: University of Chicago Press, 1989).

FOUR

The Language of Human Nature

Roger Smith

HISTORIANS AND THE SUBJECT OF HUMAN NATURE

The attention given to human nature, eighteenth-century observers and modern historians might agree, makes further discussion superfluous. On the contrary, this chapter argues that closer analysis of the category of "human nature" is central for a history about "inventing human science." A focus on human nature makes it possible to avoid anachronism in talking about "the origins" of psychology, anthropology, linguistics, and so forth. Keeping human nature firmly in view as the historical subject may enable us to write history about what we would identify, for instance, as social, psychological, or political phenomena, without distortion by modern disciplinary categories.[1] It also conceptualizes a sense in which we can perhaps legitimately refer to the Enlightenment as a unity. However various the purposes of eighteenth-century writers, and however various the content attributed to human nature, the category of human nature set the terms in which these writers contested what it was to be human and what it was to prescribe social arrangements. The category, in brief, had a priori status for the organization of knowledge about the human subject. As the abbé de Mably claimed, "Let us study man as he is, in order to teach him what he should be."[2] "What 'man' *is*": these were the grounds on the basis of which daily experience, ethics, government, or aesthetics were to be brought to order.

Historical attention to reflexive claims about human nature suggests a variety of concrete projects. The most straightforward of these, though it has barely been undertaken, is to provide more knowledge about the language of human nature.[3] "Human nature" was a commonplace term in eighteenth-century English, with David Hume's *A Treatise of Human Nature*

(1739–40) now—but not then—its most famous monument. This usage certainly goes well back into the seventeenth century, but it is not clear when it became common. The Oxford dictionary, for example, cites John Dryden referring, in 1668, to "a just and lively image of Humane Nature," in a context in which Dryden recommended a literature that used such images to portray the shared and inherent qualities of all human beings.[4] This sense lasted through the eighteenth century and beyond. When Samuel Johnson, Bishop Joseph Butler, or Scottish writers such as Adam Smith, Adam Ferguson, or Hume himself referred to human nature, they invoked a ground defining what it was to be human. Thus a reviewer of Smith's *The Theory of Moral Sentiments* in 1759 referred to "the principle of Sympathy, on which he founds his system, [which] is an unquestionable principle in human nature."[5]

For these moralists, concerned that understanding should start from and return to common experience as a basis for civil society, "human nature" was an a priori category. They discussed the category's content, not its abstract form or rational legitimacy. At the end of his now much-cited comparison between the connection of ideas and attraction in physical nature, Hume wrote: "Its effects are everywhere conspicuous, but as to its causes, they are mostly unknown, and must be resolv'd into *original* qualities of human nature, which I pretend not to explain."[6] When Butler delivered sermons on human nature, he stressed that the conscience had natural supremacy as a power to guide conduct in each person; thus the possibility of moral conduct was grounded in our God-given nature.[7] Butler believed that his responsibility as an Anglican clergyman was to inspire his people with an empirical account of God's design in human nature.

Quoting references to human nature in the eighteenth century is a bit like quoting references to God in the Bible. It is necessary, however, lest the very commonplace quality of the language have the effect of hiding its significance for forms of knowledge. To provide a contrast and hence to argue for the significance of what I am proposing, I will first sketch four influential accounts of the origins or conditions of possibility for psychology in the period. Each account has its own strengths and weaknesses, but the point here is to throw into relief what a focused attention on human nature might achieve.

E. G. Boring's *A History of Experimental Psychology* (1929), which has served over the last twenty years as a stalking horse for a revisionist history of psychology, articulated a thesis concerning the conditions of emergence for his subject in the second half of the nineteenth century.[8] Boring described two intellectual traditions that, he held, came together at that time. The first, itself bifurcated, involved philosophical inquiry into the nature of mind, grounded in what was claimed to be the right exercise of reason or the right observation of its workings. The second was the tradition

of experimental inquiry associated with both medicine and natural philosophy and, by the mid–nineteenth century, exemplified in sensory physiology. Wilhelm Wundt and others of his generation argued that a rigorous
experimental methodology could be adapted to suit psychological topics,
including many of those which had become topics through earlier philosophical and introspective practices. Psychology as a science, Boring implied, was thus created by applying scientific method to topics previously
made distinct by philosophical writers.

This thesis had straightforward consequences for understanding psychology in the eighteenth century. (At no stage did it occur to Boring or
his epigones to ask whether there was such a category of knowledge to be
understood.) What was required was description of the grand philosophical traditions, rationalism stemming from G. W. Leibniz on one side of
the English Channel, and empiricism stemming from John Locke on the
other, in as far as they discussed the mind's workings and its consequences
for conduct. One topic in particular, associationism, appeared to stand
out as a psychological strand in the philosophical context. The history
of the association of ideas, correlated with the pleasure-pain principle of
behavior, which was traced from Locke and David Hartley to Alexander Bain, appeared to be the clearest case of a philosophical concern with
knowledge and reflection transforming itself into a psychological concern
with knowing and action. "Enlightenment" meant precisely such an evolution of metaphysics into empirical science. It made possible descriptive
categories (sensation or ideas), natural laws describing causal processes
(associations), and a presentation of mental agency as natural (the motives of pleasure and pain), framing mind as a conceivable object of experimental analysis. Alongside this, Boring described an emerging scientific
interest in the body, an interest that was then still inseparable from medicine. Lastly, Boring emphasized that both philosophical and physiological
strands (respectively the content and the method of psychology) were direct consequences of the scientific revolution, and the later psychology
therefore appeared to be this revolution's natural completion.

The representation of eighteenth-century psychology as the twin traditions of philosophy and physiology is linked to argument about the consequences of Cartesian dualism. Historians have often stressed dualism,
implying that eighteenth-century psychology was constrained by the seventeenth century, meaning that knowledge was constrained in the most literal sense of being confined by belief about the basic ontological categories. This leads to arguments advanced in different ways by E. A. Burtt
and A. N. Whitehead concerning the consequences of the new physical science in the seventeenth century for human self-understanding.[9]
Burtt's and Whitehead's intentions were ultimately metaphysical, and what

concerned them was the absence of a nondualistic ontology, one where quality, value, and purpose, as immediately existing to human consciousness, could be ascribed irreducibly to being. Such a metaphysics appeared ungraspable, they argued, precisely because the great architects of seventeenth-century physical science—Galileo, Descartes, and Newton—had succeeded only by developing abstract forms of knowledge which excluded what was most fundamental to human consciousness from rational discourse. Cartesian dualism, they thought, legitimating physical science by ontological exclusion, gave this mixed blessing its most systematic but also most obviously vulnerable expression. Taking Descartes seriously meant accepting that the mind, and thus those topics likely to be of central interest to psychology, could not be a subject of science, though Descartes himself believed that the soul was systematically knowable.

Yet there is no doubt that Enlightenment writers intended to study human nature in both mental and physical aspects. A common consequence, given the authority and imagistic richness of the new physical science, was the extension of the physical to encompass the mental, rather as Descartes had expanded his account of physiological hydraulics to encompass the passions.[10] Thus Hartley's description of vibrations in the nerves, modeled on Newton's ethereal mechanism for light, entered into the content of what he claimed for the association of ideas. Physical theories not only suggested analogies but provided what Kurt Danziger has identified as "generative metaphors" for psychological concepts, that is, metaphors that influenced judgments about the nature of coherent understanding and that fostered cognitive novelty.[11] It appears that reference to human nature increasingly signified a physical content in that nature, whether or not it was intended to explain mind by matter.

Burtt and Whitehead confronted dualism with its philosophical untenability and human costs from a perspective attempting to assimilate belief in the evolutionary foundation of human existence. They were responding to the contrast between the continuity principle embedded in evolutionary thinking and the discontinuity between physical and mental categories, paralleled by fact and value and by quantity and quality, in the Cartesian inheritance. Robert M. Young returned to this theme in the 1960s with a series of incomplete but highly suggestive analyses of the intellectual parameters relevant to the modern psychological and social sciences.[12] He focused on nineteenth-century evolutionism as the core topic, since it appeared to be there, most profoundly, that human nature was conceptualized as continuous with nature. This assumption about the core significance of the nineteenth century set the agenda for historical work in the eighteenth century: it possessed a dualistic legacy from the seventeenth century on the one hand, and it witnessed the beginnings of a

unifying naturalism on the other. This naturalism, exemplified by association psychology and utilitarianism, it was argued, began the process of
reinterpreting mind as a feature of nature.

The third thesis is associated with Gladys Bryson, Lester G. Crocker,
Peter Gay, and other historians who have argued that the Enlightenment
is of overwhelming significance for theories of human nature since it established modern liberal notions of that nature.[13] This thesis has many
sides, though the most relevant is the historical claim that the Newtonian revelation of the laws of nature inspired both the substance and the
method to establish the laws of human nature. These historians have described how the eighteenth century pioneered the modern psychological
and social sciences that, in their view, represent a rational and secular attempt to ameliorate the human condition through a just understanding
of that condition. Unlike Boring or Burtt, they dignified the eighteenth
century with foundational status for the modern world. In Gay's view, it
was the search for unified natural *law* behind human mental, cultural, and
physical diversity which constituted human nature as a subject for science.
This is an argument of evident power: the origins of the sciences of the
human subject are to be sought not in particular ideas or metaphysical
frameworks or in methods of investigation but in the adoption of an explanatory mode that makes generalization and perhaps even prediction
possible. This mode acquired both form and authority, it appears, from
Newtonian natural philosophy mediated through Locke's seminal *Essay
Concerning Human Understanding* (1690).[14]

This argument, or one like it, has become commonplace in writing
about Enlightenment thought and enters into many accounts of the origins of the modern psychological and social sciences. It merges with arguments about the progressive naturalization of terms describing the human
mind and conduct and hence with what is often portrayed as the process
of secularization.[15] The extensive secondary literature about political, economic, and social thought in the eighteenth century offers tacit support
by portraying such thought as part of a systematic explanatory project.
Liberal political theory and utilitarianism, the history of which is traced
from Thomas Hobbes and Locke, through association psychology, to Jeremy Bentham and beyond, exemplifies the point. Utilitarianism, thus understood, is an applied social science based on knowledge of the laws of
human nature. It is a strength of the thesis, however, that it can encompass more than French, Scottish, and English political economy. It addresses a mode of explanation, not particular thought. It perhaps provides
a framework that is able to integrate German rationalist thought with the
sources more often presented as foundational for the human sciences.
Though rationalists understood knowledge of laws differently from Locke
and his followers, they also searched for laws encompassing the human

condition. J. G. Herder or J. N. Tetens, for example, gave substantial accounts of the knowable order in the human sphere. With Immanuel Kant, rigorous refinement of what rational or scientific knowledge meant left theories of human nature without absolute authority. Nevertheless, Kant too gave public lectures aimed at providing a descriptive and practical guide to human nature and conduct.[16]

The fourth thesis that I will mention is associated with Michel Foucault. There are special difficulties in placing Foucault's work alongside the theses already outlined since it clearly must be assessed by different criteria. All the same, Foucault did specifically identify an intellectual system in the eighteenth century. Writing contemporaneously with Gay, he launched a scathing critique of the history of ideas, arguing that it gratuitously presupposed continuity, whereas a deeper "archaeology" would seek to reveal discontinuity between systems of thought, that is, rupture in the conditions of possibility for knowledge. Foucault made his point by distinguishing the long eighteenth century (beginning about 1650) as the classical age, an age that created knowledge through the analysis of identity and difference and by representing knowledge in a precisely ordered language. He concluded that this was a form of reasoning separated from the modern age beginning in the first decade of the nineteenth century. The human sciences, he argued, became possible only in the modern age and, in striking contrast to the historians of ideas, he identified institutional practices as the site at which the conditions for the truth of modern human science emerged. The implication for the notion of "inventing human science" in the eighteenth century is devastating: the notion is simply ignorant, presupposing as it does continuity in the nature of truth claims between Enlightenment accounts of natural history, language, or wealth and the present. Foucault was explicit that the Enlightenment interest in human nature was not to be equated with the modern human sciences. He used the terms "resemblance" and "imagination" to represent the conditions of knowing, the mind's analytic ordering of nature, and he specifically opposed the view that there was a science of human nature. "The very concept of human nature, and the way in which it functioned, excluded any possibility of a Classical science of man."[17]

This work remains largely unassimilated into eighteenth-century intellectual history, not least because of an entrenched belief in the English-speaking world in the origins of the human sciences in the eighteenth century, following the theses discussed earlier. Where Foucault has inspired impressive work, this is most often in relation to histories of what is literally the present and where the question of the eighteenth century is unimportant. For example, Nikolas Rose's studies of twentieth-century Anglo-American psychology begin with a brief sketch of "the origins," taking seriously Foucault's notion of a break at the beginning of the nineteenth century.[18] Rose grasped the richness of Foucault's manner of relating the conditions of knowledge to material practices, as institutionally embodied, but he considered few of the elements (such as associationism) that historians usually believe entered into the modern human sciences. To do so would have required him to say something about the eighteenth century.

No one, to my knowledge, defends the idea of an epistemic break in the late eighteenth century in the way that Foucault originally formulated it, and any defence would have to have a theoretical rather than an empirical character. Nevertheless, Foucault was undoubtedly correct that institutional or social transformations made possible new forms of knowledge and that previous historians all too superficially assumed continuity between eighteenth-century and present knowledge. It is difficult to escape the conclusion that there are elements of both continuity and discontinuity between the eighteenth century and the later human sciences. These elements can be clarified, I suggest, by attention to the language of human nature. This language reveals the presence of a human science in the Enlightenment, but it is one which cannot be subsumed, as a prologue, to modern disciplines.

Generalizations of the magnitude promoted by all four of these theses have gone into decline as detailed contextual studies gain prominence. Such studies may be in danger of writing the Enlightenment out of existence. This encourages me to explore the language of human nature, understanding meaning by reference to context while at the same time permitting something to be said about structural elements in the thought of a period. The question is not how seventeenth-century metaphysics influenced thought about human nature or how nineteenth-century human science disciplines originated in the Enlightenment. Rather, I seek to know what sort of constructive projects eighteenth-century actors were engaged in in being reflexively human.

HUMAN NATURE AND ITS MEANINGS

The particular expression "human nature" did not exist independently of the much vaunted science of man projected in the seventeenth-century masterpiece by Thomas Hobbes. Neither Hobbes, nor indeed Locke, referred to "human nature" as Hume was to do when he straightforwardly identified human nature as the subject of "the science of Man."[19] It is thus not clear to what extent reference to human nature became common in tandem with a systematic project on the science of man, or whether this reference had multiple roots (of the kind that Dryden's usage indicated) and writers such as Hume adapted and spread an already existing vocabulary. Nevertheless, there are strong structural features in common between Hobbes or Locke and the Enlightenment writers, not least because of the inspirational role of mathematical and natural philosophy in moral philosophy.

Hobbes himself demanded that "he that is to govern a whole Nation, must read in himself, not this, or that particular man; but Man-kind," and he then proceeded to ground his idea of a commonwealth in a science "Of Man."[20] Dividing science ("that is, knowledge of consequences") into natural history and civil history, using a Baconian sense of history as the descriptive means to knowledge, "man" became a subheading of natural history. The science of man concerned the effects of "the qualities" of our nature—the senses, the passions, and speech. There is no clearer example of the relativity of Hobbes's and our own modern disciplinary categories than Hobbes's list of the divisions in this science of man: optics, music, ethics, poetry, rhetoric, logic, and "the science of just and unjust."[21] This list might prove suggestive as a guide to where to look in the seventeenth century for writings on human nature. Rhetoric, for example, though a practical rather than a formal science, centrally concerned itself with how leadership and control could be achieved given the qualities of individual nature.[22] James G. Buickerood has argued that another of Hobbes's divisions, logic, was the subject of Locke's *Essay*, which was thus not a contribution to a proto-psychology.[23] Locke's work, insofar as it treated of what later writers referred to as human nature, drew on travelers' tales and, like Hobbes, took inspiration from Baconian natural history. G. A. J. Rogers has stressed that such a natural history made sense as a project only because Locke presupposed that there was a human nature waiting to be uncovered.[24]

The origins of the English usage "human (or humane) nature" therefore in part concerned hopes for a science of man and the transformation of Ancient or Renaissance disciplines and scholarship into a modern idiom. Once we step beyond the English language, the matter becomes even more complex since there were not direct and obvious equivalents in other European languages. While French writers certainly engaged with *la science de l'homme*, it is not clear that *la nature humaine* had the same resonance or frequency of use as the English-language equivalent. In German, an eighteenth-century reference to *Natur*, as in *Natur des Menschen*, was likely to connote the body and its material relations, often with implicit contrast to the world of *Geist*. It may be that, to study something comparable to the English "human nature," it would be necessary to examine uses of *Wesen* with its rich range of meanings (being, quality, disposition, conduct, and so forth). A comparative study of linguistic usage, however, remains a task for the future.

Heightening consciousness about language leads to four issues of interpretation concerning human nature. The first is the complex and constructive ambiguity in references to "nature," whether the reference is to

the essential quality of being some thing, or to "Nature" as a general reality with which human nature may or may not be identified. The second
point concerns the fundamentally normative as well as descriptive denotation of references to human nature. The third point introduces the central significance for Enlightenment writers of history as an imaginative
resource for debating the constitution of human nature. The fourth concerns what recent historians—though not eighteenth-century writers—distinguish as questions of gender, since we want to inquire whether "man"
or "the science of man" referred to only half of humankind. (As this last
point is dealt with elsewhere in this volume, I shall consider it only
briefly.)

"Nature" and "natural" did not convey one meaning or even one range
of meanings.[25] They were the key words of a framework of thought in
terms of which basic issues were contested. Ambiguity was intrinsic rather
than a matter of confusion, different denotations providing the currency
of intellectual debate. On the one hand, some thing's nature was its essential qualities, those that made it what it was and differentiated it from
other things. Christian thought generally sustained an everyday familiarity with man's or woman's nature in this sense. Butler grouped some of
his sermons together as "upon human nature, or man considered as a
moral agent," believing in the reality of moral agency and considering it to
be definitional, because God-given, of being human.[26] Similarly, the early
modern humanistic disciplines of rhetoric or jurisprudence grounded their
approach to ordering social or political affairs with a taken-for-granted reference to these qualities or natures.

On the other hand, it became increasingly common to refer to nature
(often with a capital "N") as a state or reality in itself, making it possible to
draw contrasts with culture, artificiality, or society in the manner that was
so important to critical political, moral, or aesthetic sensibility. Reference
to human nature thus became a way of including humankind, or at least
some of its attributes, in nature. Nature herself thus set the conditions,
Enlightenment writers argued, which made experience and history possible, and the language of nature set the terms in which man was to be understood. This usage also made possible powerful moral appeals to "a state
of nature" or to "natural man." Such rhetorical appeals preceded the innovations in natural philosophy in the seventeenth century and had close
associations with the biblical record of paradise and the fall. Nevertheless,
the intellectual power of the new mathematical and experimental analysis
gave knowledge of nature an authority it had never previously enjoyed—
and hence authority to ground knowledge of human nature in that nature
or, more subtly, in discoverable laws of the kind demonstrated for physical
nature.

The ambiguity made reference to human *nature* problematic and highly charged in a Christian civilization. If there was a human essence, understood by and in relation to the divine, then knowledge of natures external to humankind but not, at least directly, of God could not ground knowledge of that essence. Christianity had in multitudinous ways recognized that humanity had a nature that partook of the mundane world, but the shift, on such a scale, to representing human nature foundationally as a this-worldly nature was something new. Subsequent to the Enlightenment, a reference to human nature most often represented a belief in understanding human identity by reference to nature and not to God, or, at least, only indirectly to God. It is therefore plausible to claim that Enlightenment writers, whether deliberately or not, played on the ambiguity of the word *nature* and thereby tended to secularize theories of human essence.[27]

The two meanings of the word *nature* ran into each other, and it would miss the whole point of usage to seek tight definitions and clear distinctions. The ambiguity is historical evidence for a shift in representations of belief, and this shift is part of what is meant by "the Enlightenment." There was a shift to redescribe an essential Christian nature, originally represented in Adam and Eve, in terms that owed more to nature. Increasingly the qualities that made men and women what they are, that is, their natures, were understood to be qualities of nature transmuted by history and experience.

It may be that human nature became such a valued category in part because the ambiguity of the word *nature* enabled belief to change slowly without too great a sense of personal loss or too great a fear of social disruption. The enterprise of studying human nature was one on which the widest spectrum of opinion could agree. There were the greatest differences of view within the overall enterprise, but these differences fostered a sense of common debate rather than of splitting into incommensurable discourses. Different audiences distinguished different resonances in the same words and listened to those that most suited their purposes and flattered their values. In this way, the call to study human nature attracted little surprise or opposition. Studying that nature had in certain senses long been central to Christian and humanistic culture. Yet the Enlightenment project to study human nature as "a science of man" reconstructed a new view of that nature, one that is intrinsic to modernity.

Eighteenth-century writers continued to refer to humankind's nature as a reference to what it *is*, its essence, identity, or qualities. At the same time, an often apostrophized reference to "Nature" established a generalized contrast to culture or art. The further claim that human nature was grounded in nature therefore had the most fundamental character, leading to the identification of man's essence with the qualities of nature. The authority that this claim achieved in various quarters in the eighteenth century contributed substantially to what we would now identify as human science.

The language of human *nature* precipitates many other key questions. If the meaning of nature involved a contrast with art, how far did knowledge of nature—through this contrast—implicate knowledge of human nature? Did usage of the term "human nature" necessarily involve a degree of conflation between nature, meaning the natural world, and nature, meaning human essence, and, if so, should we interpret "human nature" as a linguistic condition making possible a science of man—attributing human science to a pun? Or was there an element of appropriation, even opportunism, when writers favored the language of human nature in order to encompass humans by categories appropriate for the natural world?

It is conventional wisdom about the Enlightenment that it modeled its notions of human nature on the physical nature represented in Newtonian philosophy. This is why Locke was such a key figure, since it was he, it appeared, who elaborated an understanding of mental mechanisms compatible with learning from and responding to nature in the way that Newton had described it. Later writers then began from where Locke had left off, describing mental events in terms of the lawlike relations of sensations deriving from physical motions. Historically, many qualifications are needed, notably that Locke's plans for his *Essay* belong to the period before he was acquainted with Newton's work and that "Newtonian" natural philosophy contained very diverse notions of physical reality. Nevertheless, it was the superimposed image of Newton and Locke which encouraged later critics to accuse Enlightenment psychology of materialism. Romantic writers, notably Samuel Taylor Coleridge, believed that eighteenth-century sensationalist theories of human nature denied the active, transformative qualities of spirit.[28] It appeared to them that modeling human nature on material nature had reduced the self to a passive reflection of matter. This judgment, that sensationalist writers propagated an image of human nature as a passive state empty of anything besides physical properties, has lasted.

All the same, this judgment is limited. I am arguing that reference to "nature" in "human nature" permitted beliefs about qualities intrinsic to humankind and about the dependency of human on physical nature to exist side by side. So-called sensationalist philosophers—Locke obviously but also those whose views were more extreme such as the abbé de Condillac or Claude-Adrien Helvétius, presupposed that there were qualities intrinsic to human nature which made experience possible and generated the conduct that followed from it. It was this a priori in knowledge about human beings which was referred to as human nature.

This perspective derives in large measure from a reading of Ernst Cassirer's interpretation of the Enlightenment. As a neo-Kantian philosopher who took for granted the epistemological weaknesses of empiricism, he was sensitive to the fact that few (if any) post-Lockeans conceded mental passivity. In Cassirer's Enlightenment, it was reason that made possible efforts to achieve coherent sciences in all spheres—whether natural philosophy, psychology, ethics, jurisprudence, or aesthetics.[29] As he explained, eighteenth-century writers assumed that processes of reasoning, embedded in human nature, united mankind and that a science of man was therefore indeed possible. Locke took for granted shared capacities of experience and reflection. Condillac equipped his metaphor for human nature, the statue which at first glance appears to be the most passive of objects, with a nature able both to receive sensations and to think about them.[30] Locke, Condillac, and their followers discussed sensation as the source of the mind's content, but their arguments required them to deploy an a priori category, construed sometimes as capacities of mind and sometimes as the needs of living organization. This a priori was "nature."

Eighteenth-century writers shared a conceptual ground and, in the most abstract terms, a common language, and this made possible diverse claims about what human nature was while permitting communication about a common endeavor. Thus, J. O. de La Mettrie represented human nature as the organizing powers of living matter, deliberately earning himself a shocking reputation as a materialist.[31] By contrast, Tetens represented human nature as the teleological activity of the apperceptive soul.[32] Yet both writers conceived of a science concerned with the qualities of what it was to be human, and both described this "nature" as an a priori ground bringing order and meaning to experience. The religious and metaphysical form of this a priori dominated the writings of some authors, such as Leibniz. Later philosophers, such as Thomas Reid, who similarly rejected Lockean empiricism, were less inclined to be metaphysical about the a priori, and it is therefore more straightforward to label what they were discussing as human nature. Reid's fellow Scotsmen, such as Smith or Ferguson, described that nature without any philosophical self-consciousness, treating the a priori as a component in commonsensical beliefs about the social person and the conditions of virtue.

No one was more emphatic than Hume that his subject was human nature—not reason, experience, mind, or body, and certainly not anything resembling a modern human science subject like psychology or sociology. He systematically described the order observable by ourselves in our experience, habits, and actions, and in the conduct of others, and he attributed this order to our shared nature: "'Tis evident, that all the sciences have a relation, greater or less, to human nature."[33] Famously skeptical of the possibility of knowledge of essences, including knowledge of the powers and qualities supposedly causing experience, and equally skeptical of "any hypothesis, that pretends to discover the ultimate original qualities of human nature," Hume was ready in practice to describe innate powers and to attribute them to human nature.[34] It was from such knowledge that he aimed to establish the moral sciences. Even Hume accepted an a priori of the kind I have described. In Cassirer's words, "nature and knowledge are to be placed on their own foundations and explained in terms of their own conditions."[35] Hume's skepticism was directed toward certain reasoning procedures but not toward what he took to be the conditions of human nature. The conditions that Hume located in this nature suggested the possibility of a unified moral science. Hume's "a priori," however, had a content describing the capacities of man which he believed he could derive from "a cautious observation of human life."[36]

This discussion about the ambiguity of "nature" in "human nature" has led from the claim that the ambiguity is emblematic of a transition from a Christian to a secular discourse to the claim that the language of human nature signals an a priori in eighteenth-century thought about the human subject. If human nature was a category in terms of which people approached topics such as government, aesthetics, or education, then it sustained the possibility of a unified intellectual life at the same time as divergent values pulled it apart. Everyone addressed human nature, most frequently as if it were a self-evident basis on which to found moralistic argument—whether of a Christian or a secular variety.

This leads to the second interpretive issue concerning discourse about human nature: language was intrinsically and not merely contingently normative in scope. The point is well captured in the English term *moral philosophy* used in the eighteenth century (and long after) to describe those divisions of knowledge concerned with the human subject.[37] Knowledge about humans was *moral* knowledge. Moral philosophy covered both powers of reasoning (Reid's "intellectual powers") and powers of action (the "active powers"). Locke, in introducing his *Essay*, had stated that "our business here is not to know all things, but those which concern our conduct . . . [to] find out those measures whereby a rational creature, put in that state in which man is in this world, may and ought to govern his opinions and actions depending thereon."[38] "Inventing" human science reformulated normative discourse and did not fundamentally separate descriptive fact from evaluative decision.

When Enlightenment writers—whether of a Christian or of a secular disposition—described "nature," in its fully ambiguous sense of both essence and physical reality, they sought a ground determining judgment. It was precisely the hope that knowledge would reveal value that fostered belief that it was an enlightened age. Empirical knowledge of human nature, replacing superstition, ignorance, and dogma, was grasped as the foundation for improvement and progress. Writers, showing remarkable agreement, reiterated that knowledge of the qualities, powers, and capacities of humankind's nature, collectively and individually, was knowledge of what it was both possible and right to do. Smith's account of our response to murder was typical:

> And with regard, at least, to this most dreadful of all crimes, Nature, antecedent to all reflections upon the utility of punishment, has in this manner stamped upon the human heart, in the strongest and most indelible characters, an immediate and instinctive approbation of the sacred and necessary law of retaliation.[39]

For Smith, there were two questions concerning morals: "First, wherein does virtue consist? . . . And, secondly, by what power or faculty in the mind is it, that this character, whatever it be, is recommended to us?" His response to the second question was "sympathy," "which Providence undoubtedly intended to be the governing principle of human nature."[40]

The antireligious *philosophes,* as well as a moralist like Smith who was firmly within the British providentialist tradition, described moral action as something growing out of human nature. Human nature had the status of being the shared ground on which writers of many persuasions erected moral standards of universal validity. Thus, in a sense, theories of human nature developed historically from and supplanted theories of natural law. Natural law theories, most influentially reexpressed in the seventeenth century by Hugo Grotius, had located an objective right and wrong in the nature of things, that is, in the created world. Human nature theories described this objective ground in increasingly naturalistic terms, as the specific qualities of man.[41] Smith's description was inseparable from religious belief. Helvétius's description, which reduced human nature to a capacity to react to pleasure and pain, emptied ethical argument of any vestige of Christianity.[42] The normative dimension present in claims about human nature was thus a significant condition for a secular ethics.

Argument about "the state of nature," from Hobbes to Jean-Jacques Rousseau, was a major idiom expressive of the wider theme. There was debate about the actual historical reality of this state and whether empirical methods permitted any knowledge of it, notably, by comparison between living "civilized" and "primitive" peoples. Empirical questions were secondary, however, to the logical position accounts of this state held in establishing judgment about what was good and right. The state of nature, it was understood, exhibited human nature in its essential form and did not necessarily exist in a historical or present form.

Even a figure such as Ferguson, who decried historical speculation about the earliest state of mankind, assumed that that state exhibited features of human nature—sociability, for example—and that this was the basis for the subsequent foundation of government. More distinctively, scorning the opinion that pleasure and pain encompassed human motivation, he discerned in human nature a restlessness and drive that had made improvement possible and to which he attributed what was good in human character.[43]

In great contrast, Denis Diderot observed in the natural feelings of the body the grounds for legitimating freedom of expression in sexual matters.[44] Neither the conservative Ferguson nor the libertarian Diderot, however, focused on the relation between claims about fact and claims about value as a philosophical topic in its own right. The eighteenth-century discursive framework did not have space for this, since it constructed value in and through narratives of human nature. Such narratives always had a point, in the way that myths have a point, and that point was knowledge of the good as embedded in the nature of things and knowledge of the good life as embedded in the nature of being human. Once again, it is significant to note how easy it was in these terms to sustain both Christian and secular versions of the Enlightenment.

For many modern readers, Diderot is at one and the same time the most profound and the most amusing writer to embrace embodied human nature as a guide to life. "Embrace" and "embody" create the right associations since Diderot played with sexual mores as play on civilization's distance from natural truths, artfully mixing malice and delight. Historically, it must be remembered, though, that the most exploratory writings were in his letters to his mistress, Sophie Volland, or in the very posthumously published *Rameau's Nephew and D'Alembert's Dream*.[45] His own major publishing achievement was of course the *Encyclopédie*. There he had written: "It is the presence of man which makes the existence of things meaningful" and "Man is the single place from which we must begin and to which we must refer everything."[46] This was a radical, secular humanism that made everything hinge on knowing what man *was*. He sought answers to this by conceiving of nature and human nature as one and the same. Writing about his fictional character Jacques the Fatalist, he commented, perhaps also referring to himself: "The distinction between a physical and a moral world seemed to him empty of meaning."[47] Far from implying materialism in the simple sense of reducing reality to dead matter, Diderot in fact explored physiology for ideas on how to revivify nature, developing organic metaphors for the natural that projected the feelings of the heart into nature rather than cold nature into human nature.[48] By accepting his own nature more than most, Diderot saw further into something of what perhaps followed if that nature was to become the sole source of moral value.

The way in which the study of human nature was foundational for eighteenth-century moral philosophy can be taken further by reference to the third interpretive issue. This concerns the role attributed to history in constituting human nature. In the earlier discussion, I have tended to refer to human nature as a category that was itself not questioned, that indeed appeared unquestionable, however much effort was expended in describing its content. This portrays eighteenth-century writers as accepting human nature as an atemporal given. The eighteenth-century intellect, however, is remembered for temporalizing nature and for its view of civil society as a historical process. Elsewhere in this volume, Robert Wokler and David Carrithers emphasize the shift in analysis from *l'homme physique* to *l'homme moral*, representing a new understanding of man as a cultural being constituted through a historical process. As they show, this shift was a major part of what was novel ("invented") in late Enlightenment thought about the human subject and has claim to be recognized in retrospect as a foundation of both social anthropology and sociology.

Advocates of a science of man intended their science to be an empirical one founded in common knowledge of mental powers and conduct in self or mirrored in others. Most writers saw little difficulty in principle in describing human nature, implying that it was something constant and known, if not articulated, by all people. They valued classical authors highly for their wealth of experience about human nature. These same eighteenth-century writers, however, made considerable play with a historical dimension that was not the subject of empirical knowledge in the way that human conduct could be said to be. Using a historical mode of expression, they debated the causes and values of improvement, refinement, liberty, and, in short, the whole range of positions between natural and artificial or between savage and civilized in human life. The historians of Greece and Rome exemplified, inspired, and forewarned. As Wokler also points out, in the eighteenth century it also became fundamental to historical imagination to compare living non-Western "primitive" peoples with the early stages of civilization. Comparative and historical methods became inextricable, together contributing to a properly *social* social science.

This science was "conjectural," in Dugald Stewart's famous description of Smith's history of moral sentiment.[49] Its focus was on relations between causes and effects in social experience, insofar as they could be generalized into an understanding of the conditions of social achievement and failure, rather than on the particular historical facts of unique events. History writing was, above all, a literary mode for expressing the moral content of human experience, often by an account of culture supplementing or even supplanting nature. Generalized claims about human nature fitted well into this intellectual style. The literature of conjectural history took over the language of human nature but, in the process, introduced a new and significant issue. Historical thinking inevitably raised the question whether human nature itself stood outside the historical process, as a prior cause, or whether it changed and was thus, at least to a degree, a product of history. But this question does not appear to have been framed in quite this way in the eighteenth century. Conjectural histories did debate the historical relationship between *l'homme physique* and *l'homme moral,* but they did not express themselves in terms of an evolving human nature.

For some writers, human nature was a cause that specifically lay outside history and could therefore be cited as an explanation for history. This supposition lay behind the deeply influential studies, initially by Hobbes and Baron Samuel Pufendorf and later by Montesquieu, which conjectured about the material stages through which Western people had passed on the way from barbarism to civilization.[50] Pufendorf (as Wokler points out) postulated a natural sociability in man, alongside a natural selfishness, and argued that this sociability enabled people to cooperate to satisfy their needs and thus to establish society and culture, a process that then acquired its own momentum. Some later conjectural historians, among whom Ferguson has pride of place with historians of the social sciences, began to treat man's nature as self-constituted through his history. Ferguson was profoundly aware that "of all the terms we employ in treating of human affairs, those of *natural* and *unnatural* are the least determinate in their meaning." Thus, he understood, "we speak of art as distinguished from nature; but art itself is natural to man." And, as he continued, "he is in some measure the artificer of his own frame, as well as his fortune, and is destined, from the first age of his being, to invent and contrive."[51] Ferguson, however, did not then go on either fully to historicize human nature, since such a supposed nature continued to do much explanatory work in his subsequent account of social progress and decline, or simply to drop reference to it. However, it can perhaps be suggested that as social and historical accounts of human life acquired prominence, so human nature as a topic in its own right declined in significance.

Generalizations are always vulnerable to exceptions, nowhere more so than with the intrinsically speculative genre of eighteenth-century historical writing. It is widely held, for example, that Giambattista Vico's intellectual originality lay precisely with implying that human nature is historical and that there are forms of consciousness proper to each age. These historical forms, he argued, were traceable through the development of legal systems and language.[52] This historicized view of human nature then reappeared as a fundamental strand of German idealist argument, running from Herder into the nineteenth century. This assessment raises complex matters for my interpretation, notably whether this historicism perpetuated assumptions about an a priori which can be legitimately identified with an atemporal essence or "nature."

The main conclusion is to qualify a picture of the Enlightenment as a historicizing movement of thought. A fully historicized human science treats the human subject, from whatever perspective, as a historical subject. Such a science, as a collective enterprise, did not exist in the eighteenth century. Rather, the category "human nature" remained largely unquestioned and provided the ahistorical language in terms of which historical change was intelligible. The capacities or essential qualities within mind—not the mind's content which was indeed dependent on historical experience—retained their status as a priori elements in the structure of the science of man.

The fourth and last major interpretive point concerns the gendered meaning of language. Eighteenth-century authors wrote about "the science of man," about *l'homme,* or about *der Mensch.* Was this usage intended, and understood, to refer to men, to men and women, or to some combination of both, and were these usages context dependent? How much sensitivity is needed to the different connotations of different, but apparently gendered, words in different languages (*Mensch,* notably, having more universal connotations that "man")? Gender is a modern and not an eighteenth-century category. To what extent, then, was human nature discussed in relation to sexual differences and to the social expression or creation of such differences? Further, how were sexual differences fitted into other systems of classification, such as those differentiating nations or status? After all, any theory that had pretensions to uncover the universal in human nature also required a vocabulary for describing differences.

Ludmilla Jordanova's chapter in this volume makes clear the range of discussion and the difficulties facing any attempt to generalize about eighteenth-century opinions. Silently gendered language did not exclude fascination with the topic of differences between women and men. This fascination became so strong for some writers that it turned into a desire for a systematic science, even "a science of women." Both women and men contributed to this.[53] The science of woman addressed women's nature in ways comparable with the literature on human nature in general, revealing the same ambiguity about "nature," the same normative structure, and similarly historicizing the content but not the capacities of that nature.

This chapter has explored interpretive questions rather than presented empirical detail. It started by rejecting a "pillarized" approach to the human sciences in the eighteenth century, an approach that excavates foundations for each of the modern psychological or social sciences, falsely projecting back socially constructed categories into another age. Not only were there no disciplines in the modern institutional sense in the eighteenth century, but the terms and investigative activity making possible such differentiated scholarship did not exist. I have argued that the category "human nature" held together rather than dispersed knowledge about the human subject and that it was fundamental to the desire for a unified moral science. It was not necessarily foundational for modern categories—though it may in fact have been so. Human nature remained an essentially irreducible category in terms of which observed phenomena were to be explained. The business of human science was to describe its qualities. Some authors attempted to explain those qualities by some other ground, such as God or physiology, but this was a secondary undertaking in that body of work distinguished as the Enlightenment. The descriptive study of human nature distinctively identifies the eighteenth-century endeavor in human science.

ACKNOWLEDGMENTS

I should like to thank Ludmilla Jordanova and especially Stephen Pumfrey for their readings of an earlier version of this essay. A short version appeared as "'Human Nature' as an Enlightenment Category," in *New Studies in the History of Psychology and the Social Sciences. Proceedings of the Tenth Meeting of Cheiron: European Society for the Behavioral and Social Sciences, Madrid, September 1991*, ed. Helio Carpintero, Enrique Lafuente, Régine Plas, and Lothar Sprung (Valencia: "Revista de Historia de la Psicologia" Monographs 2, 1992), 247–252.

NOTES

1. For my reflections on the sense in which "psychology" as a subject can be said to exist before it gained a modern social identity, see Roger Smith, "Does the History of Psychology Have a Subject?" *History of the Human Sciences* 1 (1988): 147–177. See also Kurt Danziger, "Origins of the Schema of Stimulated Motion: Towards a Pre-history of Modern Psychology," *History of Science* 21 (1983): 182–210; idem, "Generative Metaphor and the History of Psychological Discourse," in *Metaphors in the History of Psychology*, ed. David E. Leary (Cambridge: Cambridge University Press, 1990), 331–356. For forceful, parallel criticism of Buffon's status as the founder of anthropology: Claude Blanckaert, "Buffon and the Natural History of Man: Writing History and the 'Foundational Myth' of Anthropology," *History of the Human Sciences* 6 (1993): 13–50. For the complexities of eighteenth-century linguistics: Hans Aarsleff, *From Locke to Saussure: Essays on the Study of Language and Intellectual History* (Minneapolis: University of Minnesota Press, 1982).

2. Quoted in Lester G. Crocker, *Nature and Culture: Ethical Thought in the French Enlightenment* (Baltimore: Johns Hopkins University Press, 1963), 480. For a survey of national divergencies, see Roy Porter and Mikuláš Teich, eds., *The Enlightenment in National Context* (Cambridge: Cambridge University Press, 1981).

3. "Psychology" has attracted more attention: Christopher Fox, "Defining Eighteenth-Century Psychology: Some Problems and Perspectives," in *Psychology and Literature in the Eighteenth Century*, ed. Christopher Fox (New York: AMS Press, 1987), 1–22; Graham Richards, *Mental Machinery: The Origins and Consequences of Psychological Ideas, Part 1: 1600–1850* (London: Athlone Press, 1992); G. S. Rous-

seau, "Psychology," in *The Ferment of Knowledge: Studies in the Historiography of Eighteenth-Century Science*, ed. G. S. Rousseau and Roy Porter (Cambridge: Cambridge University Press, 1980), 145–210; Fernando Vidal, "Psychology in the 18th Century: A View from the Encyclopaedias," *History of the Human Sciences* 6 (1993): 89–119.

4. John Dryden, "Of Dramatick Poesie, an Essay," in *The Works of John Dryden*, ed. Samuel Holt Monk, vol. 7 (Berkeley, Los Angeles, London: University of California Press, 1971), 15.

5. Quoted by the editors of Adam Smith, *The Theory of Moral Sentiments* (1759; ed. D. D. Raphael and A. L. Macfie, Oxford: Oxford University Press, 1976), 27.

6. David Hume, *A Treatise of Human Nature* (1739–40; ed. L. A. Selby-Bigge, Oxford: Clarendon Press, 1888), 13; emphasis in Hume.

7. Joseph Butler, "Upon Human Nature, or Man Considered as a Moral Agent," sermons I–III (first published 1726), in *The Works of Joseph Butler*, ed. W. E. Gladstone, vol. 2 (Oxford: Clarendon Press, 1896), 31–76.

8. E. G. Boring, *A History of Experimental Psychology* (1929; 2d ed., New York: Appleton-Century-Crofts, 1950). For the context in which Boring wrote, see John M. O'Donnell, "The Crisis of Experimentalism in the 1920's: E. G. Boring and His Uses of History," *American Psychologist* 34 (1979): 289–295. For the wider context of twentieth-century U.S. accounts of Wundt, see Mitchell G. Ash, "The Self-Presentation of a Discipline: History of Psychology in the United States between Pedagogy and Scholarship," in *Functions and Uses of Disciplinary Histories*, ed. Loren Graham, Wolf Lepenies, and Peter Weingart (Dordrecht: D. Reidel, 1983), 143–189.

9. E. A. Burtt, *The Metaphysical Foundations of Modern Physical Science* (1924; 2d ed., London: Routledge and Kegan Paul, 1932); A. N. Whitehead, *Science and the Modern World* (1926; reprint, Cambridge: Cambridge University Press, 1953).

10. R. Descartes, "Les passions de l'âme" (first published 1649), in *Oeuvres de Descartes*, ed. Charles Adam and Paul Tannery, vol. 11 (Paris: J. Vrin, 1967), 291–497.

11. David Hartley, *Observations on Man, His Frame, His Duty, and His Expectations* (1749; facsimile reprint, 2 vols., Hildesheim: Georg Olms, 1967); Danziger, "Generative Metaphor." On the ether theory, see John W. Yolton, *Thinking Matter: Materialism in Eighteenth-Century Britain* (Oxford: Basil Blackwell, 1983), 177–184.

12. Robert M. Young, "Animal soul," in *The Encyclopedia of Philosophy*, ed. Paul Edwards (New York: Macmillan and Free Press, 1967), vol. 1, pp. 122–127; idem, *Mind, Brain, and Adaptation in the Nineteenth Century: Cerebral Localization and Its Biological Context from Gall to Ferrier* (Oxford: Clarendon Press, 1970); idem, *Darwin's Metaphor: Nature's Place in Victorian Culture* (Cambridge: Cambridge University Press, 1985).

13. Gladys Bryson, *Man and Society: The Scottish Inquiry of the Eighteenth Century* (1945; facsimile reprint, New York: Augustus M. Kelley, 1968); Lester G. Crocker, *An Age of Crisis: Man and World in Eighteenth Century French Thought* (Baltimore: Johns Hopkins University Press, 1959); idem, *Nature and Culture*; Peter Gay, *The Enlightenment: An Interpretation* (1966–69; reprint, 2 vols., London: Wildwood House).

14. John Locke, *An Essay Concerning Human Understanding* (1690; ed. Peter H.

Nidditch, Oxford: Clarendon Press, 1975). Locke's thoughts for the *Essay* dated from the 1660s, but many Enlightenment writers understood Locke's work to be an exploration of Newtonian themes. See G. A. J. Rogers, "The Empiricism of Locke and Newton," in *Philosophers of the Enlightenment,* ed. S. C. Brown (Brighton: Harvester Press, 1979), 1–30.

15. "Secularization" is a problematic historical description since it presupposes the conclusion that it sets out to explain. For a survey of the variety and complexity of Enlightenment discussions of science and religion, see John Hedley Brooke, *Science and Religion: Some Historical Perspectives* (Cambridge: Cambridge University Press, 1991), chap. 5.

16. I. Kant, *Anthropology From a Pragmatic Point of View* (trans. Mary J. Gregor from 2d German ed. of 1800, The Hague: Martinus Nijhoff, 1974). See Katherine Arens, *Structures of Knowing: Psychologies of the Nineteenth Century* (Dordrecht: Kluwer, 1989), 59–84.

17. Michel Foucault, *The Order of Things: An Archaeology of the Human Sciences* (trans. from French of 1966; London: Tavistock, 1970), 309; cf. 71. For a commentary on this argument and for its background in French philosophy of science, see Gary Gutting, *Michel Foucault's Archaeology of Scientific Reason* (Cambridge: Cambridge University Press, 1989).

18. Nikolas Rose, *The Psychological Complex: Social Regulation and the Psychology of the Individual* (London: Routledge and Kegan Paul, 1985), chap. 1.

19. Hume, *A Treatise of Human Nature,* xix.

20. Thomas Hobbes, *Leviathan* (1651; reprint, ed. Richard Tuck, Cambridge: Cambridge University Press, 1991), 11 and part 1.

21. Ibid., 61.

22. Historical studies of rhetoric focus more on the sixteenth century than on its continuing life in the seventeenth century. For background on the rhetorical tradition, see Brian Vickers, *In Defence of Rhetoric* (Oxford: Clarendon Press, 1988). For the contributions of jurisprudence, preeminently the ordering science of human affairs, see Donald R. Kelley, *The Human Measure: Social Thought in the Western Legal Tradition* (Cambridge, Mass.: Harvard University Press, 1990).

23. James G. Buickerood, "The Natural History of the Understanding: Locke and the Rise of Facultative Logic in the Eighteenth Century," *History and Philosophy of Logic* 6 (1985): 157–190.

24. G. A. J. Rogers, "Locke, Anthropology and Models of the Mind," *History of the Human Sciences* 6 (1993): 73–87. Voltaire's oft quoted remark that Locke had written "the natural history" of the human soul has more depth than is usually recognized; see Voltaire, *Lettres philosophiques* (1734; ed. Gustave Lanson, rev. André M. Rousseau, Paris: Marcel Didier, 1964), 1:168–169.

25. Andrew Benjamin, Geoffrey Cantor, and John Christie, eds., *The Figural and the Literal* (Manchester: Manchester University Press, 1986); Ludmilla Jordanova, ed., *Languages of Nature: Critical Essays on Science and Literature* (London: Free Association Books, 1986).

26. Butler, "Upon Human Nature."

27. Such shifts in Christian belief, particularly as they affected notions of the good, led Crocker among others to refer to "an age of crisis." I cannot do justice

here to the range of opinion about the religious implications of the Enlightenment; rather, I point out only the significant sense in which the language of human nature tied in with these issues. See also note 15.

28. Samuel Taylor Coleridge, *Biographia Literaria or Biographical Sketches of My Literary Life and Opinions* (1817; ed. George Watson, London: Dent, 1956).

29. Ernst Cassirer, *The Philosophy of the Enlightenment* (1932, in German; trans. Fritz C. A. Koellin and James P. Pettegrove, Boston: Beacon Press, 1955).

30. Locke, *Essay Concerning Human Understanding*, Book II, chaps. 6 and 7; Étienne Bonnot, abbé de Condillac, *Condillac's Treatise on the Sensations* (1754, in French; trans. Geraldine Carr, London: Favil Press, 1930), 227–236. In fact, Condillac barely considered the problem of reflection in developing his metaphor of the statue, though earlier he had treated reflection as an independent power: *Essai sur l'origine des connaissances humaines: Ouvrage où l'on réduit a un seul principe tout ce qui concerne l'entendement* (1746; ed. Raymond Lenoir, Paris: Armand Colin, 1924), 38–41. Condillac thought such reflection became active with the fixing of attention made possible by language: Hans Aarsleff, "Condillac's speechless statue," in Aarsleff's *From Locke to Saussure*, 210–224; Isabel F. Knight, *The Geometric Spirit: The Abbé de Condillac and the French Enlightenment* (New Haven, Conn.: Yale University Press, 1968), 29–33.

31. Aram Vartanian, *L'homme machine: A Study in the Origins of an Idea* (1747; critical ed., Princeton, N.J.: Princeton University Press, 1960). The medical as opposed to Cartesian context of La Mettrie's works is stressed in Kathleen Wellman, *La Mettrie: Medicine, Philosophy, and Enlightenment* (Durham, N.C.: Duke University Press, 1992).

32. Tetens's main work was his *Philosophische Versuche ueber die menschliche Natur und ihre Entwicklung* (1777); see Cassirer, *Philosophy of the Enlightenment*, 125–131. Tetens is mentioned here also because of the position claimed for him by the historian of psychology G. S. Brett, that he provided "the first clear statement of a purely psychological method": *Brett's History of Psychology*, abridged, ed. R. S. Peters (London: George Allen and Unwin, 1962), 482. A German-language example such as this raises questions about the extension of my analysis beyond the English-language Enlightenment.

33. Hume, *Treatise of Human Nature*, xix.

34. Ibid., xxi. The target of Hume's skepticism has been reassessed by John P. Wright, who stated:

> A central aim of the first book of Hume's *Treatise of Human Nature* is to show how certain fundamental beliefs about the world are generated. A fundamental thesis of the book is that these ontological beliefs do not arise solely on the basis of rational or scientific considerations but that, on the contrary, they rest upon what Hume calls "human nature."

Wright, *The Sceptical Realism of David Hume* (Manchester: Manchester University Press, 1983), 38. Wright (especially pp. 188–233) stressed more than I have done that Hume thought of human nature as grounded in a physiological reality, and that, in this sense, he was in a Cartesian tradition.

35. Cassirer, *Philosophy of the Enlightenment*, 97.

36. Hume, *Treatise of Human Nature*, xxiii.

37. For moral philosophy, see Roger L. Emerson, "Science and Moral Philosophy in the Scottish Enlightenment," in *Studies in the Philosophy of the Scottish Enlightenment*, ed. M. A. Stewart (Oxford: Clarendon Press, 1990), 11–36.

38. Locke, *Essay Concerning Human Understanding*, 46.

39. Smith, *Theory of Moral Sentiments*, 71.

40. Ibid., 264, 326.

41. For discussion of natural law, see Crocker, *Nature and Culture*, chap. 1; Cassirer, *Philosophy of the Enlightenment*, 234–253; Richard Tuck, "The 'Modern' Theory of Natural Law," in *The Languages of Political Theory in Early-Modern Europe*, ed. Anthony Pagden (Cambridge: Cambridge University Press, 1987), 99–119; Kelley, *Human Measure*.

42. Claude-Adrien Helvétius, *De l'esprit* (first published 1758), in *Oeuvres complètes d'Helvétius* (facsimile reprint, Hildesheim: Georg Olms, 1969), 4:37–46, 124–138; idem, *De l'homme* (first published 1773), in *Oeuvres complètes d'Helvétius*, 7:205–223 and 8:1–9. For the striking way that Helvétius, while accepting human modifiability, still presumed that there was an essential identity in regard to human nature, see Crocker, *Age of Crisis*, 189.

43. Adam Ferguson, *An Essay on the History of Civil Society* (1767; ed. Duncan Forbes, Edinburgh: Edinburgh University Press, 1966).

44. Diderot's commitment to sexual expression was especially evident in his *Supplément au voyage de Bougainville* (written in 1772): *Diderot's Selected Writings*, ed. Lester G. Crocker (New York: Macmillan, 1966), 223–251. See Gay, *The Enlightenment*, vol. 2, *The Science of Freedom*, 194–200.

45. There is a selection in English of Diderot's letters in *Diderot's Letters to Sophie Volland*, trans. Peter France (London: Oxford University Press, 1972). He died in 1784. The publishing history of his essays is complex: *Le neveu de Rameau* (written in 1761 or later) appeared first, in an edition based on his manuscript, in his complete works in 1823. The first printed edition of *Le rêve de d'Alembert* appeared in 1830 (written in 1769). For modern critical editions, see *Oeuvres complètes*, vols. 12 and 17 (Paris: Hermann, 1975–). See *Rameau's Nephew and D'Alembert's Dream*, trans. L. W. Tancock (Harmondsworth: Penguin Books, 1966); Arthur M. Wilson, *Diderot* (New York: Oxford University Press, 1972).

46. Article "Encyclopédie" from the *Encyclopédie*, in *Oeuvres complètes*, 7:212–213, translated in Gay, *The Enlightenment*, vol. 2, *The Science of Freedom*, 162.

47. Quoted in C. C. Gillispie, *The Edge of Objectivity: An Essay in the History of Scientific Ideas* (Princeton, N.J.: Princeton University Press, 1960), 181.

48. For Diderot's physiology, see especially: *Pensées sur l'interprétation de la nature* (1753), in *Oeuvres complètes*, vol. 9, partly trans. in *Diderot's Selected Writings*, ed. Lester G. Crocker (New York: Macmillan, 1966), 70–87; *Le rêve de d'Alembert*; the notes on *Éléments de physiologie* (written 1774–1780) in *Oeuvres complètes*, vol. 17, part trans. in *Diderot's Selected Writings*, 269–282.

49. Dugald Stewart, *Account of the Life and Writings of Adam Smith, LL.D.* (first published 1794), ed. I. S. Ross, in Adam Smith's *Essays on Philosophical Subjects*, ed. W. P. D. Wightman and J. C. Bryce (Oxford: Clarendon Press, 1980), 293. P. B. Wood has suggested that the extension of the term "conjectural" to cover a general class of historical writing may need qualification: Wood, "The Natural History

of Man in the Scottish Enlightenment," *History of Science* 28 (1990): 89–123, especially 113–114. See also H. M. Höpfl, "From Savage to Scotsman: Conjectural History in the Scottish Enlightenment," *Journal of British Studies* 17 (1978): 19–40; Robert Wokler, chap. 2 in this volume.

50. Hobbes, *Leviathan*, part 1; Samuel Pufendorf, *Of the Law of Nature and Nations, Eight Books* (1672; translated from the Latin edition of 1712 by Basil Kennett, 3d ed., London: R. Sare, 1717, 3 vols. bound in 1), Book 2, chaps. 1–3; idem, *On the Duty of Man and Citizen According to Natural Law* (first published 1673), ed. James Tully, trans. Michael Silverthorne (Cambridge: Cambridge University Press, 1991), Book 2, chap. 1; Montesquieu, *The Spirit of the Laws* (first published 1748), trans. and ed. Anne M. Cohler, Basia Carolyn Miller, and Harold Samuel Stone (Cambridge: Cambridge University Press, 1989).

51. Ferguson, *Essay on the History of Civil Society*, 6. See David Kettler, *The Social and Political Thought of Adam Ferguson* (Columbus: Ohio State University Press, 1965), 187–196. The most influential remark about Ferguson's significance was made by Karl Marx, who claimed that Ferguson anticipated Smith's principle of the division of labor: Marx, *The Poverty of Philosophy* (written 1846–47; London: Martin Lawrence, n.d.), 110. He repeated the remark in *Capital: A Critique of Political Economy*, vol. 1, trans. Eden and Cedar Paul from 4th German ed. of 1890 (London: George Allen and Unwin, 1928), 103, 373, 383.

52. See Peter Burke, *Vico* (Oxford: Oxford University Press, 1985), 54: "Vico . . . asserted that human nature had changed in the course of time in quite fundamental ways, so that 'three kinds of nature' correspond to the three ages into which his historical cycles are divided." See Giambattista Vico, *The New Science of Giambattista Vico*, translation of 3d Italian ed. of 1744 by Thomas Goddard Bergin and Max Harold Fisch (Ithaca, N.Y.: Cornell University Press, 1984); Leon Pompa, *Vico: A Study of the "New Science,"* 2d ed. (Cambridge: Cambridge University Press, 1990), chaps. 3 and 4; Isaiah Berlin, *Vico and Herder: Two Studies in the History of Ideas* (London: Hogarth Press, 1976).

53. Different views are held about the timing and distinctiveness of such a science of woman. Compare Ornella Moscucci, *The Science of Woman: Gynaecology and Gender in England, 1800–1929* (Cambridge: Cambridge University Press, 1990), 2–5, and Sylvana Tomaselli, "Reflections on the History of the Science of Woman," *History of Science* 29 (1991): 185–205.

FIVE

The Gaze of Natural History

Phillip Sloan

In the magisterial 1749 discourse on method commencing the *Histoire naturelle, générale et particulière,* the French naturalist Comte de Buffon wrote:

> The first truth which issues from this sober examination of nature is a truth which is perhaps humbling to man. This truth is that he ought to range himself in the class [*classe*] of the animals, which he resembles in everything material. Even their instincts will perhaps appear to man even more certain than his own reason, and their industry more admirable than his arts. Then, examining successively and by order the various objects which compose the universe, and placing himself at the head of all created beings, he will see with astonishment that it is possible to descend by almost imperceptible degrees from the most perfect creature to the most formless matter, from the most perfectly organized animal to the most inert [*brut*] matter. He will recognize that these imperceptible gradations are the great work of Nature, and will find these gradations not only in the size and shape of things, but in the motion, generation, and successions of every species.[1]

In several respects, the exploration of the full significance of this quotation defines the general problem to be considered in this chapter. Making this claim at an early date in the history of eighteenth-century human science, Buffon's comment was intended to imply something novel, a new insight of the middle of the century. But what was the character of this novelty? Surely there was a venerable tradition before the eighteenth century, almost coextensive with the spread of Aristotelianism, which had considered man as the "rational animal." The notion of human beings as forming part of a continuous *scala natura* was also of ancient vintage. Nor was the notion of a human science, an "anthropology," itself a novel idea. A long list of works of a scientific character can be cited which employed some variant on the term *anthropology* or *anthropography* in their titles.[2] Other chapters in this volume display the rich and varied sources of Enlightenment "human science." Authors can be cited who studied the relations of human beings to animals and discussed human anatomy and physiology. Speculations had been made on the origins of races; David Hume and several others had presumed to draw attention to the need for a science of "human nature"; classifications of the human species, ranging human beings in the animal kingdom, had been published previously by Linnaeus.

To understand the full importance of the revolution in the human sciences encompassed in the comment by Buffon, I will focus on the concept of a "natural history" of the human species. To borrow an insight from Michel Foucault, I am concerned with determining the character of what might be termed the "natural historical" gaze, a *regard* that can be distinguished from medical, moral, political, and medicoanatomical inquiry into human beings. It is this *regard* that, I would suggest, is one of the most fundamental developments in the human science of the Enlightenment. Going beyond the naturalism that the eighteenth century inherited from Paduan Aristotelianism, revived Epicureanism, and Renaissance nature philosophy, intellectual movements that had indeed "secularized" human beings to a good degree by 1700, the transformation I wish to focus upon implied a new relation of the human species as a whole to time and space, to geography and history. It is this novel development that separates the *science de l'homme* of the seventeenth century from the physical-geographical anthropology of the nineteenth. The work of J. F. Blumenbach, J.-J. Virey, Paul Broca, William Lawrence, and Charles Darwin is difficult to conceive without these developments of the previous century.

To develop these claims, I shall initially explore the origins of the idea of a "natural history" of man in the late seventeenth and early eighteenth century, and display the extension of this in the systematic work of the Swedish natural historian Carolus Linnaeus (1707–1778). As the product of the most cohesive and programmatic enterprise in eighteenth-century natural history, the Linnaean natural history of human beings constituted one prominent source of subsequent reflections on the human sciences. I shall then analyze the character of Linnaeus's contemporary Buffon's self-conscious effort to construct an alternative "natural history" to that represented by the well-entrenched Linnaean program.

Concentration on the views of Buffon and Linnaeus is not to claim that these were the exclusive or even the most penetrating reflections on human science to emerge from the eighteenth century. The importance of these two programs lies more in the fact that unlike the reflections on the human sciences of many *philosophes,* Buffon and Linnaeus were able to create dynamic research programs with substantial institutional and material support, one centered at the University of Uppsala, and the other at the *Jardin du Roi* in Paris. Their competing conceptions of human science were part of institutionalized science rather than isolated philosophical reflection, and in this respect their insights could be given concrete implementation by understudies and successors.

In this historical conjunction of Buffonian and Linnaean anthropology, eighteenth-century reflection on the natural history of human beings was presented with two conflicting models of human science. Successors to the personal and philosophical conflicts between Buffon and Linnaeus could neither ignore the disputes between these two scientific titans nor easily resolve them. By the close of the century many sought to combine the insights of the two men, who "continually inspired the desire to turn from one to the other."[3] The synthesis of these two approaches provided much of the structure of scientific anthropology by the end of the century.

The philosophical and methodological disputes between Buffon and Linnaeus were taking place at a time when the eighteenth century was confronted with a welter of new anthropological data from the eighteenth century's "new world"—the South Pacific—as it was revealed in a series of remarkable exploratory voyages after midcentury by George Anson, John Byron, Samuel Wallis, Philip Carteret, and Louis Antoine de Bougainville and by the three epoch-making voyages of James Cook.[4] These late-century explorations opened a veritable "laboratory of human nature," which Buffonian and Linnaean natural history explored. The result was the establishment of a human science that institutionally, as well as conceptually, focused upon a "zoological history" of the human species, now abandoned to the vicissitudes of time and space. This naturalized empirical outlook, as it developed the fragmenting implications of ethnography, historical geology, animal biogeography, and cultural history, was to undermine the early Enlightenment ideal of a human science based on the uniformity of "human nature."

ANTHROPOLOGY AND ENLIGHTENMENT
NATURAL HISTORY

Etymological inquiries into the use of the term *anthropology* in scientific contexts have established with decisiveness that its original employment in the early modern period was within the context of medical, and specifically anatomical, discussion.[5] The focus of this science was upon those definable and generalizable features of the human *corpus*, delimited by an inquiry into form and function. This anatomical *regard* was often, even typically, placed in opposition to the tendency to "animalize" man which one can trace in the Aristotelian and Epicurean traditions. Since the beginning of the ritualized opening of the dead human body in the public dissections of the Italian medical schools in the thirteenth century, human beings had formed the subject of an objectified scientific inquiry. But it was an inquiry that by the seventeenth century was to be specifically focused on human anatomy. It did not imply an effort to draw human beings into a more generalized cosmology or natural history. Andreas Vesalius (1514–1564), the Flemish anatomist turned Paduan master dissector, had made the distinction of the anatomy of human beings from that of other animals central in his polemic against Galen's anatomical descriptions in the *De fabrica humani corporis* of 1543. The errors of Galen were, claimed Vesalius, directly the result of the attribution to man of structures found in other animals, particularly the North African apes that had been available to Galen.[6]

Medical "anthropology" after Vesalius was forced to deal with the tension between the Vesalian separation of human and animal anatomy, and the comparative approach of the Aristotelian tradition. Some workers, such as the Paduan anatomist Fabricius ab Aquapendente (1537–1619) and the Neapolitan surgeon and occupant of the Professorship of Anatomy and Medicine at the University of Naples, Marco Aurelio Severino (1580–1656), continued to draw together the anatomies of human beings and animals.[7] But for the true heirs of Vesalius, medical anatomy was a science that emphasized the distinction, rather than the similarity, of humans and animals.

This claim can be narrowed by a more specific look at select aspects of the impact of Cartesianism on the human sciences in the late seventeenth century. Cartesian philosophy, expounded not only by Descartes, but also by his many medical disciples, provided philosophical justification for the "objectification" of man already present in the anatomical tradition. By the radical distinction of two substances, *res extensa* and *res cogitans,* Descartes liberated the material human body, even in life, from its integration with the substantial form-as-soul of the Aristotelian tradition. The *corpus humani* could be studied as a mechanical machine, down to the workings of its least parts. The hypothesis of the machine-man which opened Descartes's posthumous *Traité de l'homme,* first published in Florentine Schuyl's Latin edition of 1662, described a statue "made like us" to resemble all of our actions, but with no other principle of life than the "fires within inanimate bodies."[8]

Descartes's "mechanical-physiological" approach to human science represents, I would suggest, a culmination of the objectified medical gaze that originated with the work of the Italian anatomists.[9] Whether his mechanization of life be taken as a heuristic "hypothesis," as assumed by some of his medical disciples, or as a literally true account, a claim defended by others, the Cartesian man-machine was disconnected from nature except to the extent that the human body formed part of the domain of the *res extensa,* and was subject to its same natural laws.

But I emphasize the *disconnectedness* of human beings from other forms of life as a consequence of the Cartesian analysis. By making the body of man part of the mechanical system of *res extensa,* Cartesianism surely made human beings part of nature. But "nature" in general meant for Descartes nothing more than "God himself, or else the order and disposition that God has established in created things."[10] Such a notion neither connected human beings integrally to one another nor connected them to other forms of life.[11] Furthermore, there was no evident connection of human existence with any temporal *process* in the domain of extended substance. Although Descartes speculated privately on the generation of man by natural laws, his published works simply presented human beings as true analogues of fully formed earthen machines, "that God has deliberately formed to be most similar to ourselves."[12]

I have suggested that the anatomical perspective of the main tradition of post-Vesalian anatomists deemphasized comparative anatomy. The Cartesian concept of the animal machine did not necessarily support this anticomparativist view. But when Cartesianism was then combined by Nicolas Malebranche and others with an occasionalist metaphysics in the late seventeenth century, congenial to the neo-Augustinian theology of both the Reformed and Catholic traditions of France and the Lowlands, the consequence was to atomize biological relationship in the name of mechanical philosophy through a novel account of the way in which organic beings are generated on mechanical principles.

"Really Little Men"

The expression of this I wish briefly to explore is the formulation of extreme preformationist (preexistence) theories of embryological development in the late seventeenth century. This development was to bear directly on the concept of a science of the human species. Achieving wide currency in the decades after the publication of the French edition of Descartes's *Traité de l'homme* in 1664, which had as an appendix Descartes's *De la formation du foetus,* preexistence theories were typically embraced by those who otherwise were enthusiasts for the "mechanical philosophy."[13]

The preexistence theory of generation formed a theory or collection of theoretical accounts which can be traced through the scientific and major medical texts of the early eighteenth century. Reinforced by observations of the greatest microscopists of the period, this theory formed an important aspect of the extension of mechanical philosophy to the organic domain. At the same time, it effectively denied any *integration* of organic, and more specifically, human life with the spatiotemporal processes that were operative in the physical world generally. Organisms were created directly by God *ab origine mundi,* and not by natural forces or immanent vital agencies.[14] They could, for this reason, have only accidental and superficial relationships to such variables as climate and geography. Some of my point can be seen in the words of the prominent eighteenth-century British physician Richard Mead (1673–1754):

> Geometricians have been long intent on contriving a machine that may be endued with perpetual motion; but . . . it is God alone who can complete such a machine; and was pleased that our body should be a fabric of that sort, but disposing all its powers in such a manner, that they should form a kind of circle, in which at the same time that they perform their respective functions, they should constantly and mutually repair each other.
>
> Hence it manifestly appears, that the animal machine is made, not by parts, but all together; seeing it is impossible, that a circle of motions, some of which depend on others, be compleated, without all their instruments being in their proper places. . . . Wherefore the animalcula, which by the help of microscopes we discover swiming [*sic*] in the *semen masculinum,* are really little men; which being received into the womb, are there cherished as in a nest, and grow in due time to a proper size for exclusion. Therefore Hippocrates said very justly: *In the body there is no beginning, but all the parts are equally the beginning and end.*[15]

It is not difficult to envision the importance of such theories of generation for numerous issues in the human sciences. As an initial observation, they worked directly against any assumptions of environmentalism, even to the degree the eighteenth century could find such views expressed in classical authors. Color differences between humans, for example, themselves became a problem to be explained by God's creative action rather than by means of traditional accounts of climatic alteration. Particularly when reinforced by anatomical evidence that seemed to show a deeper anatomical basis to skin color than purely environmental conditions would suggest, this provided a metaphysical basis for the distinction of races.[16]

In summary, the assumptions underlying the medical-anatomical tradition of "anthropology" in the early eighteenth century did not encourage historical and geographical analyses of human beings. Reinforced by pre-existence embryology and Cartesian dualism, it provided grounds for emphasizing the distinctness, rather than the connection, of human beings to natural process. It is in contrast to this collection of assumptions that we can distinguish the "natural history of man." The gradual replacement of medical by "natural historical" anthropology was terminologically accomplished by the late eighteenth century.[17] The important conceptual changes date from the middle decades.

ANIMAL AMONG ANIMALS

The formation of a "natural history" of the human species in the eighteenth century can be followed in three principal stages. First, there was the development of classificatory systems in which human beings for the first time were arranged, as a taxonomic group, with the rest of organic nature. Such systems supplied a rational classificatory framework into which existing varieties of human beings could be systematically ordered and organized in a form similar to that employed for other organisms.

Second, one can follow a reinterpretation of the *meaning* of these classifications, in which they ceased to be logical arrangements of forms and were assumed to display instead temporal and geographical relationships of human beings.

Third, this "natural history" of the human species was drawn into contact with the greatly expanding fund of information on the range and diversity of human beings made available in the latter half of the eighteenth century by the great expansion of exploratory voyages to the more remote regions of the world. By the end of the century geographical ethnography would become a primary problem facing the human sciences.

Within the System of Nature

The early modern classifiers, the Renaissance Encyclopedists, had traditionally excluded human beings from their systematic arrangements of animals.[18] For understanding the new dimensions of eighteenth-century inquiry, the classifications of the Cambridge divine and Royal Society virtuoso John Ray (1627–1705) are immediately relevant. In his landmark *Synopsis methodica animalium quadrupedam et serpentini generis* of 1693, Ray had divided the animals in the following schema:[19]

Animals
    Blooded
        Respire by Lungs,
            Heart with Two Ventricles
                Vivipara
                    Aquatic (Cetacea)
                    Terrestrial (Quadrupeda)
                Ovipara (Aves)
            Heart with One Ventricle (Serpents and Viviparous
            Quadrupeds, e.g., lizards)

    Bloodless
        Major
            Mollia (Polyps, Squid)

Crustacea (Crabs, Lobsters)
Testacea
    Univalves
    Bivalves
    Turbinates
Minor (Insecta)

Ray's division of the viviparous quadrupeds of the first section was further broken down as follows:

Hoofed (*Ungulata*)
    Single Hoofed (Solipeda) (*Equus, Zebra*)
    Four-Hoofed (Quadrusulca) (*Rhino, Hippo*)
Nailed (*Unguiculata*)
    Two Digits (*Bifido*) (*Camel*)
    Multiple Digits (*Multifido*)
        —Undivided digits (*Elephas*)
        —Separated digits
            —Flat Nailed (Anthropomorpha) (*Simiae*)
            —Narrow Nailed
                —Incisors only on front maxilla
                —Multiple teeth
                    —Large size
                        Short muzzle, round skull (*Felis*—cats)
                        Long muzzle (*Canis*, etc.)
                  —Small size, long body, short legs (*Mustelus*)
            —Two incisors, plant eating (*Leporium*—rabbits,
            hares)

Although claiming comprehensiveness in this general outline of groups, Ray excluded human beings from his arrangement, with no attempt to draw them into his newly named group, the Anthropomorpha—that is, the simians comprising the monkeys and baboons—that was to replace the older *Simia* used in previous arrangements.

Following Ray's proposals by only a few years, his fellow Englishman, the Oxford physician Edward Tyson (1650/51–1708), expanded the classificatory problem with his landmark *Orang-outang, sive Homo sylvestris: Or the Anatomy of a Pygmie Compared With That of a Monkey, an Ape, and a Man* of 1699.[20] In this work Tyson detailed the comparative anatomy of a novel subject—a newly acquired specimen of the "man of the woods" of Africa—previously described by the Dutch anatomist Nicholas Tulp in 1641 under the name of *Satyrus indicus*.[21]

Tyson's work was self-consciously a comparative, rather than a species-restricted anatomy. Almost as a critique of the Vesalian tradition we have

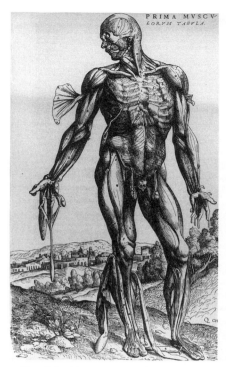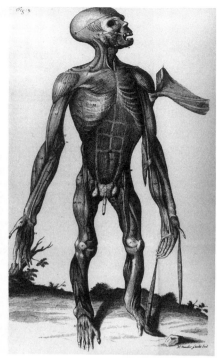

Fig. 5.1. Two comparative plates: (left) Vesalius's *De humani corporis fabrica libri septem* (1543; reprint, Brussels, 1963); (right) Edward Tyson's *Ourang-outang, sive Homo sylvestris* (1699; reprint, London, 1966). Courtesy of the University of Notre Dame Library

spoken of previously, the dissections of the chimpanzee are presented in virtually the same stark visual displays of anatomical exposure utilized in depicting the "muscle men" of Vesalius's *De fabrica* (fig. 5.1). Rather than maintaining the distinction of animal and human, Tyson fit his "pygmy" into the traditional *scala natura*, neatly filling the gap between man and animals. This form provided for Tyson the ideal "Nexus of the Animal and Rational."[22] But the implications of this comparative anatomy for the classification of man were not immediately evident. This remained the task of Linnaeus to work out in detail.

Ranged within the Three Kingdoms

In 1735 at Leyden the young Swedish medical student Carolus Linnaeus (1707–1778) published the eleven broadsheet pages that constituted the first edition of the *Systema naturae sive regna tria naturae*. This work initiated the Linnaean era in eighteenth-century science, a research tradition that would in many respects transform the practice of natural history by the end of the century. Linnaean natural history would create a cohesive social enterprise, with a specific network of institutions and museums engaged in its perpetuation, disseminated by a cadre of evangelical pupils who devoted their lives—at times literally—to its prosecution in all parts of the globe.[23]

The novelty of Linnaeus's classifications, particularly when compared to the influential systematic arrangements of predecessors like Ray and the botanist Joseph Pitton de Tournefort (1656–1708), lay particularly in the comprehensive scope of the Linnaean system, uniting in one plan the plants, animals, and minerals. From the standpoint of the human sciences, the *Systema* was a revolutionary and provocative work. For the first time human beings were explicitly included within a formal classification of animals and plants. In the preliminary schema presented by the first 1735 edition, Linnaeus included Ray's Anthropomorpha as an Order under the Class Quadrupedia, and expanded it to include not only the apes and monkeys but also the genus *Homo*, with a single species, *sapiens,* along with the sloths. Anteaters would soon join this noble company in 1740.[24] Linnaeus further differentiated this *Homo sapiens* into four varieties—europaeus albus, americanus rubescens, asiaticus fuscus, and africanus niger, with variety implying the local character and definability that his least groups in other forms of life suggested[25] (table 5.1).

Expanding Horizons

Following his appointment in 1741 to the chair of practical and theoretical medicine at the University of Uppsala, Linnaeus was in position to expand and develop his program in natural history into a major scientific enterprise over the next thirty-seven years. With specific reference to the human sciences, Linnaeus's classifications were also in a historical position to reflect, if only to a limited degree, the remarkable expansion of information through which the earth's "geographical space"—the construction of a physical map of the globe through the European explorations of the New World and eventually the far Pacific—was transformed in the eighteenth century into a "human space," defined as much by a map of peoples and tribes as it was by physical coordinates.[26] New anthropological, botanical, and zoological data from explorers and travelers reached new proportions in the eighteenth century. Collected by expeditions dispatched with at least partially scientific, as well as commercial or military, intent, the scientific component of voyages to remote areas reached new levels.[27] After 1735 it was common to include scientists and naturalists aboard long voyages with purely scientific tasks. Longitudinal location, the persistent

TABLE 5.1   Linnaeus's Classification of Anthropomorpha, 1735

Genus	Specifying distinction	Varietal distinctions
Homo	Reason (sapiens)	H. sapiens europaeus albus H. s. americanus rubescens H. s. asiaticus fuscus H. s. africanus niger
Simia	5 Anterior Digits and Posterior Digits	tailless (S. papio, S. satyrus) tailed (S. cercopithecus, S. cynocephalus)
Bradypus	2–3 Anterior Digits 3 Posterior Digits	Ai (2-toed Sloths) Tardigradus (3-toed Sloths)

problem facing navigation of the south seas and the Pacific, was generally solved in the mid–eighteenth century with the invention of a sufficiently accurate marine chronometer by John Harrison in 1741, further perfected in the 1760s. Old and inaccurate methods of dead reckoning or more cumbersome determination of location by astronomical observations made on land could be replaced with accurate determinations made aboard moving ships.[28]

As the principal comprehensive taxonomic program in position to make at least partial assimilation of the new anthropological data acquired by these explorations, Linnaean classification was forced into an expanding series of revisions. New species of monkeys and baboons were discovered, specimens of which were often sent to Uppsala for Linnaeus's examination.[29] There was also new information on the American and South American Indians, and new and extended encounters with Oriental peoples, East Indians, and Africans in many distinguishable tribes and associations. The continuing run of tantalizing, if intellectually disturbing, reports of what seemed to be outlandish humanoid creatures—Patagonian giants, Pygmies, Hottentots, intermixed with tales of feral men and women found among wild animals in Europe and wild "men of the woods" from Sumatra—continued into the late century.[30] Particularly after the midcentury, there were new encounters with the Tierra del Fuegans and South Pacific islanders to contend with. Pierre de Maupertuis, urging his French contemporaries to turn their scientific attention to the south seas and Pacific in the 1750s, relates how earlier travelers in these regions had spoken of finding "wild men, hairy men, bearing tails . . . midway between apes and us," and comments that he would rather have "an hour of conversation with them than with the greatest mind of Europe."[31] The human space opened up for the eighteenth century was to be a very complex one, raising the prospects of a plurality of human species in these remote areas.

Tracing the formal development of the Linnaean classification of human beings in the thirteen editions of the *Systema* that appeared between 1735 and 1788–93 displays the difficulties presented by this new anthropological world.[32] Although little change occurs in the first five editions, in the greatly expanded sixth edition of 1748, the genus *Homo* remained intact, but the genus *Simia* was expanded to include sixteen different species, including the genus *Satyr*—Tyson's "Pygmy" (our chimpanzee). In the next major revision, the expanded tenth edition of 1758, the Order Anthropomorpha was for the first time replaced by a new Order, Primates, and its internal contents were rearranged. In addition to the four previously recognized varieties of the species *Homo sapiens,* feral "wild man"—*Homo sapiens ferus*—was given full varietal status on the basis of the reports of such famous discoveries as that of Marie-Angelique LeBlanc, found in 1731 near Châlons-sur-Marne, and the Wild Boy of Hanover, discovered in 1724. Most remarkable is the insertion of a new species of genus *Homo,* the "nocturnal" man (*Homo troglodytes*), reported to live underground in caves on the island of Ambiona in the East Indies, under which Linnaeus synonymized Jakob de Bondt's *Homo sylvestris* from Borneo.[33] With this recognition of at least two, and possibly several, species within the genus *Homo,* Linnaean natural history was embarked upon a slide into polygenism. In a subsequent revision of Linnaeus's classification, affecting only the thirteenth (1788) edition of the *Systema,* Linnaeus's student Christian Hoppius removed *H. troglodytes* and the other anthropoids from *Homo* to the subgenus *Simia,* locating the *Homo sylvestris* of George Edwards (a chimpanzee) and the *Simia eucadata subtus nuda abdomine* (a chimpanzee) within the simian subgroup *Pygmaeus.* The *H. troglodytes* of the tenth edition of the *Systema* was moved to form the simian subgenus *Troglodytes,* and Jakob de Bondt's ape, the *Homo caudautus vulgo dictus* was placed in the subgenus *Lucifer.*[34] Some of these remarkable changes in the Linnaean classifications are summarized selectively in table 5.2. The plate from Hoppius's dissertation of 1760 (fig. 5.2) illustrates several of these problematic forms in strikingly human poses.

But what did these nomenclatural revisions imply metaphysically? The answer was not immediately evident. Linnaeus's decision to locate man among the animals was framed within the metaphysical hierarchy of a graded series, the traditional "great chain of nature," which could be pursued from man downward to the plants.[35] Linnaeus did not see that his arrangements in any way detracted from human dignity, although he was attacked on these grounds by others. He replied to these charges publicly in the *Fauna Suecia* of 1746: "But there is something in us, which cannot be seen, whence our knowledge of ourselves depends—that is, *reason,* the most noble thing of all, in which man excels to a most surprising extent all other animals."[36]

But if reason was to be the only defining mark separating man from

TABLE 5.2   Linnaeus's Classification of Anthropomorpha (Primates) 1744–1788

Genus	4th Ed. 1744	6th and 9th Eds. 1748, 1756	10th Ed. 1758	12th Ed. 1766	13th Ed. 1788
Homo	sapiens europaeus albus	s. europaeus albus	s. ferus (6 synonyms)	Homo ferus (9 synonyms)	H. ferus (9 synonyms)
	s. americanus rubescus	s. americanus rufescens [*sic*]	s. americanus	s. americanus	s. americanus
	s. asiaticus fuscus	s. asiaticus fuscus	s. europaeus	s. europaeus	s. europaeus
	s. africanus niger	s. africanus niger	s. asiaticus	s. asiaticus	s. asiaticus
			s. afer	s. afer	s. afer
			s. monstrosus	s. monstrosus	s. monstrosus
			Alpini [=Patagonian]	Alpini	Alpini
			Monorchides [=Hottentot]	Monorchides	Monorchides
			Macrocephali	Macrocephali	Macrocephali
			Homo troglodytes	H. troglodytes	Plagiocephali
			(=H. nocturnus, &	(=H. nocturnus,	
			H. sylvestris [Bontius 1658]	H. sylvestris [Bontius], &	
			[=orang])	H. lucifer of Hoppius, 1760)	

Genus	4th Ed. 1744	6th and 9th Eds. 1748, 1756	10th Ed. 1758	12th Ed. 1766	13th Ed. 1788
Simia	S. mammis quaternis (apes) S. satyrus S. cercopithecus S. cynocephalus	S. eucadata subtus glabra (= Satyrus indicus [chimpanzee] of Tulp and H. sylvestris [orang] of Bontius, 1658) S. eucadata (3 additional species) S. semicaudata (1 species) S. caudata (11 species)	S. satyrus (= Satyrus indicus Tulp [chimpanzee]) S. sylvanus S. sphinx S. apedia S. silenus S. faunus S. panicus S. diana S. cephus S. aygula S. hamadryas S. jaccus S. oedipus S. aethiops S. midas S. cynamolgos [sic] S. apella S. morta S. capucina S. sciurea S. syrichta	S. satyrus (= H. sylvestris Edwards [orang]) S. sylvanus S. inuus S. nemestrina S. apedia S. sphinx S. maimon S. hamadryas S. veter S. silenus S. faunus S. belzebul S. seniculus S. panicus S. cynomolgus (plus 18 additional species)	S. satyrus (= H. sylvestris Edwards) S. troglodytes (= H. troglodytes) S. sylvanus S. inuus S. nemestrina S. apedia S. sphinx S. maimon S. mormon S. hamadryas S. porcaria S. veter S. silenus S. cynosurus S. faunus S. belzebul (plus 29 additional species)

Fig. 5.2. From Christian Hoppius's dissertation, *Anthropomorpha* (1760),
in *Amoenitates academicae* (Leyden, 1764). Courtesy of the
University of Notre Dame Library

animal, this was, for Linnaeus, a graduated reason, in which one could follow a clear line of descent within the human species from *Homo sapiens albus* to *sapiens afer.*

The natural historical approach of Linnaeus provided the Enlightenment with one form of scientific discourse about human beings which had
enormous impact in the eighteenth and early nineteenth centuries. Linnaean classifications provided a framework on which one could assimilate
and organize existing and new materials related to the Anthropomorpha
and the genus *Homo.* As the experience with *H. troglodytes* and the pluralization within *H. ferus* and *H. monstrosus* suggested, the operating definition of genus *Homo* was to be primarily morphological, based on differences of constant character. Once such ambiguities in classification were
historicized, as Rousseau would suggest in 1755,[37] Linnaean systematics
contributed to a profound blurring of the human-animal distinction which
could be exploited by his contemporaries for philosophical purposes.

THE BUFFONIAN REVOLUTION

The Linnaean program in natural history was forced to share the Enlightenment stage with a rival version of the natural history of man, one that
ran at a more profound level in its implications. In Buffon's *Histoire naturelle, générale et particulière,* the location of human beings among the animals was combined with a radical historicizing and naturalizing of the hu-

man species that would pursue a zoogeographical analysis of humanity in connection with a gradually developing schema of a naturalized account of cosmological and geological history. Buffon's research program in natural history provided a self-conscious alternative to the well-entrenched enterprise of Linnaeus. Natural history of the later century was thus confronted with the consequences of a prominent rivalry in methodology, forms of analysis, and conceptual frameworks with important implications for the human sciences.

Buffon's treatment of the human species will be analyzed in terms of three issues: (a) his conception of "physical" truth and its relevance for his attack on Linnaean classification; (b) his novel reconceptualization of the concept of species as an entity distributed in time and space; and (c) his application of these principles to the question of the geographical distribution of species, particularly that of the human species.

Two Orders of Truth

Judged against common eighteenth-century patterns of intellectual formation, Buffon's entry into the study of anthropological questions was a highly unusual one. Virtually all other individuals who wrote or otherwise contributed specialized treatises to the field of "the natural history of man" in the eighteenth century had been trained as physicians. By contrast, Buffon entered these issues through early training in the law, which, except for a very brief and abortive stint as a prospective medical student at the University of Angers, was followed by intensive studies in mathematics, Newtonian mechanics, English philosophy, and probability theory. Buffon's exploration of these mathematical issues in the 1731–40 period stands directly in the background of the novel developments he was to initiate when he was appointed in 1739 to serve as the administrative head of the royal botanical garden and natural history collections in Paris.[38] He was in a unique position to make a direct transfer of the conceptual issues he developed in this early mathematical work to concrete problems of biology and natural history.

The circumstances that led Buffon to devote such considerable attention to the sciences of man are not immediately apparent. Upon his appointment to the directorship of the *Jardin du Roi*, Buffon began writing a comprehensive natural history. But judging from what can be reconstructed of the first public discussion of the goals of his future work on natural history in a discourse delivered to a *séance* of the Académie Royale des Sciences in winter 1744–45,[39] it did not appear that human beings were to be a particular focus of interest. Buffon's motivation for dealing with the human sciences seems to have been generated more by epistemological than empirical interests.[40]

To establish himself as a credible authority in a field where he was an unknown outsider, Buffon defined his program by opposition, an antagonism reflected in the polemical posture of the "Premier discours de la manière d'étudier et de traiter l'histoire naturelle" that opened the *Histoire naturelle* of 1749.

Central to Buffon's approach to natural history was a critique of traditional classification, especially as this was practiced by Linnaeus and his disciples. This criticism developed his earlier polemic against mathematical abstractions of the late 1730s. It was now fashioned in the 1749 discourse into a rejection of abstract universals generally.[41] Arrangement of organisms in a logical ordering of genera and species of the Linnaean hierarchy required the placement of real, existent entities under abstract universals on the basis of a flimsy presumption of distinguishable essential differentiating characters. The flavor of this often-misunderstood polemic can be gained from the following quotation:

> This pretension that botanists have for establishing general, perfect and methodical systems is thus weakly grounded. Consequently, their labors have tended to give us only defective methods [*méthodes*], which have been successively destroyed by one another, and have sustained the common fate of all systems [*systèmes*] founded on arbitrary principles. And that which has contributed most to this process of successive overthrow by one another is the freedom which botanists have allowed themselves of choosing arbitrarily a single part of the plant to make the specific character.[42]

Linnaean anthropological classifications are subjected to particularly pointed sarcasm: "It is necessary to be obsessed with making classes in order to place together beings as different as man and the sloths, or the ape [*singe*] and the pangolins."[43]

The difficulty with Linnaean classification was that it remained, for Buffon, purely at the level of "abstract" truth, without connection to the material and concrete order of nature. Physical connection to reality was to be achieved by means of an application to natural history of the conclusion he had earlier arrived at in his studies of the mathematics of probability. Just as the key to attainment of epistemological certitude from probabilistic trials depended upon the repetition of singular events, a similar solution would provide access to the true order of the concrete physical world, including genuine knowledge of the true animal and plant relationships.

The importance of this curious, even paradoxical, transferral of concepts from mathematics to biology is illuminated by close attention to the discussion that closed the "Premier discours" on the distinction of two orders of truth—physical and mathematical. Positing a distinction between these two is unusual, and it would seem to be quite unexpected from one originally enamored with Newtonian mathematics and mathematical physics. Mathematical truth, at least in the sense of the reasoning of geometry, is only "abstract" and concerns only the relation of ideas. Such abstractions have no immediate contact with reality. Reality is reached by what Buffon terms "physical" truth. This truth is a different sort of entity, attained by the mathematics of probability calculus, rather than geometrical deduction.[44] Such truth is not confined to propositions about "relations of ideas." It involves instead the constant repetition of real physical events of the same kind which, as they are repeated sufficient numbers of times, generate access to the true order of nature:

> There are several species of truths, and it is customary to place in the first order mathematical truths, which are, however, only truths of definition. . . . Physical truths, on the contrary, are not arbitrary, and do not depend on us. Instead of being founded on suppositions which we have made, they rest only upon facts. A series [*suite*] of similar facts or, if you wish, a frequent repetition and uninterrupted succession of the same events constitutes the essence of physical truth. That which one terms physical truth is thus only a probability, but a probability so great that it is equivalent to a certitude. . . . One proceeds [*va*] from definitions to definitions in the abstract sciences, but one progresses [*marche*] from observations to observations in the sciences of the real [*Sciences réelles*]. In the first case one attains evidence, in the latter certitude.[45]

From the perspective of any primary philosophical tradition feeding into the eighteenth century, these are unusual distinctions.[46] Nonetheless they are critical for illuminating the way in which the human sciences entered the purview of Buffon's natural history. The overriding concern of Buffon's "physical truth" was to achieve some kind of immanent, connected understanding of phenomena. This is exactly what "classification" in the Linnaean sense did not do. Instead of the attempts of his contemporaries to create rational systems of classification, Buffon preferred the unsystematic approach to the arrangement of organisms one finds in Aristotle's *History of Animals*. There one begins first with the species known best—the human being—and then moves outward from this anthropocentric starting point to consider other forms in relation to the human.[47] The same plan of organization was to govern his grand *Histoire naturelle*. In other words, concern with the human sciences enters Buffon's natural history as the epistemological starting point for a new kind of natural understanding, one that would emphasize relation and material continuity rather than rigid categorization. Self-reflective understanding of the human being is necessary if anything else really is to be known.

The novel implications of this anthropocentric epistemology are dramatically displayed as we follow the consequences Buffon proceeds to draw. Starting inquiry with the human being as an epistemological center rather than as a link in a ladder of being does not lead obviously to the consideration of the apes and monkeys at all. Quite otherwise. The creatures closest to man in terms of this "relational" epistemology are those of most immediate epistemological acquaintance—the familiar domestic animals and plants near to us in our own locality and climate: "[One] will come to judge the objects of natural history by the relations that they have with him. Those which are most necessary and most useful will hold the first rank, for example, he will give preference in the order of the animals to the horse, the dog, the cow, etc., and he will always know best those with which he is most familiar."[48] This is the ordering of objects which comes naturally as experience would write itself upon a *tabula rasa* of an Adamic creature confronted with the world of sensation.[49]

The organizational plan of the subsequent volumes of the *Histoire naturelle* would pursue the consequences of this unusual principle of natural order, commencing with the analysis of the human being "considered as an animal, the customs which are natural to him, according to the different races and climates,"[50] and then moving to the large and useful domestic animals of western Europe. This ordering implied that the animals of Asia, contiguous with Europe, would be treated before moving to the large wild animals of Africa and eventually those of the New World. As a direct consequence of this plan, the apes and other anthropomorphs would only be treated in the final volumes of 1766 and 1767, at the most remote distance from the opening discussion of the human species.

The natural history of man was to form a major portion of the second and third volumes of the *Histoire naturelle,* immediately following preliminary discourses on the nature of the earth and theories of cosmological formation and a lengthy discourse on the general features of reproduction in plants and animals. Buffon's analyses of human beings were supplemented by an extended discussion of human anatomy by Buffon's collaborator, Louis Jean-Marie Daubenton (1716–1800). In the combination of Buffon's and Daubenton's discussions, the eighteenth century was supplied with its longest single discussion to date of the human species as a scientific, zoological object.[51] Commencing with an analysis of human nature and the stages of life—infancy, adolescence (*la puberté*), adulthood (*l'age viril*), old age, and death—Buffon continued with a discourse on the senses. But the "histoire de l'individu" was still not that of the species as an object of separate inquiry in itself. This was to be the task of Buffon's long "Variétés dans l'espèce humain," which occupied the bulk of volume three of the *Histoire naturelle.*

Buffon's self-conscious focus on "l'espèce humain," divorced from discussions of the apes and comparative anatomy, the first being in a universe created and sustained by natural forces, is indeed novel when judged against the historical context of 1749. Some readers viewed such a naturalistic analysis as evidence of Buffon's hidden atheism, and equated him with the worst materialists of the age.[52] Others were more favorably disposed to Buffon's anthropology precisely because he had not allied himself with Linnaean systematics, maintaining a crucial metaphysical distinction between humans and animals that he did not blur by introduction of data from simian sources.[53] But neither party seemed to understand his underlying point nor its consequences. To follow this requires attention to his redefinition of the meaning of a "species" in natural history.

A Species in Time and Space

The unusual character of Buffon's natural history of the human being is most clearly revealed when it is viewed in terms of his alteration of the notion of a species. This directly flows from his concept of physical truth and his concern to replace abstractions by ontologically grounded concepts. Traditionally, the term *species* had several standard uses in the literature, none of which captured Buffon's meaning in using the term. Traditional employments included that of a sense datum; a term denoting external aspect; a universal applied to more than one individual; or one of the five predicables of traditional logic.[54] The latter was the meaning Linnaeus gave to the term, and the uses by all of Buffon's contemporaries are captured by one of these senses. But in Buffon's utilization of this concept, he oddly attributes to it adjectives like *concrete* and *real*, placing it directly in opposition to the other classificatory rankings of kingdom, class, order, and genus.[55]

Buffon's unusual meaning is clarified in a passage in his discourse on the nature of animals and plants in the second volume of the *Histoire naturelle*, also published in 1749:

> However marvellous [the individual] appears to us, it is not in the individual that we find the greatest marvel. It is in the succession, in the renewal and in the duration of species that Nature appears almost inconceivable. This faculty of producing its likeness, which resides in animals and plants, this kind of enduring unity which appears eternal, this procreative power which is perpetually exercised without ever being destroyed, is a mystery for us. . . .
>
> [. . .]
>
> This power of producing its likeness, this chain of successive existences of individuals . . . , constitutes the real existence of the species.[56]

I draw attention to the close tie of the language of this passage with the definition of "physical truth" in the "Premier discours." Such truth was to be grounded upon "a sequence of similar facts or, if you prefer, a frequent repetition and uninterrupted succession of the same occurrences." For Buffon, a "species" in organic beings is neither a class, nor a universal concept, nor a predicable in the traditional hierarchy of classes of the Neoplatonist Porphyry. It is a material chain of reproduction in which its reality lies in the historical succession of recurrent forms reproducing one another by material connection.

This point was made with greater clarity in 1753 when, after delay created by the condemnation of certain claims of the initial volumes of the *Histoire naturelle* by the Sorbonne theologians in 1751, Buffon published the first volume of the *Histoire naturelle des quadrupèdes*. In his longest discussion of the concept of organic species in the article on the ass, he explicated the new connotation he was instituting. Speaking initially of the more familiar notion, he writes:

> An individual is a creature by itself, isolated and detached, which has nothing in common with other beings, except in that which it resembles or differs from them. All the similar individuals which exist on the surface of the globe are regarded as composing the species of these individuals.[57]

But this definition, he quickly adds, is only an "abstract" meaning, the notion used by classifiers like Linnaeus, which is to be opposed to the new "physical" meaning of a species as the physical succession of self-reproducing individuals:

> However, it is neither the number nor the collection of similar individuals which forms the species. It is the constant succession and uninterrupted renewal of these individuals which comprises it. For a being which would last forever would not be a species, no more than would a thousand similar beings which would last forever. The species is thus an abstract and general term, for which the thing exists only in considering Nature in the succession of time, and in the constant destruction and renewal of creatures.[58]

This new definition of a biological species, subsequently reprinted as the body of the article "Espèce: Histoire naturelle" of Diderot's *Encyclopédie*,[59] directly underlies Buffon's unusual analysis of the human species.

At least three implications follow from this successional definition of a biological species. First, it implied that the reality of the species was to be found only in *material connections* between its members. Two beings are members of the same species not because they "look alike" or even because they share essential defining properties in the traditional Aristotelian (or Linnaean) conception. They are specifically identical only if they have a material relation to one another.

Second, the primary defining relationship satisfying such requirements is biological reproduction. Because inanimate beings cannot reproduce, they cannot form a species in Buffon's sense. To decide if two beings belong to the same species, one can apply the reproductive test. This overrides any other form of similarity or difference.

In making this claim, we see the importance of Buffon's well-known break with the reigning preformationist embryology. In 1750 this was still the predominating theory of generation. Whereas preformationism had rendered the relations of organisms purely occasional, Buffon's theory, relying on the immanent continuity of the *moules intérieures* and the *molécules organiques*, required a literal material continuity of forms in relations of true generation of like by like in historical time. By reinterpreting the issue of generation in epigenetic terms, Buffon provided a means by which the contingencies of geography and climate, acting upon the *molécules*, could affect the actual reproductive lineage of the species.[60] The action of external causes in modifying the species, conceptually blocked for the eighteenth century by the preformation theory of generation, could now be reinstituted in a more subtle form.

Third, Buffon's notion of species suggested a necessary dimension of *temporality* in a sense not associated with any of the other connotations of the term *species* current at the time. A single individual cannot constitute a species in this physical sense. Only a *succession* of individuals in time generates a physical species.[61]

In treating the human species in light of this redefinition of a natural species, Buffon on the one hand could avoid polygenism—the thesis that there is more than a single human species.[62] As we have seen previously, pluralization of species within the genus *Homo* was a persistent implication of the Linnaean classifications, particularly if one coupled such arrangements, as many in the period were doing, with some version of preformationist embryology. But on Buffonian principles, the fact that all humans can interbreed with fertility ensures their specific identity, whatever might be their definable morphological differences. Differences between peoples must necessarily be accounted for by some kind of diversifying process, never by independent origins.

Oegenerating Humanity

Buffon's overriding concern to analyze the human species in terms of a "real and physical" understanding of organisms in their concrete, multidimensional relationships in time and space directed the emphasis of his program in natural history toward such factors as geography, climate, food, reproduction, and habits of life. Furthermore, because he had sought to analyze the reproductive process itself in terms of the continuity of material *molécules*, the analysis achieves a more fundamental level than the environmentalism one encounters in the work of his contemporary Montesquieu, for example, whose *De l'esprit des lois* had appeared only shortly before the *Histoire naturelle*. One need only compare the discussion of a given animal in Buffon's works with that in a Linnaean treatise of the same approximate date to see this marked difference. Instead of emphasis on a set of specific morphological differences for the definition of a natural species, Buffon sought to characterize organisms by a complex interweaving of behavioral, biological, geographical, and relational properties that set one species apart from another.

Understanding this difference clarifies the initially confusing fluidity in Buffon's use of terms otherwise reasonably fixed in the literature of the natural historians of the period—species, genus, family, variety, race.[63] These familiar categories of hierarchical classification, initially rejected by Buffon as "abstractions," were subsequently introduced in Buffon's natural history with altered, "physical" meanings. *Genres* and *familles* are oddly subordinated to *espèces*.[64] Some species vary widely over geographical space, forming physical genera and families of related forms, while others remain remarkably resistant to such variation, forming nondegenerating *espèces nobles* or *espèces isolées*, able to maintain their form and specific identity in opposition to the surrounding degenerating causes.[65] Buffonian physical species, whether forming radiating genera, or remaining relatively fixed and detached, are more adequately represented by geographical maps, or even three-dimensional solids, than by a hierarchy of subordinating classes.[66] The relationships within and between species are intimately connected to such issues as postulated migrations and spreading from primordial originating locales.

In turning to the human species in the course of articles written between 1749 and 1777,[67] Buffon's horizon was necessarily expanded as he, like the Linnaeans, was forced to deal with geographical variation and with the mushrooming body of anthropological data obtained from new explorations.[68]

The new practice of including designated scientific personnel on these voyages gave heightened authority to reports from voyagers. The botanist Philibert Commerson (1727–1773) had accompanied Bougainville's circumglobal transit.[69] The great British natural historian Joseph Banks (1743–1820) traveled on the first of Cook's voyages, and the famous father-son team of Johann Reinhold Forster (1729–1798) and his son Georg (1754–1794) accompanied the second. These expanding explorations also created significant new problems for the human sciences.

"From What Continent, from What People Have These Islanders Come?"

Philibert Commerson's query, reflecting his puzzlement on encountering the aboriginal population of Tahiti,[70] underlined the problem for late Enlightenment contemplation created by the existence of human beings on the remote islands of the South Seas, Australia, New Zealand, and Tasmania.[71] Human beings could be postulated to have peopled the New

World by land connections, at least connections of a recently distant past. Populating Tahiti, Easter Island, the Solomons, the Carolines, and Hawaii was less easily solved in this way. Polygenic theories of the human species, assuming a plurality of human stocks, provided an attractive naturalistic solution to this question, which was advanced with increasing frequency in the last decades of the eighteenth century.[72] In connection with this issue, George Stocking has spoken of the growing importance of the concept of race in the anthropology of the end of the century.[73] But the focus on race has a different importance for the two traditions we are considering. For the Linnaean tradition, constant morphological difference readily implied distinctions of species. Human beings could be viewed as endemic in the same way as other organisms, specific to biogeographical regions.[74] By contrast, for those accepting Buffon's physical conception of the human species, the problem had to be solved by expanding the range of morphological diversity possible within a single true physical species. Buffon remained committed to the thesis that there can be no more than a single species of human beings. But this must be a species that can be diversified by geography and climate and extend itself by unusual and unknown means to far distant parts of the globe.

Since 1755, Buffon had been aware of Rousseau's suggestion that the relation of hominoids was, at least conjecturally, transformist. Originally primitive "men of the woods"—*Homo sylvestris*—had become modern Europeans through a process of historical change in which reason, language, and society developed by gradual stages.[75] Buffon explicitly rejected Rousseau's suggestion in his 1758 article on the carnivorous animals.[76] But even before the appearance of Rousseau's famous conjectures, Buffon had already raised the option in his 1753 discussion of the ass that physical species could possibly create new species by a relation of *dégéneration,* implying a decline, weakening, and degradation of an original ancestral form.

Emphatically rejecting this possibility when he initially considered the relations of the horse and the ass, Buffon had claimed that true physical species formed independent spatio-temporal lineages that could not be placed in degenerative relations to one another.[77] However, by the 1760s, Buffon concluded that within such physical species, quasi-permanent degenerative change from an original stock could take place in response to the vicissitudes of climate, geography, and most importantly food, all factors that were able to affect the *molécules organiques* and the *moules intérieures,* the basis of Buffon's solution to the problem of reproduction.[78] This concept provided the primary framework within which Buffon subsequently dealt with geographical variation. By the fixation of environmentally induced changes within the reproductive process itself, the basis was supplied for his physical interpretation of the concept of a race, a notion that seems to gain its first influential currency in his works.[79]

Buffon's thesis concerning varying degrees of degeneration within the original primitive stock of humankind had expanding consequences as he dealt with the new information available to him after 1750 from expedition and traveler's reports. In 1761 in the important article "Animaux commun aux deux continents," he was forced to consider explicitly the physical relationships between the species of the New World and the Old. The probability of an earlier land bridge between the two continents across the Bering Straits, given further support by the Russian expeditions accompanied by J. G. Gmelin, supplied the means for maintaining such material connections of the fauna.[80] Human beings formed one aspect of this larger problem, and the relations between New and Old World peoples were dealt with in the same terms as other animals. In this first analysis of the problem, Buffon's data seemed to suggest that the mammals of the New World were generally smaller, less robust, and less fertile than their Old World cognates. This he attributed to a degeneration, under the action of climatic influences acting upon the reproductive process, from a primordial originating state in the upper latitudes of the Old World. Paralleling these changes, human beings also displayed a similar degradation:

> There is therefore in the combination of the elements and other physical causes something contrary to the elaboration of living Nature in this new world. . . . Because although the aborigine [*Sauvage*] of the new world would be almost of the same stature as man of our world, this does not suffice to make an exception to the general fact of the depletion of living Nature in all this continent. The Savage is weak and small in the organs of generation; he has neither beard, nor attraction for the female . . . : he is also less sensitive and more fearful . . . he has neither vivacity, nor activity in his soul. . . . he will rest stupidly in repose on his haunches or sleep for the entire day. It is not necessary to seek for the cause of the dissipated life of the aborigines and its extension to society. The most precious flame of the fire of Nature has been refused to them.[81]

This thesis of geographical *dégéneration* provided the framework upon which Buffon developed subsequent analyses of the relationships within and between species. Utilizing the distinction between "degenerating" and "isolated" species, distinguished primarily by their different degrees of geographical variation, Buffon proceeded to work out in more detail the historical relations of forms in his later volumes.[82]

Following the unusual organizational plan of the *Histoire naturelle*, the anthropoid apes were treated for the first time in any detail only in 1766 and 1767 in the final two volumes of the initial series. In the long and complex articles, "Nomenclature des signes" and "Les Orang-outangs, ou le Pongo et le Jocko," which opened the fourteenth volume of the *Histoire naturelle*, Buffon explored the many ramifications following from the obvious anatomical similarities between human beings and the great apes.

Accompanying these articles were the anatomical accounts by Daubenton, who was now in position to make direct anatomical comparison between human anatomy and that of the other anthropoids.

In several respects, the problem that Buffon and Daubenton confronted was much the same as that they had considered in 1753 in the articles on the domestic horse and ass. In these earlier articles they had first considered the implications of the close anatomical similarity of two seemingly related forms in terms of Buffon's physical notion of a species. In the 1753 discussion, the issue had been resolved with apparent finality by the appeal to infertile interbreeding, which ensured the specific distinctness of the horse and ass, presumably to the first origins of the world. But by 1766, Buffon's personal investigations into the relative degrees of fertility between crosses of species he had earlier considered fully distinct, such as the horse and ass and dog and wolf, had rendered reproductive fertility a complex and uncertain sign of specific identity.[83] By all principles he had laid down on the definition of an organic species, Buffon had to accept the fact that his "espèces physiques" often exceeded the bounds of ordinary perceptions of affinity and included forms with varying degrees of reproductive fertility between them. It is within this expanded framework that he was then in position to deal at last with the manlike apes.

The 1766 articles on the "Nomenclature des signes" and on the "Pongo" (orangutan) and "Jocko" (chimpanzee) represent Buffon's most sustained discussion of the relationship between humans and the higher apes.[84] His awareness of the contemporary literature on this point is extensive, and he quietly accepted Linnaeus's revision of human taxonomy in the tenth edition of the *Systema naturae* (1758) in which Linnaeus introduced his *Homo troglodytes* and *Homo ferus*.

Buffon's discursive analysis of these forms, accompanied by Daubenton's anatomical analysis, pointed out the striking similarities between human beings and the higher apes. If the solutions worked out in the earlier article on the ass were still operative, the issue of specific identity and distinctness would be decided by interfertility rather than by morphological resemblance. But in a surprising statement, Buffon was even willing to report, without outright rejection, on the "forced or voluntary intercourse [*mélanges*] of Negresses with apes, the produce of which has penetrated into one or the other species."[85]

This possibility of a *material* association of men and apes satisfied the definition of a physical species. Is it then possible that human beings could have degenerated so far as to become apes? The possibility was clearly before his mind in these articles. The recurrent problem case for the eighteenth-century human science—the Hottentot of Southern Africa— with "mother and father sitting squat on their hams, both hideous, and besmeared with corrupted grease,"[86] suggested that the distance between such human beings and Linnaeus's *Homo troglodytes,* or *Simia sylvestris* was less than Buffon would have once led readers to assume.

This possibility of an analogous fertile hybridization of species between humans and apes, similar to that between the wolf and the dog; the strikingly similar anatomy of men and the "orang-outang"; the similar processes of "degeneration" producing similar racialization within the species— suggested the extent to which Buffon was being drawn into a complete reduction of human existence to the conditions of animal existence. Only Buffon's unshakable Cartesian dualism preserved for him the distinction of man and animals at this point. Apes can neither speak nor display genuine rational action, whereas the most bestial of humans can. In the end this internal condition overrides *both* reproductive fertility and physical resemblance to preserve human autonomy in an otherwise naturalistic cosmos.[87]

Buffon's final detailed treatment of anthropological questions occurred in two contexts, the first his 1777 supplement to the 1749 article "Variétés dans l'espèce humain," and the second his grand synthesis of cosmology, geology, and biology, the *Epoques de la Nature,* which reached the bookstands in 1778.[88] These works were separated chronologically from his earlier discussions by the period of greatest influx of new material from the South Pacific and the Arctic and South America.[89] In light of this information, Buffon was concerned to correct errors in his earlier anthropological discussions. This new data supplied strong reason to discount some of the earlier reports of bestial aspects of aboriginal peoples, and it cast doubt on the reports of giantism and extreme diminutiveness within the human species. Even his own earlier claims about the "degenerate" character of the American aborigines had to be modified. Local conditions might indeed produce small peoples of low energy in some regions. But Buffon now admitted that there were also tall and robust peoples in other areas of the New World.[90]

The timing of the introduction of this new data prevented Buffon from taking more than a cursory glance at its implications, however. To maintain monogenism in view of the known distribution patterns of humans available by the 1770s required an even more ambitious temporal and geographical spreading from an original site than Buffon had envisioned in his articles of the 1760s. Except for a few conjectures, the problem is conveniently left unexamined in his published writings.

Buffon's final published discussion of the human species in the *Epoques* inserted humankind into a fully naturalistic cosmology. Integrating Buffon's speculations on cosmological formation and geology with an explicit historical view of life, the work was a remarkable and revolutionary treatise.[91] Except in the symbolic division of the origin of the world into seven historical epochs, the *Epoques* is without reference to sacred history. The earth has formed by natural forces, and by its own inherent penetrating forces within matter, plants and animals have originated by the clumping together of matter, establishing the original *moules intérieures* of the various species.

Discussion of humankind in this work is suggestive and enigmatic. Human beings presumably have some different origin—one left purposely vague—from the rest of animated nature, but from the time of this event they are subject to the same vicissitudes of geography and time as any other species. Humanity originated in the high latitudes of Asia and migrated to Europe, North and South America, and Africa as the earth cooled. The indirect determinism of form via the alterations of the *molécules organiques* has resulted in the historical racialization that is displayed in the varieties of the human species. Some groups, under the action of temperate climates, have been able to improve by the development of the arts and sciences to the point that they can resist the degenerating forces of nature and in this respect form at least a temporary resistance to the determination by circumstance. Other human beings, in more extreme climates, have been unable to resist these forces of degeneration within the metaphysical limits of a common human species, and have become weak and degenerate peoples, lacking civilization and the sciences.

With this public closure on his reflections on the "natural history" of man, the human species had become fully integrated into temporal history and geographical space within a naturalistic history of the world. Buffonian anthropology, in contrast to Linnaean, compelled those adopting its perspective to emphasize geographical continuity, "degeneration" from common sources of origin, and the formation of quasi-permanent races by the action of causes operating at the most fundamental physiological level. Natural connections, rather than rational classifications, form the backbone of this methodology. The emphasis upon physical species and material relations of creatures, in dialectical interplay with an expanding body of anthropological information available to the late eighteenth century, suggested that the zoogeography of the human species presented few, if any, differences from that of other natural species. Only a residual Cartesian emphasis on reason as a distinct property of human beings prevented a complete naturalization.

AFTERWORD

The anthropologies of Buffon and Linnaeus were promulgated by their authors from two of the most important "centers of calculation" of eighteenth-century history, Uppsala and Paris."[92] Standing above other natural historians as "nature's spokesmen,"[93] Buffon and Linnaeus were uniquely positioned to define the course of later human science.

Linnaeus's *Systema* went through thirteen editions by the end of the century and was translated into several languages. Buffon's writings, also broadly translated, were printed under imperial sanction by the Imprimérie Royale at the same time the works of Montesquieu, Rousseau, Diderot, and the *Encyclopédie* were being suppressed. As a result of this privilege, Buffon became one of the more widely read and circulated authors of the Enlightenment.[94] Although the anti-Buffonian reaction that followed upon the Revolution for a time weakened the authority of his natural history in France, his tradition in human science would be revived under the Directory by Jean Baptiste Lamarck, Bernard de Lacépède, and Julien-Joseph Virey.[95] In the eyes of many nineteenth-century investigators, particularly in the French tradition, Buffon was the creator of the discipline of physical anthropology.[96]

The fragility of the special status preserved for human beings within the naturalized classificatory and zoogeographical frameworks created jointly by Buffon and Linnaeus is displayed by the subsequent course of events. If distinct faunas and floras were confined to specific geographical regions, on what warrant could one then deny that the different races of humans formed similar "endemic species," produced in separate centers of creation, rather than descending from a single pair or stock?[97]

Buffon's orthodox followers—that is, the monogenists—continued to emphasize the unity of the human species and common origin of mankind, whatever might be the degree of geographical differentiation taking place. Cook's naturalist on the second voyage of the *Resolution*, Johann Reinhold Forster (1729–1798), directly drew upon Buffon's arguments, buttressed by more orthodox religious appeals, to resolve the problem of human biogeography with a monogenetic account, which he supported by a massive study of comparative philology.[98]

Buffon's more radical French successors of the Directory period were willing to draw quite different conclusions from Buffon's naturalistic approach and the Linnaean tendency to polygenism.[99] Representative of this potential development of Buffon's program is the work of the pharmacist, fellow traveler of the Parisian *idéologues,* and later frequent contributor to the important *Nouveaux dictionnaire d'histoire naturelle,* Julien-Joseph Virey (1775–1846). An associate of the Parisian *Société des observateurs de l'homme* that flourished in the Directory period, his *Histoire naturelle du genre humaine* of 1801, dedicated to Buffon, illuminates the new naturalistic anthropology that was emerging at the end of the century. Combining Rousseau's historical developmentalism, biological naturalism, and Buffon's combined historical and zoogeographical approach, Virey viewed the human species to be "abandoned" to the vicissitudes of time and space, completely "subjected to that eternal chain of restoring and conserving actions which encompasses the entire series of beings."[100] Claiming to synthesize the work of "naturalists, physiologists, physicians, historians, voyagers, antiquaries, philosophers, political thinkers and literary authors," Virey drew together the human science of the century in a fully naturalistic scenario. Without hesitation he asserts that "one can affirm that savage man belongs to the natural family of the apes, which consists of several genera."[101] Rousseau's and Monboddo's conjectures on the development of man from the orangutan are accepted by Virey as literal scientific truth rather than as traditional conjectural history. Human beings have simply emerged by historical transformation from apes in tropical regions on at least two occasions, giving rise to two separate species of men.[102]

Virey's synthesis, combining taxonomic and physical-historical perspectives, displays some of the ways in which the Buffonian and Linnaean programs in their combination could be united in a single "natural-historical gaze" upon human beings, a view that eventually rendered human beings a purely zoological object, subjected to all the fragmenting powers of history and geography operative on any other species. The noble creature extolled by the Psalmist with whom John Ray could still feel some deep affinity at the end of the seventeenth century[103] had become a curious animal that a new generation of natural historians could presume to study with detached scientific objectivity by the opening of the nineteenth.

ACKNOWLEDGMENTS

I wish to thank Claude Blanckaert, Robert Wokler, and my colleagues Lynn Joy and Julia Douthwaite for comments on an earlier draft of this paper. Support for aspects of this project was supplied by a travel grant from the Institute for Scholarship in the Liberal Arts of the University of Notre Dame.

NOTES

1. Georges-Louis Leclerc, Compte Buffon, "Premier discourse de la manière d'étudier et de traiter d'histoire naturelle," Vol. I of *Histoire naturelle générale et particulière*, 14 vols. (Paris: Imprimérie Royale, 1749–67), as in *Oeuvres philosophiques de Buffon*, ed. J. Piveteau (Paris: Presses Universitaires de France, 1954), 10a, hereafter cited as *O.P.* except where reference to the original Imprimérie Royale edition is necessary. The "First Discourse," and several other items cited below, are also available in English translation in *From Natural History to the History of Nature: Readings from Buffon and His Critics*, ed. and trans. J. Lyon and P. R. Sloan (Notre Dame, Ind.: University of Notre Dame Press, 1981).

2. Georges Gusdorf (*Introduction aux sciences humaines* [Paris: Ophrys, 1974], 155–156) cites Magnus Hundt, *Anthropologia, de hominis dignitate, nature et proprietatibus* (1501); Otto Casmann, *Psychologia anthropologica sive animae humanae doctrina* (1594); Jean Riolan, *Anatomica seu anthropographia* (1626); H. F. Teichmeyer, *Anthropologia* (1739); James Drake, *Anthropologia nova: or, a New System of Anatomy,*

Describing the Animal Oeconomy, and a Short Rationale of Many Distempers Incident to Human Bodies (1707); Wilhelm Friedrich Struve, *Anthropologia naturalis sublimior* (1754); Ernst Platner, *Anthropologie à l'usage des médecins et des philosophes* (1772). A computerized review of the *Eighteenth-Century Short Title Catalogue* revealed no further entries for "anthropology," "anthropologia," "anthropologie," and "anthropographica."

3. G. Cuvier, "Prospectus," to *Dictionnaire des sciences naturelles*, ed. F. Levrault (Strausbourg: Levrault, 1816), I: vii.

4. Alan Frost, "The Pacific Ocean: The Eighteenth Century's 'New World,'" *Studies in Voltaire and the Eighteenth Century* 152 (1976): 779–822; see also P. J. Marshall and G. Williams, *The Great Map of Mankind: Perceptions of New Worlds in the Age of Enlightenment* (Cambridge, Mass.: Harvard University Press, 1982), chap. 9.

5. See Denis Diderot, "Anatomie," in *Encyclopédie: ou Dictionnaire raisonné des sciences, des arts et des métiers, par une société de gens de lettres*, 17 vols. (Paris: Briasson, 1751–65; reprint, New York and Paris: Pergamon Press, 1969), vol. 1, 416; and idem, "Anthropologie," in *Encyclopédie*, vol. 1, 497. On the history of the early usage of the designation, see also M. Duchet, *Anthropologie et histoire au siècle des lumières* (Paris: Maspéro, 1971), 12, and the exhaustive history of French usages of the term by C. Blanckaert, "L'*Anthropologie* en France: Le mot et l'histoire (XVI–XIX siècle)," *Bulletin et mémoires de la Société d'Anthropologie de Paris* 1 (1989): 13–44.

6. Andreas Vesalius, *De fabrica humani corporis* (Basel, 1543), Book 2, chap. 9, p. 42. See discussion by Charles Singer in notes to Galen, *On the Anatomical Procedures*, vol. 1, trans. C. Singer (London: Oxford University Press, 1956).

7. See F. J. Cole, *The History of Comparative Anatomy* (London: Macmillan Publishers, 1944), 132–149.

8. René Descartes, *L'Homme de René Descartes*, ed. Claude Clerselier (Paris, 1664), 107, as reprinted in Descartes's *Treatise of Man*, ed. T. S. Hall (Cambridge, Mass.: Harvard University Press, 1972).

9. Descartes's own positions were possibly developed under the influence of his contacts with the Italian medical schools, most likely with the University of Bologna, during his residence in Italy for an uncertain time between 1619 and 1625. T. S. Hall's extensive commentary upon the *Treatise of Man* details Descartes's reworking of contemporary medical anatomy.

10. René Descartes, *Meditations*, VI, in *Oeuvres philosophiques de Descartes*, ed. C. Adam and P. Tannery (Paris: Cerf, 1904), 9: 64.

11. Descartes continues by speaking of his own nature as "the complex or assemblage of everything God has give me." Ibid.

12. Descartes, *L'Homme*, 1. On his private reflections on human generation, see Jacques Roger, *Les sciences de la vie dans le pensée française du xviiie siècle*, 2d ed. (1971; reprint, Paris: Michel, 1993), especially 150–154.

13. Ibid., especially part 2, chap. 1.

14. See especially George Garden's review, "A Discourse on the Modern Theory of Generation," *Philosophical Transactions of the Royal Society* 192 (1691): 474–483.

15. Richard Mead, *Medical Precepts and Cautions*, translated from the Latin by T. Stack (London: Brindley, 1751), 10–11. Emphases in original.

16. "Ovist" preformationists, attempting to explain the different races, at times held that God must have created different colored eggs encapsulated in the ovaries of Eve! See the review of Pierre Barrère's treatise *Dissertation sur la cause physique de la couleur des Nègres* (Paris, 1741) in *Journal des Sçavans* 132 (May 1742): 23–45.

17. Michèle Duchet has identified the thirteen-volume manuscript "Anthropologie ou science générale de l'homme," by Alexandre-César Chauvannes (1788, Bibliothéque cantonale de Lausanne, MS A909) as the first work to undertake an extended discussion of this new meaning of a science of "anthropology." I have not consulted this document. See also Blanckaert, "L'*Anthropologie*," for other uses in this sense in the late Enlightenment.

18. For example, in the influential arrangements of animals by the Oxford physician Edward Wotton, the human species is discussed in a separate book from the known apes and monkeys (*De Differentiis animalium libri decem* [Paris, 1552]). On the history of the early modern classifications of human beings and apes, see C. Blanckaert, "Premier des singes, dernier des hommes?" *Alliage* 7–8 (1991): 113–129.

19. John Ray, *Synopsis methodica animalium quadrupedam et serpentini generis* (London: Smith and Walford, 1693), 53, 60.

20. Tyson's direct comparison of men and apes in a Vesalian format provides an obvious exception to my earlier generalization that the medical-anatomical tradition after Vesalius was opposed to drawing relationships with animals.

21. Nicolai Tulpii, *Observationum medicarum* (Amstelodami: Elsevier, 1641). The same form was described by Olfert Dapper in his *Description de l'Afrique* (Amsterdam, 1686). See Blanckaert, "Premier des singes," 114–119. Confusions are common between the chimpanzee of Africa, named the "Jocko" by Buffon, and the true orangutan of Borneo and Sumatra, commonly designated the "Pongo," first described and drawn by the voyaging Dutch physician Jakob de Bondt (1592–1631). The distinction of the orangutan from the chimpanzee was only made decisively by Petrus Camper in 1799 and Richard Owen in 1835. The gorilla was only formally described and distinguished from the chimpanzee and orangutan in 1847 by Thomas Savage and Jeffries Wyman ("Notice of the External Characters and Habits of Troglodytes Gorilla, a New Species of Orang from the Gaboon River") and Wyman ("Osteology of the Same," *Boston Journal of Natural History* 5 [1847]: 417–443). See R. Owen, *Memoir on the Gorilla Troglodytes Gorilla Savage* (London: Taylor, 1865), and the introduction by Ashley Montagu to the reprint of Edward Tyson's *Anatomy of a Pygmie* (London: Dawson, 1966), 10.

22. Tyson, "Epistle Dedicatory," in *Anatomy of a Pygmie*, 3. For discussions of Tyson, see Robert Wokler, "Tyson and Buffon on the Orang-utan," *Studies on Voltaire and the Eighteenth Century* 155 (1976): 2301–2319. See also W. F. Bynum, "The Anatomical Method, Natural Theology, and the Functions of the Brain," *Isis* 64 (1973): 445–468, especially 463–465.

23. Frans Stafleu, *Linnaeus and the Linnaeans: The Spreading of Their Ideas in Systematic Botany, 1735–1789* (Utrecht: A. Oosthoek, 1971). Linnaeus is estimated by Stafleu to have had over 186 pupils under his immediate supervision during his teaching career at Uppsala between 1741 and 1776.

24. The first edition of 1735 recognized two species under the genus *Bradypus*,

distinguishing the two- and three-toed sloths. These would remain in the Anthropomorpha until the tenth edition of 1758, when Linnaeus introduced the new Order *Primates*. The Anteaters, genus *Myrmecophaga*, were first included in the Anthropomorpha in the second edition of the System of 1740, and would remain in this group through the fourth edition of 1744.

25. The adoption of the binomial form of specific designation as the "proper name" of a species was instituted by Linnaeus only in the tenth edition of the *Systema* in 1758. Prior to that time the essential definition was given by a polynomial. Hence the designation *Homo sapiens europaeus albus* is to be read as a generic designation (*Homo*) followed by specifications of three essential differentiae of increasing specificity. The final designations *albus*, *niger*, etc. were dropped in the tenth and subsequent editions with *europaeus*, *asiaticus*, etc. designating formal varieties.

26. See on this, Duchet, *Anthropologie*, chap. 1.

27. This era commences with the commissioning of the expeditions to Peru and Lapland in 1735 by the French Académie des Sciences to measure the size of the degree of the meridian. For useful summaries of French and British explorations in the Pacific in the eighteenth century, with maps of routes, see especially Robert J. Garry, "Geographical Exploration by the French," and Richard I. Ruggles, "Geographical Exploration by the British," in *The Pacific Basin: A History of its Geographical Exploration*, ed. Herman R. Friis (New York: American Geographical Society, 1967), chaps. 12, 13.

28. See J. C. Beaglehole, "Eighteenth Century Science and the Voyages of Discovery," *New Zealand Journal of History* 3 (1969): 107–123.

29. See G. Broberg, "*Homo Sapiens:* Linnaeus's Classification of Man," in *Linnaeus: The Man and His Work*, ed. T. Frängsmyr (Berkeley, Los Angeles, London: University of California Press, 1983), 156–194, and Broberg, *Homo sapiens Linn* (Uppsala: Almquist and Wicksell, 1975), English summary.

30. A sample of the conflicting information available to western Europeans by midcentury can be gleaned from Thomas Astley's influential *A New General Collection of Voyages and Travels*, 5 vols. (London, 1745–47).

31. Pierre de Maupertuis, *Lettre sur le progrès des sciences* (1752), reprinted in *Oeuvres de Mr. de Maupertuis*, new ed., 4 vols. (Lyon: Bruyset, 1756), 2:350–351. See note 33 below.

32. Twelve editions appeared in Linnaeus's lifetime, with a posthumous thirteenth edition, edited by J. G. Gmelin, commencing publication in 1788. The latter forms the basis of the William Turton English edition of the *Systema* of 1802–06.

33. The most developed examination of these issues undertaken under Linnaeus's supervision is the doctoral dissertation by his student Christian Hoppius, *Anthropomorpha* (Uppsala, 1760), reprinted in *Amoenitates academicae* vol. 6 (Leyden: Westernium, 1764), 184–187. Maupertuis's creature (note 31) is located under *Homo troglodytes*.

34. For further details, see Broberg, "*Homo sapiens*." I am also indebted to my colleague, Julia Douthwaite, for an illuminating discussion of Linnaean anthropology in her "Rewriting the Savage: The Extraordinary Fictions of the 'Wild Girl of Champagne,'" *Eighteenth-Century Studies* 28 (1994–1995, 163–192).

35. C. Linnaeus, *De sexu plantarum* (1760), trans. J. E. Smith (Dublin, 1786), quoted in *Readings in Early Anthropology*, ed. J. S. Slotkin (Chicago: Aldine Publishing Co., 1965), 180.

36. C. Linnaeus, *Fauna Suecia* (Holmiae, 1746), as quoted in Slotkin, *Readings in Early Anthropology*, 178. Linnaeus was responding to criticisms by the Danzig naturalist J. T. Klein (*Summa dubiorum circa classes quadrupedum et amphibium in Linnaei systemate naturae*, 1743). See Broberg, "*Homo Sapiens*: Linnaeus's Classification," 170–171.

37. See discussion of Rousseau below, p. 135.

38. On this background, see J. Roger, *Buffon: Un Philosophe au Jardin du roi* (Paris: Fayard, 1989), chaps. 2–3; for more detail, see Lesley Hanks, *Buffon avant l'histoire naturelle* (Paris: Presses universitaires, 1966).

39. In a letter of 2 August 1745 to his friend the Genevan Academician Jean Jallabert (*O.P.*, viii), Buffon described his plan to make an attack on Linnaean classification in his opening discourse, which would serve as a preface to a "*Catalogue raisonée du cabinet du Jardin du Roi.*" The collection of materials at the Paris Jardin included anthropological specimens.

40. His friendship with Pierre de Maupertuis in the late '30s and early '40s was probably important as well, although I have been unable to document the effect of this on Buffon's shift of attention to anthropological questions. Maupertuis had encountered the Laplanders in his expedition to Nova Zemblya in 1735 and made his own conjectures on the origins of the races in 1744 following the exhibit of a live albino African in Paris that year, reported in his *Dissertation physique a l'occasion du nègre blanc* (Leyden, 1744) and in his *Vénus physique* (Paris, 1746). See also comments in his 1752 *Lettre sur le progrès des sciences*, above, note 31.

41. See my "From Logical Universals to Historical Individuals: Buffon's Conception of Biological Species," in *Histoire du concept d'espèce dans les sciences de la vie*, ed. J. L. Fischer and J. Roger (Paris: Fondation Singer-Polignac, 1986), 101–140.

42. Buffon, "Premier discours," *Histoire naturelle* I (1749), in *O.P.*, 10a. Hereafter, citations given in the form *HN*, volume, year, with references to *O.P.* when possible.

43. Ibid., 19a. The pangolins are scaly anteaters of Africa. See note 24 above.

44. See my "From Logical Universals," 112–115.

45. Buffon, "Premier discours," *HN* I (1749), *O.P.*, 236–246.

46. Elsewhere I have discussed the probable connection of Buffon's views to the Wolffian philosophy as this had been expounded in 1740 by Buffon's friend Emilie Gabrielle Lomont Du Châtelet (Sloan, "L'Hypothétisme de Buffon," in *Buffon 88*, ed. J. Gayon [Paris: Vrin, 1992], 207–222) and more recently in my article "Natural History" for the *Cambridge Encyclopedia of Eighteenth-Century Philosophy*, ed. Knud Haakonssen (in press).

47. Aristotle, *Historia animalium* I.vi.491a, 15–23.

48. Buffon, "Premier discours," *HN* I (1749), *O.P.*, 17a.

49. On Buffon's relational epistemology, see Roger, *Buffon*, chap. 6.

50. Buffon, "Prospectus" for the *Histoire naturelle, Journal des sçavans* (October 1748): 639.

51. I exclude the medical anatomies and "anthropologies" from this general-

ization (see note 2). Daubenton's series of articles occupy pages 12–304 of the third volume of the original Imprimérie Royale edition, and lead the reader through a detailed discussion of normal and pathological anatomy, principally of the skeletal system and the separate internal organs. There is no effort in this to compare human anatomy with that of other animals. Buffon's discussions occupy pages 305–530 of the same volume.

52. For example, the Jansenist *Nouvelles ecclésiastiques* (6 February 1750: 21) allied Buffon with Pope, whose *Essay on Man* was seen as the nadir of modern materialism. See translation in Lyon and Sloan, *From Natural History*, 238.

53. Review of *Histoire naturelle*, vols. 2–3, *Journal des sçavans* (March 1754): 155.

54. See Ephraim Chambers, "Species," in *Cyclopedia: Or an Universal Dictionary of Arts and Sciences* (London: Midwinter, 1741), Vol. II (no p. number); John Harris, *Lexicon Technicum*, "Species" (London, 1710), Vol. I (no p. number).

55. See, for example, Buffon "Premier discours": "il n'existe réellement dans la Nature que les individus, & que les genres, les ordres & les classes n'existent que dans notre imagination." *HN* I (1749), *O.P.*, 19a.

56. Buffon, *HN* II (1749), *O.P.*, 233, 238. I have analyzed this in relation to Aristotle's notion of the perpetuity of the *eidos* and given evidence for Buffon's awareness of this Aristotelian understanding, via discussions of William Harvey, in my "From Logical Universals."

57. Buffon, "L'Asne," *HN* IV (1753), in *O.P.*, 355.

58. Ibid., 355b–356a.

59. *Encyclopédie*, Vol. 5 (1755), 956–957 (unsigned).

60. See John Eddy, "Buffon, Organic Alterations, and Man," *Studies in History of Biology* 7 (1984): 1–45; I have also discussed this in my "The Idea of Racial Degeneracy in Buffon's *Histoire naturelle*," *Studies in Eighteenth-Century Culture* 3 (1973): 293–321.

61. See Hans-Jörg Rheinberger, "Buffon: Zeit, Veränderung und Geschichte," *History and Philosophy of Life Science* 12 (1990): 203–223. I have also discussed this issue in my forthcoming "Natural History" (see note 46 above).

62. His work is praised for maintaining the specific unity of the human species. See *Journal des sçavans* review, March 1754, p. 159.

63. The grouping *Famille* is not part of the original Linnaean hierarchy but is frequently used in French sources.

64. See my "From Logical Universals."

65. On the distinction of "noble" or "isolated" from "degenerating" species, see "Le Lion," *HN* IX (1761), and "De la dégénération des animaux," *HN* XIV (1766).

66. Linnaeus developed the image of the two-dimensional geographical map as a representation of "natural" relationships of forms in his later lectures. See Caroli a Linné, *Praelectiones in ordines naturales plantarum*, ed. J. C. Fabricius and P. Giseke (Hamburg: Hoffmanni, 1792). Buffon's temporal and spatial view was more complex. As he wrote in 1770, organic relationships seem best represented by an "immense tableau, in which all orders of beings are each represented by a chain which . . . is not a simple filament extended only in length, [but] is a large network [*faisceau*] or bundle which, from interval to interval, casts branches to the side into order to be joined with the network of another order." Buffon, "Oiseaux

qui ne peuvent voler," *HN des Oiseaux* VI (1770), *O.P.*, 417a. For a general discussion of these graphic representations of natural relationship, see G. Barsanti, "Buffon et l'image de la nature: De l'échelle des êtres à la carte géographique et à l'arbre généalogique," in *Buffon 88*, ed. J. Gayon, 254–296.

67. Important anthropological discussions are to be found in "Les Animaux sauvages," *HN* VI (1756); "Animaux communs aux deux continens," *HN* IX, (1761); "De la nature: première vue," *HN* XI (1764); "Nomenclature des signes," *HN* XIV (1766); "Les orang-outangs, ou le Pongo et le Jocko," *HN* XIV, (1766); "Addition aux différents articles de l'*Histoire naturelle de l'homme*," *HN Supplément* IV (1777), (reprinted in M. Duchet, *Buffon: De l'Homme* [Paris: Maspero, 1971]). The additions made to "Les Orang-outangs" in the seventh supplementary volume, published posthumously in 1789, do not continue the discussions of the man-ape relationship.

68. These included reports of the northern latitudes by French, Russian, and British expeditions to Siberia, Kamchatka, and the Bering Straits, conveniently summarized in vols. 18–19 (1768–1770) of the abbé Prévost's *Histoire générale des voyages*, edited by Prévost's continuers Meussnier de Querlon and Rousselot de Surgy. See Duchet, *Anthropologie*, 54–59. Buffon utilized Prévost as a frequent source of data in the preparation of the *Histoire naturelle des oiseaux*, and was probably relying on it earlier as a source of information. See letters to his collaborator, the abbé Leopold-Charles Bexon, of 2 and 5 February 1778 in *Correspondance générale*, in *Oeuvres complètes de Buffon*, ed. J. L. Lanessan (Paris: Le Vasseur, 1885), 13: 374–376. Buffon's earlier conclusions on the relations of the Old and New World, set forth in his articles of 1761, had been severely attacked for inaccuracy by Cornelius De Pauw in his *Recherches philosophiques sur les Américains*, 2 vols. (Berlin: Decker, 1768–69). On this dispute, see especially A. Gerbi, *The Dispute of the New World: The History of a Polemic, 1750–1900*, trans. J. Moyle (Pittsburgh: University of Pittsburgh Press, 1973), chap. 1. The South Sea expeditions of John Byron, Philip Carteret, and Samuel Wallis, and James Cook's first voyage of 1768–71, were conveniently summarized for the period in John Hawkesworth's *An Account of the Voyages Undertaken by the Order of His Present Majesty for Making Discoveries in the Southern Hemisphere*, 3 vols. (London: Cadell, 1773).

69. Louis Bougainville, *Voyage autour du monde* (Paris: Saillant and Nyon, 1771; English edition, London: Norse, 1772). Commerson's biological and anthropological observations remained in manuscript and are not cited by Buffon, but surely would have been known to him following the return of the expedition to France in 1769.

70. "Lettre de M. Commerson . . . sur la découverte de la nouvelle isle de Cythère ou Taïti," *Mercure de France* (November 1769), 197–207, especially p. 201. I am indebted to my colleague Julia Douthwaite for this valuable reference.

71. See Marshall and Williams, *Great Map of Mankind*, chap. 9.

72. On this, see especially Claude Blanckaert, "Monogenisme et polygenisme en France de Buffon à P. Broca," doctoral thesis, Université de Paris I, 1981. I wish to thank Dr. Blanckaert for making this available to me.

73. George Stocking, Jr., "French Anthropology in 1800," in his *Race, Culture, and Evolution* (Chicago: University of Chicago Press, 1982), 38–39.

74. See on this, James L. Larson, "Not without a Plan: Geography and Natural

History in the Late Eighteenth Century," *Journal of History of Biology* 19 (1986): 447–488.

75. Rousseau's conjectural history of the *Second Discourse* of 1755 posits a transformist history of humanity that commences with a creature resembling the docile *Homo sylvestris* of Java and Sumatra, and terminates with modern European man in civilized society. The dating of his work excludes the awareness of Linnaean classifications beyond those of the sixth edition of 1748, which remained constant through the ninth edition of 1756 (see table 5.2). Rousseau derived much of his information on the anthropoid apes from Antoine François Prévost's *Histoire générale des voyages* (Paris: Didot, 1746–91), vol. 5. See Rousseau, *Discours sur l' origine et les fondements de l'inegalité parmi les hommes* (1755), "note j." On the further extensions of Rousseau's conjectural developmentalism in the late Enlightenment in conjunction with the later revisions of Linnaean classifications, see especially R. Wokler, "Apes and Races in the Scottish Enlightenment: Monboddo and Kames on the Nature of Man," in *Philosophy and Science in the Scottish Enlightenment,* ed. P. Jones (Edinburgh: Donald, 1988), 145–168. For an update on the Buffon-Rousseau relationship with reference to the issue of degeneration and ascent, see A. Cherni, "Dégénération et dépravation: Rousseu chez Buffon," in *Buffon 88,* ed. J. Gayon, 143–154.

76. Buffon, "Les Animaux Carnassiers," *HN* VII (1758), *O.P.,* 373–374.

77. Buffon, "L'Asne," *HN* IV (1753), *O.P.,* 353–358.

78. See "Le Cerf," *HN* VI (1756), Imprimérie Royale edition, 86–88. For this reason Buffon regards the direct effect of climate and geography as superficial. See also "De la dégénération des animaux," *HN* XIV (1766), *O.P.,* 395.

79. See Duchet, *Anthropologie,* 270–273. It is common to trace the origins of modern notions of race to Blumenbach and Kant, but Buffon was the originating source of this concept; from him Kant and later Blumenbach seem to have derived it. A *race* in Buffon's sense typically denoted the physical and material relationships within a degenerating species, forming a subdivision of a degenerating *espèce physique.* It was characterized by "constant and general characters by means of which one recognizes the races and even the different nationalities of the human genus." (Buffon, "De la Dégénération des Animaux," *HN* XIV [1766], *O.P.,* 395b.)

80. "Animaux communs aux deux continens," *HN* IX (1761), Imprimérie Royale edition, 101. Buffon is drawing upon Johann Georg Gmelin's *Reise durch Sibirien,* first published in German in four volumes in 1751–52. This was translated into French in 1767.

81. "Animaux communs aux deux continens," *HN* IX (1761), Imprimérie Royale edition, 103–104.

82. Buffon, "De la dégénération des animaux," *HN* XIV (1766), *O.P.,* 408–409.

83. The relevance of these new complexities surrounding the interbreeding criterion for issues in the human sciences, set forth in "De la dégénération des animaux" in the same volume as the Pongo and Jocko discussions, could scarcely escape the attentive reader.

84. The relationship between the chimpanzee of Africa and the orangutan of southeast Asia remained uncertain in these discussions. Buffon is undecided whether one is only the juvenile form of the other, or if these are two different

races within a single species. In the seventh *Supplément* volume, edited posthumously by Bernard de Lacépède from Buffon's manuscripts in 1789, Buffon concluded that the great apes of Africa and the Indies formed two separate species.

85. "Nomenclature des signes," *HN* XIV (1766), Imprimérie Royale edition, 32. Buffon is apparently attempting to take account of Linnaeus's new intermediate *Homo troglodytes* in asserting this point. His immediate source for this account is evidently the report of the voyager Charles de Brosses, who described the capturing of young girls by orangutans in Angola in his *Histoire des navigations aux terres australes* (Paris: Durand, 1756). See also P. Alletz, *Histoire des singes et autres animaux curieux* (Paris: Duchesne, 1752), 40. Further reference to this can be found in James Burnett (Lord Monboddo), *Of the Origin and Progress of Language*, 2d ed. (Edinburgh, 1774; reprint, New York: Garland, 1970), 1: 277; and Cornelius De Pauw, *Recherches philosophiques* (London edition of 1771), 1: 17. Reports of human-ape hybridizations had been made in the first accounts of the orangutan by Jakob de Bondt in 1658 and by Olfert Dapper in 1686. See Blanckaert, "Premier des singes," 114–116. Cornelius De Pauw attacked Buffon and others for accepting such claims in the absence of firm evidence. Given the importance Buffon had previously placed on the interbreeding criterion, his acceptance of this possibility, without critical examination of the sources of these reports, is indeed surprising.

86. Buffon, "Nomenclature," *HN* XIV, Imprimérie Royale edition, 32. Buffon was aware of the accounts of the Hottentots in the abbé Prévost's *Histoire générale des voyages*, vol. 5 (1748), and de Brosses's *Histoire des navigations*. In the *Supplément* he updates his discussion with specific references to the reports on the Hottentots from the voyages of James Bruce, James Cook (first voyage), Robert Gordon, and other reports summarized in John Hawkesworth's compendium *An Account of the Voyages Undertaken by the Order of His Present Majesty for Making Discoveries in the Southern Hemisphere* (3 vols., London: Cadell, 1773).

87. As he continued to reiterate in his last works:

> One will not fail to tell us that analogy seems to demonstrate that the human species has followed the same march and that it dates from the same time as the other species, that it is even more universally distributed; and that if the epoch of its creation is posterior to that of the animals, nothing has proven that man is not subjected to the same laws of Nature, the same alterations and the same changes. We will acknowledge that the human species does not differ essentially from other species by its corporeal faculties, and that in this respect its destiny has been almost the same as that of other species. But can we doubt that we differ remarkably from the animals by the divine ray which it has pleased the sovereign Being to grant to us. (*Des Epoques de la Nature, Supplément HN* V, reprinted in *O.P.*, 175–176).

88. Although published in 1778, the detailed study of the text by Jacques Roger has revealed that the *Epoques* was primarily composed in the 1760s, explaining the fact that it ignores the expedition reports of the 1770s. In the *Epoques*, Buffon makes one reference to reports of the presence of chickens and pigs on Tahiti, commenting that "ces espèces aient suivi celle de l'homme dans toutes ses migrations," Buffon, *Epoques* (*O.P.*, 194), without further discussion of the means of such migration. On the history of the text, see J. Roger, ed., *Buffon: Les Epoques de la Nature* (1962; reissue, Paris: Editions du Muséum, 1988), xxxvii–xli.

89. Volumes 18 and 19 of Prévost's *Histoire,* dealing with the Arctic regions, appeared in 1768 and 1770. Cornelius De Pauw's *Recherches philosophiques sur les Américains* appeared in its first volume in 1768; A. F. J. Fréville's *Histoire des nouvelles decouvertes faites dans la mer du sud en 1767, 1768, 1769, & 1770,* was published in Paris in 1774; Johann Gmelin's *Reise in Sibirien* appeared in French in 1767. The report from Cook's first voyage, with a new account of the Hottentots, appeared in 1774. Buffon also used John Byron's descriptions of Patagonia, printed in the collection by Hawkesworth of 1773. He also frequently cites Timothé Merzahn von Klingstod's *Mémoire* on Nova Zemblya of 1762. Buffon and the abbé Bexon were jointly conducting a review of all available travel literature in the 1770s for the preparation of his *Histoire naturelle des oiseaux,* which commenced publication in 1770. Buffon appears to have had knowledge of at least some of the unpublished results from Cook's second voyage as summarized in Georg Forster's unpublished "Observationes Historiam naturalem spectantes" and possibly some version of Johann Forster's draft of the *Observations* prior to its publication. On the circulation of the Forster manuscripts, see Michael E. Hoare's introduction to *The Resolution Journal of Johann Reinhold Forster, 1772–1775.* (Works of the Hakluyt Society, 2d series, no. 152 [London: Hakluyt Society, 1982], 1: 64–67.)

90. Buffon, "Supplément" to "Variétés dans l'espèce humaine," reprinted in Duchet, *Buffon Anthropologiste,* 388.

91. See J. Roger, "Buffon et l'introduction de l'histoire dans l'*Histoire naturelle,*" in *Buffon 88,* ed. J. Gayon, 193–205, and M. J. S. Hodge, "Two Cosmogonies (Theory of the Earth and Theory of Generation) and the Unity of Buffon's Thought," in ibid., 241–254.

92. I am drawing here on Bruno Latour's concept of a "center of calculation," which he used to characterize the relation of the urban scientific institution to the eighteenth-century exploratory voyage. In this the cartographer and the European natural history museum were able to systematize the complexity of distant nations and people. See *Science in Action* (Cambridge, Mass.: Harvard University Press, 1987), chap. 6, and Dirk Stemerding, *Plants, Animals, and Formulae: Natural History in the Light of Latour's Science in Action and Foucault's The Order of Things* (Enschede, Holland: University of Twente Press, 1991).

93. See Dirk Stemerding, "How to Make Oneself Nature's Spokesman," *Biology and Philosophy* 8 (1993): 193.

94. Daniel Mornet's valuable quantitative survey of the catalogues of 392 eighteenth-century French libraries revealed Buffon's *Histoire naturelle* to be third in frequency (220/392), exceeded only by the *Dictionnaire* of Pierre Bayle (288) and the writings of the sixteenth-century poet Clément Marot (252). This can be compared to the frequency of Rousseau's *Discours sur l'Inégalité* (76) and the French translation of Locke's *Essay* (156). D. Mornet, "Les Enseignements des bibliothèques privées," *Revue d'histoire littéraire de la France* 17 (1910): 419–496. An exhaustive analysis of the various editions and commentaries on Buffon's work is to be found in E. Genet-Varcin and J. Roger, "Bibliographie de Buffon," in *O.P.,* 521–530.

95. On the attempts at the restoration of Linneanism in France and the reaction against Buffon in the Convention period, see P. Corsi, *The Age of Lamarck,* trans. J. Mandelbaum (Berkeley, Los Angeles, London: University of California

Press, 1988), chap. 1, and G. Beale, "Early French Members of the Linnean Society of London, 1788–1802: From Estates Générale to Thermidor," *Proceedings of the Western Society for French History* 18 (1991): 272–282.

96. For a critique of this historiographic tradition, see Claude Blanckaert, "Buffon and the Natural History of Man: Writing History in the Face of Anthropology's 'Foundational Myth,'" *History of the Human Sciences* 5 (1993): 13. For the later history of Buffon's role in French anthropology, see Joy Harvey, "Buffon and Nineteenth Century French Anthropologists," in *Buffon 88*, ed. J. Gayon, 649–665.

97. Larson, "Not without a Plan." For remarks on the relation of the notion of "centers of creation" to polygenicism, see Blanckaert, "Monogenisme et polygenisme," 245–260.

98. For details on Johann Forster, see introduction by Michael E. Hoare to Forster's *Resolution Journal*. Johann Forster seems to have been the first to attempt a detailed monogenetic explanation of the origin of the South Sea islanders. By comparative philological analysis of the language of the Pacific islanders, he concludes that they can be derived by migration from the Malay peninsula, rather than from the Americas. See J. R. Forster, *Observations Made During a Voyage Round the World on Physical Geography, Natural History, and Ethic* [sic] *Philosophy* (London: Robinson, 1778), chap. 6, pp. 283–284. Forster notes his debt to Buffon's geographical approach (preface, p. i). Unlike Buffon, Forster was concerned with maintaining the orthodox biblical account of Creation from a single pair in this extensive analysis of the origin of the Pacific islanders. On some of the struggles of his son Georg with the problem of remote islanders, see Hugh West, "The Limits of Enlightenment Anthropology: Georg Forster and the Tahitians," *History of European Ideas* 10 (1989): 147–160.

99. The German and Scottish readings of Buffon followed different paths leading beyond the bounds of this essay. See Peter Reill, "Buffon and Historical Thought in Germany and Great Britain" in *Buffon 88*, ed. J. Gayon, 667–679; P. B. Wood, "Buffon's Reception in Scotland: The Aberdeen Connection," *Annals of Science* 44 (1987): 169–190; and idem., "The Natural History of Man in the Scottish Enlightenment," *History of Science* 28 (1990): 89–123. The great importance of Linnaeus for Scottish anthropology is not discussed by Wood.

100. Julien-Joseph Virey, *Histoire naturelle de genre humain, ou, recherches sur ses principaux fondements physiques et moraux, precedées d'un discours sur la nature des êtres organiques* (Paris: Dufart, an 9 [1801]), 1: 15. On Virey, see C. Blanckaert, "J. J. Virey, Observateur de l'homme (1800–1825)," in *Julien-Joseph Virey: Naturaliste et Anthropologue*, ed. C. Benichou and C. Blanckaert (Paris: Vrin, 1988), 97–182, and Stocking, "French Anthropology in 1800." Virey situates his anthropological discussions in the context of a general physiological and metaphysical theory based on the creative power of nature. Employing the dynamic materialism of French medical vitalism, he develops an ascending, rather than degenerating, history of the human species.

101. Virey, *Histoire naturelle*, 1: 92.

102. Ibid., 229.

103. John Ray, *The Wisdom of God Manifested in the Works of the Creation*, 5th ed. (London: Walford, 1709), part 2, pp. 255ff.

SIX

Sex and Gender

Ludmilla Jordanova

In a particularly striking passage at the beginning of *Rameau's Nephew*, written between 1761 and 1774, Diderot suggests an unexpected way in which sex and gender might be linked with the human sciences of the Enlightenment. To set the scene for this extraordinary dialogic tour de force, the character known only as "I" describes his regular afternoon visits to the Palais Royal:

> I hold discussions with myself on politics, love, taste or philosophy, and let my thoughts wander in complete abandon, leaving them free to follow the first wise or foolish idea that comes along, like those young rakes we see in the Allée de Foy who run after a giddy looking little piece with a laughing face, sparkling eye and tiptilted nose, only to leave her for another, accosting them all, but sticking to none. In my case my thoughts are my wenches.[1]

It is a witty way of suggesting that thought is an erotic act. Yet if we look at the passage more closely, two other points emerge. A specific kind of eroticism is invoked; first, it is simultaneously transgressive and flirtatious, and second, it is autoerotic in a special sense. The logic of what "I" says makes it clear that part of him, or to be more precise, of his mind, is male and another part of it is female. Indeed the idea of talking to oneself, which is what makes this gender split possible, is a recurrent theme in this dialogue.

Diderot's text suggests something of the complexity of the subject under discussion here. Perhaps it is misleading to associate it with a field called human science—we will come to that particular term shortly—but it does indicate that sex and gender pop up in the least obvious places, and that they are present as much in metaphor as in subject matter. As happens so often, Diderot's writings serve as a dramatic reminder of the impossibility of constructing simple stories or comforting consensuses around

152

eighteenth-century ideas. Sex and gender pose special problems to historians which it is essential to acknowledge. This essay accordingly begins with some methodological reflections on "human science" and on the manner in which sexual difference was conceptualized during the Enlightenment. In order to examine these issues in more depth, I shall turn to a limited number of well-known thinkers. The subject is vast, and since matters pertaining to sex and gender are not confined to particular branches of science, there are no natural limits to the places where these themes may be found. The selection of materials is thus inevitably arbitrary. I have made a particular set of choices, to concentrate on a small group of well-known writers. This restriction seemed necessary if an appreciation was to be gained of how sex and gender work as concepts. Furthermore, the secondary literature in this field is still small, suggesting that primary sources have most to offer at this stage.[2] It is customary to associate the idea of a human science with that distinctively eighteenth-century formulation "the science of man," and with the Enlightenment quest for secure knowledge of the human condition to match that of nature. The first version stresses a concept of the period itself (the science of man), and the second places its focus on the generous epistemological claims made on behalf of natural knowledge (it can properly embrace "man" too). By contrast, the phrases "human science" or "human sciences" imply the existence of well-defined scientific disciplines and seem more apt when applied to the nineteenth and twentieth centuries than to earlier periods. They also imply universalism; "human science" is a modern phrase that purports to fit diverse times and places.[3] As it is quite legitimate to define terms in different ways according to the project they are serving, I shall propose a definition of "human science" to suit this particular exercise, for which the idea of a science of man is too restrictive. Since it was used in the period, but only by specific groups, to extend it more widely seems anachronistic. The formula that stresses epistemology is too loose, since to be concerned with knowing about "man" encompasses just about everything.

Human science is a scientific endeavor that has humanity or human nature at its center. But this begs the question of how we define "scientific endeavor." Four principal criteria are appropriate to the Enlightenment: first, "scientific" suggests that the object of enquiry is *in nature*—neither supernatural nor mere custom or convention; second, the object of enquiry is regulated by natural law, and its study is primarily a search for regularities; third, the phenomena in question can only be known through observation and experiment, hence the importance of methodological rigor; and finally, the aim of the whole enterprise is to produce a stable and coherent body of knowledge. Any field where all four of these closely related and overlapping features obtain can confidently be called a human science, and a number of other areas fulfill some if not all these criteria.

The phrase "science of man" contains a significant ambiguity, since we have come to suspect that "man" was really used to talk about men, rather than the whole of humanity. Some light can be shed on this by a brief consideration of the science of *woman*. Ornella Moscucci has argued that this idea underpinned the early vision of gynecology and that in the first half of the nineteenth century, some people aspired to a total knowledge of the female sex that was explicitly analogous to the goals of a science of man.[4] The search for such total knowledge reminds us of the importance of holistic approaches to human nature; it also explains why anthropology—the core of the science of man—is so important in scientific traditions that study sexual difference.[5] Two conclusions follow from the delineation of a new science of woman: first, that medical practices were seen as secondary to, indeed consequent upon, a more general theoretical knowledge of woman/women; second, that the ambiguity surrounding the concept "man" was recognized at that time. It was implicit in the gynecologists' claims both that women were profoundly different from men and that they had not been properly understood previously. The science of man neither paid them sufficient attention nor adequately conceptualized sexual difference. It was possible for nineteenth-century writers to see this because, as several modern scholars have pointed out, there was a growing scientific literature during the eighteenth century on the nature of woman.[6] Pierre Roussel's *Système Physique et Moral de la Femme* is often cited as a seminal text in this genre.[7] Roussel was a medical practitioner, interested in the same range of issues that also concerned the early gynecologists. Discussions of menstruation, childbirth, female diseases, and so on were occasions for reflections upon the social and moral position of women, their history, and the cross-cultural differences and similarities between them. Roussel contributed to a large body of writings by philosophers and natural philosophers, natural historians, conjectural historians, novelists, poets, and others. Clearly not all such writings could be seen as coming under the umbrella of the human sciences, but it is worth noting the range of authors who addressed such questions, and the existence of a continuum between writings that fully meet the criteria set out above and those that touched on similar questions but from a "nonscientific" viewpoint. The broad historical *context* of human science, where there was constant interchange between domains, no sense of the "apartness" of science, and continual interaction between theory and practice made such diversity possible.[8]

In relating human science to sex and gender, a wide range of endeavors is relevant. Medicine plays a special part here, because it, uniquely, could claim to root its knowledge about women in the anatomy and physiology of human beings and to have an area of practice that constantly generated new observations and findings. While not all claims to secure knowledge about gender were based on anatomy and physiology, these fields were central, and as a result, medical language was pervasive and practitioners could assert their professional and intellectual dominance. The empirical basis of knowledge about sex and gender is crucial, because it affects the role assigned to fields such as natural history and medicine on the one hand and "economics" and political theory on the other. These areas drew upon different kinds of evidence, despite deploying similar concepts and exploring similar preoccupations. Diverse fields of interest in the eighteenth century bore on the scientific understanding of sex and gender: in addition to those already mentioned, we can cite political arithmetic and political economy; geography, anthropology, and psychology (to use three anachronistic terms); and also physiognomy, legal theory, possibly theology, but certainly natural theology. There is also much relevant material in philosophical writings.

Having defined human science in a way that emphasizes systematizing accounts of human nature, a word needs to be said about sources. I have used writings that deliberately strove to give a coherent account of matters pertaining to sex and gender, even if these subjects were not central to the text in question. This has not restricted the genres represented, since, to take an outstanding example, Montesquieu's epistolary novel *Lettres persanes* (1721) aimed at such coherence even as it was simultaneously playful. The point certainly applies to the writings of Diderot, who, while he undermined settled positions on human nature, especially in the dialogues, nonetheless tackled them with seriousness and rigor—indeed his satire depended on this.[9] However, most of the works used here are treatises of some kind, which, furthermore, were largely written by men. This situation is an indication both of the current state of scholarship and of the gendering of genres in the eighteenth century. We are in the early stages of discovering eighteenth-century writings by women; to date most research has been done on fiction, poetry, diaries, and autobiographies.[10] Of these genres, fiction bears most centrally on the human sciences as defined here. Some attempts have been made to examine women scientists of the period, and these will doubtless continue to bear fruit, although few of the women whose work has been recovered so far were primarily concerned with the science of human nature.[11] At the level of widely disseminated treatises in medicine, natural history, and natural philosophy, the majority were written by men.

I should not like my concentration on male writers to be misunderstood. It does not imply a lack of interest in female authors.[12] It reflects a particular interest in why so many male writers privileged "woman" at this time. This did not occur only at an intellectual level; there was a cult of male writing about women that contained strong aesthetic and voyeuristic elements. A concentration on relatively well-known figures is inevitable at such an early stage in both the history of the human sciences, especially in relation to their concepts of sex and gender, and the history of women as nonfiction writers. For all these reasons it is appropriate to use an outstanding female intellectual, Mary Wollstonecraft, as an example. Although her writings have become extremely well known over the last two decades, they are rarely seen, as I believe they should be, in the context of the human sciences. I shall also consider an earlier anonymous pamphlet, "Woman Not Inferior to Man," 1739, which we can take to be by a female hand, and which addresses the issue of how sex differences should be conceptualized.

The concentration on a small number of thinkers makes it possible to appreciate better their conceptual strategies. The argument is that sexual difference is an abstract idea with a complex history. Its role in the human sciences of the Enlightenment is one strand of that history, which can only be written in terms of the detailed way ideas function: the manner in which specific abstractions were formed, sustained, and put to work in particular historical situations. By comparing related yet distinct abstract ideas, we get a better grip on sex and gender in Enlightenment human science. The phrase "sexual difference," like "social difference," is used to draw attention to the ways in which generalized rather than empirically derived categories are used to delineate groups. Current research on the social construction of race, class, and gender, and on the interplay between them, challenges claims that such distinctions are in nature, that they can be measured and used to make a whole range of judgments.[13] Abstract ideas, such as race and gender, are elements generated by the principles of ordering that a given society has available to it. This is, in effect, to use an anthropological perspective, and to suggest that the basic cultural building blocks—boundaries, categories, systems of kinship, taboos—make some, but not other, forms of social differentiation sayable and plausible.[14] Man/men and woman/women are best examined in the context of the child/children, groups defined by age, slaves, servants, rulers, racial distinctions, and concepts such as mind, reason, and the soul in order to gain a rich historical picture.

But to compare fully the sets of abstract ideas listed above, we cannot simply consider *writings* in isolation from social practices. Many political theorists of the period struggled with the relationship between men and women and the implications of this for the domestic sphere and for the nature of the state. They often did so by drawing on accounts of many countries and regions, by exploring the state of nature and its transformation into civil society. At the same time, in the law, there existed an amalgam of theory and practice about these very questions, so that the status of married women in common law as "femmes couverts" or the use of the charge of petty treason when women murdered their husbands gave tangible form to the concept of woman, both in relation to the domestic world and to the state.[15] The work of writers like Locke and Rousseau had a central bearing on sex and gender in the eighteenth-century human sciences. They attempted to think more or less systematically about gender and sex, to discern patterns, not only in their own but in other cultures, and thereby to generate and draw upon a body of data. But if we want to use such writings, and examine and tease apart the tangle of overlapping abstractions, we have to recognize that abstractions are felt as well as thought, that they are practiced as well as theorized. The point also applies to "psychology" and education, where theories of human growth and development are best understood in terms of associated educational practices.

Another pertinent example concerns the relationships between eighteenth-century studies of sexual "man" and the manner in which legal systems dealt with sexual transgressions. It is now well known that "the sexual life of savages" was of widespread interest in the period, and that this was closely connected with responses to European sexuality.[16] The study of sexual phenomena was certainly part of human science. The context of concern with deviant sexuality is quite central to the matter in hand. General debate about individual morality was widespread, and so indeed were philanthropic reactions to what were seen as moral breaches—prostitution, illegitimacy, venereal disease, and so on. The legal framework is central here, since in England, for example, male homosexuality was a capital offence and men were indeed hanged for it in the period.[17] The question of gender is brought into sharp relief here. The act under which prosecutions were made concerned a whole range of unnatural connections, including between human beings and animals. The act was not applied to women. This case reveals some crucial boundaries—between humans and animals, between men and women, between men and men—pertaining to sex and gender in the period, in both theory and practice.

The law and its applications are not self-evidently part of human science but are nonetheless relevant. First, law provides one important setting within which distinctions acquire their felt quality, where a society reworks its fundamental categories, albeit within fairly firm constraints. Second, law, as theorized and as practiced, aimed at a certain consistency, a systematic quality that makes it akin to the project of a human science. In the process, it relied on assumptions about human nature, which aspired to be more than the *opinions* of a select few and to be based upon a deeper understanding of humanity. Those who tried to theorize sexual behavior and human nature had both legal codifications and legal practice available to them as part of their mental armory.

"Gender" was not, however, an explicit part of that mental armory. The value of this term lies in its capacity to act as a modern analytical tool; it encapsulates our interest in the distinction between masculine and feminine, an interest shared by many in the eighteenth century but not named by them in this way. "Gender" alerts us to the complexities of sexual difference in diverse periods and places. For over ten years scholars have used gender to signal something that they consider is socially constructed; sometimes a contrast with sex is implied, where the latter is construed as "natural," pertaining to biology. This strategy is designed to effect certain political goals, principally to uncouple any potential link between claims about anatomy and physiology and those about the social, political, economic, and cultural capacities of women.[18] It may be that the sex/gender distinction has little relevance for the eighteenth century, although there certainly were attempts to differentiate between inherent and acquired characters. But the idea that there were two kinds of difference (gender and sex) between men and women was foreign to them. Yet this was a period so preoccupied with sexual anatomy, with reproduction, with erotic experiences, and with the nature of masculinity and femininity that we can usefully deploy the terms "sex" and "gender" in exploring those preoccupations.

At this point we need to consider, in general terms, the place of sex and gender in the kind of natural knowledge we are calling human science. This is not straightforward; our understanding of this area can only be advanced by recognizing the difficulties of tracing the history of sex and gender in the human sciences. Some of these have already been referred to; it is time to make them explicit. The absence of disciplinary boundaries of the kind that existed from the early nineteenth century onward is significant—it meant that in earlier times there were no major scientific fields that principally or explicitly focused on these areas. Furthermore, the metaphorical power of sex and gender is so great that it cannot be contained; in the eighteenth century these ideas were far from being restricted to areas where they were the ostensible subject matter. These areas were, indeed are, inherently hard to define; as highly charged, even scandalous, terrain, there was considerable collective anxiety, tension, and conflict, especially around their boundaries. Such boundaries cannot be understood in purely cognitive terms; they were closely bound up with a range of practices, especially social, moral, and legal ones, that were exceptionally controversial in the period: infanticide, marriage, prostitution, cross-dressing, and homosexuality are obvious examples.[19] Given the significance of sex and gender, it is not surprising to find that numerous groups claimed to speak authoritatively about them, creating a situation where overlapping discourses competed with one another. Inevitably, there were no secure resting points. Assumptions about social difference were being increasingly destabilized over the period, and the more extensive use of other cultures and races in debates within the human sciences made a significant contribution to this, as did political upheavals that called into question the capacity of human beings to conduct themselves in an orderly, reasonable manner. As a consequence it was hard to give sexual difference any fixed meaning.[20] The constant reliance on "nature" provided a semblance of stability, although in fact it was notoriously hard to pin down.

Scholars who see gender as a useful analytical category are concerned with the nature of dualisms, with the ways they can be seductive means of clarifying, simplifying, organizing, and managing complexity. They recognize that binary pairs are rarely symmetrical or equivalent. In the eighteenth century, talk of relations between the sexes tended to focus more on women than on men. Woman held a fascination that man did not. One interpretation is that this indicates (male) concern about (potential and/ or actual) sexual misdemeanors by women; the desire to control women makes them simultaneously fascinating and threatening. Sometimes this is the driving force behind what is said—concern about women's adultery and the consequent birth of illegitimate children is a classic example from this period. But another way of looking at gender asymmetries in the eighteenth century focuses on the kinds of abstractions involved. "Feminine" and "masculine" expressed distinct levels of generality.

When writers spoke generally about human nature, and especially about the soul and the intellectual capacities of "man," gender rarely entered the picture—there was no useful work that such a focus on the different kinds of humanity could do; it would have been an inappropriate specificity. Hence, relations between the sexes were invoked only in order to stress differences between male and female that served quite specific ideological purposes. But masculine and feminine were not accorded equivalent status; the male side being pulled toward the general, the universal, the female side to the particular. And since difference was required at that stage in the argument, emphasis was placed on women as the problematic, the contentious side, as a designated *branch* of humanity—the concept of "woman" carried the burden of difference. Furthermore, discussions of sex and gender within the human sciences were invariably linked with the family, itself a naturalized concept through which the social, political, and economic manifestations of sexual differences were mediated.[21] However skeptical some thinkers were becoming in the eighteenth century about the state/family analogy, or perhaps precisely because there was such skepticism, talk of the family usually concentrated on women and children. "The family" occupied a particular place in ways of thinking about collective life. Clearly a more specific concept than society or the state, it was more general than the individual or the citizen. Unlike the citizen, the family was directly connected with reproduction, both biological and social, and was thereby allied with the domestic—the domain of women in this mental universe. Certain familial issues were construed as "male"— ones that were connected with matters of property or lineage.

It is apparent from the kinds of topics that writers on the human sciences discuss in relation to women that there were gendered sets of social and moral questions—chastity, modesty, and marital fidelity, for example. They are gendered in that concepts were used primarily of one sex and not of the other, so that to use them was to remind readers of sexual difference. Thus the pair "male and female" was not composed of two equivalent terms—its constituent ideas were associated in the eighteenth-century mind with distinct levels of generality/abstraction, with distinct social-cum-political categories, and by extension with distinct practices and experiences. The double standard exemplifies the point.[22] Although not given this name in the eighteenth century, the phenomenon itself was clearly recognized. Legal theorists, for example, noted that the notion of *flagrante delicto* applied only to wives, who had no right to harm their husbands if they caught them in a compromising position.[23] The practice of the courts was rooted in concepts of male and female, even if these were not fully articulated as such. Similarly, the intimate link between concepts of gender and social practices may be found in the eighteenth-century concern with reputation, which manifested itself largely in an interest in women's sexual probity. At the level of practice it was visible in the workings of church courts. At the level of concepts it formed a central part of writings, especially fictional ones, that explored female desire. Defoe's *Roxana* (1724) is a case in point.[24] In an extraordinarily sustained, if ultimately unresolved, examination of the female mind, Defoe made Roxana's sexual reputation her main preoccupation, while relating her pursuit of sexual and worldly pleasures. He cast her fear of being thought a whore at the center of her existence, and probed the relations between desire and identity. This conceptual frame could never have been applied to a man. Such an inquiry into the nature of female subjectivity properly forms part of the human sciences.

We can put more flesh on these arguments by taking a series of specific texts, noting the places in the argument and the manner in which sexual difference is emphasized. I shall discuss briefly eight authors: Montesquieu, Hume, Kant, "Sophia," Wollstonecraft, Cabanis, Smith, and Malthus. Since this chapter contains no claims about chronological change, I shall not discuss their works in order of publication. Rather my interest is in certain key themes and in the forms of reasoning employed. These writers worked in different national, intellectual, and social contexts, although the ubiquity of a limited number of topics and motifs is striking. Montesquieu's *De l'esprit des lois* (1748) serves as a convenient starting point.[25] First, we must ask, where is gender in this text? Taking topics in the order in which they appear, the most obvious ones associated, in one way or another, with the differences between men and women are luxury and sumptuary laws (7/1); slavery and the family (16/2); marriage customs (16); modesty (16/12); marriage, family, and population (23). Although related issues arise in other contexts, they are nowhere else as prominent as in the cases cited. Questions like the nature of law, political principles, education, military issues, relations between the state and citizens, and so on did not require Montesquieu to register this form of social difference. A pattern emerges; concern with gender, which generally takes the form of discussions of women, was present when the family/household was at issue, especially when population—the distinctively feminine type of production—was discussed. If a particular level of social organization was associated with sexual difference, so a particular aspect of the economy was associated with women. Montesquieu linked women with consumption, and with *over*-consumption, as is implied by their association with sumptuary laws and luxury. The title of book 7 is revealing: *Conséquences des différents principes des trois gouvernements, par rapport aux lois somptuaires, au luxe et à la condition des femmes.*

The final chapter of book 7, "De l'administration des femmes" (chap. 17), could stand as an epitome of how gender appears in the human sciences of the Enlightenment. Montesquieu argued that it is not natural for women to run households, but it *is* permissible for them to govern an empire. He sustained this position in two ways. First, he employed a common metaphor of the period to claim that women's state of feebleness (*faiblesse*) is the reason for his assertion. This quality makes them tender and moderate rulers, which is a good thing. The link between the nature of women and the kind of power they can exercise is effected through word associations. Second, he cited other countries in support of his position—in a chapter of less than a page he mentions Egypt, the Indies, Africa, Muscovy, and England. These areas are invoked as if to merely mention their names sufficed.

Montesquieu is often celebrated as a pioneering environmentalist. Eighteenth-century beliefs about the capacity of the milieu—natural and social—to shape human beings were central to their concepts of gender. The family/household was itself understood as an environment, which determined the attributes of each generation, particularly with respect to their mental competence. Such competence included sexual behavior and moral propriety. Indeed, since naturalistic explanations of human variations were sought so enthusiastically in the period, it was perfectly logical to turn to the environment to understand sex and gender better. This accounts for two central features of eighteenth-century thinking about sexual difference: the language of environmental medicine and the use of comparative methods.

Commonplace medical assumptions were of fundamental importance in sustaining the idea that human beings—at the physical, mental, and moral levels—were highly variable, that such differences could be systematically understood, and that their surroundings had potent effects, and hence possessed explanatory power. In pointing to climate as a factor that affected humankind, Montesquieu drew upon long-standing medical commonplaces, and his arguments depended on the metaphorical associations of qualities like hot and cold. Such commonplaces included the importance of diet and the capacity of the nervous system to vary according to external conditions (i.e., sensibility). These medical traditions can be traced back to their classical sources, especially in Hippocrates and Galen. Scholars now agree that during the eighteenth century the concern with the systematic relations between internal (physiological) traits and external (environmental) factors took on fresh significance.[26]

The environmentalist interest in habit, born out of concern with "philosophical psychology," stimulated thinking about the mechanisms of the mind. It offered a vocabulary through which to express the links between external factors and internal traits, and by that token implied a naturalistic explanation of them. Environmental medicine analyzed what we think of as lifestyle. Although conceptually lifestyle was an aspect of the environment, it was nonetheless distinct from areas like climate, which appeared less problematic because less amenable to human control. All we can do, conceded Montesquieu, is legislate appropriately, taking the environment into account. When it comes to habits and lifestyle, the responsibility of individuals and groups becomes a serious issue. Furthermore, it was in the interests of medical practitioners to stress the reversible nature of the ills that allegedly resulted from an unhealthy lifestyle, while maintaining that the success of any attempts at reversal depended on patients themselves.[27]

These points help to establish the preoccupation of the period not only with the nature of differences between people, but also with how they could be explained according to the current canons—of logic, of evidence, of scientific theory. The whole tenor of Enlightenment thinking led to widespread interest in what was common to all human beings, and, by extension, to attempts to conceptualize differences between them—a fundamentally comparative project. At the same time, the relevant empirical base grew tremendously over the eighteenth century, and it would thus be tempting to suppose that accounts by travelers, systematic geographical exploration, and the growth of scholarship in history contributed, above all, *data* to the debates about human nature. I believe this was not true. Such sources were decisive, but not as data; these issues were not empirical ones at all. Montesquieu himself exemplified the point; on climate, he was remarkably unspecific. Climates for him were either hot, cold, or temperate—an unnuanced set of categories. This was not due to geographical ignorance, but to the level of abstraction at which his arguments were pitched, which did not require empirical detail. His aim was to establish clear, systematic connections between climate and human traits and social organizations. *De l'esprit des lois* set out to achieve certain ends, which had to do with the *political* arguments of the text.

Montesquieu needed to establish where and how legislators can and should intervene. In his project various kinds of human differences were invoked, precisely which one depending on the stage his argument had reached as well as on his broad ideological position. Clearly, the kinds of abstraction put to work depended on the intellectual project of the author. In Kant's *Critique of Pure Reason* (1781), for example, human difference plays a negligible role because the entire work revolves around a philosophical analysis of the qualities of the human mind. The point becomes abundantly clear in the two references to anthropology in the book; in the first it is designated as the study of "prejudices, their causes and remedies" and in the second it is equated with "simply observing" and with "a physiological investigation into the motive causes of [human] actions." In both cases Kant makes it clear these areas are *not* his concern; they are less abstract than his concerns.[28] As we have already noted, among those who worked within the human sciences, questions of human difference break in only sometimes; they pertain to some levels of generality but are deemed irrelevant to others.

Thus, eighteenth-century environmentalism depended upon the possibility of comparing individuals, groups, and societies in relation to a wide range of variables, from diet to political structures, from climate to religion. Comparative approaches, and areas like lifestyle medicine that supported them, were of fundamental significance in relation to sex and gender—gender is one of the most basic terms of comparison. Comparative methods occupied an especially prominent place in the eighteenth century, which saw, after all, the birth of comparative anatomy.[29] Although it would be a mistake to exaggerate the novelty of the comparative enterprise, there is something distinctive about comparative thinking in the eighteenth century, which perhaps consists in its centrality in a wide range of intellectual concerns—medicine, law, physiognomy, natural history, anthropology, social thinking, and so on. Comparative methods rested on three intellectual procedures. First, comparison between forms was an analytical device for the purposes of classification, that is, for identifying the distinguishing properties of each taxonomic unit, for differentiating customary or artificial characteristics from natural ones, varieties from species, and so on. This exercise could be carried out on virtually anything—plants, animals, languages, nations, faces, or pictures. Second, firm bases and clear criteria for comparison had to be established; sometimes this took the form of morphological traits or ideal types, or normative social structures—English democracy, American republicanism, the "nuclear" family. Third, series were elaborated into which forms were fitted, both to demonstrate more vividly their similarities and differences, and to generate a natural/ized hierarchy. These procedures were applied to sex and gender.

It was possible to compare relations between the sexes, or the nature of marriage, or female development at different times and places. In such cases historical and or geographical variations came to the fore, and social-cum-moral differences were highlighted, using matters pertaining to sex and gender as case studies. Male and female could be treated as the two central terms in the comparison. Eunuchs, cross-dressers, castrati, homosexuals, and so on were invoked to make the comparisons more rich. Abstract qualities were often the focus of male/female comparisons: strength, beauty, skills, intellectual capacities, and virtues.[30]

Descriptions and illustrations of sex and gender in various times and places tended to be passed from author to author, a textual form of Chinese whispers. Arranging abstract qualities in a series and establishing norms and ideals readily generated visual representations.[31] Although aesthetic considerations were certainly present in travelers' accounts and in historical writings, they were more prominent in analyses of gendered abstract qualities. This partly explains the extraordinary force of depictions of ideal male and female beauty in the work of physiognomists and comparative anatomists. These were based on elaborate sets of assumptions about the anatomy and physiology of sexual differences, and about the moral qualities latent in or associated with such differences. An excellent example is Cabanis's *Rapports du physique et du moral de l'homme*. In the fifth section of his influential work, on "the influence of sex on the nature of ideas and on moral feelings," Cabanis moved between the bone structure of women and their social position and responsibilities.[32] From our perspective this constitutes a confusion between descriptive and prescriptive statements. The more interesting point, however, is that representations of male and female had strong aesthetic dimensions, which are inseparable from the sense of rightness that was felt in relation to the images and examples writers on the human sciences deployed. Thus Hume's association with men and a male familial line with greatness and importance, and of women with smallness, operates at a number of levels, including the mobilization of common metaphors and aesthetic preferences. Images of this kind were pervasive—in the associations of women with luxury, with superstition, and with unreliable desires. These were not trivial associations; the human sciences had such metaphors and assumptions at their heart. In using them writers and artists could draw support and gain credibility not so much at an intellectual as at a felt level.

The writings of David Hume provide an exceptionally rich exemplification of these points. A number of attempts to analyze Hume's treatment of women address philosophical rather than historical issues. Nonetheless, on the basis of such work, we can see that some central issues arise in

Hume, found also in other writers, issues that constitute the most difficult and controversial areas raised by gender in the period. Among the most obvious is the claim that chastity is a distinctively female virtue, principally because of the need for men to have an absolute assurance that the children they acknowledge and support are indeed theirs—a theme to be found in Rousseau, too, and expressed by him with characteristic force.[33]

Hume possessed qualities that make him an ideal example of the "invention of human science." He was willing to embrace the idea of a science of man, to think naturalistically, to draw upon examples from his own society, to invest ideas like the natural and the artificial with fresh significance, and to seek pertinent examples in both history and geography. Hume's consideration of gender, sex, and family is not designated as such by the titles of books or chapters. It is claimed there are more than one hundred references to women in the *Treatise* and the *Enquiries*, yet in neither case has the standard edition included "women" in the index.[34] References to women appear in a variety of places; the casual quality of Hume's treatment of gender makes his remarks all the more revealing.

Hume's views can be analyzed in a number of different ways. For some feminist philosophers, the existence of a double standard, or of a profound compatibility between the nature and the content of Hume's reasoning on women, has been the main source of interest in his work, while others have been concerned quite simply with what they see as Hume's sexism.[35] For a historian these are not fruitful avenues. Another, more rewarding possibility is to look at Hume's language. A. Baier, for example, has argued that Hume's use of the language of kinship reveals a (hitherto unrecognized) unifying principle in his work.[36] She has drawn out the implications of this claim for a modern philosophical understanding of Hume. For a historian it is worthwhile to extend the study of Hume's language to general questions about common assumptions and usages of the period. It is true that Hume places considerable weight on notions like "relation," or "the association of ideas" (T 511), often in connection with "natural." Thus, when speaking of the ways in which property passes between generations, "natural" and "relation" refer to both kinship and our ideas of kinship (T 510–513). A further way of approaching Hume is to examine, as we did with Montesquieu, where in his arguments gender and related issues come up and what he says on the matter.

Explicit treatments of family, sex, and gender do not appear in the *Treatise* in book 1, *Of the Understanding*, but appear in books 2 and 3, which deal with the passions and morals respectively. In book 2, part 1, "Of pride and humility," Hume cites the antiquity of a family as a source of pride, especially where this can be traced through the male line. This is explicable for him by the fact that the mind is naturally drawn first to what is "great," "important and considerable," rather than to what is "small." Furthermore:

'Tis easy to see, that this property must strengthen the child's relation to the father, and weaken that to the mother. For as all relations are nothing but a propensity to pass from one idea to another, whatever strengthens the propensity strengthens the relation; and as we have a stronger propensity to pass from the idea of the children to that of the father, than from the same idea to that of the mother, we ought to regard the former relation as the closer and more considerable. (T 309)

Hume offers further support for his view in naming practices. Readers will be struck by the way in which Hume's argument treats thoughts and persons in the same terms.

Part 2, "Of Love and Hatred," contains three references to the family. In the first Hume explains that if we love or hate a person, we tend to extend this to that person's family, and again "natural relations," in both senses, are invoked (T 341). In the second he takes the love between parents and children, based on "the relation of blood," as "the strongest tie the mind is capable of" (T 352). For him consanguinity provides an unambiguous example of one end of the spectrum of love, and can thus be used as an unproblematic base for his arguments, presumably because it is rooted in both nature and our ideas of nature. The third reference, in the chapter devoted to "the amorous passion, or love betwixt the sexes" (T 394–396), discusses not so much the family, or even gender, but sex. It is worth considering this brief chapter in more detail.

Hume's intention was to analyze "amorous passion" as a compound passion. He resolved it into three components: "the pleasing sensation arising from beauty; the bodily appetite for generation; and a generous kindness or good-will" (T 394). Although he spoke of bodily appetite in terms of desire, it is significant that he characterized it by its association with "generation." Beauty is associated with sexual pleasure because it mediates between the refinement of kindness and the physicality of the sexual appetite. Naturally, Hume discussed this matter from an explicitly male position, as is clear when he says: "One, who is inflamed with lust, feels at least a momentary kindness towards the object of it, and at the same time fancies *her* more beautiful than ordinary" (T 395, my emphasis). Hume simultaneously undertook the abstract analysis of a feature common to all humanity, placed men at the center of it, associated women with male aesthetic pleasure, and linked sexuality and procreation.

The third book of the *Treatise*, *Of Morals*, contains five significant references to sex, gender, and the family. The first (T 486–487) considers the central role of sex and the family in the formation of society. The second and fourth ones pertain, again, to the passing of property between generations of men (T 510–513, and 559). The third examines the relationship between patriarchal and state authority (T 541), while the final one returns to the common concern about the modesty and chastity of women

(T 570–573). The whole thrust of the discussion was directed at defending different moral standards for women, standards appropriate to their character and position. Hume argued that these rested on the differing responsibilities toward children that fall to men and to women. In doing so he repeated the prevalent anxiety about the legitimacy of children, for which a woman's chastity stood as guarantee.[37] He continues:

> if we examine the structure of the human body, we shall find, that this security is very difficult to be attained on our part; and that since, in the copulation of the sexes, the principle of generation goes from the man to the woman, an error may easily take place on the side of the former, tho' it be utterly impossible with regard to the latter. From this trivial and anatomical observation is derived that vast difference betwixt the education and duties of the two sexes. (T 571)

The passage illustrates Hume's attempt to find a secure reference point for sexual differences in anatomy. At the same time, he clearly wanted to move on to other, less trivial, more philosophical matters, yet he apparently could not do so in this particular case without anatomy. When treating the same questions in a more open-ended manner in the Dialogue at the end of the *Enquiries concerning the Human Understanding,* Hume went into historical and geographical mode, with anecdotes and stories pertaining mostly to the family. These served to clarify distinctions between the natural and the artificial, and to explore different customs and different utilities (E 337), but they did not offer the kind of secure legitimation that references to the structure of the human body did.

An early, pre-Critical work by Kant can usefully serve as a further brief case study. An exceptionally good example of the themes of this essay may be found in Kant's *Observations on the Feeling of the Beautiful and Sublime,* written in 1763, and published the following year.[38] Kant addressed directly the nature of human nature, using two case studies to develop in greater detail his more general points; these concern "the Interrelations of the Two Sexes" and "National Characteristics." The structure of this short work is revealing. The first section established the contrast between the sublime and the beautiful: the sublime combines enjoyment with horror, it induces high feelings, it moves where the beautiful charms, it is night to the day of the beautiful, which Kant associated with joy and gaiety. Section 2, "Of the Attributes of the Beautiful and Sublime in Man in general," rooted the distinction between these two qualities in human behavior, virtues, attributes, even appearance—the sublime is dark, while the beautiful is fair. As if further embedding in the human frame were required, Kant then linked these two feelings with the four temperaments; he noted the harmony between the sublime and the melancholy frame of mind, and between the beautiful and the sanguine. The choleric temperament has a touch of the sublime in it, but only superficially—what Kant called a gloss of virtue. The phlegmatic, dismissed as the opposite of the sublime, possessed none of the finer sentiments. Thus before discussing relations between the sexes, Kant established the links between two abstract aesthetic categories and virtues, frames of mind and body types. That he associated the beautiful with women and the sublime with men was clearly overdetermined.

Section 3 began with women as the fair sex, and with the differences between men and women—"the charming distinction that nature has chosen to make between the two sorts of human being."[39] A list of the main attributes of women follows, all of them totally familiar to students of the eighteenth century: women are beautiful, elegant, decorated; they are associated with delicacy, pleasantries, trivialities, modesty, and sympathy. About men, little is said directly, other than to associate them with nobility. Kant extended his analysis to mental faculties; women do have understanding, but it is beautiful where men's is deep, that is, sublime. It followed that women were unsuited to dry (Kant's word) knowledge—diligent, fundamental, abstract, deep—and to learning that concerned fortresses and battles. There are, then, two kinds of knowledge (and ancillary virtues): that which pertains to sense and to moral feeling (of women) and that of reason and memory (men). The first can be understood in terms of the development of so-called adoptive virtues; the second, genuine, noble virtues. Kant's discussion included numerous other qualities commonly given to women (e.g., neatness, simplicity, innocence), culminating in his assertion that in marriage, the couple should become "a single moral person."[40] This formulation of matrimonial unity gave emphasis to a central theme of Kant's discussion—men and women have profoundly different natures, which are complementary to one another.

Throughout this section, an active nature is present—choosing, willing, hinting, asserting order, carrying out purposes. Hence it is *nature* that underwrites the differences between men and women, which rest on a marked asymmetry between the sexes. This is neatly revealed in the claim, "the man should become more perfect as a man, and the woman as a wife"—a statement that evokes Rousseau's *Emile* (1761), especially Book V (it is known that Kant had read *Emile*).[41] In the *Observations*, the distinctions between men and women are developed through metaphor. Kant can, as a result, both talk abstractly about male and female, as if he were basing this on the actual condition of men and women, and link a naturalistic understanding of the sexes to aesthetic categories, to morality, and to the temperaments. His understanding of human nature blends together description and prescription, aesthetics and physical attributes, morality and gender, national characteristics and qualities of mind. A generous view of nature permitted these maneuvers; it is a nature that acts as the stable point of unity as well as the source of extraordinary human diversity. Kant's project can properly be designated a part of human science; it is one in which naturalism, natural dualities, the metaphorical richness of nature, and the natural base of moral qualities come together to form a microcosm of the role of sex and gender in the human sciences of the Enlightenment.

Kant drew upon comfortable associations, on commonplaces of his time, in order to forge arguments about the sublime and the beautiful as gendered. So did writers who analyzed sex and gender in explicitly moral and social terms, while seeking to ground their views in nature's order. The challenge for those who wanted to understand gender differently was to find ways of breaking up comfortable commonplaces and of exposing the intellectual inadequacies of conventional arguments that rooted morality in naturalized sex differences. This was the strategy used by writers retrospectively designated "feminist."[42]

A particularly persuasive example is "Woman Not Inferior to Man," a pamphlet published some fifteen years before Kant's treatise.[43] In it "Sophia" went to the heart of debates about sex and gender in the eighteenth century. While not denying that females and males are different, she insisted that souls are not sexed. In the area that makes humanity special, gender is not a relevant category. She deduced from this that male views of women as profoundly inferior have no rational basis; their brains are identical, while other bodily differences pertain only to "the propagation of human nature."[44] At the same time, she also suggested that the bodily refinement of women conveys a certain superiority on them. The female body is physiologically superior to the male in its delicacy, which made it better able to carry out the operations of the soul. Furthermore, as persons, mothers deserved special respect, not contempt. The fact that men refused to acknowledge the importance of the office of mother was one instance among many of the unreasonableness of men. Although men claimed superiority in the matter of reason, in practice they were passionate and irrational, as the manner in which they maintained power over women revealed. "Sophia" both denied and affirmed gender differences in her argument that women had equal rights to public employments and esteem with men. She made one of the most eloquent cases in the period for women being allowed leadership positions in the army, law, science, medicine, and university teaching; having equal educational opportunities; and receiving esteem in their nurturing roles.

This pamphlet is a nice manifestation of the conceptual difficulties that gender posed. It sought to dispose of commonplaces like the frivolities and incapacities of women by exposing the inadequate and contradictory arguments that lay behind them. One way was to argue that women were essentially like men, except that having been denied opportunities, especially educational ones, they had been rendered inferior. If women were kept in their place by force, this was evidence of male irrationality. It was consequently impossible for men to sustain their claims to rational and moral superiority. Nonetheless, sexual difference had to be conceptualized in a convincing way for such arguments to be successful. "Sophia" claimed that in what really mattered—souls and brains—human beings were not sexed. Yet she insisted that female organs were more refined, and took this as an "indication of our souls being also in a state of greater delicacy."[45] This could be understood as a rhetorical device; the case for women is so strong that claims simply for equality appear less persuasive. But the issue of motherhood remained. For virtually every thinker of the period, male or female, it placed a unique responsibility upon women.[46] The resulting asymmetry between the sexes could not be resolved by locating sexual difference in the reproductive organs alone because the whole notion of motherhood was thoroughly permeated by moral assumptions. Those writing on behalf of women could not neglect its potential for asserting women's special claims, while those who allocated women a clear and limited domestic role needed to associate the moral high ground of motherhood with female physiology.

There is no better example of the resulting conceptual difficulties for "feminist" writers than Wollstonecraft's *Vindication of the Rights of Woman* (1792), a work fully in human science traditions.[47] As a Lockean, Wollstonecraft had a clear commitment to a particular model of the human mind and the manner in which it could be changed. From this grew her interest in education, in both theory and practice, which enabled her to present "woman" as a fabricated being, constructed by education and custom. It followed that any changes to the female condition, whether political, social, or economic, involved remaking women or making them anew. Changing customs and education were fundamental in improving not just the position of women, but of other groups who had been deformed by their social relations—soldiers, sailors, slaves. There is an occupational model here, which is closely related to the notion of lifestyle implicit in environmental medicine—the marks of a person's formation endure throughout that person's life. By treating womanhood as a specialized, full-time job, women's status as persons had been neglected. For Wollstonecraft, this became a political argument: existing relationships involving massive power inequalities require urgent change. Women are distortions from the ideal of the virtuous, active, responsible, rational citizen. At first sight this is a genderless figure, an impression that is reinforced by her theological argument that it would be impious to imagine God gave reason only to men.[48] Two key terms—reason and virtue—are apparently ungendered. In fact, Wollstonecraft's position is more complex. She had a special commitment to mothers, who shape the citizens of the future and so have a special kind of power and of virtue. She never fully explored the relationship between apparently ungendered concepts, like reason, and social roles, like motherhood, that are female but not simply by virtue of anatomy. This tension, similar to the one we discerned in "Sophia," hinges on the interpretation of "nature."

Despite Wollstonecraft's emphasis on the making of social roles, she privileged the domain of nature. She took it for granted that women should rear their own children, including breast-feeding them, and was dismissive of those who employed others to do so. There is no evidence that fathers come into the picture at all; she assumes that women are inherently better suited to bringing up children than men, and that they should receive enhanced respect as a result. Thus women are taken, unproblematically, as the socializers of the next generation, making them central to the political virtues of their society. At the same time, these key virtues are rooted in a universal, God-given reason, and sanctioned by a genderless human capacity to learn. In the *Vindication*, advice-book writers were castigated for treating women as innately inferior to men.[49] Although her argument—that traits that are in actuality inculcated are treated as inborn—found its mark, she did not achieve a reconceptualization of motherhood in naturalistic terms. Since medical writers could treat the body as prior (where Wollstonecraft treats the soul and reason as prior) and deduce social roles from it, theirs was the easier task. The abstract qualities of both sexes could appear to be rooted in, deduced from, the order of nature, although, as we saw with Kant, these qualities were contemporary commonplaces projected onto nature.

It might be assumed that medical thinkers were concerned with the reproductive organs. In fact, the general approach taken, especially in the late eighteenth century, was not to search for a seat of femininity but to understand the whole body as gendered. This orientation was nurtured by two aspects of eighteenth-century thought. First, the increasing interest in the nervous system discouraged the location of sex differences in specific organs. The nervous system united disparate body parts, enabling organisms to act as organized wholes. The nervous systems of men and women were seen as distinctive, with the result that the entire body, and its diseases, were seen as gendered. This trend is especially noticeable in the discussions of female illness. Hysteria, for example, was no longer about the uterus, but about the sensibility of women, where sensibility was a property of the nervous system, not a body part.[50] Second, as we have already noted, medical environmentalism was a dominant framework. This built on associationist models to make habit a key medical concept, and it was closely linked with a growing sympathy for Hippocratic approaches.[51] Thus both body and mind were thought of as being molded by constant interaction with their setting. These trends were powerfully expressed in the writings of the *idéologue* Cabanis. His *Rapports* are of particular importance because they constitute his most elaborate exploration of "the science of man."[52] This work is organized around the major variables that determine human characteristics—age, sex, temperament, illness, habit, and climate—and is designed to provide a systematic overview of "man."

Cabanis was not uninterested in the specifics of anatomy and physiology. He presented the differences between men and women in terms of their nervous and their glandular systems, both of which affect the entire body. Accordingly, he saw puberty as the decisive moment in sexual differentiation. Until then, boys and girls were similar; afterward they became strikingly different in every respect. Yet, there is, once again, a significant asymmetry at work. Femininity is much more all-engulfing than masculinity; it severely limits what a woman can do and be, while masculinity is not seen as producing curtailments. Cabanis united sex and gender, in our sense, when he considered women. A female body, mind, and social role were all one. Male tasks and lives are not similarly dependent on their special natural properties. This was part of a pattern, summed up by the phrase "the sex," which implies a unique association between women and sex as a form of human particularity. Abstract notions of sexual difference served to delineate the specificity of women, a specificity underwritten by nature.

I have suggested that women's specificity was inextricably linked to notions of female domestic roles. The family was central to the human sciences of the Enlightenment by virtue of its dual status as a natural entity and a fundamental social unit. It was an area where concepts and practice were closely linked, allowing writers to test out their ideas about sex and gender through examples from family life, in their own context and in relation to other times and places, including ideal ones. The family was also important because it was the level of social organization at which questions of sexual difference seemed most urgent. It was closely linked to other concepts, such as population, which were treated as subject to natural laws and hence to scientific analysis. Writings on political economy, where these themes came together, constitute our last case study.

In theorizing population in terms of natural laws, Thomas Malthus included in his *Essay on the Principle of Population* a general proposition about sexuality—namely, that the passion between the sexes was constant.[53] This suggested to him that people were naturally drawn to form unions, that any inhibitor of this process would cause pain, but that it was nonetheless essential to stop new families from forming unless they could be self-supporting. The family represented the basic economic and reproductive unit. The animating force behind his theories was the cost of poor relief. In attempting to bring together his general criticisms of the management of poverty and his ideas about the natural history of population, it was inevitable that he should enter into a discussion of sexuality and the family. Yet he placed most emphasis on population as an entity, because his conceptual strategies did not require a sustained discussion of the family as such—other analytical levels served him more effectively. Only when explaining the importance of marrying at the correct point in the life cycle, did the family, rather than population, come to the fore. Yet his whole book is informed not only by a particular understanding of sex as a natural force but also by assumptions about gender roles. As with Adam Smith, assumptions about gender were built into Malthus's mode of thought; these were not a primary focus of interest but simply part of his conceptual baggage. Both political economists assumed that males were the main breadwinners, not just because they commanded, as Smith correctly noted, higher wages but because a greater measure of civic responsibility was attributed to them. Malthus's trenchant remarks about "disgraceful poverty" were clearly directed at male workers, while in *The Wealth of Nations*, Smith associated women with luxury, and with a specific form of civic frivolity:

> Barrenness, so frequent among women of fashion, is very rare among those of inferior station. Luxury in the fair sex, while it inflames perhaps the passion for enjoyment, seems always to weaken, and frequently to destroy altogether, the powers of generation.[54]

The capacity of women to be good mothers was, as we have noted, a recurrent theme of the human sciences in this period. In Smith's formulation, two dimensions of humanity are clearly distinguished: passion and generative powers. He implied that these powers pertain to some inner bodily vitality. This is confirmed by a further distinction between the capacity to *bear* and the capacity to *rear* children, which is about differences of class, between the poor who can bear but not rear, the rich who often cannot bear, but if they can, rear them more successfully, and those "of better station" who care well for their children (which presumably includes middle-class people). In effect Smith was suggesting that "external" determinants of child health (incomes and the like) could be analytically separated from internal ones (barrenness, generative powers), although particular circumstances created links between them.

Smith's discussion of these matters in his chapter "The Wages of Labour" was assisted by the use of "facts" about infant mortality. "One-half the children born . . . die before the age of manhood," he said matter of factly.[55] The accuracy of his claims is not the issue. Such statements enabled him to make calculations about family life: how many children were needed in order to raise a given number to adulthood, how much children cost, how valuable they are to their parents and so on. For others the same claims about infant mortality were the jumping off point for discussions about the quality of motherhood, which were rooted in assumptions about femininity, lifestyle, and custom—all treated naturalistically. Political economists gave these arguments a distinctive cast by placing them in the context of natural economic laws:

> in civilised society it is only among the inferior ranks of people that the scantiness of subsistence can set limits to the further multiplication of the human species; and it can do so in no other way than by destroying a great part of the children which their fruitful marriages produce. . . . The liberal reward of labour . . . naturally tends to widen and extend those limits. If this demand [for labour] is continually increasing, the reward of labour must necessarily encourage . . . the marriage and multiplication of labourers. . . . If the reward should . . . be less than what was requisite for this purpose, the deficiency of hands would soon raise it; and if it should at any time be more, their excessive multiplication would soon lower it to this necessary rate. . . . It is in this manner that the demand for men, like that for any other commodity, necessarily regulates the production of men; quickens it when it goes too slowly, and stops it when it advances too fast. It is this demand which regulates and determines the state of propagation in all the different countries of the world.[56]

Smith's argument suggested that the analysis of human beings as commodities, subject to the laws of the market, is geographically universal yet socially restricted to "labourers." By treating children as products, it played down the agency of parents in making children, and it ignored the significant lag time between decreases in the supply of labor and the availability of children to increase it. And, if agency is denied to working people, it is readily given to the "scantiness of subsistence"—an economic abstraction with the power to destroy children.

Political economy developed abstract languages for talking about family, gender, and sexuality. They fitted into and drew upon other such languages, produced, for example, by medicine, philanthropy, and law. As a result, the human sciences had a range of registers to draw upon, which provided different kinds and levels of abstractions to suit a variety of intellectual and moral strategies. The particular forms that quantitative arguments took in the period is a case in point—rammed home by Smith in his repeated use of "multiplication" in relation to population. Other kinds of generalizations were also important. Take, for instance, geographical abstractions, which may sound like an absurd juxtaposition of terms, since for us "geography" evokes the particularity of place. But in the eighteenth century places/regions were used quite differently. For example, the passage by Smith quoted above continues, "in North America, in Europe, and in China" in order to cite three cases in which population grows at different rates—fast, slowly, and not at all, respectively.[57] In this case—and there are many others—regions are used as types. As types, they are generally defined, by invoking a few qualities, that sum up an area, as did Montesquieu's simple climatic categories, hot, cold, and temperate. His arguments did not demand further exactitude, but rather brief generalizing characterizations of whole zones in order to convince readers that laws and conditions do indeed correlate. In summing up areas in this way, their characteristic family forms and relations between the sexes were included.

Many writers compared relations between the sexes in different geographical areas in a search for the principal "natural" variables of the human condition. It enabled different marriage customs, or practices relating to children, to be treated as either the products of geographical variation, or as indicative of some underlying unity within human nature. In one sense it did not matter which, since either way sex and gender were understood naturalistically, as if they were illuminated by empirical research, although in fact it was a question of typologies. We can illuminate this by turning to one of the most influential treatments of population of the century. Montesquieu's novel the *Lettres persanes*, published anonymously in 1721, was a sustained attempt to think about gender and sexuality, using the contact between two vastly different cultures as a tool for bringing out their differences.[58] The epistolary format enabled him to evoke the complex social and psychological dynamics involved in relations between the sexes in various geographical areas and imaginary zones. This worked especially well in relation to the Persian harem, since Montesquieu could probe relations between *three* sexes (men, women, and eunuchs). As this was a study of power dynamics, he was able to explore the experience of women in remarkable depth, by examining the ways in which they exercised power in the seemingly unpromising situation of a harem—the antithesis of a European family. The style, format, and structure of the book allowed him both to portray individuals with fairly full characterizations, and to offer generalizations about the roles of men and women in different societies.

The work reveals how a number of themes were closely bound together. In the *Lettres persanes* he used a doubly comparative approach when he set both cultures and sexes next to one another. This enabled him to link gender, sex and sexuality, family, and population, and to examine power in relation to the sexes. As the other case studies already mentioned confirm, it was precisely the lack of equivalence between men and women in respect of power that led eighteenth-century commentators to struggle over the relations between the sexes and the kinds of power at issue. Despite being a satire, the novel contains the clear assumption that naturalistic explanations of cultural/sexual differences were most appropriate. The book rehearsed many of the key debates of the century. Yet there was hardly full consensus on these matters. If there is a certain repetitiveness both in the topics discussed and in the languages used of them, sex and gender were also topics to be fought over during the Enlightenment, although this is not always apparent. Much of the time sex and gender lurk in writings on human science, in metaphors, in discussions of other issues, in models of human nature and of thought processes.

CONCLUSION

I have examined the presence of sex and gender, not in areas of natural knowledge that might be expected to tackle them directly, such as the study of generation, but in fields that were more explicitly grappling with distinctively human qualities, in which these concepts played a complex and less obvious role. Nonetheless, fields that did deal with sex and gender directly, and that means medicine above all, were enormously influential on those pursuing the so-called human sciences. A medical or quasi-medical approach was often apparent, in references to anatomy or the temperaments for instance. It offered a vocabulary that was widely disseminated, easily available, and generally plausible for expressing differences between the sexes, which were, invariably, rooted in "nature." Medical practitioners formed a growing constituency that reserved the right to speak with authority on these matters. The burgeoning literature on woman in the second half of the eighteenth century was dominated by them, and it demonstrates the ways in which moves were made between empirical claims about women and generalizations about *woman* as a special case among human beings. It was wide-ranging in the subjects it considered—morals, desire, marriage, child rearing, population, work, and so on.

In referring here to writings on woman/women or to discussions of them in larger treatises, I am not making the mistake of confusing the categories women and gender. Rather I suggest that when they invoked female characteristics, writers were pointing up the differences between men and women, between male and female, masculine and feminine. Sometimes this was done directly, at others it was implied; to examine one side of the pair is, silently, to invoke the other. Writers on human nature turned to women either when they wanted to bring social differences to the fore or when they wanted to consider a particular form of social organization that was associated with women, the domestic domain, the family. This was because sex and gender represented a certain kind or level of generality that was a suitable vehicle for thinking about some issues, such as luxury, but not others, such as the soul.

The issues that matched well with sex and gender, conceptually speaking, can also be characterized in terms of their felt quality. They were dense with associations from everyday life, with customary modes of being. We cannot separate the history of such concepts from the practices that gave them meaning. This felt quality also accounts for the strong aesthetic dimension in writings on sex and gender, which partly derives from the drive to ground aesthetic distinctions in nature. Male and female were so intimately bound up with a sense of rightness, decorum, and propriety that they acquired aesthetic connotations and could be used in aesthetic discourse. A rather generous interpretation of "human science" has been used here, and I am conscious of the dangers of anachronism in using terms such as "gender" and "human science." It is important not to impose twentieth-century presuppositions on the past. This was not a society dominated by nature *versus* nurture, heredity *versus* environment, sex *versus* gender. Medical models, especially those that took seriously the impact of lifestyle and environment on human bodies, made such apparently clear-cut dichotomies implausible. Eighteenth-century savants were intensely conscious of the complexity of masculinity and femininity, and of the social, political, economic, and moral entailments of these concepts. They sought to bring this complexity within the domain of natural knowledge. Our job is to understand the enterprise in which they were engaged, and to appreciate the diverse modes—medical, moral, epistemological, geographical, and aesthetic—in which it operated.

ACKNOWLEDGMENTS

For their help, I would like to thank Roy Porter, Christopher Fox, and Roger Smith, and the members of the Historical Geography Seminar, Institute of Historical Research, London, and of the Department of History and Philosophy of Science, Cambridge. I owe a special debt to Catherine Crawford, both for her generous help with this essay, and for sharing her knowledge of eighteenth-century science and medicine with me over many years.

NOTES

1. D. Diderot, *Rameau's Nephew and D'Alembert's Dream* (Harmondsworth: Penguin Books, 1966), 33.

2. S. Tomaselli, "The Enlightenment Debate on Women," *History Workshop Journal*, no. 20 (1985): 101–124; L. Schiebinger, *The Mind Has No Sex? Women in the Origins of Modern Science* (Cambridge, Mass.: Harvard University Press, 1989); B. Duden, *The Woman beneath the Skin: A Doctor's Patients in Eighteenth-Century Germany* (Cambridge, Mass.: Harvard University Press, 1991); M. Benjamin, ed., *Science and Sensibility* (Oxford: Basil Blackwell Publisher, 1991); C. Gallagher and T. Laqueur, eds., *The Making of the Modern Body* (Berkeley, Los Angeles, London: University of California Press, 1987); T. Laqueur, *Making Sex: Body and Gender from the Greeks to Freud* (Cambridge, Mass.: Harvard University Press, 1990). An exemplary study of an earlier period is I. Maclean, *The Renaissance Notion of Woman* (Cambridge: Cambridge University Press, 1980).

3. P. Jones, ed., *The Science of Man in the Scottish Enlightenment* (Edinburgh:

Edinburgh University Press, 1989), especially chap. 2; G. Bryson, *Man and Society: The Scottish Inquiry of the Eighteenth Century* (1945; reprint, New York: Augustus M. Kelley, 1968); M. Staum, "Cabanis and the Science of Man," *Journal of the History of Behavioural Sciences* 10 (1974): 135–143, and "Medical Components of Cabanis's Science of Man," *Studies in History of Biology* 2 (1978): 1–31; G. Gusdorf, *La Conscience Révolutionnaire: Les Idéologues* (Paris: Payot, 1978); T. Hankins, *Science and the Enlightenment* (Cambridge: Cambridge University Press, 1985), chap. 6.

4. O. Moscucci, *The Science of Woman: Gynaecology and Gender in England, 1800–1929* (Cambridge: Cambridge University Press, 1990), especially chap. 1; see also S. Tomaselli, "Reflections on the History of the Science of Woman," *History of Science* 29 (1991): 185–205.

5. On eighteenth-century anthropology, see G. Stocking, *Race, Culture, and Evolution* (New York: Free Press, 1968), chap. 2; W. Jordan, *White over Black: American Attitudes toward the Negro, 1550–1812* (Baltimore: Penguin Books, 1969); M. Duchet, *Anthropologie et Histoire au Siècle des Lumières* (Paris: Maspéro, 1971); Gusdorf, *La Conscience,* section 2, chap. 4, and section 3, chap. 3; Moscucci, *Science of Woman,* makes the link between anthropology and the study of "woman," as does P. Hoffmann, *La Femme dans la Pensée des Lumières* (Paris: Ophrys, 1977), part 1, chap. 5; part 4, chap. 4; which also contains an extensive bibliography.

6. C. MacCormack and M. Strathern, eds., *Nature, Culture, and Gender* (Cambridge: Cambridge University Press, 1980), chaps. 2 and 3; M. Le Doeuff, "Pierre Roussel's Chiasmas: From Imaginary Knowledge to the Learned Imagination," *Ideology and Consciousness,* no. 9 (1981/2): 39–70; V. Jones, ed., *Women in the Eighteenth Century* (London: Routledge, 1990); Hoffman, *La Femme*; Yvonne Kniebiehler and Catherine Fouquet, *La Femme et les Médecins* (Paris: Hachette, 1983).

7. P. Roussel, *Système Physique et Moral de la Femme* (Paris, 1775, and many subsequent editions); MacCormack and Strathern, *Nature, Culture, and Gender,* chaps. 2 and 3; Le Doeuff, "Pierre Roussel's Chiasmas"; Hoffmann, *La Femme,* 141–152.

8. Recent scholarship on "science and literature" in the eighteenth century makes this point effectively; see, for example, L. Jordanova, ed., *Languages of Nature* (London: Free Association Books, 1986), especially part 1, although this approach can be problematic, as Tomaselli points out in "Studying Eighteenth Century Psychology," *History of Science* 29 (1991): 102–104; a similar impression of the cultural integration of natural knowledge and concepts of gender may be gained from the two outstanding anthologies prepared by Roger Lonsdale, *The New Oxford Book of Eighteenth Century Verse* (Oxford: Oxford University Press, 1984) and *Eighteenth-Century Women Poets: An Oxford Anthology* (Oxford: Oxford University Press, 1989).

9. Diderot, *Rameau's Nephew and D'Alembert's Dream*; the best short introduction to Diderot is P. France, *Diderot* (Oxford: Oxford University Press, 1983).

10. M. Mahl and H. Koon, eds., *The Female Spectator: English Women Writers before 1800* (Bloomington and London: Indiana University Press, 1977); L. Brown and F. Nussbaum, eds., *The New Eighteenth Century: Theory Politics English Literature* (New York and London: Methuen, 1987), especially chap. 5; F. Nussbaum, *The Autobiographical Subject* (Baltimore: Johns Hopkins University Press, 1989), especially chaps. 1, 2, 6–9; M. Poovey, *The Proper Lady and the Woman Writer* (Chicago: University of Chicago Press, 1984); J. Spencer, *The Rise of the Woman Novelist* (Oxford:

Basil Blackwell Publisher, 1986); V. Jones, *Women in the Eighteenth Century,* chaps. 4 and 5.

11. Schiebinger, *The Mind Has No Sex?*; P. Abir-Am and D. Outram, eds., *Uneasy Careers and Intimate Lives: Women in Science, 1789–1979* (New Brunswick, N.J., and London: Rutgers University Press, 1987).

12. See my forthcoming *Testaments of Women, 1720–1780* (Oxford: Oxford University Press).

13. N. Stepan, "Race and Gender: The Role of Analogy in Science," *Isis* 77 (1986): 261–277; L. Davidoff and C. Hall, *Family Fortunes: Men and Women of the English Middle Class* (London: Hutchinson, 1987); F. Nussbaum, ed., *The Politics of Difference,* special issue of *Eighteenth Century Studies,* vol. 23, no. 4 (1990); S. Mendus and J. Rendall, *Sexuality and Subordination* (London and New York: Routledge, 1989), especially chap. 3. Although some of these works are largely concerned with nineteenth-century issues, they indicate some of the general arguments about the social construction of social differences.

14. While historians often claim to be influenced by anthropology without being more specific, the work of Mary Douglas had a quite precise influence on historians of science, and it remains inspiring; her *Rules and Meanings* (Harmondsworth: Penguin Books, 1973) contains a succinct statement of her position; see also her *Purity and Danger* (1966; reprint, Harmondsworth: Penguin Books, 1970).

15. V. Jones's *Women in the Eighteenth Century* contains some contemporary accounts of women's legal status; see also J. Beattie, "The Criminality of Women in Eighteenth-Century England," *Journal of Social History* 8 (1975): 80–116; S. Okin, *Women in Western Political Thought* (London: Virago, 1980); J. Elshtain, *Public Man, Private Woman* (Oxford: Basil Blackwell Publisher, 1981); E. Kennedy and S. Mendus, eds., *Women in Western Political Philosophy* (Brighton: Harvester Press, 1987). A. Clark, *Women's Silence, Men's Violence* (London: Pandora, 1987), considers the specific case of rape.

16. G. Rousseau and R. Porter, eds., *Exoticism in the Enlightenment* (Manchester: Manchester University Press, 1990), especially 117–144; G. Rousseau and Roy Porter, eds., *Sexual Underworlds of the Enlightenment* (Manchester: Manchester University Press, 1987), especially chap. 10; C. Barash, "The Character of Difference: The Creole Woman as Cultural Mediator in Narratives about Jamaica," *Eighteenth-Century Studies* 23 (1990): 406–424.

17. A. Gilbert, "Buggery and the British Navy, 1700–1861," *Journal of Social History* 10 (1976/7): 72–98; A. Harvey, "Prosecutions for Sodomy in England at the Beginning of the Nineteenth Century," *Historical Journal* 21 (1978): 68–79; R. Trumbach, "London's Sodomites: Homosexual Behaviour and Western Culture in the Eighteenth Century," *Journal of Social History* 11 (1977): 1–33.

18. The journal *Gender and History,* published by Basil Blackwell, contains a wide range of approaches to gender by scholars from many different countries; see J. Scott, *Gender and the Politics of History* (New York: Columbia University Press, 1988), and her chapter in *New Perspectives on Historical Writing,* ed. P. Burke (Cambridge: Polity Press, 1991), which examines recent changes in women's history, including the interest in the concept of gender; see also Davidoff and Hall, *Family Fortunes,* especially part 3; L. Jordanova, *Sexual Visions: Images of Gender in Science and Medicine* (Hemel Hempstead: Harvester Wheatsheaf, 1989).

19. On infanticide, see O. Ulbricht, "Infanticide in Eighteenth-Century Germany," in *The German Underworld*, ed. R. Evans (London: Routledge, 1988), 108–140; M. Jackson, "New-Born Child Murder: A Study of Suspicion, Evidence, and Proof in Eighteenth-Century England," Ph.D. dissertation, University of Leeds, 1992; on marriage, see R. B. Outhwaite, ed., *Marriage and Society* (London: Europa, 1981), especially chaps. 6–8; J. F. Traer, *Marriage and the Family in Eighteenth-Century France* (Ithaca, N.Y.: Cornell University Press, 1980); S. Okin, "Patriarchy and Married Women's Property in England: Questions on Some Current Views," *Eighteenth Century Studies* 17 (1983/4): 121–138; on prostitution, see C. Jones, "Prostitution and the Ruling Class in Eighteenth-Century Montpellier," *History Workshop Journal*, no. 6 (1978): 7–28; D. Andrew, *Philanthropy and Police, London Charity in the Eighteenth Century* (Princeton, N.J.: Princeton University Press, 1990), chap. 4; D. A. Coward, "Eighteenth-Century Attitudes towards Prostitution," *Studies on Voltaire and the Eighteenth Century* 189 (1980): 363–399; on cross-dressing, see L. Friedli, "'Passing women'—A Study of Gender Boundaries in the Eighteenth Century," in *Sexual Underworlds*, ed. Rousseau and Porter, 234–260; R. Dekker and L. van de Pol, *The Tradition of Female Transvestism in Early Modern Europe* (London: Macmillan Publishers, 1989).

20. The preeminent example here is the French Revolution; see H. Mills, "Recasting the Pantheon? Women and the French Revolution," in *The French Revolution in Perspective*, ed. C. Jones, special issue of *Renaissance and Modern Studies* 33 (1989): 89–105, and H. Applewhite and D. Levy, *Women and Politics in the Age of the Democratic Revolution* (Ann Arbor: University of Michigan Press, 1990), which contains many contributions on gender.

21. L. Jordanova, "Naturalising the Family: Literature and the Bio-medical Sciences in the Late Eighteenth Century," in *Languages of Nature*, ed. Jordanova, 86–116; on concepts of family in the period, see J.-L. Flandrin, *Families in Former Times* (Cambridge: Cambridge University Press, 1979), introduction and chap. 1.

22. K. Thomas, "The Double Standard," *Journal of the History of Ideas* 20 (1959): 195–216.

23. J. Fournel, *Traité de l'Adultère Considéré dans l'Ordre Judiciaire* (Paris, 1778), e.g., xv–xvii.

24. D. Defoe, *Roxana the Fortunate Mistress* (Oxford: Oxford University Press, 1964). On women's "reputation," see, e.g., Anna Clark, "Whores and Gossips: Sexual Reputation in London, 1770–1825," in *Current Issues in Women's History*, ed. A. Angerman, G. Binnema, A. Keunen, V. Poels, and J. Zirkzee (London: Routledge, 1989), 231–248.

25. C. de S., Baron de Montesquieu, *De l'esprit des lois*, 2 vols. (Paris: Garnier, 1973). Subsequent references consist of the book number followed by the chapter number.

26. See Roy Porter's chapter in this volume.

27. The best introduction to medical practice in this period is R. Porter's *Disease, Medicine, and Society in England, 1550–1860* (London: Macmillan, 1987); unfortunately, nothing comparable exists for other countries.

28. I. Kant, *Critique of Pure Reason* (London: Macmillan Publishers, 1933), 17, 474.

29. W. Coleman, *Georges Cuvier Zoologist* (Cambridge, Mass.: Harvard University

Press, 1964), chap. 3; L. Schiebinger, "The Anatomy of Difference: Race and Sex in Eighteenth-Century Science," *Eighteenth Century Studies* 23 (1990): 387–405. This was part of a more general interest in comparative methodologies, especially in the nascent social sciences.

30. Such comparisons are to be found in many different kinds of eighteenth-century writings. They are treated more systematically in philosophical discourse, as we shall see in relation to Kant; in the visual arts, as I show in *Sexual Visions*, especially p. 60; in medicine, as is clear from examples already given; and in physiognomy, as is evident in J.-G. Lavater, *La Physiognomonie ou L'Art de Connaitre les Hommes* (Lausanne: Delphica, 1979), 190.

31. For example, Lavater, *Physiognomonie*, plates 12–14, 25, 49, 53, 118–119. The last two plates contain the well-known example that goes, in numbered sequence, from a frog to a classical *male*, showing the head in profile. See also G. Tytler, *Physiognomy in the European Novel* (Princeton, N.J.: Princeton University Press, 1982), and M. Cowling, *The Artist as Anthropologist* (Cambridge: Cambridge University Press, 1989), on the dissemination of these ideas.

32. P. J. G. Cabanis, *Oeuvres Philosophiques*, 2 vols. (Paris: Presses Universitaires de France, 1956), 1:105–631, which uses the 1805 edition of the *Rapports*: these were originally read to the Institut National des Sciences et Arts in years IV and V of the Revolutionary calendar. The fifth *Rapport* concerned sex, pp. 272–315; the points about bones, feminine roles, and women's soft roundness are made on p. 275.

33. On Hume, see L. Clark and L. Lange, eds., *The Sexism of Social and Political Theory* (Toronto: University of Toronto Press, 1979), 53–73; A. Baier, "Good Men's Women: Hume on Chastity and Trust," *Hume Studies* 5 (1979): 1–19; idem, "Helping Hume to 'Compleat the Union,'" *Philosophy and Phenomenological Research* 41 (1980): 167–186; C. Battersby, "An Enquiry concerning the Humean Woman," *Philosophy* 56 (1981): 303–312. On Rousseau, see Okin, *Women*, part 3; Elshtain, *Public Man*, 148–170; J. Schwartz, *The Sexual Politics of Jean-Jacques Rousseau* (Chicago: University of Chicago Press, 1984).

34. Clark and Lange, *Sexism*, 60. The standard editions are both edited by L. Selby-Bigge: *A Treatise of Human Nature* (Oxford: Oxford University Press, 1888) and *Enquiries Concerning the Human Understanding and Concerning the Principles of Morals* (Oxford: Oxford University Press, 1902).

35. E.g., Clark and Lange, *Sexism*.

36. Baier, "Helping Hume," especially p. 170: "[T]he concept of the natural family is the root concept dominating all Hume's thought, generating the explanatory principles he appeals to." Subsequent references to Hume's works are identified by *T* for *Treatise*, and *E* for *Enquiries*, together with page numbers from the editions cited in note 34.

37. One of most powerful explorations of this theme may be found in D. Diderot, *The Nun* (Harmondsworth: Penguin Books, 1974); it was also present in Rousseau's writings; see note 33 above.

38. I. Kant, *Observations on the Feeling of the Beautiful and Sublime* (Berkeley and Los Angeles, University of California Press, 1960). Susan Mendus discusses Kant's view on women as citizens in "Kant: 'An Honest but Narrow-Minded Bourgeois'?" in *Women in Western Political Philosophy*, ed. E. Kennedy and S. Mendus (Brighton: Wheatsheaf, 1987), 21–43. It would be instructive to compare Kant's work with

Burke's *A Philosophical Enquiry into the Origin of Our Ideas of the Sublime and Beautiful* (1757), with respect to gendered aesthetic categories.

39. Kant, *Observations*, 77.

40. Ibid., 95.

41. Ibid., 7, 11. J.-J. Rousseau, *Emile* (1762; reprint, London: Dent, 1974).

42. The question of the appropriateness of using the term *feminism* of the eighteenth century remains, to my mind, unresolved. This hinges on the precise manner in which the term is defined. See, for example, K. Rogers, *Feminism in Eighteenth-Century England* (Brighton: Harvester Press, 1982); A. Browne, *The Eighteenth-Century Feminist Mind* (Brighton: Harvester Press, 1987); V. Jones, *Women,* chap. 5; Tomaselli, "Reflections," 189ff.

43. "Sophia," *Woman Not Inferior to Man* (1739; reprint, London: Brentham Press, 1975).

44. Ibid., 23.

45. Ibid., 61.

46. C. Duncan, "Happy Mothers and Other New Ideas in French Art," *Art Bulletin* 60 (1973): 570–584; R. Perry, "Colonizing the Breast: Sexuality and Maternity in Eighteenth-Century England," *Journal of the History of Sexuality* 2 (1991): 204–234; F. Nussbaum, "'Savage' Mothers: Narratives of Maternity in the Mid–Eighteenth Century," *Cultural Critique* 20 (1992): 123–151.

47. M. Wollstonecraft, *Vindication of the Rights of Woman* (1792; reprint, Harmondsworth: Penguin Books, 1975).

48. Ibid., 93–94.

49. Ibid., chaps. 2–5. Many advice books appealed to nature as the authority for their claims about gendered responsibilities; their popularity meant that these ideas were widely disseminated.

50. The idea that mental illnesses in particular are gendered is now commonplace. The pioneering work on hysteria is I. Veith's *Hysteria: The History of a Disease* (Chicago: Chicago University Press, 1965); see also E. Showalter, *The Female Malady* (London: Virago, 1987), introduction. I discuss gender and sensibility in *Sexual Visions*, 27–28, 58–60.

51. F. Sargent, *Hippocratic Heritage* (Oxford: Pergamon Press, 1982), parts 3 and 4.

52. Staum, "Cabanis"; idem, "Medical Components."

53. T. Malthus, *An Essay on the Principle of Population* (1798; reprint, Harmondsworth: Penguin Books, 1970). A convenient introduction to Malthus is D. Winch, *Malthus* (Oxford: Oxford University Press, 1987).

54. A. Smith, *The Wealth of Nations* (1776; reprint, Harmondsworth: Penguin Books, 1970), 182. On Smith, see also J. Rendall, "Virtue and Commerce: Women in the Making of Adam Smith's Political Economy," in *Women in Western Political Philosophy*, ed. Kennedy and Mendus, 44–77.

55. Smith, *Wealth*, 171. Many commentators used infant mortality as an index of social trends: G. Rosen, "The Slaughter of the Innocents: Aspects of Child Health in the Eighteenth-Century City," *Studies in Eighteenth-Century Culture* 5 (1976): 293–316; J. Taylor, "Philanthropy and Empire: Jonas Hanway and the Infant Poor of London," *Eighteenth-Century Studies* 12 (1979): 285–305.

56. Smith, *Wealth,* 182–183.

57. Ibid., 183.

58. C. de S., Baron de Montesquieu, *Persian Letters* (1721; reprint, Harmondsworth: Penguin Books, 1973). Hankins, in *Science,* sees the novel as reformist, and an exposition of comparative method, pp. 8, 160, 162. See also S. Pucci, "The Discrete Charms of the Exotic: Fictions of the Harem in Eighteenth-Century France," in *Exoticism,* ed. Rousseau and Porter, 145–176.

SEVEN

Remaking the Science of Mind

Psychology as Natural Science

Gary Hatfield

Let us agree that "psychology" may be defined as the science of the mind or of mental phenomena, and that the subject matter of this science includes sense perception, imagination, memory, understanding or reasoning, feeling, and will.[1] If we then interpret the term "natural science" (or "natural philosophy") as it was understood in the early modern period, psychology considered as a natural science already had a long history as the eighteenth century began. The prescribed domain of subject matter was investigated by Aristotle under the name "logon peri tes psyches," of which it formed a proper part. This Aristotelian discipline was widely studied and taught in the early modern period under the title of "de anima," or, with some frequency, "psychologia."[2] Aristotelian textbooks of philosophy placed the study of the soul, including the rational soul and intellect, under the rubric of physics or natural philosophy, together with the study of basic physical principles, body in general, and the heavens.[3] Although the "new philosophers" of the seventeenth century uniformly rejected (in their various ways) the Aristotelian theory of the soul as the substantial form of the body,[4] they did not always deviate from the Aristotelian conception of physics as the science of nature in general, including the human mind. As the eighteenth century opened, then, it was an academic commonplace that the science of the mind or soul belongs to physics or the science of nature.

Eighteenth-century writers made many proposals for changing or newly founding the study of the human mind. A few contended that the study of the mind could not be made sufficiently rigorous to rank as a science.[5] The most famous was Immanuel Kant, though he nonetheless put empirical psychology under the rubric of physics (*physiologia*) and remained committed to the applicability of the law of cause to all psychological phenomena.[6] But many authors, British, French, Swiss, and especially German, proposed and sought to practice an "experimental"—that is, an "empirical" and "observational"—"science of the mind," a scientific psychology. Quantitative study, though rare, was not entirely absent, and there was a large body of systematic theorizing based on appeals to immediate experience and to observations of ordinary behavior. This activity was surveyed by F. A. Carus in his *Geschichte der Psychologie* of 1808, in which he discussed more than 125 eighteenth-century authors, mostly German, but also British, French, Swiss, Italian, Spanish, and Swedish, who wrote psychological works of some type, the majority placing psychology under the rubric of natural science.[7] Max Dessoir, writing a century later in his history of modern German psychology, maintained that "in the eighteenth century psychology assumed the same position as natural science in the seventeenth century and epistemology in the nineteenth," that is, the position as the central "philosophical" discipline.[8] The psychologies of the eighteenth century retained vitality, especially in Britain and Germany, into the second half of the nineteenth century, when a "new psychology" was proclaimed.

This description of psychology in the seventeenth and eighteenth centuries contradicts received historiography. Recent general histories of psychology, written by psychologists, agree that natural scientific psychology arose only in the second half of the nineteenth century.[9] Other historians, taking their cue from this historiography, have sought to explain why psychology did not arise in the previous centuries.[10] Only a few recent studies treat the earlier calls for a "natural scientific" psychology as anything but empty rhetoric.[11] And I have found no recent author who acknowledges that psychology was considered a natural science as the eighteenth century opened, that it had been so considered in Europe for several centuries, and that offshoots of the tradition in which it was so considered remained vital, even among figures deemed important in the standard historiography, into the second half of the nineteenth century.

The contradiction between my description of eighteenth-century psychology and the traditional historiography arises partly from differing understandings of the concepts *psychology* and *natural science*. In the past half-century, since the writings of E. G. Boring, there has been a decided tendency to equate "natural scientific psychology" with "quantitative, experimental psychology," and to contrast the "scientific" character of this psychology with the "metaphysical" character of its earlier namesake.[12] This tendency is not surprising: the growth of psychology as a scientific discipline has been built on its claim to have applied quantitative experimental rigor to subject matters about which philosophers and metaphysicians only talked and speculated. If one equates modern science with quantitative science, then there seemingly was no scientific psychology prior to the well-known uses of quantitative experimental techniques after 1850. If one attempts to confine modern science to its ostensibly nonmetaphysical moments, then patently metaphysical theorists and experimentalists must be excluded, or their work must be "sanitized" of the offending content. These two constraints on legitimacy conjointly explain why the great body of eighteenth-century literature claiming to found a natural scientific psychology has been ignored by historians of psychology, despite the historical continuity between the eighteenth and nineteenth centuries in the faculty tradition in Germany, and in the associationist traditions in both Germany and Britain.

The equation of natural science with antimetaphysical, quantitative experimentation is problematic on two counts. As an approach to history, it partakes of the worst failings of "presentism" or "Whig" history: it ignores the self-understanding of earlier figures who considered themselves practitioners of natural science, and it redescribes their cognitive activity and intellectual products from the standpoint of the presently ruling party, in this case, the community of experimental psychologists and their historians and apologists. Philosophically, it makes a crude positivist assumption that all progress in science is progress in the quantitative description of natural phenomena. This philosophical position should be resisted: not all natural scientific achievements are fundamentally quantitative, including achievements in two sciences that are closely related to psychology, namely, physiology and biology (consider the discovery of neurons, or the development of the theory of evolution). Moreover, in the early history of physics an important role was played by conceptual innovation as opposed to quantitative prediction or modeling, as exemplified in Descartes's contribution to the development of the concept of a unified celestial and terrestrial physics, (metaphysically) grounded on a small set of basic concepts, laws, and patterns of explanation.[13] One should not rule out the possibility that in psychology, too, important conceptual work preceded quantitative experimentation. Moreover, we may well find that although quantitative, experimental psychology became widespread under that name only in the second half of the nineteenth century, a continuous tradition of quantitative observation in sensory physiology and psychology stands behind that development.

A CONTEXTUALIST APPROACH TO THE ORIGIN OF "NATURAL SCIENTIFIC" PSYCHOLOGY

My approach to the historical question of whether there was an eighteenth-century scientific psychology[14] is to begin with the concepts of *psychology* and *natural science* as they were understood in that century. During that time, psychology was the science of mind or soul, or of mental phenomena; as such, it was known under many names, deriving from "psyche," "anima," "soul," "mind," and their cognates.[15] Mind and soul were often, but not always, equated. The mind or soul was considered by many to be a natural being, a thing in nature. "Science" was applied to any systematic body of thought, and need not have connoted an empirical basis. "Natural science" was equated with "physics," in the etymological sense of that term; it was the science of nature.[16] In the seventeenth and throughout much of the eighteenth centuries this science included the whole of nature, comprising a subject matter that we would now range under the headings of physics, physical astronomy, chemistry, biology, physiology, and psychology. It might or might not have been ascribed metaphysical foundations by its practitioners.

Given these understandings of the terms and the areas of study they denote, psychology was considered by a great many eighteenth-century authors to be a science. This was so whether psychology was treated as a science of mental phenomena or of mental substance. Many considered it to be a natural science based on experience, including those who considered themselves to be studying an immaterial substance. A minority of the latter group followed Christian Wolff in placing psychology under the rubric of metaphysics rather than physics. This fact, however, requires careful interpretation, for Wolff also placed cosmology (general physics, including planetary astronomy and the laws of motion) under metaphysics, and he allowed that metaphysical principles could and should be established empirically.[17] Thus, if one takes eighteenth-century conceptions of psychology seriously across the board, as I intend to do, one is committed to allowing immaterial substances as a (putative) object of empirical study.

This last observation, even cushioned as it is by the surrounding contextualist historical methodology, is likely to shock modern sensibilities. This shock is another manifestation of our use of present standards (and mythologies) to judge past materials. Immaterial substances are not in the list of likely theoretical posits in current psychology and physiology. One way of interpreting this fact is to think that such posits were part of a religious worldview that was overcome with the Enlightenment rejection of superstition and authority.[18] "Reason," so the story often goes, has shown us that dualism and other mind-positing ontologies are empty or incoherent.

This way of understanding the Enlightenment and the dictates of reason is itself unreflective and simplistic. It is true that many an Enlightenment *philosophe* is justly portrayed as rejecting God and the soul on rational grounds, in opposition to tradition and authority. But one should not leap to the converse conclusion, for it is not true that all those who posited immaterial substances were blind followers of tradition and authority. Indeed, a chief characteristic of many who were metaphysical realists about the soul was their appeal to reason or intellect in establishing their ontologies: Descartes is the most notorious example. In any event, if one believes that immaterial entities exist and that some of them inhabit human bodies, it makes good sense to seek to determine the powers and capacities of such substances empirically, by studying the manifestation of the mind in the behavior of others and in one's own experience of mental phenomena. From this point of view, taking an empirical approach to immaterial substances is an extremely rational undertaking. How else is one to determine their powers?[19]

My thesis in this chapter is that psychology as a natural science was not *invented* during the eighteenth century, but *remade*. As the century opened, the science of the mind included several dimensions: charting the "faculties"—the capacities and powers—of mind was foremost. Associated with this task were metaphysical questions about the ontology of the mind and its faculties, and about their relation to body and to specific bodily organs, especially the brain. These questions were posed within various metaphysical frameworks; the three most widely discussed were the Aristotelian, Cartesian, and Leibnizian. As the century proceeded, new conceptions of psychology were proposed or implicitly adopted. The Aristotelian ontology of form and matter faded; most psychological authors adopted some version of mind-matter dualism. But the faculty-based approach continued to dominate the most prevalent form of dualistic psychology, "Ehrfahrungsseelenlehre," or the empirical doctrine of the soul or mind. Ontological questions were bracketed in order to concentrate on study of mental faculties through their empirical manifestations in mental phenomena and external behavior. This approach arose prior to midcentury in Britain, Switzerland, France, and Germany. It was pursued most extensively in the latter, where there were numerous calls for an autonomous empirical psychology. Psychological theorizing was only rarely pursued as part of an attempt to cast doubt on (or to secure) the existence of immaterial souls or their connection with things divine.[20]

An alternative to faculty psychology began to be widely discussed in the middle of the eighteenth century: the associationist theory of mind. Hume, David Hartley, and others attempted to explain many or all phenomena of mind by appeal to laws of association.[21] The organization of their discussions largely followed the faculty-based division of psychological phenomena into sense perception, imagination, memory, and will, but a new explanatory schema was applied to these phenomena, one that promised explanatory unification under a few basic laws. Associationists reduced the powers of the mind to one, the ability to receive impressions, and they sought to explain the interactions among these impressions by appeal to the laws of association (which often numbered three). At first pursued most vigorously in Britain and France, with the translation of associationist works into German this approach came to be acknowledged in German psychology and found several German adherents. A variant of the associationist approach found a vigorous German proponent just after the turn of the century in a quantitative statement by J. F. Herbart.[22]

In support of my thesis I first describe the state of psychology as the eighteenth century opened, and then chart the development of various new or modified natural scientific conceptions of or approaches to psychology and its subject matter.

PSYCHOLOGY CIRCA 1700

The science of the soul in its *De anima*–inspired form was discussed in four literatures in the seventeenth century: it constituted a considerable chunk of the typical seventeenth-century university textbook in Aristotelian physics, occupying from a fourth to a third of the total number of pages;[23] it was the subject of numerous commentaries on Aristotle's *De anima*;[24] it was found in separate treatises labeled "psychologia," which might or might not be closely tied to an exposition of Aristotle's *De anima*;[25] and it constituted one part of works on "human nature" or "anthropology" intended for the natural philosophy curriculum, which part was sometimes labeled "psychologia," by contrast with anatomy or "somatotomia."[26] "Soul" or "anima" was, in the Aristotelian tradition, understood quite broadly, to include the principles of growth and development, or the "substantial forms," of both plants and animals, including the human animal. The Aristotelian physics textbook began with a discussion of general physical principles, such as the four causes, and the general properties of bodies, including their constitution from form and matter. It then divided all bodies into "specific kinds": first, into celestial and terrestrial; terrestrial into simple (namely, the four elements) and mixed; mixed into inanimate and animate. Animate beings were then divided according to the type of soul, which was denominated by its highest power. Thus, plants have only a vegetative soul, while nonhuman animals have sensitive souls (also possessed of vegetative powers), and human animals have rational or intellective souls (also possessed of sensitive and vegetative powers).

As is apparent, the Aristotelian concept of soul did not entail consciousness or rationality; at its most general, it required only life. For this reason, the seventeenth-century Aristotelian discipline named "de anima" cannot strictly be equated with the "science of mind," and hence with "psychology" as defined herein. But the science of the phenomena that we now denominate as "mental" dominated this discipline. In standard textbooks and commentaries, the vegetative soul received comparatively brief coverage; much greater space was given to the sensitive and rational souls.[27] More importantly, the activities of the sensitive and rational souls were grouped together under the denomination "cognitive," and the sensitive and intellectual faculties were seen as cooperating in the process of cognition. Indicative of their close relation, their modes of operation were often compared and contrasted.[28] So although the Aristotelian discipline of the soul is broader than the science of the mind, effectively it contained the study of the cognitive faculties as a subdiscipline.

The treatment of the sensitive and rational souls, exclusive of certain general (and significant) ontological questions, was organized so that the reader followed the chain of cognition according to the famous Aristotelian dictum "nothing in the intellect that was not first in the senses." Under the rubric of the sensitive soul, the five external senses were discussed first and at greatest length, including the transmission of color via light, its reception in the sense organ and the subsequent transmission along the optic nerve, and the discriminative acts of the sensitive power. Then came discussion of the internal senses, including the "common sense," imagination, memory, and the estimative power (the latter explained the undeniable, though limited, abilities of nonhuman animals to learn and to anticipate), followed by discussions of appetite and the motive power (which controls locomotion).[29] Under the rubric of the rational soul, considerable discussion often was devoted to problems about the spirituality and immortality of the soul; other questions concerned the production of the rational soul at the time of conception. Especially in the commentaries, the role of the intellectual faculty in cognition was analyzed extensively, focusing on its power to extract intelligible species (common natures, universals) from phantasms present in the internal senses. The power of abstraction was attributed to the "agent intellect," which, together with the phantasm, produces an intelligible species that is received in the "patient intellect," completing the act of intellection.[30]

All of these discussions were considered to pertain to the physics or natural science of the soul, with the exception that some authors assigned to metaphysics discussion of the spirituality and immortality of the human soul.[31] Accordingly, most authors contended that the study of the soul could be approached through "natural human reason" alone, without appeal to scriptural authority or divine inspiration. The subject matter belongs in "natural science" on the simple grounds that it pertains to "natural" things, or things possessed of natures, that is, intrinsic principles of motion or change. The class of "natures" was somewhat wider than we now include within the proper scope of the terms "natural" and "physical," because it included the rational soul. At the same time, throughout the eighteenth century many authors included the soul, conceived as an immaterial substance distinct from the body, to be a thing in nature.

We would now classify the material covered in Aristotelian psychology under several headings, including physiology, psychology, metaphysics, and epistemology. The discussion of the external senses included the material characteristics of sensory qualities in bodies, the transmission of qualities to the sense organs, the characteristics of the sense organs and the physics and physiology of the reception of transmitted qualities, nervous transmission to the brain, and the experience and discrimination of the quality by the mind or soul. The discussions of the internal senses included what we would call the physiology and psychology of memory, imagination, feeling, appetite; many would today consider these discussions as properly "naturalistic." The theory of the rational soul seems least properly naturalistic from our perspective. Within the Aristotelian tradition, there had been a dispute over whether intellection is a natural function of the human soul or derives from a higher intelligence. The majority opinion, however, included intellection among the natural, if immaterial, powers of the human soul, and hence as proper to the subject matter of the part of physics that treats of the human animal.[32] In sum, although only a portion of the material found in the *De anima* discussions would now be considered proper to the natural science of psychology, in Aristotelian terms these discussions did constitute a natural science of soul, including the cognitive powers of the soul.

Although the Aristotelian physics continued to be taught well into the eighteenth century (especially in France), it was being displaced. The force for this displacement came first from the "mechanical philosophy," championed by Hobbes and Descartes (among others). Although in general the advocates of the new mechanical philosophy understood the scope of physics along Aristotelian lines, to encompass all of nature, they differed among themselves on where to place mental phenomena or mental substance. Their differing ontologies partly explain their divergent attitudes toward psychology: the materialist Hobbes unproblematically placed the phenomena of mind under the rubric of physics, while substance dualists who distinguished mental from bodily substance faced a decision about where to put mind in the system of sciences. Ontology was not determining: some substance dualists placed mind under physics, some assigned it to metaphysics, and some baptized a new science of mind, coordinate with but distinct from physics.

In his *Elements of Philosophy* (1656), Hobbes forthrightly placed the treatment of "Sense and Animall Motion" in part 4, "Physiques, or the *Phaenomena* of Nature."[33] On the surface, this placement of the text was unremarkable; it departed not in the least from Aristotelian practice. But given the content of Hobbes's discussion, it was a radical departure. In this chapter he discussed the phenomena of sense and imagination, the faculties that Aristotelians (and Cartesians) held to be shared by humans and beasts. He departed from the Aristotelians in contending that these phenomena should be equated with material motions in the bodies of animals and humans.[34] Hobbes's thorough break with both Aristotelian and

Cartesian theory becomes apparent when we recall that in his *Leviathan* of 1651 he had reduced understanding or intellect to imagination: "The Imagination that is raysed in man (or any other creature indued with the faculty of imagining) by words, or other voluntary signes, is that we generally call *Understanding*; and is common to Man and Beast."[35] The only major materialist in the seventeenth century, Hobbes took the radical step of bringing the science of mind within the domain of physics by reducing physics to matter in motion and equating mental activity with the latter. Of greater importance for the history of psychology, though, was his analysis of the regularities of imagination. As later authors were to notice, Hobbes described the activity of the imagination in terms of a principle of association: the faculty governs the production of "traynes" of images according to the principle that "we have no Transition from one Imagination to another, whereof we never had the like before in our Senses."[36] Current transitions in imagination are limited to prior actual transitions, although, by Hobbes's lights, this was not much of a limitation because of the great variety of successions found in the senses: the combinations presented to the senses are so diverse, he thought, that "when by length of time very many Phantasmes have been generated within us by Sense, then almost any thought may arise from any other thought."[37] As Hobbes explained, the development of rational thought depends not on any special faculty of the mind or immaterial agency but on proper control of the trains of imaginations, through their regimentation under the rules of language or the use of signs. This attitude toward the human mind was to serve as an inspiration to several eighteenth-century thinkers (in Britain and on the continent), though a direct debt to Hobbes is difficult to establish because of citation practices (including penalties of disfavor for acknowledging Hobbesian influence).

The most prominent body of seventeenth-century physics was that spawned by Descartes and spread in numerous books by his followers. In his *Principia philosophiae,* Descartes had intended to cover the full range of the traditional physics, including "the nature of plants, of animals, and above all, of man." He was forced to cut his treatment short because of lack of means to carry out "all the experiments that I would need in order to support and justify my reasonings."[38] In the extant portions of the *Principia* devoted to physics (parts 2–4), he discussed the bodily side of sensory activity and the creation of sensations in the mind, but not the essentially mental faculties of intellect and will.[39] The latter were discussed in his "metaphysical *Meditations*" and in the corresponding part 1 of the *Principia,* and it is not clear whether they would have been discussed under the rubric of "physics" in a completed version of the latter work. But there is evidence to suggest that Descartes had intended his earlier book on physics, entitled *Le Monde,* to extend at least to the union of soul and body: the posthumously published *Traité de l'homme* (originally part of *Le Monde*) covered human physiology, including the bodily mechanisms involved in sense perception, imagination, memory, bodily motion, sleep, dreams, and emotions, and was to have examined the mind-body union.[40] Further, in his *Dioptrique*, Descartes examined the physiological processes and mental judgments involved in the perception of size, shape, distance, and motion.[41] Subsequent Cartesian treatises on physics incorporated discussion of sense perception—including its mental aspect—within physics, but they split on whether to place discussion of the rational soul in physics or metaphysics.

Jacques Rohault produced the most widely distributed textbook of Cartesian physics, which was used well into the eighteenth century. He followed the extant *Principia* in limiting physics primarily to the material world, though he included discussion of both the bodily and mental aspects of sensory perception in treating of the qualities of bodies. Among the senses, he again followed Descartes (and tradition) in treating vision most extensively, including the perception of color, size, and distance, the production of an "*immaterial* Image" in the soul through brain activity, and the "judgments," based on that image which result in size and distance perception.[42] Antoine Le Grand produced the first comprehensive rendering of Descartes's philosophy.[43] Within physics, he followed scholastic practice in dividing physics into general and special, and inanimate and living.[44] Following the Aristotelian order, Le Grand included the whole of what he termed the science of "Man" in his physics, divided into two parts, considering first the human body, then the mind (agreeing with the usual division in the literature on "anthropologia"). The part on the body covered various bodily functions as well as the operation of the senses, including the production of sensations, or "Spiritual Images," in the soul.[45] The chapter on "Mind" proper covered the essential nature of the mind, its union with the body, and its faculties, taking care to observe that its acts of intellection can be exercised independently of brain processes.[46] In academically orthodox fashion, Le Grand classed these discussions under the rubric of physics or natural philosophy. Pierre Regis produced a popular "system" or "entire course" of Descartes's philosophy, again covering logic, metaphysics, physics, and morals.[47] Five of seven volumes were devoted to physics, and of these, two and one-half to living things, of which more than one full volume was devoted to the senses, the other cognitive faculties, and the passions. He emphasized especially the brain processes—or as he put it, the "causes physiques"—associated with sense, imagination, judgment, reason, and memory. Of these topics, Regis devoted the greatest attention to vision, including extensive discussion of color perception, the formation of a "spiritual image," the basis of binocular single vision, size and distance perception, and the so-called moon illusion. He treated all of these "psychological" topics under physics; he reserved discussion of the existence and nature of mind (and body), and the mind-body union, for metaphysics (three-fourths of one volume).

Cartesian textbook philosophy fostered the development of psychology as the science of the mind in two ways. Implicitly, its dualist ontology abetted the perception that the phenomena of mind form a single disciplinary unit. Descartes's starkly drawn dualism grouped the phenomena of sensation and intellection (and feeling, and willing) together as "thoughts" or "mental" states, joined by virtue of their common containment in "consciousness," and united ontologically as modifications of thinking substance. Although most of these phenomena were associated in Aristotelian philosophy under the rubric of "cognitive operations," they were not ontologically divorced from other bodily functions. Second, Cartesian textbook physics reinforced the inclusion of at least portions of the science of the mind within natural science by including the study of the corporeal and bodily conditions of sense perception, and especially vision, within the "physics" part of the curriculum. In the Aristotelian curriculum, optics was a "mixed mathematical" science (which meant that it applied mathematical principles to physical subject matter); although optical treatises themselves typically included extensive discussion of the "psychological" portions of the theory of vision (such as size, shape, and distance perception), very little discussion of such topics was included when the senses were examined in *De anima* commentaries and the corresponding portions of the physics textbook, which focused on the ontology of sensible species and of the act of sensing. By contrast, all three of the major Cartesian textbooks placed the psychology of vision—which would later be the mainstay of the new experimental psychology—squarely within physics or natural science. This second contribution stands in tension with the first, because it mixes the discussion of a purely mental subject matter (perceptual experience itself) with the discussion of brain processes. This fact can serve to remind us that despite substance dualism, Cartesian physics treated those mental processes that depend on the bodily processes in the chapters on *body*.

Near the end of the seventeenth century, Newton's new mechanics presented itself as a rival to Cartesian physics. It would be several decades before it clearly displaced the Cartesian physics, and several more (until near the century's end) before the older conception of physics as the science of nature in general, including psychology, was displaced by the narrower conception of experimental, mathematical physics familiar to us now.[48] Newton himself wrote as if his work in mechanics and optics were just two instances of a new approach that could be extended to other areas of the science of nature.[49] He promoted this extension of physiology in the Queries to the *Opticks*, where he speculated on the vibratory character of both sensory and motor nervous transmission. Also in the Queries, he expressed a commitment to a "sensitive substance" that he implicitly characterized as "incorporeal."[50] Newton thus opted for mind-matter dualism. The most prolific textbook writers among his followers, 'sGravesande and Musschenbroek, made this commitment explicit. Willem Jacob 'sGravesande equated the subject matter of physics with "natural things," by which he meant "all bodies"; within the division of sciences, he placed the human mind under metaphysics.[51] His Netherlandish friend and colleague Petrus van Musschenbroek developed a more elaborate partition of philosophy, which included the logic, metaphysics, physics (limited to space and body), and moral philosophy of the traditional curriculum, augmented by teleology and by pneumatics, or the science of spirits.[52] Unlike scholastic Aristotelian psychology, pneumatics comprehended all spirits, finite and infinite. It also comprehended the union of spirit with body, which Cartesian dualists had sometimes placed in physics, sometimes in metaphysics.

In displacing the reigning Aristotelian natural philosophy, the Cartesian and Newtonian systems affected psychology in two ways. First, they ushered in dualism as the reigning ontology of the mind-matter relation. Second, they disrupted the traditional classification of mental phenomena under physics, creating uncertainty about where the study of the mind fit into the system of sciences; some placed it within physics, while others distributed the discussion between physics and metaphysics, and still others subsumed the human mind under pneumatics. Substance dualism thus did not necessarily lead to the divorce of psychology from its previous position within natural science: it did among the close followers of Newton, but not among all Cartesians.

The physics curriculum proper was not the only locus for discussion of the mind or mental phenomena. Throughout the seventeenth century and into the eighteenth these phenomena were discussed in a great many disciplinary contexts. In the traditional philosophical curriculum, moral philosophy applied the physics of mind in moral psychology; logic (Aristotelian and non-Aristotelian) discussed the faculties or powers of the mind in relation to their proper use, including especially the cognitive faculties relevant to the logical acts of conception, judgment, and reasoning. In other contexts, the mind and mental phenomena were studied empirically as part of the domain of nature, but the relation to physics proper was indefinite or secondary. Optics, which was classically defined as the theory of vision, was throughout the eighteenth century considered by many to be a branch of applied mathematics.[53] Long after Newton published his own *Opticks,* which focused narrowly on the physics of light, optics continued to be pursued as a complete theory of vision, including perceptual phenomena and the mind's contribution to perception.[54] Further, medical physiology had long included discussion of the operation of the senses and other cognitive faculties. Others studied the mind in order to determine the grounds and limits of human knowledge. Locke's *Essay* is the most noted example of an empirically based ("plain, historical") approach to the human mind considered as a cognitive power. Although his project has often been characterized as an early attempt at natural scientific psychology, Locke himself clearly distinguished his inquiry into the "Original, Certainty, and Extent of humane Knowledge" from a "Physical Consideration of the Mind," as well as from the (metaphysical) consideration of the mind's essence and its interaction with body.[55] More generally, Descartes had called for an investigation of the knowing power in the *Regulae* (circulated in manuscript and published in 1701), without implying that this was a "physical" or "natural philosophical" investigation.[56]

PSYCHOLOGICAL LOCI IN THE EIGHTEENTH CENTURY

The study of the mind, displaced from its subdisciplinary status in the Aristotelian curriculum, was refounded and pursued along many lines in the eighteenth century. A Christian apologetical approach was pursued in works by gentlemen and divines on the soul.[57] In discussions of Enlightenment psychology, the diametrically opposed materialism of the *philosophes* and their Scottish counterparts—including Diderot, d'Holbach, Helvétius, Priestley, and Bentham—has received recent attention, as part of the conventional story of the Enlightenment banishment of spirits and the alliance of materialism with progressive thought and politics.[58]

Between these two extremes lay the largest and richest body of literature, that of the manifold programs for adopting an empirical approach to mind and its relation to body. There was not one program for studying the mind empirically, and there was not a single disciplinary matrix for doing so. Rather, in diverse established, relocated, and newly created disciplinary matrices, the empirical study of mental phenomena was proposed, projected, recounted from books, attempted for real, and sometimes achieved. The disciplinary matrices included the traditional Aristotelian structure and the various replacements for it, including the study of the mind as an attempt to understand the basis of human knowledge; the newly founded and widely influential Wolffian matrix in Germany; various midcentury projects to bring new methods to the study of the soul, including that of the Swiss naturalist Charles Bonnet and those of the French physician Guillaume-Lambert Godart and the German physician Johann Gottlob Krüger; the "science of the mind" allied with Scottish moral philosophy; the avowedly nonmetaphysical "Ehrfahrungsseelenlehre"; and treatments of mind in the established contexts of medical physiology, optics, and anthropology. The contexts in which new empirical or conceptual results were achieved included medical physiology and optics, appeals to common experience organized by new theoretical structures, and demonstration measurements to illustrate the possibility of quantitative handling of mental phenomena. Appeals to Newtonian method were legion and varied, exemplifying the many possibilities for claiming "Newtonian" heritage in the eighteenth century, many of which did not require quantitative data or mathematical derivations, but simply an empirical (Newtonian) as opposed to a metaphysical (Cartesian) starting point.[59] Medical physiology provided an even more general model for natural science: that of natural history and clinical observation. This model was operative in Locke, David Hartley, and Thomas Reid, and in physiologists such as Albrecht von Haller and Johann Blumenbach, who discussed the mental faculties extensively in their physiological lectures.

Charting a detailed road map through this diverse material would require discussion of nearly one hundred different works. What I aim for here is a survey of the most visible empirical approaches to the mind, an account of their main features, and a report and analysis of their self-ascribed disciplinary locations. This survey will provide a reasonably accurate overview of natural-scientific psychology remade during the eighteenth century. Omitted are some self-avowed empirical approaches to the mind that treat it as a knowing or truth-discerning power rather than as an object of natural science, even if such approaches contain psychological material. Especially noteworthy among those omitted are the purely naturalistic analyses of the abbé de Condillac and Johann Christian Lossius. Also omitted are nonnaturalistic considerations of the knower, such as that of Kant.[60]

WOLFFIAN PSYCHOLOGY

Christian Wolff created the paired disciplines of empirical and rational psychology, which he ordered coordinately with ontology, rational cosmology, and natural theology under metaphysics.[61] His efforts have been the butt of many jokes in the history of psychology, most notably of Wilhelm Wundt's famous jest that Wolff's rational psychology "contains about as much experience as the empirical, and the empirical about as much metaphysics as the rational."[62] In the standard historiography, Wolff is part of the metaphysical past of psychology's prehistory. In fact, Wolff's work was of paramount importance for the development of empirical psychology during the eighteenth century and beyond.

Wolff's imposing row of textbooks (in German and Latin) contain an interesting conception of philosophical method and a novel division of the sciences. Wolff separated all knowledge into three types: historical, or knowledge of bare facts; philosophical, or knowledge of reasons; and mathematical, or knowledge of the quantities of things. According to Wolff, philosophy is related to the other two sorts of knowledge in the following way: it is grounded in facts, and its method of reasoning is like that of mathematics.[63] Wolff's works are organized according to a highly articulated division of the sciences (or the branches of demonstrative knowledge). Most generally, he retained the Aristotelian division between "philosophical" disciplines, which in his case included "physics," and "mathematical" disciplines, in which he included "mechanics" (taken as the theory of machines).[64] Central components of the philosophical disciplines included "logic" (or "the science of directing the faculty of cognition in cognizing truth"), metaphysics, physics, and practical philosophy. Physics was the science of corporeal nature in general and included general physics, empirical cosmology, orycthology (science of fossils), hydrology, phytology, physiology and pathology, and teleology. Metaphysics was much expanded over its Aristotelian and Cartesian counterparts, to include ontology, general cosmology, psychology, and natural theology (the latter two constituting pneumatology).[65] General cosmology extended to the nature of body and of the elements, the laws of motion, and the distinction between natural and supernatural.[66] Ontology, general cosmology, and psychology, although classed as divisions of metaphysics, were nonetheless advertised as empirically based. Metaphysics did not imply for Wolff, as it had for Descartes and would for Kant, a body of knowledge known through reason alone, independent of experience. Rather, it was defined by its subject matter, as "the science of being, of the world in general, and of spirits."[67] Metaphysics, as all philosophical knowledge, is based in "historical cognition," that is, in the cognition of facts.[68] Wundt's jest about the intermixture of empirical and metaphysical content, as clever as it may seem, betrays a total lack of comprehension of Wolff's position, simply repeating an earlier and mistaken interpretation that most likely resulted from reading Kantian terminology (regarding metaphysics and the pure a priori) back onto Wolff.

Thus, although Wolff placed psychology within metaphysics rather than physics, he nonetheless held it to be an empirical science. Indeed, contrary to later interpretations of his work, Wolff maintained that empirical was more basic than rational psychology, because it provided the first principles from which the latter constructed its demonstrative arguments. Within empirical psychology, the chief problem was to chart the faculties of the soul. Rational psychology then sought to find principles in empirical psychology such as could guide demonstrative explanations of the phenomena. Thus, where empirical psychology established that the soul or mind perceives or represents external objects, it fell to rational psychology to give an account of the representational relation, which Wolff explained in terms of similitude (drawing liberally on other portions of empirical psychology and on ontology).[69] And where empirical psychology established that sensations arise through alterations in the sense organs and that light causes alterations in the organ of sight, rational psychology explained the basis of spatial representation in general, gave an account of the means by which external objects affect the sense organs, and sought to explain vision by appealing to the relation between such effects and the consequences for sight (drawing on optics).[70] Psychological topics pertaining to individual mental faculties and their empirical characteristics were considered under other divisions of Wolffian philosophy. Wolff's physics provided a summary discussion of the senses, as did his experimental physics for selected problems. His optics examined the theory of vision, including optical anatomy; color; the perception of size, shape, position, and motion; and single vision with two eyes. His physiology, understood as the study of the uses of the parts of living things, discussed the construction of the senses, nerves, and brain and their service as instruments of sensation.[71]

Wolff's psychology is paradigmatic of the allegedly regressive tendencies of prescientific, speculative or metaphysical psychology: it is organized around the study of mental faculties, and it adopts a realistic attitude toward the soul considered as an immaterial substance. Histories of psychology typically take a dismissive attitude toward faculty psychology, an attitude that usually stands without argumentative backing, except as conveyed through allusions to Molière's joke about the dormitive virtue of opium. Such histories are also openly dismissive of the posit of immaterial substances, sometimes "explaining" such posits by mentioning the assumed religious convictions of past thinkers.[72] In each case, historians have failed to take a properly empirical and contextualist approach to past thinkers.

In the context of the eighteenth century, Wolffian psychology was a progressive research program. It promulgated an empirical approach to the mind, a kind of empiricist realism. It was "realistic" in that it took seriously its theoretical posits; it was empiricist in that it claimed to base its posits on repeatable observation or "stable experience." In organization, the general framework of Wolffian empirical psychology was similar to that of Cartesian psychology: it divided the faculties of the soul into cognitive and appetitive and distinguished "higher" and "lower" species of each. In content, however, it was closer to Aristotelian theory, because it treated volition as a species of cognition rather than as a separate mental power. Its basic conformity to the Aristotelian and Cartesian denumeration of faculties, including sense, imagination, memory, and intellect, does not conflict with the empirical nature of Wolff's psychology; the attribution of these faculties to humans is surely based on experience. But this much empirical content was shared by many discussions of the soul or mind from Aristotle onward. What, then, was new with Wolff?

Wolff's psychology had novel features in both content and methodology. Its major methodological innovation was the explicit enjoinder to adopt a metaphysically modest empiricist attitude toward mental faculties and phenomena: they were to be studied by attending to their operations while holding metaphysical speculation in abeyance. When rational psychology seeks to explain the facts thus attained, it draws upon empirically established generalizations rather than allegedly pure a priori metaphysical insights into the essences of things in order to determine appropriate explanatory (we would say "theoretical") principles.[73] Within this scheme, the empirically based attribution of mental faculties to human cognizers is not intended to be *explanatory* (as was the dormitive virtue of Molière's joke), but to be *descriptive* of a unified capacity of the mind. Such descriptions, being classificatory, are not atheoretical, but because they were not intended to be explanatory, they are not subject to Molière's joke (any more than are current psychological investigations of cognitive and perceptual capacities).[74] Within his empiricist program, Wolff claimed that psychological states, and particularly those pertaining to pleasure and pain, are subject to quantitative measurement and mathematical laws, although he did not himself formulate a calculus of pleasure. He also suggested that the goodness of one's memory can be estimated by the temporal latency of response to a memory demand, from the number of tries it takes to retrieve from memory, and from the number of acts it takes to fix an item in memory. He suggested a corresponding quantitative estimate for the size of memory.[75]

In content, the Wolffian psychology was noteworthy for its analysis and discussion of the faculties of imagination, attention, and reflection. Wolff distinguished imagination proper, which simply reproduces sensory materials, from the faculty of "feigning" or producing new representations (*faculte figendi*). He described the "law of imagination," a law of association through simultaneity. And he discussed attention and its subspecies, "reflection" (or attention to the content of one's perceptions), including impediments to their exercise.[76]

The Wolffian system was widely influential on the Continent, where it displaced the fading Aristotelian and Cartesian school philosophies. Its influence was strongest in Germany, where Wolff's works or the numerous textbooks that arose in their wake were used even by authors who no longer subscribed to their precepts, including Immanuel Kant.[77] The system was rendered into French by the Berlin Wolffian, Jean Deschamps.[78] Wolff's psychology was discussed with appreciation in the article on the soul (*Ame*) in the *Encyclopédie,* and his classification of psychology under metaphysics and his division of the discipline into empirical and rational were featured prominently in the article on "Psychologie."[79]

NEW EMPIRICAL APPROACHES TO MIND:
KRÜGER, GODART, BONNET

Near midcentury there was a burst of new psychological activity in Scotland, France, Switzerland, and Germany, with various authors essaying to apply the methods of natural history, natural philosophy, or medicine to the study of the mind. I will take up the Scottish work, including that of Hartley, in the section following. In the present section we will consider the new psychologies of the physicians Krüger and Godart and the naturalist Bonnet.

Johann Gottlob Krüger, in his *Versuch einer Experimental-Seelenlehre* of 1756,[80] set himself the task of showing "how the soul can be known through experiment," that is, of creating an experimental science of mind coordinate with the experimental science of body. This was, he recognized, a formidable task. At the same time, he believed that his experience as a physician would be of help, for it gave him access to "natural experiments" that arise in brain-damaged patients. More generally, he wanted to show philosophers that medicine could make a contribution to philosophical knowledge of the soul, and also that mathematics could be applied to this subject matter. Indeed, in his earlier *Naturlehre* (1740–49), he had already proposed a mathematical (proportional) formulation of the relations among the force with which external objects affect the nerves, the resultant nerve activity, and the liveliness of the resulting sensation.[81] In essence, he attempted to bring the methods and results of physics (in the broad sense), the knowledge of the brain provided by physiology, and the case-history knowledge of the clinic together in order to form an experimental psychology, one that eschewed (as too difficult) metaphysical questions about the substance of the soul or its immortality.[82] At the same time, he openly acknowledged his admiration for Wolff's work in philosophy (including psychology), dedicating to Wolff his medical dissertation, which treated the "physical" topic *De sensatione* (1742), and praising Wolff in his later "physical" works on sensation and his experimental work on the soul.[83]

Krüger expected his experimental psychology to be met with skepticism: "Experiment, one will say, can be done only with bodies. Is it being suggested that spirits [*Geister*] be brought under the airpump, that their shapes be viewed under the microscope, that their forces can be weighed?" This particular sort of skepticism, he countered, rests on the mistaken conception that "no other instruments can be used in experiments with the soul, except those that we find in the instrument cabinet of the physical scientist [*Naturforschers*]." But in Krüger's view, "if the soul is considered to be so very different from the things that one studies in physical science, then completely different experiments will have to be undertaken."[84] In any case, the skeptic might rejoin, experiment depends on observation. Is the soul observable? Certainly not by the senses, in the manner of external objects: we do not see, hear, taste the soul. Yet, Krüger maintained, we can become aware of the states of our soul through "inner sense." We can also know the soul through its connection with the body, as when we come to know someone's mental states through their reflection in her countenance.[85]

Krüger distinguished experiment from observation, and he did not intend to rely merely on observations of the soul's natural expression in inner experience and outer comportment; he was proposing a genuinely experimental study of the soul. Experiment, as he understood the term, differed from mere observation in the following way: observation requires only the possession of working sense organs and a willingness to pay attention, while true experiment requires that we "put things into circumstances in which they would not otherwise come to be, and thereby ask Nature to show us, what she had resolved to conceal from our eyes." Again, the link between soul and body makes it reasonable to seek such experiments: from changes in the soul, changes in the body are known (in perception), and from changes in the body, changes in the soul are known. There is also the close relation between mind and brain. Krüger allowed that the investigator could not cut open human heads and selectively invade the brain to see what happens, but he remarked that such experiments could be undertaken with animals, and also that physicians have a chance to observe the effects of natural "experiments" in patients who have suffered brain damage.[86]

An "experimental" science did not imply for Krüger, or for other eighteenth-century thinkers, an atheoretical collecting of facts, or the piecewise construction of theory from facts. In good empiricist fashion, Krüger held that all knowledge and all concepts derive from sensory experience. They arise, though, through the operation of reason.[87] Krüger did not develop a theory of scientific method to account for the interaction of sensory experience and reason in the development of scientific theory. From his practice, it is clear that he drew heavily on currently accepted theory in interpreting experimental results. In psychology, he drew on a physical understanding of external objects and their effects on the senses, on physiological knowledge of the nerves and brain as interpreted in accordance with a "mechanical" approach to nature, and on the theoretical framework available in previous works on psychology, including that of Wolff.

Krüger's debt to Wolff and his ability to press beyond his senior colleague are both evident in one of Krüger's applications of mathematical reasoning to psychology. Krüger adopted a vibratory conception of nerve activity, supporting his position with experimental results obtained by Giorgio Baglivi in vivisections of dogs.[88] Given that sensations depend on the activity of nerve fibers, he postulated that the strength or liveliness of the sensation will vary with the force produced by the vibrating nerve fiber. This force in turn will vary with the force of the external object. One might then suppose that the liveliness of the sensation will vary directly with the force of the external object, and this in fact is what Wolff had proposed, based on his own assumption about the vibratory nature of nerve activity.[89] Krüger, however, went beyond Wolff in the depth of his theoretical analysis (articulated most fully in his *Naturlehre*). Appealing to the physics of vibrations, he contended that the action of external bodies on individual nerve fibers will depend on the "tension" (*tensione, Spannung*) of those fibers. The liveliness of the sensation will therefore depend on both the force of the external object and the tension of the nerve. He formulated the relation as a mathematical proportion: allowing S and s to represent the liveliness of two sensations, V and v the action of the external object, and T and t the tension of each nerve fiber, then, in Krüger's formulation, $S : s = VT : vt$. Thus, if V is three times v and T is twice t, S will be six times livelier than s. Individual differences in T-values might be found in the sensory apparatus of a single perceiver or in comparisons between or among perceivers. While he had clear conceptions of how V might be determined (based on the physics of light and sound), he gave no indication of how S was to be measured or how sensations were to be compared to establish one as "six times" livelier than another, other than through the determination of V and assumptions about T.[90]

As Krüger acknowledged in the preface of his *Experimental-Seelenlehre*, it did not contain much that was new.[91] Most of the experimental results he reported were extant in the literature: his real contribution was to introduce medical observations and mathematical formulations to psychology. He did not, however, accept the mathematical formulations of others uncritically: he used experience to evaluate extant theoretical claims. In his treatment of vision in the *Naturlehre*, Krüger initially followed a tradition in the optical literature—rendered with mathematical rigor by Wolff—according to which the apparent sizes, horizontal distances, and motions of objects vary directly with visual angle or angular velocity.[92] Although this definition of "apparent" magnitudes was found in many technical works in optics, those writers with a keen sense of visual experience—including Descartes, George Berkeley, and Krüger's French contemporary, Claude Nicolas Le Cat—observed that objects often do not seem to have the sizes, horizontal distances, and velocities assigned by this theoretical formulation, and so they introduced additional psychological considerations, including unnoticed judgments or associative connections, to explain the character of perceptual phenomena.[93] Krüger knew at least the portion of this literature that discussed the horizon moon (the so-called "moon illusion"), and he added, almost as an afterthought to his mathematical treatment of "apparent" size, the observation that sometimes apparent size does not follow visual angle but is influenced by apparent distance, such that of two objects falling under the same angle, that judged to be further away is judged to be and appears larger than the other.[94]

Krüger often made good use of the extant natural philosophical, physiological, and clinical literature in discussing the relation between nerve activity and sensations or the role of experience in the development of perceptual abilities. He presented the experiment of the natural philosopher Edmé Mariotte, who used two white dots on a black wall to demonstrate the existence of a "blind spot" at the point where the optic nerve enters the eye. Mariotte had interpreted his results as showing that the choroid, rather than the retina, is the seat of optical sensation, on the grounds that the retina, but not the choroid, is present in the blind spot. Krüger appealed to his own previous arguments that the outer membrane and not the medulla (or marrow) of the nerve is the sensitive portion, in order to argue that the retina is not truly present in the blind spot, which, he argued, contains nerve marrow but not nerve membranes.[95] However, although Krüger adopted a vibratory conception of the effect of objects on the nerves, he did not believe that such vibrations would be carried by delicate nerve membranes along the circuitous path to the brain. Moreover, he held that the nerve fluid or animal spirits are necessary for sensations. He thus concluded that sensations arise at the locus of the vibrations, when the latter set the animal spirits in motion.[96] In support of this conclusion, he cited the observations of John Woodward on decorticized, decapitated, decardate, or otherwise vivisectioned pigeons, chickens, eels, snakes, frogs, flies, wasps, and spiders. He used Woodward to support his conclusion that "sensibility" is found in the parts of animals themselves, even if separated from the brain, and that this sensibility is lost when the nerves dry out (and hence could not depend on vibrations of membranes alone, but requires the presence of nerve fluid). At the same time, he held that in ordinary circumstances perception depends on the conveyance of motion to the brain via the animal spirits in the medulla of each nerve, while also contending that the speed of transmission, which he thought likely to be equal to the speed of sound, was too rapid for investigators to be able to detect any noticeable difference between reports of sensations originating in the foot and in the head.[97] Krüger also reported the famous Cheselden case, to support the point that if newborns saw things inverted because of the inverted retinal image, they could soon learn through experience to see things upright.[98] Finally, in discussing the imagination, he reported as a generally accepted "law of imagination" the regularity with which, in imagining one thing, we come to imagine things that we previously experienced simultaneously with that thing, or things that are similar to that thing. As an example, he offered the case of a microscopist who formed an aversion to cheese through the action of this law: having studied cheese mites under the microscope, he could not help but imagine those mites when eating cheese, an image that spoiled his appetite.[99]

Not long after Krüger had completed his dissertation on the senses at Halle, Guillaume-Lambert Godart submitted a medical dissertation at Reims entitled *Specimen animasticae medicae* (1745), which he later developed under the title *La physique de l'ame* (1755).[100] The framework of Godart's thought was largely Aristotelian: he attributed to humans a "rational soul" that is a "vivifying principle" that accounts both for the life functions of the body and for its power of thought;[101] after considering the nature and seat of the soul (in part 1), he successively treated (in part 2) the "vital functions" (section 1), including nutrition and generation, and the "animal" and "intellectual" functions (section 2), including sensation, perception, imagination, judgment, the passions, memory, sleep, dreams, and the "metamorphosis" of man through his terrestrial, spiritual, and eternal stages of life. But he approached this subject matter with the empirical attitude and metaphysical chagrin characteristic of many eighteenth-century natural philosophers and natural historians: he abandoned any attempt to know the nature of the soul, admitting that we have no more conception of its nature than we have of that of matter.[102] Further, he devoted special attention to his use of the word "physical" in the title of his book: "although the word *physics* comes from *physis* which signifies *nature* and nothing more, a book that treats of the nature of the soul may receive the name of physics." Indeed, he allowed, etymologically the word suggests the treatment of corruptible things, but natural philosophers treat of incorruptible atoms, so he may be allowed to consider the incorruptible soul under the same title. In any event:

> that which seems to me principally to authorize that name, is the manner in which I consider my object: my treatise is neither pneumatological nor moral, but physical. It concerns, it is true, a spirit, but this spirit is not considered according to its substance, but in the physical relation it has with the body, and when it comes to its actions, that which concerns merit and demerit is left to the moralists.[103]

His chief "physical" contribution was his discussion of the seat of the soul, which, relying on observations made by François de la Peyronie, he located in the *corpus collosum*.[104]

The Swiss naturalist Charles Bonnet was more prolific and more influential than either Krüger or Godart. Although his early years were devoted to the natural history of insects, during which time he had little patience with metaphysics, around 1750 he came to see the interest in turning the techniques of natural history to the principal object of study for human beings, human beings themselves; his first psychological work, the *Essai de psychologie,* appeared anonymously in 1754, followed by the *Essai analytique sur les facultés de l'ame* in 1760.[105] As he said in the latter work, "I consecrated my first years of reason to the study of natural history; I am consecrating those of its maturity to more important study, that of our being. I have tried to study *Man* as I have studied insects and plants. The spirit of observation is not limited to a single genre." Although he often referred to psychology as a "metaphysical" discipline by contrast with physics, he also averred that he had put in his book "much physics and little of metaphysics," a decision he defended by suggesting that very little can be known of the soul "considered in itself." Like Godart, he intended to apply the method of physics (in the wide sense) to the study of the soul. He found two points of methodological analogy. First, he assigned two parts to psychology, one "historical" and one "systematic": "the first contains the exposition of facts; the second, their explanation" (similar to Wolff's "empirical" and "rational" psychology). Second, the only method he found viable for the purposes of investigating a new subject matter (rather than providing instruction in a well-known one) was the "method of analysis." This method consisted in "anatomizing each fact, decomposing it down to its smallest parts, and examining separately all of these parts"; then "seeking the connections that tie these things to one another and to analogous things, and to find results that can turn into principles."[106] Starting from facts of consciousness and behavior, Bonnet sought to establish the general principles that govern the flow of ideas and the formation of motor habits, as governed by principles of association that direct the formation of habits in accordance with the laws of pleasure and pain.[107]

Bonnet's psychology shared many features characteristic of the new psychological naturalism: he accepted dualism and the immateriality of the soul, without claiming to achieve an analysis of the substance of the soul; his arguments for the soul's immateriality sprang from the unity of consciousness as contrasted with the conglomerate nature of material mechanisms; like Krüger, he approached the activity of the mind through its connection with vibrations of nerve fibers and motions set up in nerve fluid; and he assigned the origin of all our ideas to sense.[108] Some aspects of his thought are more particular: he developed the "mechanics" (brain-fiber physiology) of each sense with special thoroughness; he developed the theory of association extensively, using it as a key to understanding the course of thought, and dwelling on the "mechanics" of association with an intensity similar to that of Hartley's slightly earlier treatment; he analyzed the role of attention in strengthening certain ideas by "reacting" on nerve fibers in the brain; he held that the formation of intellectual ideas depends on language, and that exposure of language results in the formation of "intellectual fibers" that are the bodily counterpart to abstract notions; and he explored the implications of his psychology with respect to the power of education in the cognitive development of each person.[109] Because of his heavy emphasis on the role of brain fibers in all thought processes, Bonnet's work raised a suspicion of materialism; he was by no means a materialist, having devoted considerable effort to showing that the mind must be immaterial. At the same time, he placed questions about the substantial nature of the mind and its ideas, and about the mode of interaction between mind and body, beyond the pale of human reason.[110]

The newly sounded call for a "physical" science of the mind, or for the application of the methods of natural history and natural philosophy to the subject matter of mind, was not lost on generations subsequent to Krüger, Godart, and Bonnet. Especially in Germany, their work was incorporated as part of the founding literature of the *Ehrfahrungsseelenlehre* and empirical anthropology that developed in the second half of the century and continued through the following century, conditioning and being continued by philosophical and natural-scientific psychology and the self-proclaimed "new" experimental psychology of Wundt and others.[111] We will return to these developments in Germany after examining the Scottish scene, which itself strongly influenced nineteenth-century developments in psychology in both Britain and Germany.

SCOTTISH SCIENCES OF MAN AND MIND

In the Scottish Universities of the first half of the eighteenth century the mind was studied in three areas of the revised Aristotelian curriculum: logic, metaphysics, and moral philosophy (which discussed appetite). By midcentury, a peculiarly Scottish phenomenon had occurred: within the university arts curriculum, the study of the mind in general became the special preserve of moral philosophy (as might be expected of the "moral sense" school). Thomas Reid, professor of moral philosophy at Glasgow, transformed moral philosophy into the examination of the "powers" of the mind. At Edinburgh, the connection between mind and morals had been forged even earlier: from 1708, the University had reserved a chair for the professor of moral philosophy and pneumatics; while the motivation may have been the relation between morals and the study of spiritual beings, when Adam Ferguson filled this chair in 1764 he answered to his title by making the "theory of mind" a proper part of his basic textbook, the *Institutes of Moral Philosophy*.[112]

The fact that the study of the mind fell largely under moral philosophy in the Scottish arts curriculum does not imply that the mind was considered to be distinct from nature or from natural scientific methods of study and modes of explanation. Indeed, it was characteristic of Scottish philosophers to adopt a naturalistic attitude toward the mind and its powers. Hutcheson compared the moral sense, and the internal senses more generally, to other natural human capacities, and sought to investigate them by appeal to experience.[113] Hume signaled his naturalistic intentions in the subtitle to his *Treatise of Human Nature: Being an Attempt to Introduce the Experimental Method of Reasoning into Moral Subjects*; in the introduction to the work, he explicitly compared his methods and modes of explanation to those of Newton. By the "experimental method" he meant no more and no less than an appeal to experience in support of his claims; by "moral subjects" he included not only the study of the passions and of morals proper (virtue and vice) but also, and fundamentally, the "science of human nature."[114] Hume portrayed his analysis of perceptions into impressions and ideas, simple and complex, and his appeal to the laws of association in explaining their interactions, as having revealed the basic elements and laws of the human mind.

Hume was not unique in claiming to be the Newton of the mind; he shared invocation of Newton with David Hartley, Reid, and Ferguson.[115] Hartley, like Hume, was not a university professor; like Krüger and Godart, he was a physician. He shared with the other Scottish naturalists the division of phenomena pertaining to human beings into two realms: bodily and mental. His major work, *Observations on Man,* was an attempt to ground the operation of the mind in association, and to explain association as the result of sympathetic vibrations among nerve fibers in the brain.[116] Reid, who was a physician as well as professor of moral philosophy, divided all of the objects of human knowledge into two realms, material and intellectual, and grouped the sciences that study the first under the heading of natural philosophy, while reporting that the branch of philosophy "which treats of the nature and operations of mind has by some been called Pneumatology."[117] He allowed that the study of mind was less advanced than that of natural philosophy (aided as the latter had been by Galileo, Evangelista Torricelli, Johannes Kepler, Bacon, and Newton) and commended the hope that "human genius" would, in time, "produce a system of the powers and operations of the human mind, no less certain than those of optics or astronomy."[118] Reid portrayed the "philosophy of the human mind" as awaiting its Newton, but hinted that the time might well be nigh.[119] Adam Ferguson, in his telegraphic *Institutes of Moral Philosophy,* formulated natural laws of both matter and mind, distinguishing the latter from properly moral laws. He defined moral philosophy as "the knowledge of what ought to be" and declared that "pneumatics, or the physical history of mind, is the foundation of moral philosophy." The term "physical" is not used here to announce a physicalist or reductionist theory of mind; rather, it is used to mean "any general expression of a natural operation, as exemplified in a number of cases." The natural laws of mind were named "physical" by Ferguson in order to contrast them with the moral laws that serve to guide conduct: the physical laws of mind are the natural laws of its operations. Under this usage, pneumatics "treats physically of mind or spirit"; the branch of pneumatics pertaining to human minds is designated simply as the "theory of mind." It is equated with "the knowledge of physical laws collected from fact, and applicable to explain appearances."[120] Examples of the laws of mind include the facts that we are conscious of our "existence, operation, and will" and that perception takes place via media that do not resemble the object of perception.[121]

To these Scottish theorists of mind must be added Erasmus Darwin, whose *Zoonomia; or, the Laws of Organic Life* of 1794–96 was dedicated, among others, to those who "study the Operations of the Mind as a Science."[122] In this work, Darwin presented a sophisticated version of the associationist theory, replete with novel empirical observations, including some famous ones on after-images. Darwin stands out among the Scottish authors noted thus far for his materialistic theory of mind. He allowed that the whole of nature may be "supposed" to consist of "two essences or substances," namely, "spirit" and "matter." Spirit "possesses the power to commence or produce motion," matter "to receive and communicate it." Living and sentient things possess a "spirit of animation," which is a vital principle residing in the brain and nerves, and subject to "general or partial diminution or accumulation" (and hence material).[123] Darwin's treatment of sensory perception and associative learning were particularly astute. His works were translated into German and republished often, helping to introduce a sophisticated associationism into German psychological writings. He is virtually singular as an eighteenth-century materialist (even if vitalist) who actually contributed to the development of psychological theory.

Although the theory of the mind, or psychology, was pursued vigorously by Scottish philosophers and physicians, Scottish writers came regularly to denominate this branch of knowledge "psychology"—as opposed to pneumatics, theory of mind, science of mind, or philosophy of mind—only in the nineteenth century. Dugald Stewart, who undertook an introductory textbook on the subject, chose the title *Elements of the Philosophy of the Human Mind.*[124] He dedicated his work to Reid, and drew upon the mainstream Scottish tradition. He placed himself in opposition to Erasmus Darwin and Joseph Priestley, whom he classified as materialists. Priestley himself did not contribute to psychology, but brought out an abridgement of Hartley's *Observations.*

EHRFAHRUNGSSEELENLEHRE

While in the Scottish context investigators sought to make the mind an object of empirical investigation and to discover its "physical laws" as a prolegomena to morals, in Germany the science of the soul (or mind) was treated as an autonomous discipline—or as a subdiscipline of the science of man—within the theoretical (as opposed to moral) sciences. The framers of "Seelenlehre," "Ehrfahrungsseelenlehre," and "empirische Psychologie" aspired to such an empirical approach to the soul or mind. Developed instances are found in the work of J. F. Abel and K. C. E. Schmid. Abel and Schmid placed empirical psychology within natural science proper, distinct from metaphysics; they considered psychology to be the branch of anthropology or *Menschenlehre* that searches for the general laws of the mind and its relation to the body.[125]

Abel's book exhibits a typical psychological textbook organization, with roots in the *De anima* tradition. After brief preliminary methodological remarks, it considers first the nature of the mind, its basic powers and organs, and especially its relation to the brain, and then it systematically surveys the chief faculties of mind: sense, imagination, attention, thought, feeling, and bodily motion. Throughout, Abel attempts to show how all of the various powers and capacities of the mind can be reduced to one basic power, the power of representation, and how the materials on which the power of representation operates must all derive from sensory ideas aroused through stimulation of the sense organs. As had become common in the eighteenth century, he showed an interest in quantitative measures where these were available; indeed, he gave quantitative values for the "briefest still perceivable duration" of an impression on the sense organs. But the primary theoretical interest of the work was the discovery of "laws" governing the various faculties, including laws of association and attention.[126] The laws of attention assumed an all-or-none "conquest" (*siegen*) of attention by one or another representation. Originally, the currently liveliest or most pleasant representation wins out, but through experience it may happen that a less lively or pleasant representation that has in the past been followed by more pleasant representations will win out; the attentional faculty then comes to be guided by means-ends considerations in choosing which representations to enhance through its own power.

Many of the topics of Abel's textbook, such as the perception of size, shape, location, and distance, and attentional "conquest," can be found in nineteenth- and in early– and late–twentieth-century textbooks. But one set of questions would no longer be found after circa 1930: those pertaining to the existence and nature of the soul. The framers of *Seelenlehre* typically argued that the soul is a separate substance from the body, and they did so on philosophical as opposed to religious grounds. Abel repeated the widely used argument that the unity of consciousness requires a unified substance as its vehicle; but body is essentially conglomerate; hence, the simple substance that is mind must be distinct from body. He took this argument to be an example of empirical investigation. He divorced his investigation from "metaphysical" considerations that transcend experience, for example, about mind-body interaction. Historians of psychology typically lump together talk of a separate thinking substance and of mind-body interaction as "metaphysics." Here, an eighteenth-century author asserts a different dividing point. He holds that empirical considerations can be brought to bear on the existence and nature of the soul. He does not mean that one can simply introspect and discover the simple substance of the soul. An argument is required: a theoretical structure must be fit to the "data" of inner sense. But he considered these questions on the soul to be empirically tractable, by contrast with the problem of mind-body interaction, which admits of multiple hypotheses that "save" the phenomena without differing empirically. He excluded the latter, empirically undecidable problem from his *Seelenlehre*.[127]

Schmid's *Empirische Psychologie* is a more advanced textbook than Abel's, and in particular it is filled with rich and detailed methodological discussions that are informed by previous writings, including those of Wolff and Kant. These discussions include a precise delimitation of the disciplinary boundaries and relations of empirical psychology to anthropology more generally, a discussion of the empirical object and form of explanation of psychology, and a division of psychology itself into distinct subareas. Schmid observed that some would limit the subject matter of psychology to the data of inner sense alone (as in fact Kant had done), but he argued that it should be defined more broadly, to include those "outwardly" observable phenomena of body that have a lawful relation with inner sense. He thus included not only the introspective data of inner sense but observations of the behavior of other humans and indeed the historical record of human behavior within the subject matter of psychology. Again, he acknowledged that some would limit a science "in the strict sense" to those fields that could derive their main conclusions a priori (as Kant had maintained), but he chose to employ a concept of science "in the wide sense," as a "systematic body of knowledge, that is, one ordered according to principles"; when the concept of science is so understood, *Seelenlehre* can be a science. It seeks empirical generalizations (*Regeln*) and universal laws (*Gesetze*) of mental life, which, Schmid is careful to observe, are to be regarded as theoretical laws of nature governing the operation of the mind, and not as the moral laws by which we seek to guide our behavior.[128]

Schmid drew the boundaries of the empirical more narrowly than had Abel. He followed Kant in removing questions pertaining to the substantiality and simplicity of the soul from the domain of empirical investigation and relegating them to "dogmatic" metaphysics—for which he reserved the names "transcendental" or "pure" psychology, or "pneumatology," thereby deviating from Kant's terminology. Included here were questions pertaining to the independence, simplicity, personhood, spirituality, immutability, and immortality of the soul, as well as those pertaining to its real causal relation to body. He used the terms "empirical" and "rational" psychology as Wolff had, to denote disciplines that are based

directly on experience (or are a posteriori) and those that are based on
the analysis of concepts that themselves are drawn from experience (and
hence are "comparatively a priori").[129] The rational part of psychology
constructs explanations for the empirical generalizations and other data
collected in the empirical part.

Having relegated the problem of the substantial nature of the mind to
the domain of dogmatic metaphysics, Schmid adopted a position of "empirical dualism."[130] Empirical dualism distinguishes soul and body on the
grounds that the properties and phenomena revealed through outer and
inner sense cannot be united under a single set of concepts. Experience
shows that the phenomena of each are lawfully related. Empirical psychology charts lawful relations within the domain of soul, spirit, or mind, and
between that domain and bodily processes. Schmid's work is particularly
impressive for its detailed analytical treatment of psychological concepts
informed by a thorough acquaintance with the psychological, anthropological, and medical literatures.

PSYCHOLOGY IN THE ANTHROPOLOGICAL, MEDICAL, AND OPTICAL LITERATURES

This is not the place to survey the diverse set of works in anthropology, or
the "Science of Man," that appeared in the eighteenth century. However,
two general points will help place the natural scientific approach to psychology with respect to the anthropological tradition. First, anthropology
was considered by many to be a more encompassing discipline than psychology: whereas the latter pertained to mind, anthropology considered
the whole human: mind, body, and their union. (Of course, anthropology
was also narrower than psychology, in that the latter might treat of animal as well as human souls.) Consequently, one trend in anthropological treatises, so denominated, was to focus on problems of mind-body
union, giving only a summary treatment of bodily functions (which were
discussed in medical physiology) and mental functions (which were discussed in psychology), a description that fits Johann Karl Wezel's *Versuch
über die Kenntnis des Menschen* (1784–85).[131] Secondly, even those, such as
Kant and Blumenbach, who took the science of man to pertain to humankind in its full empirical diversity—to include various individual, national,
and racial types—began their anthropologies with an overview of what is
common to all humans, or at least to all human minds.[132] Kant placed anthropology among the empirically based investigations of nature. He considered its evidence to come from self-observation, observation of others,
and reports of others' behavior, as found in fiction, travel literature, and
history. Yet the most extensive portion of his anthropological lectures concerns the properties and operations of the cognitive faculties in diverse

empirical circumstances, including a discussion of the roles of vision and touch in the perception of three-dimensional solid shapes.

Medical physiology had long included examination of the mental powers of humans and the physiological structure of the sense organs, nerves, and brain that serve them.[133] This practice continued through the eighteenth century, and into the nineteenth and twentieth. Albrecht von Haller's physiological lectures are noteworthy for the extensive discussion and wealth of the citation in the six books (filling one large volume) devoted to the external and internal senses.[134] These discussions referred to a great deal of literature, but were of mixed quality from a psychological perspective. Thus, like Wolff, Haller simply equated apparent size with the visual angle subtended by an object in the field of view, whereas many of the authors he cited, including Berkeley and Le Cat, recognized that perceived size may take into account the perceived distance of an object.[135] Beyond the five external senses, Haller discussed the "internal senses," under which he grouped intellect, will, and sleep. In the section on intellect, he also discussed the faculties of memory and imagination, the cognitive acts of judgment, wit, and abstraction, and the conditions leading to truth and error, delirium, and foolishness. His discussion of the intellect focused especially on the status of mental representations. In particular, he advised that four different things must be kept distinct in discussing mental representations such as perceptions: (1) the external object, (2) its impressions on the sense organs, (3) the effects of these impressions as transmitted to the cerebrum, and (4) the representation of this effect in the mind.[136]

Finally, the optical literature, which had long included psychological topics as part of a complete theory of vision, flourished under this description in the eighteenth century, even if some authors adopted the narrower Newtonian conception of optics. The theory of vision addressed the act of seeing itself, especially the perception of size, shape, distance, motion, and color. Berkeley's *New Theory of Vision,* for instance, was widely known and often admired in the eighteenth century. It introduced a new psychological theory into the theory of vision, by accounting for the connection among visual and tactual ideas via the mechanism of "suggestion" (association), which Berkeley opposed to the posited unnoticed judgments of previous optical writers, including Descartes. Berkeley's theory that touch educates vision through a process of learning was widely discussed in the eighteenth century; Berkeley and others claimed empirical support for his position from observations on the newly-sighted blind.[137]

Beyond these theoretical disputes, many authors engaged in geometrical modeling and empirical investigation of the phenomena of size, shape, and distance perception. Because it was descended from optics, a mixed mathematical science, the theory of vision inherited geometrical modeling, and as the other mixed mathematical sciences appealed ever more to experiment, optics and theory of vision became experimental disciplines. It is in optics and theory of vision, before and during the eighteenth century, that the first significant body of mathematical constructions and quantitative measurements were applied to mental phenomena. It is here that we should look for the first success in quantitative, experimental psychology, though this work in sensory psychology was not credited to the name of "psychology" until the nineteenth century.

EMPIRICALLY AND THEORETICALLY PROGRESSIVE RESEARCH PROGRAMS

According to the usual sociological measure of progressiveness, psychology was a progressive discipline during the eighteenth century: academic appointments in psychology were made, courses were taught, the number of textbooks published per decade increased, and, near the end of the century, journals were founded (even if they failed within a decade).[138]

In Britain the "theory of mind," conceived as a branch of natural science, was firmly entrenched by the end of the century, and it continued into the next. In Germany, "psychology" so called was even more firmly entrenched as a discipline, and it continued to be taught throughout the next century. There were competing conceptions, of course, and in the second half of the nineteenth century some entrepreneurs proclaimed the founding of a "new" psychology, meaning thereby to distinguish themselves from the extant discipline. This claim of novelty rested on a comparison with the old psychology, portraying it as "merely philosophical," which meant metaphysical and not experimental (i.e., not empirically based).

I would like to make a stronger claim for the progressiveness of various eighteenth-century research programs that took a natural scientific attitude toward the mind or mental phenomena. I propose as a working historical thesis that eighteenth-century work made a threefold contribution to the psychology of the nineteenth century. First, eighteenth-century faculty psychology yielded a *conceptual* framework that was more fine-grained than that of earlier centuries and that benefited nineteenth-century investigations. Second, eighteenth-century association psychology provided the *theoretical* framework that dominated much nineteenth-century psychology, the associationist framework. Third, eighteenth-century experimental work, especially in vision, provided a tradition of *experimental* practice that, although not often counted as part of "psychology" so called during the eighteenth century, was incorporated into the "new" experimental discipline of psychology during the nineteenth century. Further development of the long-standing tradition of experimental work on vision provided the primary foundation for the claims to found a new, experimental psychology.

A survey of that subset of popular late–nineteenth- and early–twentieth-century psychology textbooks that treat psychology as a natural science would reveal that the structure of these books has much in common with scholastic textbooks of the seventeenth century: the external senses, their organs and associated nervous processes, are treated first; the "internal senses" (usually not so called) are treated further on, including memory and imagination; higher cognitive faculties, including reasoning, further on; bodily motion, somewhere along the way; and appetite and will, near the end.[139] We can discover the specifically eighteenth century contribution by finding those new chapters in these textbooks that have origins in that century. The new chapters include those on attention, conception or abstraction, and association. Attention was brought into psychology by the faculty tradition, particularly by Wolff and his followers, and was further addressed in *Ehrfahrungsseelenlehre*, which proposed empirically discovered constraints on the scope and direction of attention.[140] The chapters on discrimination and on conception or abstraction, though rooted in ancient Greek philosophy, were introduced into eighteenth-century psychology books by those developing the faculty approach.[141] The added chapter on association was due largely to attempts by authors such as Hume and Hartley to make the laws of association the fundamental explanatory principles of mind.[142]

Thus far my analysis of the "progressive" tenor of eighteenth-century psychology has been restricted to changes in psychological textbooks, which may or may not have claimed novel conceptual and theoretical results, and which only sometimes claimed to present original observations. One might concede that this older tradition contributed conceptual materials to the textbooks of the new psychology of the nineteenth century, without accepting that the eighteenth century contributed to the rise of quantitative experimental psychology. In point of fact, the strongest eighteenth-century contribution to the rise of quantitative experimentation in psychology came from the mixed-mathematical science of optics.

Optics was a "mathematical" science in virtue of its use of geometrical constructions, especially in the tracing of "visual rays." As regards vision proper, these rays were used in the analysis of the perception of size, shape, distance, and motion. Mathematical (geometrical) regularities, such as that among visual angle, apparent distance, and perceived size, were typically expressed as proportions. There were few numerical values in optics (indices of refraction being one). In the seventeenth century Descartes gave estimates of the range within which accommodation and convergence could provide accurate information for the perception of distance, though he did not say how he had arrived at the values. Berkeley, who introduced a conceptual revolution into the theory of vision with his doctrine of suggestion, did not cite quantitative observational evidence.[143] The eighteenth century was replete with novel observations of sensory phenomena, including after-images and color blindness, which were not quantitative but were nonetheless important for that.[144]

Nonetheless, there were quantitative studies of visual perception in the eighteenth century, among which I give three examples. Patrick D'Arcy measured the persistence of visual impressions by devising an apparatus for presenting to an observer a luminous object (a live coal) with a circular motion whose diameter, velocity, and distance from the observer could be varied. By observing how rapidly the coal must turn in order to result in the perception of a closed circle under a constantly fixed gaze, he concluded that the impression lasts for "8 tierces."[145] Pierre Bouger examined the question of how lines must be rendered in perspective to yield an appearance of being parallel, which was a problem addressed by several mathematical theorists. He introduced into the problem the notion of the apparent (as opposed to real) inclination of the ground plane, and measured the latter.[146] Robert Smith undertook a thorough study of the moon illusion, which he explained in accordance with the hypothesis that for a given visual angle, perceived size varies with apparent distance. He contended that the moon appears larger at the horizon because it seems further away than when it is overhead. In support of this hypothesis, he undertook to measure the perceived curvature of the vault of the heavens, which informal observation suggested is flattened. He obtained numerical values by comparing the known position of the stars with the apparent bisections by visible stars of the angle between the horizon and straight overhead.[147]

The practice of seeking precise measurements in testing theories of perception became more common in the nineteenth century and was particularly highly developed in German sensory physiology and psychology. Wundt and Hermann Helmholtz drew upon earlier work when they brought sensory psychology into a position of scientific prominence, and not solely with respect to experiment; equally or more importantly, their theoretical conceptions were inherited from the highly developed theories of spatial perception that arose in the eighteenth and early nineteenth centuries.[148]

CONCLUSIONS

Psychology or the science of the mind was conceived as a natural science in the seventeenth, eighteenth, and nineteenth centuries. The notions of *psychology* and *natural science* underwent significant change along the way.

At first "psychology" was the science of the Aristotelian soul, and covered vegetative as well as sensory and intellectual powers; study of the latter, "cognitive," powers was a (dominating) subdiscipline in Aristotelian psychology. Wolffians made psychology a part of metaphysics, coordinate with cosmology. Scots placed psychology within moral philosophy, but distinguished its "physical" laws from properly moral laws (for guiding conduct). Several Germans sought to establish an autonomous empirical psychology. Meanwhile, British and French visual theorists developed sophisticated theories of spatial perception and mathematically precise theories of size and distance perception; they created instruments to test these theories, and to measure other visual phenomena, such as the duration of visual impressions. Nearly all of these investigators were dualists of one sort or another. From early to late, the trend was to bracket metaphysical questions in favor of the search for empirical regularities and empirically based systems of classification. These empirical studies were directed at mental phenomena considered as distinct from material phenomena.

This being the case, psychology was not "invented" in the eighteenth century, but remade. Subsequently, a historical narrative according to which genuinely natural scientific psychology came into existence only in the second half of the nineteenth century has been invented. It would be interesting to look into the historical conditions that gave rise to it. Wundt, in the first edition of his *Grundzüge*, admitted considerable continuity between the old, empirical and observational psychology and the new experimental psychology that drew upon the methods of psychophysics, though he toned down the talk of continuity and stressed the differences in later editions.[149] My guess is that the story of the invention of the new psychology will lead well into the twentieth century, and will include the narrative of experimentalists such as Edward Scripture and the Harvard experimental psychologist turned historian (and, perhaps in fact, founder), Edwin Boring.[150]

My sketch of the early history of psychology challenges not only the usual historiography but also the usual conception of Enlightenment progress. In the standard narrative, the heroes of the Enlightenment are materialists. If psychology is to be made a science, the story goes, mind must be equated with matter and thereby rendered subject to empirical investigation.[151] The problem is that no one bothered to tell the early practitioners of natural scientific psychology that they had to be materialists in order to be natural scientific psychologists. In point of fact, of all the major eighteenth-century authors who made contributions to the development of psychology, only Erasmus Darwin allowed that mind might be material; nineteenth-century founders of psychology, including Wundt, Helmholtz, R. H. Lotze, Hermann Ebbinghaus, William James, Hugo Munsterberg, and Alfred Binet, banished the very question from scientific

psychology.[152] These authors conceived psychology as natural scientific
without seeing the need to adopt the metaphysical position of materialism. In so doing, they would seem to be proceeding quite rationally, by
studying what can be studied on its own terms and avoiding an unnecessary commitment to the unsupported claim that mental phenomena can
be reduced to material processes. The old equation of Enlightenment Reason with materialism turns out to have been so much prejudice. It would
be interesting to discover the historical conditions in which this version of
history became entrenched. In the meantime, there is much work to be
done investigating the history of psychology considered as the science of
mental phenomena, a history in which faculty psychology is no joke, and
in which materialism is virtually nowhere to be found.

ACKNOWLEDGMENTS

The author is grateful to the Department of Special Collections, University
Library, University of Pennsylvania, for facilitating his access to the rare
books collection.

NOTES

1. "Psychology" was so defined in major textbooks into the 1920s: Eduard
Beneke, *Lehrbuch der Psychologie als Naturwissenschaft*, 2d ed. (Berlin, 1845), 1; Theodor Waitz, *Grundlegung der Psychologie*, 2d ed. (Leipzig, 1878; reprint of 1st ed.,
Hamburg, 1846), 8–9; Wilhelm Fridolin Volkmann, *Grundriss der Psychologie* (Halle,
1856), 2–3; Wilhelm Wundt, *'Grundzüge' der physiologischen Psychologie* (Leipzig,
1874), 1–3; William James, *Psychology*, Briefer Course (New York, 1892), 1; George
Trumbull Ladd, *Psychology, Descriptive and Explanatory* (New York, 1895), 1–2; Harvey A. Carr, *Psychology: A Study of Mental Activity* (New York and London, 1925), 1.

2. On the origin of the terms "psychologia" and "psychology," Francois H. La-
pointe, "Who Originated the Term 'Psychology'?" *Journal of the History of the Behavioral Sciences* 8 (1972): 328–335.

3. Seventeenth-century textbooks, early and late: Franco Burgersdijck (1590–
1636; professor of physics at Leiden), *Collegium physicum, disputationibus XXXII ab-
solutum, totam naturalem philosophiam proponens*, 4th ed. (Oxford, 1664); Pierre Barbay (d. 1664; professor of philosophy at Paris), *In universam Aristotelis philosophiam
introductio*, 6th ed. (Paris, 1700), "Compendii physici"; idem, *Commentarius in Aristotelis physicam*, 5th ed., 2 vols. (Paris, 1690); Eustace of St. Paul (1573–1640; a
Feuillant within the Cistercian Order), *Summa philosophiae quadripartita* (Cologne,
1638), part 3, "Physica"; Bartholemew Keckermann (ca. 1571–1608, Lutheran
theologian, professor of philosophy at Danzig), "Systematis physici," in vol. 1 of his
Operum omnium, 2 vols. (Geneva, 1614); Philipp Melanchthon, *Initia doctrinae physicae*, in his *Opera*, 28 vols. (Halle, 1834–1860), 13:197; idem, *Liber de anima*, in his
Opera, 13:5–9. The Aristotelian concept of *soul* (*psyche, anima*) extended to vegeta-

tive (e.g., nutritive and reproductive), as well as sensory and intellectual, powers and capacities.

4. Seventeenth-century challenges to the Aristotelian theory of the soul included Hobbes's materialistic treatment of mind, the substance dualism of Descartes and his followers, and Leibniz's theory of monadic substances in preestablished harmony.

5. Julius B. von Rohr, *Unterricht von der Kunst, der menschen Gemüther zu erforschen* (Leipzig, 1721); Charles de Secondat, Baron de Montesquieu, *De l'esprit des lois* (Geneva, 1748), book 1, chap. 1, pp. 3–5.

6. Gary Hatfield, "Empirical, Rational, and Transcendental Psychology: Psychology as Science and as Philosophy," in *Cambridge Companion to Kant*, ed. Paul Guyer (Cambridge: Cambridge University Press, 1992), 200–227. Wundt, *Grundzüge*, 6, credited J. F. Herbart with discrediting Kant's objection that psychology cannot be a natural science because mathematics cannot be applied to "inner sense," through Herbart's observation that sensations have both temporal position and intensive magnitude; oddly, Kant was himself committed to the assertion that all sensations have intensive magnitude: see *Kritik der reinen Vernunft*, 2d ed. (Riga, 1787), 207, which makes this methodological objection, expressed in the preface of his *Metaphysische Anfangsgründe der Naturwissenschaft* (Riga, 1786) especially difficult to understand.

7. Friedrich A. Carus, *Geschichte der Psychologie* (Leipzig, 1808), 522–760.

8. Max Dessoir, *Geschichte der neueren deutschen Psychologie*, 2d ed. (Berlin, 1897–1902), 358.

9. Edwin G. Boring, *History of Experimental Psychology*, 2d ed. (New York: Appleton-Century-Crofts, 1950); Duane P. Schultz and Sydney Ellen Schultz, *History of Modern Psychology* (San Diego: Harcourt Brace Jovanovich, 1987); Richard Lowry, *Evolution of Psychological Theory: A Critical History of Concepts and Presuppositions*, 2d ed. (New York: Aldine Publishing Co., 1982); Daniel N. Robinson, *Intellectual History of Psychology*, rev. ed. (New York: Macmillan Publishing Co., 1981).

10. Graham Richards, "The Absence of Psychology in the Eighteenth Century: A Linguistic Perspective," *Studies in History and Philosophy of Science* 23 (1992): 195–211.

11. Christopher Fox, "Defining Eighteenth-Century Psychology: Some Problems and Perspectives," in *Psychology and Literature in the Eighteenth Century*, ed. Christopher Fox (New York: AMS Press, 1987), 1–22; Rolf Jeschonnek, introduction to the reprint of Carus's *Geschichte* (Berlin and New York: Springer Verlag, 1990), 17–37; Eckart Scheerer, "Psychologie," in *Historisches Wörterbuch der Philosophie*, ed. Joachim Ritter (Basel: Schwabe, 1971–), vol. 7, col. 1599–1653; Fernando Vidal, "Psychology in the Eighteenth Century," *History of the Human Sciences* 6 (1993): 89–119.

12. The history of psychology may be told from different perspectives depending on the current understanding of psychology itself; cognitive or mentalistic studies are differently valued in histories written by behaviorists as opposed to cognitive psychologists: e.g., compare J. R. Kantor, *Scientific Evolution of Psychology*, 2 vols. (Chicago: Principia Press, 1963–69), with Robinson, *Intellectual History of Psychology*.

13. I. B. Cohen, *Newtonian Revolution* (Cambridge: Cambridge University Press,

1980), 182–189; Gary Hatfield, "Metaphysics and the New Science," in *Reappraisals of the Scientific Revolution,* ed. David Lindberg and Robert Westman (Cambridge: Cambridge University Press, 1990), 93–166.

14. In essence, I am asking about the presence of the *discipline* of psychology. The term "discipline" can be understood in several ways, e.g., as the province of members of a professional society, as the province of the members of a recognized institutional administrative structure such as a university department, as a subject taught in school, or as a division of knowledge characterized by its subject matter and methodology. Here I am emphasizing the latter two senses of the word.

15. Many historical investigations, including Vidal's helpful "Psychology in the Encyclopedias," have focused on the origin of the word "psychology," as opposed to the origin of psychology as a discipline. But the etiology of concepts must be distinguished from the (allied) histories of word usage. The science of the mind was known under many titles in the eighteenth century, including "the science of the mind," "the theory of mind," "psychology," "psychologie," "Psychologie," and "Seelenlehre." Related disciplines included "anthropology," or the "science of man," which often included "psychology" as a subdiscipline, and "pneumatics," "pneumatology," or "Geisterlehre," which considered spirits (immaterial beings).

16. For eighteenth-century definitions (explicit and implicit) of the terms in quotation marks in this paragraph, see Ephraim Chambers, *Cyclopaedia, or An Universal Dictionary of Arts and Sciences,* 2d ed. (London: 1738), 2 vols.; Kant, *Kritik der reinen Vernunft,* Methodenlehre, part 3 (Kant uses the Latin term "physiologia" for the science of nature).

17. Christian Wolff, *Philosophia rationalis sive logica,* 3d ed. (Frankfurt am Main/Leipzig, 1740): philosophical cognition requires "historical" cognition of facts (§50) and metaphysics is a species of philosophy (§79). Further, psychology is a part of metaphysics, and it requires cognition of facts from experience in both its empirical and rational branches: *Psychologia empirica,* new ed. (Frankfurt am Main/Leipzig, 1738), §§1–4.

18. Roy Porter, *The Enlightenment* (Atlantic Highlands, N.J.: Humanities Press International, 1990), especially chaps. 4, 8.

19. Aristotelians also quite reasonably took an empirical attitude toward the powers of the soul, considered as powers of an animating principle. A similar point might be made about the study of an immaterial supreme being; hence, the extensive practice of "natural theology" during the eighteenth century. There is a tension between characterizations of the Enlightenment as "the Age of Reason" and as anticlerical and secular. "Enlightenment" has two distinct connotations, one based on cognitive attitude or "method," another on content and conclusion. According to the first, it means "thinking for one's self"; to the second, it includes rejection of the immaterial beings posited in many religions. Tension arises because supreme rationalists such as Descartes and Leibniz "thought for themselves" and claimed to establish the existence of God and the soul through reason. This apparent conflict should, I think, serve to sensitize us to the changing content assigned to reason or "the rational" in the modern period.

20. The most notable exceptions are the French materialists, including Diderot, La Mettrie, d'Holbach, and Helvétius, though their actual contribution to the development of psychological theory is questionable. Another exception is Samuel

Strutt, whose *A Philosophical Enquiry into the Physical Spring of Human Actions, and the Immediate Cause of Thinking* (London, 1732) argues that the only conceivable cause of motion in the human body is material.

21. David Hume, *A Treatise of Human Nature: Being an Attempt to Introduce the Experimental Method of Reasoning into Moral Subjects*, 3 vols. (London, 1739–40), I.i.4, pp. 10–13; David Hartley (1705–1757; physician, philosopher, and Christian apologist), *Observations on Man, His Frame, His Duty, and His Expectations*, 2 vols. (London, 1749), I.i, 1:5–114. On the background to associationism, emphasizing its roots in Aristotle, see William Hamilton's notes in his edition of the *Works of Thomas Reid*, 2d ed. (Edinburgh, 1849), note D**, 889–910 (thanks to Suzanne Senay for this reference).

22. In Britain, beyond Hume and Hartley, associationism received a thorough statement by Erasmus Darwin, M.D. (1731–1802), in his *Zoonomia; or, The Laws of Organic Life*, 2 vols. (London, 1794–96), who used the more general term "habit," of which association formed a species (II.ii.11, 1:12–13); this work went through three German editions between 1795 and 1805. Charles Bonnet, *Essai de psychologie* (London, 1755 [1754]), chaps. 4, 8, 20, 29 (pp. 11–12, 19–20, 45–49, 87–88), discussed a principle of association, under the title "réproduction des idées," which he explained via an interaction between the soul and vibrating fibers in the brain; see also his *Essai analytique sur les facultés de l'ame*, 2d ed., 2 vols. (Copenhagen and Geneva, 1769), chaps. 25–26, and his "Sur l'association des idées en géneral," preliminary essay to his *Palingénésie philosophique*, in his *Oeuvres d'histoire naturelle et de philosophie*, 18 vols. (Neuchatel, 1779–83), 15:143–56. Johann Friedrich Herbart (1776–1841) published two important works in psychology, *Lehrbuch der Psychologie* (Königsberg and Leipzig, 1816) and *Psychologie als Wissenschaft neu gegründet auf Erfahrung, Metaphysik und Mathematik*, 2 vols. (Königsberg, 1824–25); he sought to construct mental life using a "law of reproduction," which was itself derived from interactions among representations, on which, see Gary Hatfield, *The Natural and the Normative: Theories of Spatial Perception from Kant to Helmholtz* (Cambridge, Mass.: MIT Press, 1990), 122–123.

23. Burgersdijck, *Collegium physicum*, 198–343 (out of 353 pages); Barbay, *In Aristotelis philosophiam introductio*, 210–219 (within 191–219); Barbay, *In Aristotelis physicam*, 2:305–558 (out of 985 pages); Eustace of St. Paul, *Summa philosophiae*, 3:174–308 (out of 308 pages); Keckermann, "Systematis physici," cols. 1478–1657 (within 1357–1764).

24. Francisco Toledo, S.J. (1532–1596), *Commentaria una cum quaestionibus in tres libros Aristotelis De anima* (Cologne, 1594); Coimbra College, *In tres libros De anima*, 2d ed. (Lyon, ca. 1600); Antonio Rubio, S.J., Theol.D. (1548–1615; professor of theology), *Commentarium in libros Aristotelis De anima* (Lyon, 1620).

25. For the earliest freestanding "psychology," see Rudolph Goclenius (1547–1628; professor of physics, logic, and mathematics at Marburg), *Psychologia: hoc est, de hominis perfectione, animo* (Marburg, 1594), which had little "psychological" (in our sense) content by comparison with the standard *De anima* literature, being a collection of twelve disputations, each by a different author, ten of which discussed whether the soul is transferred from the father in the semen or is infused by God, one of which discussed the philosophical perfection of man in connection with an interpretation of Plato's *Timaeus*, and one of which discussed the seat of the

human soul, and particularly whether the whole is in the whole and in each part of the whole; similarly, Fortunio Liceti (1577–1657), *Psychologia anthropine, sive de ortu animae humanae* (Frankfurt am Main, 1606), focused on the origin, substantial nature, and reproductive status of the soul. While both of these works treat topics pertaining to the soul or "psyche," they are narrowly focused compared to the usual range of *De anima* topics such as was covered under the title of "psychology" in a disputation by Johann Conrad Dannhauer (1603–1666; Lutheran theologian, professor of theology at Strassburg, 1633–66): *Collegium psychologicum, in quo maxime controversae quaestiones, circa libros tres Aristotelis de Anima, proponuntur, ventilantur, explicantur* (Argentoranti, 1630). Christoph Scheibler (1589–1653), *Liber physicus de anima*, in his *Opera philosophica*, 2 vols. (Frankfurt am Main, 1665), vol. 2, also discussed the usual range of Aristotelian topics on the soul. "Psychology" served as a thesis topic, e.g., Petrus Liungh (d. 1679), examining Laurentius Preutz, *Theoremata psychologia generalia* (Uppsala, 1655), which focused primarily on ontological, reproductive, and postmortem questions; sometimes particular topics from the subject matter of *De anima* were examined, e.g., Abraham Georg Thauvonius (ca. 1622–1679), examining Petrus Joannis, *Disputatio physica de sensibus* (Aboae, 1655), which discussed the external and internal senses; Albert Linemann (1603–1653; mathematician in the Academy of Regiomantus), examining Benjamin Crusius, *Exercitatio philosophica visiionis naturam physicis & opticis rationibus explicatam* (Regiomantus, 1662), which discussed the doctrine of visual species in connection with Kepler's theory of retinal images.

26. Otto Casmann (d. 1607; schoolmaster in Steinfurt), *Psychologia anthropologia, sive animae humanae doctrina* (Hannover, 1594), first treated "psychologia," covering the usual Aristotelian topics, and then, in *Secunda pars anthropologiae: Hoc est, fabrica humani corporis* (Hannover, 1596), Casmann discussed "somatotomia," or the anatomy and physiology of the body, including the sense organs; Fabiano Hippio (professor of physics at Leipzig), in *Psychologia physica, sive de corpore animato, libri quatuor, toti ex Aristotle desvmti, morborum saltem doctrinis ex medicis scriptis adiecta* (Frankfurt am Main, 1600), defined "psychologia physike" as "scientia corporis animati," explicitly leaving out any discussion of souls not operating naturally in a body; *Psychologia physica* was divided into four books, the first treating the parts of the body, including the brain and animal spirits (largely free from Aristotle, including his theory of the brain); the second treating general questions about the soul, its faculties, and its relation to the body; the third treating the natural operations of the soul in the body, from nutrition through intellection and appetite; and the fourth treating medical topics concerning morbidity; Gregor Horst (1578–1636), in *De natura humana, libri duo, quorum prior de corporis structura, posterior de anima tractat* (Frankfurt am Main, 1612), treated the usual Aristotelian topics on the soul in the second part (which originated as an exercise "peri tes psyches," Wittenberg, 1602) and affirmed that the soul is part of physics only when considered as an act of the body, but not as a separated substance; Tobias Knobloch (M.D. and professor of physics), in *Disputationes anatomicae et psychologicae* (Leipzig, 1612), surveyed human anatomy in 613 of the book's 713 pages, then treated the usual topics of the soul; Johann Sperling (1603–1658; professor of physics at Wittenberg), in *Physica anthropologia* (Wittenberg, 1668), contended that "anthropologia" is part of physics because human beings are a physical species, and then

in book 1 treated the usual topics (pp. 59–302), to which he added chapters on laughter and speech, and surveyed the human body in book 2 (pp. 303–780). Samuel Haworth (medical student and later M.D.), in *Anthropologia, or, A Philosophical Discourse Concerning Man: Being the Anatomy both of his Soul and Body* (London, 1680), focused in his "pneumatology" (pp. 14–73) on the ontology, immateriality, and immortality of the soul, giving scant attention to the operation of its faculties (pp. 67–73), and in his "somatology" surveyed anatomy and physiology, adding chapters on the sexes and the ages of man. The practice arose early of including "anthropologia," treating body and soul, in physics texts: Johann Freig (1543–1583), *Quaestiones physicae* (Basel, 1579), book 35, "De anthropologia et anatome" (pp. 1147–1237), book 36, "De anthropologia et anima hominis" (pp. 1237–1290). The relation between the sixteenth-, seventeenth-, and eighteenth-century discipline of "anthropology" and the physical and cultural anthropology of the nineteenth and twentieth centuries needs further study.

27. Toledo, *Commentaria*, devoted folios 65rb–73vb to the vegetative soul, 73vb–129ra to the sensitive, 129ra–169ra to the intellect, and 169rb–179rb to appetite, will, and motion; Coimbra College, *In tres libros De anima*, devoted pp. 148–161 to the vegetative soul, 160–361 to the sensitive, 360–469 to the intellect, 460–498 to appetite, will, and motion, with separate treatises on the separated soul (499–596) and on additional problems pertaining to the five senses (597–619); Rubio, *Commentarium in libros Aristotelis De anima*, devoted pp. 278–305 to the vegetative soul, 305–632 to the sensitive, 633–735 to the rational, and 735–757 to appetite, will, and motion, adding a treatise on the separated soul (758–794). The coverage was slightly more balanced in the textbooks: Burgersdijck, *Collegium physicum*, devoted 229–239 to nutrition and growth, 239–271 to reproduction, 271–302 to the sensitive soul, 302–313 to appetite and motion, 313–333 to the intellect, and 333–343 to the will and freedom; Barbay, *In Aristotelis physicam*, devoted 374–436 to the vegetative soul and power of generation, 437–529 to the sensitive soul, including appetite and motion, and 529–558 to the rational soul; Eustace of St. Paul, *Summa philosophiae*, "Physica," devoted 197–228 to the vegetative soul, 228–277 to the sensitive, including motion, and 278–308 to the rational soul, including will.

28. Toledo, *Commentaria*, II.12, quest. 32, folios 109vb–110ra, III.3, quest. 7, folios 127ra–128rb, III.7, quest. 21, folios 164va–166ra; Coimbra College, *In tres libros De anima*, III.3, quest. 2, pp. 357–360, III.4, p. 362, III.8, quest. 5, article 3, p. 443; Rubio, *Commentarium in libros Aristotelis De anima*, II.5–6, quest. 1, p. 314, quest. 2, p. 323, III.3, quest. 5–6, 8, 11, pp. 606–613, 616–632, III.4–5, quest. 2, pp. 662–663.

29. The material treated in *De anima*, II.5–III, which was covered in the textbooks and commentaries mentioned in notes 23 and 24.

30. Toledo, *Commentaria*, III.4–7, quest. 9–23, folios 129ra–168vb; Coimbra College, *In tres libros De anima*, III.4–8, pp. 360–459; Rubio, *Commentarium in libros Aristotelis De anima*, III.4–5, pp. 633–735. The doctrine of the agent and patient intellects was regularly mentioned in the textbooks, e.g., Eustace of St. Paul, *Summa philosophiae*, "Physica," III.4, disputation 2, pp. 284–300.

31. Toledo, *Commentaria*, proem, quest. 2 (folio 4), subsumed the soul in all of its operations under physics; Coimbra College, *In tres libros De anima*, proem,

quest. 1, article 2 (pp. 7–8); and Rubio, *Commentarium in libros Aristotelis De anima,* proem, quest. 1 (pp. 10–11), subsumed the study of embodied souls under physics, and the separated soul under metaphysics.

32. The orthodox view was that intellection is a natural power of the human soul, but that it differs from the sensitive powers in being immaterial; it is an immaterial power of the form of the human being, and hence of a form informing a material body. It was ascribed immateriality "in its operation" on the grounds that, in order to receive "common natures" (which are universals), it must be capable of "becoming all things," and that any power that was tied to a corporeal organ for its operations would be limited by the materiality of the organ. Orthodox authors nonetheless considered this immaterial power to be a natural power of the form of the human animal. Unorthodox authors denied that these powers could be produced by the rational soul considered as the form of the human body precisely because of its assqciation with a body; they ascribed either the agent or both it and the patient intellects to a higher being, which the early seventeenth-century commentator Jacopo Zabarella contended was God itself. Thus, as the eighteenth century opened there was in the recent Christian Aristotelian corpus a minority opinion that the intellectual powers of the mind are not "natural" to the human psyche but must be attributed to a divine power.

33. Thomas Hobbes (1588–1679), *Elements of Philosophy, the First Section, Concerning Body* (London: 1656; translation from Latin edition of 1655), chap. 25.

34. Ibid., chap. 25, article 2, pp. 291–292.

35. Hobbes, *Leviathan, or the Matter, Forme and Power of a Commonwealth Ecclesiasticall and Civil* (London, 1651), part 1, chap. 2, p. 8.

36. Ibid., part 1, chap. 3, p. 8.

37. Hobbes, *Elements,* part 4, chap. 25, article 8, p. 297.

38. The quoted phrases are from Descartes's "Lettre de l'avthevr," which first appeared in the French translation, *Principes de la philosophie* (Paris, 1647; translated from the Latin edition, Amsterdam, 1644), 26, 29; English translation, Valentine Rodger Miller and Reese P. Miller, *Principles of Philosophy* (Dordrecht, Boston, and Lancaster: D. Reidel, 1983), xxiv, xxvi. "Experiment" includes appeals to both sense experience and controlled observation.

39. Descartes, *Principia,* part 4, articles 189–198. René le Bossu, *Parallele des principes de la physique d'Aristote, & de celle de René des Cartes* (Paris, 1674; reprint, Paris: J. Vrin, 1981), noted that "l'homme même, & son ame, au moins en qualité d'ame sensitive, sera l'objet de la Physique de M. des Cartes, aussi bien que tout ce qu'il y a de matériel & d'étendu dans le monde qu'il nomme *Corps*" (p. 46).

40. René Descartes, *L'Homme de René Descartes* (Paris, 1664), 1, 29; English translation by Thomas Steele Hall, *Treatise of Man* (Cambridge, Mass.: Harvard University Press, 1972), 1, 36. It is likely that the discussion of mind-body union would have occurred after the lost or unwritten section of *Le Monde* on the soul, as described in Descartes's *Discours de la methode* (Leiden, 1637), part 5; nonetheless, it would have been a part of what Descartes termed his "physics," to Marin Mersenne, March 1637, in *Oeuvres,* 11 vols., ed. Charles Adam and Paul Tannery (Paris: J. Vrin, 1968–74), 1:348.

41. René Descartes, *Dioptrique,* part 6, published with the *Discours* in 1637.

42. Jacques Rohault (1618–1672), *Traité de physique* (Amsterdam, 1676); idem,

trans. John Clarke (Samuel's brother), *System of Natural Philosophy*, 2d ed., 2 vols. (London, 1728–29; reprint, New York: Garland Publishing, 1987), 1:248–257.

43. Antoine Le Grand (d. 1699), *Institutio philosophiae secundum principia de Renati Descartes*, new ed. (London, 1678); trans. Richard Blome, *An Entire Body of Philosophy, According to the Principles of the Famous Renate Des Cartes* (London, 1694; reprint, New York: Johnson, 1972).

44. As Descartes had himself done, Le Grand was not averse to presenting Cartesian philosophy using the Aristotelian terms, and so he attributed a "soul" to plants and animals, which turned out to be "a Heating, but not a Shining Fire" (Descartes's "fire without light"): Le Grand, *Body of Philosophy*, book 1, part 7, introduction, article 3, p. 229b.

45. Ibid., book 1, part 8, chap. 19, article 1, p. 300a. This placement of the senses mimics the Aristotelian treatises by grouping sense perception with other bodily functions.

46. Ibid., book 1, part 9, chap. 5, article 3, p. 329a.

47. Pierre Sylvain Regis (1632–1707), *Système de philosophie: contenant la logique, metaphysique, physique & morale*, 7 vols. (Lyon, 1691).

48. William R. Shea, "The Unfinished Revolution: Johann Bernoulli (1667–1748) and the Debate between the Cartesians and the Newtonians," in *Revolutions in Science: Their Meaning and Relevance*, ed. William R. Shea (Canton, Mass.: Science History Publications, 1988), 70–92; Thomas Hankins, *Science and the Enlightenment* (Cambridge: Cambridge University Press, 1985), chap. 3; Gary Hatfield, "Was the Scientific Revolution Really a Revolution in Science?" in *Tradition, Transmission, Transformation*, ed. Jamil Ragep and Stephen Livesay (Amsterdam: E. J. Brill, in press).

49. Isaac Newton, *Mathematical Principles of Natural Philosophy*, 2 vols., trans. Florian Cajori (Berkeley and Los Angeles: University of California Press, 1966), 1:13, where he stated a wish to "derive the rest of the phenomena of nature by the same kind of reasoning from mechanical principles," and acknowledged that the needed principles remained unknown.

50. Isaac Newton, *Opticks, or, A treatise of the Reflections, Refractions, Inflections & Colours of Light*, after the 4th ed. (London, 1730), ed. Duane H. D. Roller (New York: Dover Publications, 1952), Queries 12, 14–16, 23–24, 28, pp. 345–347, 353–354, 370.

51. Willem Jacob 'sGravesande (1688–1742; professor of mathematics at Leiden), *Mathematical Elements of Natural Philosophy, Confirm'd by Experiments, or An Introduction to Sir Isaac Newton's Philosophy*, 6th ed., 2 vols., trans. J. T. Desaguliers (London, 1747), 1:1–2. In his *Introductio ad philosophiam; metaphysicam et logicam continens*, 2d ed. (Leiden, 1737), he discussed the human mind in book 1, "Metaphysica," part 2, "De mente humana," covering intellect, freedom, the mind-body nexus, and the origin of ideas (pp. 38–105); in book 2, "Logica," he discussed how the mind should be directed in order to acquire a cognition of things (pp. 106–342, with an appendix on the syllogism, pp. 345–375).

52. Petrus van Musschenbroek (1692–1761; professor of philosophy and mathematics at Utrecht), *Essai de physique*, 2 vols., trans. Pierre Massuet (Leyden, 1739), chap. 1, section 2, 1:2; idem, *Elements of Natural Philosophy*, trans. John Colson (London, 1744), chap. 1, section 2, pp. 2–3.

53. E.g., Johann Samuel Traugott Gehler (1751–1795), *Physikalisches Wörter-buch*, new ed., 6 vols. (Leipzig, 1798–1801), "Optik," 3:385.

54. Even the Newtonians continued to include the theory of vision in the optical portions of their physics books: 'sGravesande, *Mathematical Elements of Natural Philosophy*, though patterning his treatment of optics after Newton's narrow view, so that he treated motion, inflection, refraction, and reflection (vol. 2, book 5), nonetheless provided a summary discussion of visual perception (2:175–181); Musschenbroek, *Essai de physique*, discussed the properties of light, refraction, and reflection (chaps. 27–31), followed by a discussion of the eye and vision, including optical anatomy and physiology and visual judgments (chaps. 32–33), to which he added the traditional optical topics of dioptrics and catoptrics, or vision by means of refracted and reflected light (chaps. 34–35).

55. John Locke, *An Essay Concerning Humane Understanding* (London, 1690), I.i.2; further discussion in Hatfield, *Natural and Normative*, 28–31.

56. Descartes, *Regulae ad directionem ingenii*, in *Opuscula posthuma* (Amsterdam, 1701), rules 8, 12, pp. 23, 32–35. A translation of the *Regulae* into Netherlandish had appeared in 1684.

57. E.g., T. E., "a gentleman," *Vindiciae mentis: An Essay of the Being and Nature of Mind* (London, 1702), and John Broughton (ca. 1673–1720; chaplain to the Duke of Marlborough), *Psychologia: or, An Account of the Nature of the Rational Soul* (London, 1703), which sought to show the immateriality and immortality of the soul by means of natural reason.

58. Simon Schaffer, "States of Mind: Enlightenment and Natural Philosophy," in *Languages of Psyche*, G. S. Rousseau (Berkeley, Los Angeles, Oxford: University of California Press, 1990), 233–290.

59. For an appreciation of the variety of senses in which a "Newtonian" approach to natural philosophy might be understood, see Chambers, *Cyclopaedia*, vol. 2, "Newtonian Philosophy"; also, I. B. Cohen, *Newtonian Revolution* (Cambridge: Cambridge University Press, 1980), part 1.

60. On Lossius and Kant, see Hatfield, *Natural and Normative*, chap. 3.

61. Wolff, *Philosophia rationalis*, §79; see also Alexander Gottlieb Baumgarten (1714–1762; professor of philosophy at Halle), *Metaphysica*, 7th ed. (Halle, 1779).

62. Wilhelm Wundt, *Grundzüge der physiologischen Psychologie*, 3d ed. (Leipzig, 1887), 7.

63. Wolff, *Logica*, preliminary discourse, chaps. 1–2.

64. Christian Wolff's most general division of philosophy and its distinction from mathematical disciplines is given in his *Cognitiones rationales de viribus intellectus humani*, new ed. (Frankfurt and Leipzig, 1740; first translated from German in 1730), prolegomena, §§10–15; mechanics and statics, considered as the sciences of motion and equilibrium, were considered together, *Elementa matheseos universae*, new ed., 5 vols. (Halle, 1733–42), vol. 2: "Elementa mechanicae et staticae." As Wolff understood the mathematical division of knowledge, it also contained portions depending on facts: the "mixed" mathematical sciences of optics, astronomy, chronology, geography, etc.

65. Wolff, *Logica*, preliminary discourse, chap. 3.

66. Christian Wolff, *Cosmologia generalis*, new ed. (Frankfurt, 1737).

67. Wolff, *Logica*, preliminary discourse, §78. In Wolff's view metaphysics uses some principles, including the principles of sufficient reason and contradiction, that are grounded in the powers of mind and not derived from observations of external objects, but the attribution of these principles as basic logical and metaphysical principles is, according to Wolff, empirically based on the mind's reflective awareness of its own operations in making judgments: *Ontologica*, §§27–29.

68. Wolff, *Logica*, preliminary discourse, §10.

69. Wolff, *Psychologia empirica*, §§23–24; *Psychologia rationalis*, §§83–91 (thanks to Alison Simmons for getting me to clarify the distinction with examples).

70. Wolff, *Psychologia empirica*, §§65–69; *Psychologia rationalis*, §§103–145.

71. Wolff, *Vernünfftige Gedancken von den Würckungen der Natur* (Halle, 1723), chap. 14; idem, *Allerhand Nützliche Versuche, dadurch zu genauer Erkäntniss der Natur und Kunst der Weg gebähnet wird*, 3 vols. (Halle, 1727–29), part 3, chap. 8 (vol. 3); idem, *Elementa matheseos*, "Elementa opticae" (3:1–100); idem, *Vernünfftige Gedancken von dem Gebrauche der Theile in Menschen, Thieren und Pflantzen* (Frankfurt and Leipzig, 1725), chap. 5.

72. Boring, *History of Experimental Psychology*, 162; Robinson, *Intellectual History of Psychology*, 259, 265, 301.

73. Wolff, *Psychologia empirica*, §§1–4; *Psychologia rationalis*, §§1–3. For English translation and discussion, see Robert J. Richards, "Christian Wolff's Prolegomena to Empirical and Rational Psychology: Translation and Commentary," *Proceedings of the American Philosophical Society* 124 (1980): 227–239.

74. Jerry Fodor jocularly defends faculty psychology in his *Modularity of Mind* (Cambridge, Mass.: MIT Press, 1983). More seriously, the organization of psychology textbooks has long born the stamp of the traditional division of faculties, as psychologists have studied the functionally characterized faculties of cognition, including perception, learning, and memory, and more specific capacities, such as visual perception, and within vision, color, shape, and motion perception.

75. Wolff, *Psychologia empirica*, §§190–194.

76. Wolff, *Psychologia empirica*, part 1, section 2, chaps. 3–4; section 3, chap. 1; *Psychologia rationalis*, part 1, section 1, chaps. 3–4.

77. The following textbooks follow Wolff in the disciplinary placement and the basic content of his empirical and rational psychology: Georg Bernhard Bilfinger, *Delucidationes philosophicae de Deo, anima humana, mundo, et generalibus rerum affectionibus* (Tübingen, 1725); Ludwig Philipp Thümmig, *Institutiones philosophiae Wolfianae*, 2 vols. (Frankfurt and Leipzig, 1725–26); Johann Peter Reusch, *Systema metaphysicum* (Jena, 1735); Friedrich Christian Baumeister, *Institutiones metaphysicae: Ontologiam, cosmologiam, psychologiam, theologiam denique naturalem complexae* (Wittenberg and Zerbst, 1738); Baumgarten, *Metaphysica*. Kant used Wolff's mathematics texts and Baumgarten's *Metaphysics* (including psychology).

78. Jean Deschamps, *Cours abrégé de la philosophie wolfienne*, 2 vols. (Leipzig and Amsterdam, 1743–47).

79. *Encyclopédie, ou Dictionnaire raisonné des sciences, des arts et des metiers*, eds. Denis Diderot and Jean Le Rond d'Alembert, 17 vols. (Paris, 1751–65), 1:338, 13:543.

80. Johann Gottlob Krüger (1715–59), *Versuch einer Experimental-Seelenlehre*

(Halle and Helmstädt, 1756). Krüger studied philosophy and medicine at Halle, receiving degrees in 1737 and 1742, becoming doctor and professor of philosophy and medicine in 1743; in 1751 he became professor of philosophy and medicine at Helmstädt.

81. Krüger, *Naturlehre*, 3 vols. (Halle, 1740–49), part 2, §§316–317, 2:568–575.

82. Krüger, *Experimental-Seelenlehre*, iii–v.

83. Krüger, *Dissertationem sollemnem de sensatione pro honoribus doctoris* (Halle, 1742), 3–6, 8–9 (the dissertation was completed in 1742, two years after Wolff's return to Halle from Marburg); idem, *Naturlehre*, part 2, §9, 2:14–16; idem, *Experimental-Seelenlehre*, ix–x, in which he said he followed the Wolffian Baumeister in metaphysics (vi).

84. Krüger, *Experimental-Seelenlehre*, 1–2.

85. Ibid., 5–8.

86. Ibid., 15–21. Earlier Krüger spoke somewhat wistfully of the days when "experiments," such as cutting out pieces of the brain to see what happens, were performed on human "delinquents," *Naturlehre*, part 2, §427, 2:726.

87. Krüger, *Experimental-Seelenlehre*, 2–3.

88. Krüger, *De sensatione*, 15–18; idem, *Naturlehre*, part 2, §§308–309, 2:551–558.

89. Wolff, *Psychologia rationalis*, §§136–141, pp. 109–112.

90. Krüger, *Naturlehre*, part 2, §§314–322, 2:567–580; discussed qualitatively, idem, *Experimental-Seelenlehre*, 101–104.

91. Krüger, *Experimental-Seelenlehre*, iii–v.

92. Krüger, *Naturlehre*, part 2, §§369–379, 2:667–675. Wolff, *Elementa matheseos*, "Elementa opticae," chaps. 5, 6, 8.

93. Descartes, *Dioptrique*, part 6; George Berkeley, *An Essay towards a New Theory of Vision* (Dublin, 1709), sections 53–60; Claude Nicolas Le Cat (1700–68; M.D.), *Traité des sensations et des passions*, 2 vols. (Paris, 1767), 2:441–484. On early modern theories of size and distance perception, see Gary Hatfield and William Epstein, "The Sensory Core and the Medieval Foundations of Early Modern Perceptual Theory," *Isis* 70 (1979): 363–384.

94. Krüger, *Naturlehre*, part 2, §380, 2:675–677; also, idem, *Experimental-Seelenlehre*, 95–101.

95. Krüger, *De sensatione*, 20–22; *Naturlehre*, part 2, §312, 2:559–563.

96. Krüger, *De sensatione*, 23–24 (where he quotes from Newton's Query), 29–31; *Naturlehre*, part 2, §331, 2:607–608.

97. Krüger, *Naturlehre*, 2d ed., 3 vols. (Halle, 1744–1755), part 2, §§330–332, 2:625–642 (on p. 641 he favorably cites Herman Boerhaave on the elasticity of the animal spirits). Krüger added several clinical reports to the second edition.

98. Ibid., part 2, §386, 2:718–724.

99. Krüger, *Naturlehre*, 1st ed., part 2, §430, 2:729–730.

100. Guillaume-Lambert Godart (ca. 1717–1794; M.D.), *Specimen animasticae medicae* (Reims, 1745); idem, *La physique de l'ame* (Berlin, 1755).

101. Godart, *Physique de l'ame*, 21.

102. Ibid., v–vi, 8.

103. Ibid., iii–iv, v–vi.

104. Ibid., part 1, chaps. 3–4.

105. Charles Bonnet (1720–1793; gentleman naturalist, psychologist, and religious thinker), *Essai de psychologie; ou, Considerations sur les operations de l'ame, sur l'habitude et sur l'education* (London, 1755 [1754]; translated into German, Lemgo, 1773); idem, *Essai analytique sur les facultés de l'ame*, 2 vols. (Copenhagen, 1760; 2d ed., Copenhagen and Geneva, 1769; translated into German, Bremen, 1770; Dutch, Utrecht and Rotterdam, 1771). New psychological material, along with a summary of the old, appeared in his masterpiece, *La palingénésie philosophique ou idées sur l'état passé & l'état futur des etres vivans*, 2 vols. (Geneva, 1769; translated into German, Zurich, 1769–70).

106. Charles Bonnet, *Essai analytique*, 2d ed., vii, xxiv, ix–x.

107. Ibid., chaps. 7, 9–11; *Essai de psychologie*, chap. 64.

108. Bonnet, *Essai de psychologie*, introduction, especially pp. 1–3; chaps. 1–6, 35.

109. Ibid., chaps. 21–26; 27–31, 61–64; 7; 8–20; 66–70. Many of the topics in the *Essai de psychologie* recur in the *Essai analytique* (which often quoted the former work); some, such as freedom, received more extended analysis, while some, such as the discussion of education, were omitted.

110. Bonnet, *Essai de psychologie*, chaps. 34–37. On Bonnet, see Lorin Anderson, *Charles Bonnet and the Order of the Known* (Dordrecht, Boston, and London: D. Reidel, 1982), and Raymond Savioz, *Philosophie de Charles Bonnet de Genève* (Paris: J. Vrin, 1948).

111. The works of Krüger, Godart, and Bonnet were regularly mentioned in overviews of the psychological literature: Karl C. E. Schmid, (1745–1799; professor of philosophy at Jena), *Empirische Psychologie*, 2d ed. (Jena, 1796), 143, 149; Carus, *Geschichte der Psychologie*, 598, 642 (Krüger and Bonnet only); Karl Hermann Scheidler (1795–1866; professor of philosophy at Jena), *Handbuch der Psychologie*, 2d ed., 2 vols. (Darmstadt, 1833), 1:295.

112. Thomas Reid (1710–1796), *On the Active Powers of Man* (Edinburgh, 1788). Adam Ferguson (1723–1816), *Institutes of Moral Philosophy*, 2d ed. (Edinburgh, 1773), part 2; the original version was entitled *Analysis of Pneumatics and Moral Philosophy*.

113. Francis Hutcheson, *De naturali hominum socialitate, oratio inauguralis* (Glasgow, 1730); *Philosophiae moralis* (Glasgow, 1745), book 1, chap. 1.

114. Hume, *Treatise of Human Nature* (see note 21 above).

115. Gladys Bryson, *Man and Society: The Scottish Inquiry of the Eighteenth Century* (Princeton, N.J.: Princeton University Press, 1945), 18–21, 138–139, 145.

116. Hartley, *Observations on Man*, 1:5, credited Locke and Newton for drawing attention to the importance of association and the theory of vibrations, respectively.

117. Thomas Reid, *Essays on the Powers of the Human Mind* (London, 1827), vi.

118. Ibid., vii.

119. Ibid., 31: This philosophy "has received great accessions from the labours of several modern authors; and perhaps wants little more to entitle it to the name of a science, but to be purged of certain hypotheses, which have imposed on some of the most acute writers on this subject, and led them into downright scepticism." This "hypothesis" is the theory of ideas and mediate perception (ibid., Essay II, chaps. 8–12).

120. Ferguson, *Institutes*, introduction, section 7; section 3.

121. Ibid., part 2, chap. 2, section 1.

122. Darwin, *Zoonomia*, 1:iii.

123. Ibid., 1:1; 41; 37.

124. Dugald Stewart (1753–1828; professor of moral philosophy at Edinburgh), *Elements of the Philosophy of the Human Mind* (Philadelphia, 1793).

125. Jacob F. Abel (1751–1829; professor of psychology and morals at the Karlsschule), *Einleitung in die Seelenlehre* (Stuttgart, 1786), Einleitung; Karl C. E. Schmid (1761–1812; professor of philosophy at Jena), *Empirische Psychologie*, 2d ed. (Jena, 1796), 8, 11–12. Earlier works included Dietrich Tiedemann (1748–1803; professor of ancient languages at the Karlsschule), *Untersuchungen über den Menschen*, 3 vols. (Leipzig, 1777–78); Johann Nicolas Tetens (1736–1807; professor of philosophy at Kiel), *Philosophische Versuche über die menschliche Natur und ihre Entwickelung*, 2 vols. (Leipzig, 1777), which, while applying the "psychological method" of observation (the method of the natural philosopher), did so to a restricted set of topics, namely, understanding, will, the nature of humankind, freedom, the nature of the soul, and the development of the soul.

126. Abel, *Seelenlehre*, §§148–163, 194–206.

127. Ibid., §§4–20.

128. Schmid, *Empirische Psychologie*, 11–17.

129. Ibid., 18–26.

130. Ibid., 189–190.

131. Johann Karl Wezel (1747–1819), *Versuch über die Kenntnis des Menschen*, 2 vols. (Leipzig, 1784–85).

132. Immanuel Kant, *Anthropologie in pragmatischer Hinsicht* (Frankfurt and Leipzig, 1799); Johann F. Blumenbach, *De generis humani varietate nativa* (Göttingen, 1775).

133. Jean Fernel (1497–1558; physician and philosopher), *Opera medicinalia* (Venice, 1566), "Physiologiae," book 1, chaps. 9–10, and book 5.

134. Albrecht von Haller (1708–1777), *Elementa physiologiae corporis humanae*, 8 vols. (Lausanne, 1757–66), vol. 5, books 12–17.

135. Ibid., book 16, section 4, §29, 5:520–522. Berkeley, *New Theory of Vision*, sections 53–60; Le Cat, *Traité des sensations*, 2:441–484.

136. Haller, *Elementa physiologiae*, vol. 5, book 17.

137. On Berkeley, see Margaret Atherton, *Berkeley's Revolution in Vision* (Ithaca, N.Y.: Cornell University Press, 1990).

138. These claims are supported by Carus's *Geschichte* and Schmid's overview of the literature, *Empirische Psychologie*, 142–156. A reviewer in the *Allgemeine Literatur Zeitung of 1787* (supplement), while panning Christoph Meiners' *Grundriss der Seelenlehre* (Lemgo, 1786), could speak of the great number of "textbooks of psychology" that are available. It has been customary for writers of psychology textbooks, from Krüger and Bonnet on, to apologize for adding to such a crowded field.

139. James, *Psychology*; Edward B. Titchener, *Outline of Psychology*, new ed. (New York and London, 1901); Hermann Ebbinghaus, *Abriss der Psychologie*, 4th ed. (Leipzig, 1912); Edward L. Thorndike, *Elements of Psychology*, 2d ed. (New York,

1915); Wilhelm Wundt, *Grundriss der Psychologie*, 13th ed. (Leipzig, 1918); Carr, *Psychology*.

140. Wolff, *Psychologia empirica*, part 1, section 3, chap. 1. Abel, *Seelenlehre*, §§194–268. Nicolas Malebranche previously had placed attention at the center of his discussion of method, *Recherche de la vérité*, book 6, part 2, in his *Oeuvres*, 20 vols. (Paris, 1958–1970), vol. 2.

141. Wolff, *Psychologia empirica*, part 1, section 3, chap. 1; *Psychologia rationalis*, part 1, section 1, chap. 4; Abel, *Seelenlehre*, §§392–436.

142. Hume, *Treatise*, book 1, part 1, section 4; Hartley, *Observations on Man*, part 1, chap. 1, propositions 10–14, and passim. Wolff described the phenomena of association and their law, *Psychologia empirica*, §§104, 117; his follower Baumgarten named "*associatio idearum*" the "*lex imaginationis*," *Metaphysica*, §561.

143. On Descartes and Berkeley, see Hatfield and Epstein, "Sensory Core."

144. Georges Louis Leclerc, Comte de Buffon, "Dissertation sur les couleurs accidentelles," *Mémoires de mathématique et de physique* 60 (Paris, 1743): 147–158. John Dalton, "Extraordinary Facts Relating to the Vision of Colours: with Observations," *Memoirs and Proceedings of the Literary and Philosophical Society of Manchester* 5 (1798): 28–45.

145. Patrick D'Arcy, "Mémoire sur la durée de la sensation de la vue," *Mémoires de mathématique et de physique* 82 (Paris, 1765): 439–451.

146. Pierre Bouger, "Recherche sur la grandeur apparente des objets," *Mémoires de mathématique et de physique* 72 (Paris, 1755): 99–112.

147. Robert Smith, *Compleat System of Opticks*, 2 vols. (Cambridge, 1738), 1:63–66. All three examples, along with others, are reported in Joseph Priestley, *History and Present State of Discoveries Relating to Vision, Light, and Colours* (London, 1772).

148. Hatfield, *Natural and Normative*, chaps. 2, 4, 5.

149. Wundt, *Grundzüge*, 1–8; ibid., 3d ed., 2 vols. (Leipzig, 1887), 1:1–8; ibid., 5th ed., 3 vols. (Leipzig, 1902), 1:1–8.

150. Edward Wheeler Scripture, *New Psychology* (London, 1898); E. G. Boring, *History of Experimental Psychology* (New York: Century, 1929).

151. Schaffer makes this position explicit in "States of Mind," 240, 263.

152. Darwin, *Zoonomia*, 1:108–109. On antimaterialistic and nonmaterialistic stances in eighteenth- and nineteenth-century psychology (including Wundt, Helmholtz, and Lotze), see my *Natural and Normative*, chaps. 6–7; James, *Psychology*, 6–7; Hugo Munsterberg, *Psychology: General and Applied* (New York and London, 1914), 39–42: Alfred Binet, *Introduction à la psychologie expérimentale* (Paris, 1894), 146.

EIGHT

The Enlightenment Science of Society

David Carrithers

In his *Treatise of Human Nature* (1739) David Hume identified "logic," "morals," "criticism," and "politics" as the "sciences" most closely connected with the study of human nature and human understanding. Within these four "sciences," Hume asserted, "is comprehended almost everything which it can anyway import us to be acquainted with, or which can tend either to the improvement or ornament of the human mind."[1] Understandably absent from Hume's classificatory scheme were such specialized human sciences as psychology, sociology, political economy, geography, anthropology, ethnology, and philology. Hume's terminology reminds us that the formal development and specialization of distinct social science disciplines was a nineteenth- rather than eighteenth-century phenomenon. Hence one commits the sin of anachronism—Giambattista Vico's "conceit of scholars"—in attempting to identify specialized human sciences prior to the nineteenth century. As Roger Smith points out in this volume, an essential concern with human nature during the eighteenth century unified lines of inquiry that have since been separated and refined. Hume's "science of man," as Ludmilla Jordanova reminds us, should not be conflated with human sciences whose contours had not yet been sharply delineated. In spite of these cautions, the literature on the Enlightenment is filled with titles celebrating the Enlightenment birth of social science and unabashedly labeling as "sociological" the major works of such figures as Montesquieu, Turgot, Condorcet, Vico, Hume, Ferguson, Smith, Thomas Reid, William Robertson, Dugald Stewart, and John Millar.[2] In his much applauded synthesis of Enlightenment viewpoints Peter Gay suggested a quarter century ago that a small group of individuals, drawing partly on the influence of travel literature and partly on the striking successes in the natural sciences, set out to apply observational methods to the study of man in society and created the early classics of social science. Gay did not hesitate to use the phrase "the first social scientists" to describe the work of Enlightenment-era *philosophes* even though the phrase *la science sociale* was nonexistent prior to the works of D.-J. Garat, P.-L. Lacretelle, and E.-J. Sièyes—all members of the Société de 1789.[3] Embracing the term *sociologie*, coined by Comte in 1839, Gay concluded that "the aims of eighteenth-century *sociology* were clear enough: to substitute reliable information and rational theory for guessing and metaphysics, and to use the newly won knowledge in behalf of man."[4]

In the last quarter century, the intellectual landscape has changed almost beyond recognition. At the time Gay composed his two-volume study, the influence of Arthur Lovejoy, the doyen of the history of ideas movement in America, was still pervasive. Lovejoy's method stressed continuity and the extent to which philosophers engage in roughly the same conversation while only the materials and their arrangement undergo modest change.[5] This perspective has now been thoroughly challenged. Discontinuity, rupture, paradigm shifts, and the end of history have displaced the old trilogy of progress, positivism, and evolution as the dominant metaphors for the prospects for both human beings and for human science. For many, disciplinary history is now dead on arrival, along with the history of ideas itself. Prominent in this new school of thought was Michel Foucault, who hinted in his *L'Archeologie du Savoir* (1969) that adherence to a notion of disciplinary continuity is a form of infantile neurosis. We fixate on foundations, he asserted, because we crave "the certainty that time will disperse nothing without restoring it in a reconstituted unity." Instead we should accept the decentering of man and the presence of "radical discontinuities" that "suspend the continuous accumulation of knowledge, interrupt its slow development, and force it to enter a new time, cut . . . off from its empirical origin and its original motivations."[6]

There is much to be said for Foucault's point of view.[7] As Heraclitus long ago remarked in a text that nudged Marx toward the dialectic, one can't step into the same river twice, and with regard to the human sciences some have asked whether the contributions of *any* Enlightenment figure may be regarded as even in the same stream of thought as *any* figure writing in the changed world wrought by the French Revolution.[8] There is a danger of distortion, however, in overdoing the discontinuity thesis. New sciences are never as new as the label implies. Even Foucault spoke of the *suspension*—rather than the *nonexistence*—of "accumulation," "development," "empirical origin," and "original motivations." Hence his radical discontinuity may presume, sub rosa, an underlying substratum of continuity whose broad rhythms and patterns must exist if only to be smashed, broken, or forgotten prior to resurfacing later. Nor should we discount the issue of perspective. There exist, Foucault acknowledged,

"several pasts, several forms of connection, several hierarchies of importance, several networks of determination, several teleologies, for one and
the same science, as its present undergoes change."[9] We need ask, then,
on Foucault's own terms, whether it is the present discontinuities we are
suffering that are causing us to project rupture back into the past, while
an earlier age produced Lovejoy's "unit-ideas" and continuity. There should
be no claim that disciplines evolve in well-ordered patterns, and certainly
there should be no positing of teleological ends for disciplines as with the
Enlightenment longing for a Tenth Epoch encapsulating perfection. But
is there no lineage at all? Can we posit no lines of development, transmission, and succession making it possible to recognize a modicum of com-
monality in work done on the same questions in different centuries, even
if the context is radically different?

Such a view seems extreme. We can appreciate that Marx reached different conclusions from eighteenth-century students of society in spite
of the once-popular arguments of Roy Pascal and Ronald Meek for the
presence of economic determinism in products of the Scottish Enlightenment.[10] But should eighteenth- and nineteenth-century explorations of
the material and moral substrata of laws and institutions at least be regarded as part of the same general flow of thought? Foucault himself offered us a way out of this impasse when he suggested that "any context
of History is the province of psychology, sociology, or the science of languages" since all men live, work, and speak. Hence history offers "each of
the sciences of man . . . a background, which establishes it and provides it
with a fixed ground and, as it were, a homeland."[11] What I aim to do in
the remainder of this chapter is to discuss the Enlightenment science of
society as the "homeland" for what was later labeled "sociology," while
avoiding any additional skirmishes on the vexing questions of origins and
disciplinarity. I consciously avoid using the anachronistic term *sociology* in
the title of the chapter, but since I do not fully subscribe to Foucault's radical epistemic break at the epoch of the French Revolution, I have not
avoided using the terms "sociology" and "sociological" to describe the orientation of a number of Enlightenment figures, although quotation marks
will always be employed. Although their science of society was, of course,
different from the sociology of later epochs reflecting a different context, it was not so completely different as to be wholly without relevance
for what nineteenth-century perspectives would produce. Furthermore, a
strong case can be made that *la science sociale* of the Société de 1789 bears
less resemblance to what we now mean by "social science" than does the
work of such figures as Montesquieu, Hume, Smith, Ferguson, and Millar.
For J.-J. Régis de Cambacérès, for example, *la science sociale* consisted of
"determining the best use for the capacities of the individual, his rights,
[and] his passions"—a usage that hardly corresponds to our own.[12]

Before there can be a science there must be a subject matter. For sociology that subject matter, most generally speaking, is society, or civil society. During the course of the eighteenth century numerous questions concerning civil society were being discussed. These included the natural, that is, noncontractual, origins of civil society; the evolutionary origins of property, government, and justice; the role of such natural sentiments as benevolence and sympathy as contributors to social bonding; the origins and implications of the social division of labor; the impact on legal systems of the advent of property and of changing modes of subsistence; the relation between governmental types and underlying psychological and social conditions; the influence of such physical causes as climate, geography, and extent of territory on human behavior and thus, indirectly, on societal development; the functionalist interaction of the structural components of society to produce a "general spirit," or "national character"; and the extent to which human character, behavior, ideas, tastes, and impressions are fashioned by what Nicolas Malebranche, Hume, and Smith all referred to as "the mirror of society."

Focus on society as a whole as the subject matter of a new science of society moved numerous eighteenth-century theorists—the physiocrats were an obvious exception—away from the methodological individualism too often considered the dominant Enlightenment model for theorizing about man and society.[13] In the writings of Montesquieu in particular and of those he influenced, it was not just the individual and individual mental processes that received attention but rather the behavior of individuals in groups of various sorts. General causes affecting large groups of people and culminating in grand historical events were what intrigued Montesquieu both in his historical investigation of the rise and fall of Rome and in his massive treatise on laws. Numerous later theorists caught the gist of this refocusing of social science inquiry from the individual to the group. Hence Adam Ferguson's famous remark, "Men have always acted in troops or companies."[14] Individuals qua individuals, it came to be understood, are not the basic building blocks of society. Rather, families, clans, and socioeconomic groupings of various sorts deriving from the earliest division of labor began to take center stage as the focal point of the "sociological" analysis emerging in the Enlightenment.[15]

Many eighteenth-century theorists, including Hume, Smith, Ferguson, and J. G. Herder tended to conflate the study of human societies with the study of human nature, believing that the study of one illumines the essentials of the other.[16] There also began to emerge, however, a more distinctly sociological focus suggesting that psychology and medicine might best treat the mind and its operations whereas the "moral philosopher," or "politician"—to use two of Hume's favorite terms—might better concentrate on social phenomena considered sui generis and beyond the influence of particular individuals. Certainly Montesquieu regarded society as much less the natural extension of certain common attributes of human nature—human nature reified—than as a realm of phenomena obeying its own laws and displaying its own patterns not directly traceable to the actions of particular individuals. He came gradually to understand that human nature, far from being the generative source defining the structure of societies, is itself a social product influenced by the complex array of moral and physical causes operative in any given society. Montesquieu and others sensed, as Ronald Meek aptly expressed the point, that "Man . . . not only made himself and his institutions: he and his institutions . . . were themselves made by the circumstances in which . . . he happened to find himself."[17] Montesquieu clearly perceived, in the words of Emile Durkheim, that "the nature of societies is no less stable and consistent than that of man" and that "it is no easier to modify the types of a society than the species of an animal."[18] Such a conception of a stable society subject to thorough investigation and exploration became central to the French tradition of sociology.

Similarly important in identifying major foci of Enlightenment social science is recognition of two distinct types of evolutionary progress theory characteristic of the epoch. The rather sober "sociological evolutionism" of the Scots inspired by Montesquieu must be contrasted with the utopian hopes of such figures as Condorcet, David Hartley, Joseph Priestley, and William Godwin for whom progress and the perfectibility of humankind became nothing short of a new social religion.[19] Such Scots as Kames, Smith, Ferguson, and Millar did not consider the discovery of historical evolution from rudeness to refinement tantamount to prediction of continued progress. Their immersion in the discourse of civic humanism kept uppermost in their minds the threats posed to altruistic patriotism by commerce, luxury, and corruption. As Duncan Forbes noted, Hume referred to historical cycles reminiscent of Polybius and Machiavelli, Smith worried over the narrowness of the commercial spirit and the extinction of the nobler virtues, and Millar focused on the debilitating effects of the division of labor as well as the likelihood that luxury would reduce population. The Scots were also less inclined to read into the tabula rasa school of empirical psychology grounds for glowing optimism concerning the potential to construct the human personality along the most desirable social lines, and this contributed to a more sober, less utopian outlook to their study of society, whereas Condorcet and others, as Frank Manuel observed, were "intoxicated with the future."[20]

METHODOLOGY AND UNDERLYING ASSUMPTIONS

It will be useful at the outset to discuss the methods the *philosophes* and moral philosophers of the Enlightenment believed appropriate for undertaking "a science of society." A pervasive secularism has often been seen as providing the broad context for the scientific study of societies, particularly in France. Whether or not such secularism approached the rabid anticlericalism of a Voltaire, a Diderot, or a Raynal, or the extreme religious skepticism of a David Hume, many social theorists of the eighteenth century, it is often asserted, followed their numerous Renaissance predecessors in putting aside the medieval search for final causes in a teleological, God-centered universe and focusing instead on man and his works. Hence numerous "theoretical," or "conjectural," historians are often seen as setting out to trace the true progress of humankind without even passing reference to Divine Providence. Even a theorist like Vico who retained a strong role for Providence in setting history on its necessitous course could nonetheless observe that it is "a truth beyond all question that the world of civil society has certainly been made by men."[21] Such generalizations concerning a natural linkage between secularism and social science should be advanced with caution. A good many Scots moral philosophers, for example, felt that in studying human nature they were doing God's work, and certainly figures like Louis de Bonald and J.-M. de Maistre in France saw no contradiction between theism and the pursuit of human science.[22]

Progress in the human sciences, then, certainly did not require rejection of the deity. It was useful, however, to separate the realms of Providence and human history in order to stake out a secular sphere open to human science. Tracing out the footsteps of God was deemed the work of theologians—not social scientists. Hence the critical importance of those early pages in Rousseau's *Discourse on the Origins of Inequality among Mankind* (1755), where he labored to separate supernatural, biblical explanations for man's early development from more strictly socioanthropological explanations so that he could explore "what the human race might have become if it had remained abandoned to itself."[23] Such concern to differentiate "socioanthropology" from theology became a defining point of the age. We find d'Alembert in his "Preliminary Discourse" to Diderot's *Encyclopédie,* for example, sharply distinguishing between "the science of God," "the science of man," and "the science of nature." At roughly the same time, Voltaire was drastically reducing the significance of Hebrew history from what it had been in Bishop J.-B. Bossuet's account of world history, Diderot was composing his article "Man" in the *Encyclopédie* without so much as a single reference to the Creation, and Hume was writing to Hutcheson rejecting emphasis on "final Causes" as "pretty uncertain and unphilosophical."[24] Hume concluded that a science of man and morals properly conceived on an experimental foundation has to rule out what he termed the "religion hypothesis," and he confidently asserted that in England religion had been pretty thoroughly discredited.[25]

The Deistic conception of a watchmaker God who set the world in

motion and then stepped back to let it function in accordance with certain natural laws made it possible to subject even religion to "sociological"
analysis.[26] Hence Montesquieu boldly declared in his *De l'esprit des lois*
(1748) that he would ignore theology in order to study religions "in relation only to the good they produce in civil society," including their tendency to "humanize the manners of men."[27] This was the same utilitarian
perspective that had earlier led him in his *Lettres persanes* (1721) to ignore
orthodoxy and decry the Catholic prohibition of divorce as completely
contrary to the important secular goal of population growth. As part of
this new utilitarian viewpoint, shared by numerous *philosophes* and moral
philosophers, Montesquieu introduced a decidedly functionalist perspective into the study of societies. He considered societies integrated wholes
whose structural components, both moral and physical, exercise a combined and cumulative influence producing an overall "general spirit," "national spirit," or "national character." This organic perspective, characteristic also of Vico and Herder, made him keenly aware of the influence of a
society's religious beliefs on its plan of government, the vigor of its laws,
and the manners of its people, all of which must be adjusted to the characteristics of the dominant religion as part of a society's homeostatic mechanism.[28] Montesquieu suggested a natural linkage between Islam and despotism, whereas Christianity accords better with moderate governments
(XXIV, 3). Generally speaking, where religion works at cross purposes
with the institutions, or principles of government, or laws of a society, im-
balance and instability will result (XXIV, 3).

From this newly emerging "sociological" viewpoint, the truth or falsity
of religious beliefs could no longer be the chief concern. It seemed far
more important during the century that produced such works as David
Hume's *Natural History of Religion* (1757) and Voltaire's and Herder's
equally naturalistic accounts of the origins of religious sentiment among
primitive peoples[29] to explore the formation of beliefs and ritual. Montesquieu was keenly interested in how the religious beliefs of a given people
are shaped by their geographical, social, political, and cultural milieu. In
Book XXIV of *De l'esprit des lois* he demonstrated a close connection between the real-life conditions of a given people and the religious rituals
they practice. The Hindu belief, for instance, in metempsychosis inclining
them to respect all living things and refrain from slaughtering cows for
food was perfectly adapted to an area of the world where such animals
were rare, exceedingly valuable as work animals, and very much needed
for the production of milk and butter. Such a belief could not have arisen
where cattle are plentiful and are consumed as a staple of the human diet,
just as offering prayers in a river like the Ganges could not have become a
religious ritual in a cold country (XXIV, 24, 26). Hence to the dismay of
his Jesuit and Jansenist critics alike, Montesquieu could conclude, "Where

a religion adapted to the climate of one country clashes too much with the climate of another, it cannot be there established" (XXIV, 26). Clearly a secular approach to a sacred subject such as religion could produce novel perspectives instrumental to the development of a "sociology" of religion.

If we take seriously the rhetoric of those practicing human science in the eighteenth century, their methods relied heavily on empirical observation and experience rather than deductive reasoning from first premises. Observation took the place of pure ratiocination as the eighteenth century witnessed a widespread revolt from the uncompromising rationalism of René Descartes, who had deduced from the single proposition "I think therefore I am" a whole universe of things and propositions he considered demonstrably true. It had been Descartes's reliance on "supposition upon supposition, without any evidence of reality," remarked Adam Ferguson, which had produced those whirling vortices of matter eliminated by the superior observations of Newton.[30] Certainly the unsuitability of the deductive approach of Cartesian philosophy to the empirical study of human societies functioned as one of the central propositions of Vico's *New Science* (1725–44).[31] Similarly, the attack on ratiocinative systems played a key role in the work of David Hume on human understanding. "Men are now cured of their passion for hypothesis and system in natural philosophy," Hume wrote in his *Treatise of Human Nature*. "Observation and experience," he noted somewhat later in his *Enquiry concerning Human Understanding*, "form the basis for moral, political, and physical subjects." Even conclusions that appear to result from purely a priori considerations of the nature of things, Hume suggested, "will be found to terminate at last in some general principle or conclusion for which we can assign no reason but observation and experience."[32]

Perhaps the key Enlightenment fallacy that inspired countless sociopolitical investigations, while at the same time dooming them to ultimate failure, was the conviction that observing individuals in society required an approach no different from what Newton had employed in analyzing nature. With a few noteworthy exceptions, including Vico's *New Science* and Smith's *Theory of Moral Sentiments* (1759), there were precious few inklings of the need for a hermeneutical approach to the study of society focusing on the ability of human scientists to comprehend the motivations and actions of past actors precisely because of their shared human nature. It was far more common to assume that the study of individuals was little different from the study of objects in nature. Francis Hutcheson, for example, called for exploration of the "natural dispositions of mankind, in the same way that we enquire into the structure of an animal body, of a plant or of the solar system."[33] The ideological goal obscuring the fundamental differences between human actors possessing free will and natural objects obeying fixed laws was the desire to believe that the condition of human beings could be substantially improved by discovering in human conduct the same level of lawfulness and order that scientists had revealed in the physical world. The perceived need was to borrow the methods of natural science in order to bolster the social prospects of humanity. This utilitarian goal was particularly evident in the investigations of the physiocrats, emphasizing the Marquis de Mirabeau's "art social" and in the work of such members of the French National Institute Class of Moral and Political Sciences, 1795–1803, as Cambacérès, C.-F. Volney, P.-J.-G. Cabanis, Destutt de Tracy, Sieyès, and P.-L. Roederer, most of whom used the phrase *la science sociale* as a synonym for a unified science of public policy focused on "administration" to foster prosperity.[34] The linkage between social science and the welfare of society, however, was certainly not a new theme discovered at the end of the eighteenth century. Rather it permeates the whole epoch, partly as a result of the popularization of a Baconian approach to nature stressing the yoking of nature to the needs of humanity.[35]

A paradigmatic example of the widespread eighteenth-century faith in induction of facts to arrive at empirically grounded "truth" is the article in Diderot's *Encyclopédie* devoted to "Observation." Making no distinction whatever between the natural and the human sciences, the anonymous author of this essay suggested that observation "is the primary foundation of all the sciences, the surest way to succeed, the principal means of extending the circumference of scientific knowledge and of illuminating all of its points."[36] The so-called facts were deemed the key. "The historian collects them, the natural philosopher [*physicien rationnel*] combines them, and experiment examines the results of their combination." Not that the facts speak for themselves. It requires an active mind to perceive the critical connections between facts that might at first seem to bear no important relation to one another so that, ultimately, one may discover the "chain that ties them all together."[37] There remained a role for system building, then, provided the theoretical construction of an explanatory system was preceded by ample observation. Hence we find Condorcet arguing that observation needs to be informed by occasional periods of brilliant insight when all the assembled truths gained by observation can be reduced to a system. This "moment of revolution must arrive more slowly in the moral sciences, where human vices add to the difficulties of nature: and Descartes had to precede Montesquieu."[38] What is particularly striking is that Condorcet did not see Descartes and Montesquieu as having embarked on fundamentally different missions. Both were seeking laws: Descartes those laws governing the universe and Montesquieu those laws governing man. The same basic method was affirmed as suitable to each domain.

As the model for the use of observation in "the sciences related to man," the author of "Observation" singled out none other than Montesquieu for acclaim. Montesquieu's history of Rome and his treatise on laws were jointly described as "an immense collection of observations made with a great deal of genius, selectivity, and sagacity, which furnished the illustrious author with reflections that are so much the more accurate because they are natural."[39] This author considered Montesquieu's treatises on laws and on Roman history so impressive that much could now be expected from "the sciences related to man." Observation held the key to progress in the human sciences since "man ultimately, from whatever angle one considers him, is the least appropriate subject for *experimentation.*" Just as in physics and astronomy, however, and just as Montesquieu's achievements revealed, enormous strides could be expected from observation alone.[40]

Many students of society in the Enlightenment era did actually suggest analogies between the study of history and the experimentation characteristic of the natural sciences. D'Alembert viewed the study of history as yielding "expériences morales" providing fundamental truths concerning an unchanging human nature.[41] Certainly experiments figure prominently in Hume's exploration of human nature and human understanding in his *Treatise of Human Nature* (1739), whose revealing subtitle was *Being An Attempt to Introduce the Experimental Method of Reasoning into Moral Subjects.* Later on, in his *Enquiry concerning Human Understanding* (1748), Hume suggested that "wars, intrigues, factions, and revolutions" are "so many collections of experiments by which the politician or moral philosopher fixes the principles of his science, in the same manner as the physician or natural philosopher becomes acquainted with the nature of plants, minerals, and other external objects."[42] Hume believed that observing man's typical responses when placed in various "situations and circumstances" would make it possible to isolate, somewhat in the manner of a lab experiment, "the constant and universal principles of human nature" conceived as "the regular springs of human action and behavior." And believing that human nature had not changed over time, Hume could confidently assert that the "experiments" in human science reported by Polybius and Tacitus remained valid sources of information centuries later.[43] Hume's view of the utility of "experiments" in the study of human nature and society was corroborated by Ferguson, who in his *Principles of Moral and Political Science* (1792) suggested that the circumstances in which men operate are sufficiently varied to reveal the effects on humankind of "external accommodations, diversity of manners, and forms of policy."[44]

Another way to fashion experiments within the domain of the human sciences was to engage in comparative analysis. The desire to compare different cultures had been strengthened during the early modern period of European history as travel accounts of strange and exotic lands flowed into Europe. Similarly helpful in giving rise to comparative methodology was the controversy raging in the seventeenth century concerning the relative merits of "ancients" and "moderns." The only way to resolve this dispute was to compare the achievements of humankind in both epochs. Hence by the Enlightenment era the habit of comparison was fully ingrained. Voltaire's article "History" in the *Encyclopédie* even suggested that the very "usefulness" of history derived from "the comparison that a statesman or a citizen can make of foreign laws, morals, and customs with those of his country."[45] And certainly Vico was substantially aware of the virtues of the comparative method. In the first book of his *New Science* he presented a comparative analysis of nations both barbarous and civilized seeking to ascertain the "human customs" common to them all.[46]

In the seventeenth and eighteenth centuries "socioanthropological" comparisons between the native tribes of America and the ancestors of modern Europeans became increasingly common, and it was assumed that existing tribes in the hunting mode of subsistence served as excellent observational evidence for European man's very first condition. Hence Bernard le Bovier de Fontenelle reported a marked similarity between native American and Greek myths,[47] and J.-F. Lafitau, in his widely read *Moeurs des Sauvages Amériquains, comparées aux moeurs des premiers temps* (1724), confidently drew comparisons between the native Americans and the earliest Greeks and Jews, while relying for explanation on a theory of diffusion from Asia to the New World.[48] In the works of William Robertson noteworthy similarities between native Americans and the early Germanic tribes became the empirical basis for a "sociological" theory suggesting that the "state of society" determines the character of a people and the nature of their beliefs and institutions. How else, Robertson concluded, could one account for the striking similarities between these two cultures—one American and one German—so geographically separate from one another. No theory of cultural diffusion, he concluded, could provide the explanation.[49]

Use of the comparative method to study society was by no means restricted to cross-cultural comparisons between distinct peoples. The method was also used to construct what would now be termed "political sociology." The progenitor and preeminent practitioner of this form of "sociology" was Montesquieu, who constructed ideal types to clarify what is characteristic of republican, monarchical, and despotic societies.[50] Surely Montesquieu was aware, as Herder noted in caustic criticism of his approach, that "No two republics or monarchies have yet been identical," just as he was surely aware, as Herder also asserted, that each government still has to be studied on its own terms.[51] Montesquieu nonetheless perceived the crucial significance of classification by types to aid comparison, an emphasis whose importance was still being touted much later by Max Weber.

As important to understanding the science of society of the Enlightenment epoch as the use of a method stressing observation, experimentation, and comparison was the conviction that social phenomena display recognizable patterns reflecting underlying causes.[52] If there are no discernible patterns in human actions, then no amount of observation can yield significant results. Once again, reference to Montesquieu is instructive since he expressed a strong conviction concerning the rational explicability of social phenomena. "I have first examined mankind," he wrote in the preface to *De l'esprit des lois*, "and I have come to believe that in this infinite diversity of laws and customs, they have not been guided purely by capricious whim." Vico was motivated by a similar conviction in rejecting the Epicurean stress on pure chance as failing to take account of the historical "facts" revealing the same succession of institutions in different countries.[53]

It is difficult to imagine a perspective more significant for the development of the social sciences. Montesquieu and Vico were both affirming that social facts display causal relations. The rationale underlying any given law or custom may not be at first apparent, but proper observation will eventually demonstrate its underlying causes. "When a law appears strange," Montesquieu asserted, "and it is not apparent that the Legislator had an interest in making it in such a manner . . . , one must assume that it is more rational than it appears and that it is based upon sufficient reason."[54] "It is not chance that rules the world," Montesquieu wrote in his history of Rome. "There are general causes, moral and physical, which act in every monarchy, elevating it, maintaining it, or hurling it to the ground. All accidents are controlled by these causes. And if the chance of one battle—that is, a particular cause—has brought a state to ruin, some general cause made it necessary for that state to perish from a single battle. In a word, the main trend draws with it all particular accidents."[55] This passage expressed what Raymond Aron has termed Montesquieu's "first truly sociological idea," the notion that the course of history can be explained following proper attention to underlying causal influences.[56]

As is well known, Montesquieu identified two basic sorts of influences shaping the behavior of men, one broadly physical and one broadly moral. Ultimately, he regarded *causes morales* as far more influential than *causes physiques*.[57] The key point of his whole discussion for his science of society, however, was his belief that when people act in groups as social and political beings, their actions result from the combined influences of the physical and moral causes to which they are exposed. This historicist view can readily be distinguished from the conviction one sometimes encounters in such figures as Voltaire, Diderot, Hutcheson, Hume, Kames, Smith, and

Ferguson that owing to the presence of certain universal characteristics in human beings, knowledge of human nature is the principal key to unlocking the mysteries of social systems and societal development.

David Hume was as convinced as Montesquieu that there is a pattern of predictability underlying human actions akin to the causal structure explaining the phenomena of nature. Such causes may be hidden at times, or may lose their effect owing to the operation of other invisible and contrary causes, but such causes exist nonetheless. Hence all that is required to explain "the actions and volitions of intelligent agents" is to learn "every particular circumstance" of a man's "character and situation." Human actions will then become predictable, Hume concluded, since "the conjunction between motives and voluntary actions is as regular and uniform as that between the cause and effect in any part of nature."[58] Indeed we count on this element of predictability in our dealings with other individuals. The more complex the society, Hume asserted, the more we enter into relations with our fellow human beings that depend on the predictability of their actions. This same element of predictability is what makes human science possible. How could there be a science of morals, Hume asked, if certain character traits did not produce certain "particular sentiments," which in turn produce certain predictable actions? And "how could *politics* be a science," Hume wondered, "if laws and forms of government had not a uniform influence upon society?"[59] The key point is that Hume shared the common eighteenth-century belief that human affairs display some of the same regular patterns Newton and others had discovered in the natural world.

Hume acknowledged that the actions of particular individuals may be unpredictable, but he was nonetheless convinced that, in the aggregate, individuals act as a result of certain ascertainable causes. When it comes to "group action," he concluded, "determinate and known causes may be sought." The reason is that groups of individuals are subject to the same causes, and most of them—though not every single individual—will therefore display the same inclinations or passions when facing the same situation or stimuli. Hence a historian will be able to discover, Hume contended, the underlying causes of such macroscopic events as the rise of the House of Commons and the flourishing of trade and industry.[60] Hume was not the only eighteenth-century figure to draw a sharp distinction between individual human actions, which may be unpredictable, and the actions of large groups, which will correspond to ascertainable causes and hence display discernible patterns. Montesquieu had a very similar point in mind when he remarked in his *Essay on Causes*, "We know better what gives a certain character to a nation than what gives a particular mentality to an individual, what modifies one of the sexes than what affects a man, what forms the spirit of societies that have embraced a way of life than what forms the character of a single person."[61] Similar in spirit was Immanuel Kant's remark in his *Idea for a Universal History from a Cosmopolitan Point of View* (1784)—a work that keenly interested Auguste Comte—that "what seems complex and chaotic in the single individual, may be seen from the standpoint of the human race as a whole to be a steady and progressive though slow evolution of its original endowment." Kant was convinced that there are patterns to human historical development just waiting to be discovered. "Marriages, births, and deaths occur according to laws as stable as those which account for the orderliness of nature."[62]

For some Enlightenment-era theorists the quest for order in the social world replicating the orderliness of the natural world and its governance by physical laws became a near obsession. The physiocrats in France, for example, constructing their "science de l'ordre" and "science de la vie humaine," firmly believed that nature would reveal her truths to the properly instructed and educated, thereby producing what François Quesnay termed a "concours des volontés," transcending both error and dissension. Positive law, Quesnay believed, should be nothing other than "the rule of all human action . . . conforming to the physical order." The "laws of the natural order," he observed, should serve as "the sovereign rule of all manmade legislation and of all civil, political, economic, and social conduct."[63] And Quesnay confidently asserted that in societies where the "natural order" does prevail, that is, where "the torch of reason illuminates the government," "an unwise law would not be put forward, for the government and the people would immediately perceive its absurdity."[64] Quesnay considered even the moral conduct of the individuals within a given society predictable rather than being arbitrary and capricious. When a sufficient quantum of "order, plenty and security" exists in the economic sphere, he concluded, then human beings may be expected to act morally and refrain from "violence and robbery."[65] Order, abundance, and security, then, are the veritable "causes" of morality.

As implied in much of the foregoing discussion, Enlightenment students of society sought not just patterns but veritable laws describing underlying regularities explaining human behavior in societies. Rather than just describing this or that human action as an isolated, particularistic event, their explanations sought to locate major events within broader patterns. Only this "sociological" mentality stressing underlying causes can transcend the particularism that reduces and splinters the comprehension of social phenomena into separate acts of cognition. If every human action is unpredictable, then there can be no pattern to human affairs, and the social scientist's researches will be unable to produce useful generalizations. There is no question that eighteenth-century figures went beyond the quest for discernible patterns and emphasized the existence of invariable "laws" descriptive of human conduct. For a number of *philosophes* of the Enlightenment, for example, self-interest was regarded as a law of the social world akin to the principle of universal gravitation in the physical world. Hence Helvétius could conclude in *De l'esprit* (1758) that moral philosophy could be modeled on experimental physics.[66]

Belief in the orderliness and rational explicability of the social realm also motivated the research and writing of those stadial theorists who believed all nations are destined to pass through the same successive stages of development. Hence Turgot could assert, "In the over-all progress of the human mind, all nations start from the same point, proceed to the same goal, follow more or less the same path, but at a very uneven pace."[67] And Lord Kames could contend, there exists "a regular system of causes and effects" from which we can conclude "that the progress has been the same among all nations, in the capital circumstances at least."[68] Vico certainly believed the "course" of history conformed to a discernible pattern "present in every nation." Nations, he contended, go through three stages of development "by a constant and uninterrupted order of causes and effects present in every nation."[69] All the progressist historians identifying stages of history were swayed by the same underlying conviction that social evolution could be both traced and causally explained.

This "sociological" conviction that causal patterns can be discovered in the social realm should be distinguished from the belief that societal results are somehow traceable to human design, or intent. Conflating the two would ignore the strong currents of thought Ronald Meek has called the "law of unintended consequences," Ronald Hamowy the "theory of spontaneous generation," and Duncan Forbes the "law of the heterogeneity of ends."[70] Basically, this very widely held viewpoint—found, for example, in Mandeville, Hume, Smith, Ferguson, Millar, Kames, James Burgh, Priestley, Turgot, Condillac, and Vico—posits that what happens in history is, as Ferguson said, "the result of human action, but not the execution of any human design." According to Ferguson, "the greatest revolutions" occur "where no change is intended." Men are led by instinct to act in certain ways, and it is with "blindness to the future" that their actions actually end up shaping the future. Hence Hume attributed English freedom to the actions of the Puritans even though that was hardly their intent. Duncan Forbes takes as the *locus classicus* of this view Vico's statement in *The New Science* that while "men have themselves made this world of nations," they have followed "narrow ends" that were only made to "serve wider ends" owing to the workings of a superior "mind" endeavoring "to preserve the human race upon this earth."[71] Such convictions of unintended consequences—whether in Vico's Providential formulation, or in Mandeville's transformation of private license into public gain, or in Smith's conception of "an invisible hand"—need not undermine belief in lawfulness and pattern. Such theories merely exclude the conscious design of individuals from being considered the true agents creating those patterns that exist.

THE ATTACK ON CONTRACT

Given both the rage for empirical observation and the widespread rejection of outright human design as explaining social and political outcomes, it was perhaps inevitable that the abstract social contract tradition would fall into disrepute among those theorists seeking to discover the natural history of society. Far from describing as a modern anthropologist would the actual behavior of individuals existing in a primitive condition, social contract theorists invented hypothetical human beings and attributed to them the essentials of human nature as they conceived them. Hence they practiced deductive philosophy rather than empirical socioanthropology. They then compounded their original rationalist error by deducing from this purely imaginary natural state of humankind the proper governmental type and organization capable of either preserving what was deemed meritorious, or overcoming the presumed liabilities of humanity's natural state. Hence both Adam Ferguson and J. G. Herder ridiculed Rousseau's *Discourse on the Origins of Inequality Among Mankind* because it was based on speculation rather than on observation. Theorists indulging in such idle speculation were responsible for "many fruitless inquiries" and "many wild suppositions," Ferguson observed. "No constitution is formed by consent," and "no government is copied from a plan." Rather forms of government have arisen from human nature. "The seeds of every form of government are lodged in human nature; they spring up and ripen with the season."[72] Unlike the conjectural historians who used whatever materials were available to construct the natural history of humankind, Rousseau had, by his own admission, begun by putting the facts aside, and this was precisely the opposite of the concrete approach favored by those committed to subjecting society and human relations to scientific scrutiny. Herder left no doubt that he regarded Rousseau's sophistical wizardry of his *Second Discourse* as almost completely useless, since, in his opinion, it was unlikely that the "golden age" extolled by Rousseau ever existed.[73]

Rejecting social contract theory was essential to clearing the ground for a "sociological" investigation of the real-life, natural evolution of societies from a rude, uncivilized condition to the advanced commercial societies of eighteenth-century Europe.[74] The attack on consensual social contract as the source of government began early and proved unrelenting. Pierre Bayle leveled one of the first barrages by asserting that ambitious and cunning men—not consent—had been responsible for the first societies.[75]

Later, Shaftesbury attacked Hobbes for making society and government "a kind of invention and creature of art rather than a natural development."[76] As the century progressed, numerous theorists concurred. Although both Gershom Carmichael and Francis Hutcheson, the first two holders of the chair of moral philosophy at the University of Glasgow, retained contract in a form amalgamating Pufendorf and Locke, Montesquieu ridiculed the notion of contract and consent in one of his *Lettres persanes* (1721), and Hume called the state of nature a "philosophical fiction."[77] Complaining of the recent advent of social contract theory, Hume remarked that "new discoveries are not to be expected in these matters." Conquest and usurpation—not consent—have been the origin "of almost all the new governments which were established in the world."[78] Both Smith and Ferguson purposefully refrained from following Rousseau in depicting individuals in a state of nature. "To be in society," Ferguson observed, is "the physical state of the species."[79] "Every infant," he noted in his *An Essay on the History of Civil Society* (1767), "is born into the society of his own family," and ties to that family and extended family become the basis of tribal or clan attachments held together by "affection, fidelity, and courage."[80] To explain government, Ferguson concluded, one need not leave the real ground of history, or at least *conjectural* history where certain "broken links," as Kames suggested, can be replaced, though a complete chain is lacking. Duncan Forbes found Ferguson's observational approach in his *Essay* so significant a departure from previous "logical reconstruction" of humanity's earliest condition in a state of nature that he suggested "this is where, in the history of social theory, one can hear a snapping of threads." Ferguson made, Forbes continues, a complete "break with the whole state of nature/contract apparatus," a step that Montesquieu, above all, encouraged him to take.[81]

As social contract theory fell into increasing disfavor, numerous eighteenth-century theorists developed a view of human nature as naturally social. Gone—with a few major exceptions such as Rousseau and Lord Monboddo—was the stark contrast between formerly asocial creatures existing wholly independently of one another in a pure state of nature and new sociable individuals transformed by the mutual swearing of a covenant binding all equally to one another and to one common rule. Instead, society was recognized as humanity's primordial natural habitat, and the widespread belief in innate sociability made it possible to return to a basically Aristotelian perspective concerning the naturalness of society and government to humankind.[82] Hence Ferguson observed, after acknowledging Montesquieu as his tutor, that "the love of company is a principle common to man with all the gregarious animals." Human beings quite naturally form "manifold troops and companies" welded together by "a social disposition, which receives with favor and love what constitutes the good of mankind, or rejects, with disapprobation and abhorrence, what is of a contrary nature." A proper synonym for this "fellow feeling," Ferguson suggested, would be "humanity," which he defined as "a feeling of good will toward all men."[83] Earlier Scots theorists—preeminently Hutcheson—had posited "universal benevolence" as the key to innate sociability. This benevolence, Hutcheson noted, provided the "ties," or "bonds" that link not just the members of families but all members of a given society. Seeking an analogy to the orderliness of the physical world, Hutcheson compared this "universal benevolence" to "that principle of gravitation which perhaps extends to all bodies in the Universe."[84]

THE PRIORITY OF THE SOCIAL

Rejection of the state of nature model as lacking in historicity was often accompanied by the growing recognition that far from actually creating societies through formal contracts, and far from societies simply reflecting and reifying man's uniform nature, societies preexist particular individuals and function as the crucibles in which human character, beliefs, and inclinations are formed. No society, it came to be appreciated, can simply be equated with the sum total of all the separate individuals who comprise it. Rather, the interaction of groups of individuals facing common needs dictated by their particular situation creates distinctive moral, political, and social structures that shape along the same lines all, or nearly all, individuals falling under a particular society's sway. Appreciation of sociocultural conditioning stood in the eighteenth century in stark contrast to the quest for a uniform science of human nature enabling an observer to deduce the social behavior of human beings from innate psychological qualities held in common with other individuals.

As is almost uniformly the case where modes of "sociological" analysis are concerned, Montesquieu provides an excellent starting point for discussion of eighteenth-century beliefs concerning the molding or shaping influence of society on individuals. He fully appreciated the extent to which "customs" and "manners" as well as the "general spirit," "general character," or "national character" influence human behavior. Already in his early *De la Politique* (1721) he was developing the notion of what he termed "a common character," "collective soul," or overall "tone" giving societies their particular identities. "In all societies," he observed, "which are really groupings of minds, a common character takes shape. This collective soul takes on a manner of thinking which is the effect of a chain of infinite causes that multiply and combine from century to century. Once the tone is set and has permeated the society, it alone governs and all that sovereigns, magistrates, and peoples are able to do or plan, whether they seem to go against this tone or follow it, is always in relation to it; it dominates until the society is totally destroyed."[85] By the time he put the finishing touches on his classic work *De l'esprit des lois* (1748), Montesquieu had narrowed the list of basic components of what he termed the "general spirit" of a society to climate, religion, laws, maxims of government, historical precedents, manners, and customs (XIX, 4). From the combined influence of all these elements, he suggested, a "general spirit" develops. As Hegel clearly perceived, such a concept of a "general spirit" was tantamount to a belief in national character.[86]

Hume, too, may be cited as one who appreciated that society shapes human nature. "We can form no wish," he wrote in his *Treatise of Human Nature*, "which has not a reference to society." None of the passions, he observed, would have "any force, were we to abstract them entirely from the thought and sentiment of others. . . . Ourself, independent of the perception of every other object, is in reality nothing."[87] Although Hume was a strong believer in the uniformity of human nature, he nonetheless considered individuals eminently malleable as far as character and conduct are concerned. In his essay "Of Commerce" he included a passage reminiscent of later pronouncements in what is now termed the sociology of knowledge. "Man is a very variable being," he suggested, "and susceptible of many different opinions, principles, and rules of conduct. What may be true, while he adheres to one way of thinking, will be found false, when he has embraced an opposite set of manners and opinions."[88]

No discussion of the shaping and molding power of society on human beings should ignore Rousseau. In his *Discourse on the Origins of Inequality Among Mankind* (1755), he suggested that many of the differences between men which are typically considered "natural" actually derive from the influence of "habit and the various types of life men adopt in society."[89] Once formed, civil society transforms original human instinct. Hence the significance of those well-known passages where he presents a thumbnail sketch of the remarkable changes society produces. As individuals move from nature to society, "the soul and human passions, altering imperceptibly, change their nature so to speak."[90] So great are the transformations wrought by society that savages and civilized beings cannot possibly agree on the path to human happiness. What pleases the one will displease the other. What explains the fundamental difference, Rousseau suggested, is that the savage exists "within himself," whereas "the sociable man, always outside of himself, knows how to live only in the opinion of others; and it is, so to speak, from their judgment alone that he draws the sentiment of his own existence."[91] Rousseau clearly comprehended, then, that society becomes the point of self-definition for the individual, a veritable mirror, as Adam Smith later expressed the point, handing individuals their images of themselves. Human nature, then, is far from being the finished product of nature prior to the organization of societies. Societies take creatures formerly governed only by instinct and instill in them what Rousseau termed "cultivated reason." Hence, Rousseau could conclude, there is no reason to expect that "the human race of one age" will resemble "the human race of another."[92]

In Rousseau's approach, as with that of Montesquieu, one encounters a strong dose of historicism defined as the sociocultural conditioning of human beings. The behavioral traits, and even the character individuals display, will be relative to societal context. No two sets of societal conditions will produce precisely the same human character. Furthermore, the same society, at different times, will produce different sorts of individuals with different dispositions, inclinations, and motivations. Rousseau did not even regard the human capacity for pity as a constant feature of human nature. A society corrupted by substantial inequality will corrupt, or even eradicate, this original instinct of pity and replace it with jealousy and calculation. Hence, Rousseau concluded, "it is the spirit of society alone, and the inequality it engenders, which thus change and alter our natural inclinations."[93] How completely natural was it, then, for Marx a century later to envision the prospect of an egalitarian society that would produce a basically new human nature by drastically changing the socioeconomic context of human life.

An equally historicist viewpoint can be found in the writings of Herder, who was even more attuned than Rousseau to the shaping influence of physical and moral environment on humankind. In his *Ideas for a Philosophy of History of Mankind* (1784) Herder referred to the history of man as "a theatre of transformation . . . in the ever-changing, ever-renewing creation." He rejected any notion of a uniform human nature constant over time. It was inconceivable to him that those occupying the earth in the advanced societies of the eighteenth century could bear much resemblance to individuals who had lived "when elephants lived in Siberia and North America, and dinosaurs roamed Ohio."[94] In his *Yet Another Philosophy of History* (1774) he remarked that "Human nature under diverse climates is never wholly the same." Rather human nature "is a pliant clay which assumes a different shape under different needs and circumstances."[95] The more stress Herder placed on the shaping influence of society, the closer he approached pure historicism. We find him contending, for example, that the collective ideas of a people will be so purely the result of their particular environment that they will be literally incapable of comprehending words in foreign cultures that correspond to objects or ideas they have not themselves experienced. "If the *Voluspa* of the Icelander were read and expounded to a bramin," Herder contended, "he would scarcely be able to form a single idea from it; and to the Icelander the *Vedam* would be equally unintelligible. Their own mode of representing things is the more deeply imprinted on every nation, because it is adapted to themselves, is suited to their own earth and sky, springs from their mode of living, and has been handed down to them from father to son."[96]

Clearly, then, it came to be understood among Enlightenment students of society that preexisting the arrival of every human being in the world is a preestablished social world that defines how individuals will act and react as social beings. The emergence of this line of thought is hardly surprising. Certainly strong emphasis on the shaping power of environment had been implicit in the sensationalist psychology of John Locke and others. Locke's rejection of innate ideas and his reliance on sense impressions for the raw materials of reflection suggested to numerous eighteenth-century figures, including Condillac, Helvétius, Morelly, La Mettrie, and d'Holbach, that human beings are infinitely malleable and likely to become whatever their environment makes them. At times this sensationalist psychology contributed to an extreme psychological determinism. Hence Henri de Boulainvilliers could characterize human beings as "machine-like being[s] determined by external causes." "External stimuli," he asserted, "account for all perceptions, affections, and actions."[97] In accordance with a similarly materialist psychology, d'Holbach concluded that all that might be necessary to achieve proper social engineering was to arrange society so that human motives and inclinations would tend toward the common good. When this was not the case, d'Holbach asserted, and antisocial behavior became widespread, the fault was chargeable to "society" so that it would be unjust to punish those who have not been able "to contract the habits necessary to the maintenance of society."[98] Not all theorists were content to follow d'Holbach in reducing whatever defects of character individuals may display to inadequacies in their social environment. As we have seen, however, there certainly existed widespread recognition that nurture can be more crucial than nature in the formation of human character. By the end of the century, what Robert Nisbet has termed "the priority of the social" had become something of a commonplace.[99]

The "sociological" viewpoint stressing society as sui generis, which one finds purest in Montesquieu and to a lesser extent in Rousseau, Hume, Ferguson, Smith, Millar, and Herder, can readily be distinguished from a contrasting psychologism suggesting that the features of society derive exclusively or mainly from principles of human nature considered uniform regardless of time or place. We find Diderot suggesting in this more psychological vein, for example, that the human characteristic of *sociabilité* is the source of "all the laws of *society*, and all our duties towards other men," as well as "the general principle of all ethical thought and of the whole of civil *society*."[100] From the presence of an assumed trait of human nature, Diderot saw fit to deduce the behavior of individuals in societies. Whereas Diderot stressed humankind's innate *sociabilité*, numerous other writers selected benevolence as the primary instinct guiding human behavior. Francis Hutcheson, for example, considered natural benevolence an adequate explanation for the strength of kinship bonding among clans in the Scottish highlands. Confronted with Hutcheson's blatantly psychological explanation, the more "sociologically" inclined Adam Smith stressed that certain societal factors above and beyond the psychological disposition of the individuals involved provide the true explanation for the strength of those kinship bonds. In particular, he concluded, it was the weakness of central authority and the constant need for self-defense that provided the proper explanation.[101] A similarly intriguing example of the advent of "sociological" explanation is to be found in John Millar's tracing of the caste system in India to "the natural separation of the principal professions," whereas John Mill would later simply attribute this system to "a legislator of genius."[102]

FUNCTIONALISM

No discussion of the Enlightenment science of society should ignore the organic conception of society now labeled "functionalism," which stresses "social statics" rather than "social dynamics," to borrow Comte's later phraseology. In direct contrast to the evolutionary perspective of the conjectural historians exploring the progressive unfolding of distinct societal stages, functionalists study societies at a given moment in time as integrated entities whose various component elements dramatically influence and shape one another. Embedded within the nineteenth book of Montesquieu's treatise on laws is the veritable credo of eighteenth-century functionalist "sociology": "Men are influenced by various causes, by the climate, the religion, the laws, the maxims of government; by precedents, morals and customs, from whence is formed a general spirit that takes its rise from these. In proportion as in every nation any one of these causes acts with more force, the others in the same degree become weak" (XIX, 4). Montesquieu assumed that the various causes and influences at work in a given society will be in a state of mutual self-adjustment so that where one of the component elements of the overall general spirit exerts a particularly strong influence, the others will recede in importance. When the moral sanctions provided by religion, for example, are strong, the laws can be weaker. Among savage peoples, nature and climate will exert the strongest influence. Among the Chinese, on the other hand, it is customs deriving from Confucianism and reinforced by numerous rites that have governed the people, whereas the same constraining role was played by laws among the Japanese and morals among the Spartans. A combination of maxims of government and morals, Montesquieu concluded, established the dominant "tone" in Rome (XIX, 4). What is significant here is to see Montesquieu adopting a holistic perspective envisioning societies as systems of interdependent and integrated structural components.[103]

Among the diverse moral causes contributing to shaping the overall general spirit of a nation, Montesquieu placed substantial emphasis on custom, morals, and manners. He was keenly aware that such nonlegal sanctions supplement law as a socializing influence directing human conduct toward certain ends. Law should regulate an individual's conduct as a citizen, he suggested, whereas conduct outside one's political and legal duties falls within the realm of custom (XIX, 16). Such matters as styles of dress, or whether men shave their beards, are issues of custom, not law. No legislator ought to consider such matters within his jurisdiction. Rather, the proper way to alter customs is to introduce new ones (XIX, 14). Montesquieu was convinced that custom can be as tyrannical in its grip as law. People, in fact, are likely to be more attached to local custom than to laws. The scorn of one's acquaintances when one acts contrary to custom will often function as a more substantial external restraint than law on human conduct, thereby providing the necessary encouragement for individuals to adhere to whatever informal rules and standards are embodied in any particular "culture." The rituals built into Chinese culture, for example, were designed precisely to create tranquil individuals displaying proper civility and regard for others (XIX, 16).

Montesquieu was not alone in his recognition of the powerful grip of morals, manners, and customs on human behavior. This became one of the central themes of Voltaire's *Essai sur les moeurs et l'esprit des nations* (1769) as he sought to describe the relative balance between nature and nurture in shaping human behavior. "It is clear that everything which belongs intimately to human nature is the same from one end of the universe to the other," Voltaire wrote in that work, and equally clear "that everything that can depend on manners is different." Ultimately, custom prevails over nature, Voltaire concluded. "The empire of custom . . . sheds variety on the scene of the universe" and produces extremely "diverse fruits."[104] Nor was the point lost on Montesquieu's avid Scots readers. In his *Theory of Moral Sentiments* (1759), Adam Smith termed custom and fashion "the chief causes of the many irregular and discordant opinions which prevail in different ages and nations concerning what is blamable or praiseworthy." In his *Wealth of Nations* (1776) he observed simply, "The difference between the most dissimilar characters, between a philosopher and a common street porter, for example, seems to arise not so much from nature, as from habit, custom, and education."[105] Lord Kames similarly observed, "manners, depending on an endless variety of circumstances, are too complex for law; and yet upon manners chiefly depends the well-being of society."[106]

As important as custom was considered to be in shaping the character, beliefs, and conduct of a given people, most Enlightenment-era theorists considered the form of government established in a given country the most pervasive influence of all. This appreciation of the shaping power of governmental form on human behavior and conduct is frequently apparent in contrasts drawn between government and climate and cautions us not to read nineteenth-century determinism back into the Enlightenment. Voltaire remarked, for example, that government is a hundred times more influential than climate, and following Montesquieu's point about climate having its maximum impact on primitive peoples, Etienne Bonnot de Condillac noted that however influential climate may be in the early stages of societal development, "The character of a people does not take permanent shape until the government has taken a fixed form."[107] In a similar vein, Diderot remarked, "Manners [*moeurs*] are everywhere the result of legislation and government. . . . Manners are good when the laws which are observed are good and bad when the laws which are observed are bad."[108]

Examples of theorists singling out government as the dominant influence on human character and human behavior could be multiplied substantially. Hume made much of the point, as did abbé Raynal, who suggested that "the human race is what one wishes it to be. It is the way in which it is governed which determines it to be good or evil."[109] Diderot asserted that even the English would lose their love of liberty if they had to endure the rule of three consecutive monarchs as despotic as Elizabeth.[110] D'Alembert, to take another example, did not discount the influence of climate and other physical factors in shaping human conduct, but he acknowledged that where governmental form remains constant over a long period of time, it can be particularly influential, as in a despotic state which causes people to be "lazy," "vain," and unable to appreciate "the true and the beautiful" or to "think great thoughts or to perform great action."[111] And to take one final example, Herder used an agricultural metaphor to establish the importance of government as a pervasive influence on human character. Likening climate and national character to seeds, he suggested that it is "the political constitution of a nation in its broadest sense—its laws, government, customs, and civic traditions" that constitute both "the sowing of the seed" and "the close tilling of the soil."[112]

THE SOCIOLOGY OF LAW

There remains a key "sociological" conception deserving emphasis in this exploration of the Enlightenment science of society. Motivating the researches of Montesquieu and the Scots whom he inspired was a quest, not for the letter of the law, but rather for the "spirit" of laws, by which he meant all the complex relations laws bear to the moral and physical substrata influencing their content.[113] If Grotius had despaired of any systematic treatment of positive as compared to natural laws, Montesquieu successfully initiated that quest. And Montesquieu shifted the emphasis from natural law rules to the positive laws arising in diverse societies, an area of investigation John Millar termed the "natural history of legal establishments."[114] In so doing, he launched what became a Scottish school of civil jurisprudence that functioned, in J. G. A. Pocock's view, as a paradigm separate from that of civic humanism.[115] Whether or not such earlier commentators as Roy Pascal, Duncan Forbes, and Ronald Meek exaggerated the extent of materialism in Montesquieu and Scots writers, as Knud Haakonssen, Andrew Skinner, and Donald Winch have all suggested,[116] there is no denying the inspiration Scots writers derived from the "sociological" discussions of law in Book I, chapter 3, and Book XVIII, chapters 8 through 21, of *De l'esprit des lois*.

Montesquieu began his discussion of laws in Book I, chapter 3, with an acknowledgment of the need to trace law in general to human reason—an act of fealty to the old natural law tradition from which he never completely extricated himself. Immediately thereafter he launched a strikingly "sociological" quest to discover the relation laws bear to the nature and principle of government, to climate, to soil quality and terrain, to territorial extent, to religion, to the inclinations of the inhabitants and their extent of wealth, to population levels, to modes of subsistence and commerce, and to the manners and customs of the people. Given all these relations between laws and underlying influences, it is very unlikely, Montesquieu concluded, that the laws of any one society will be suitable for another. He was here following a very different path from theorists who sought to deduce rightful laws from some carefully defined essence of human nature. "Sociology" was displacing "psychology." Hence Durkheim could remark of Montesquieu that he derived positive law "from the nature not of man but of societies."[117]

Laws, for Montesquieu, arise spontaneously from their natural societal settings rather than being "invented" by some ingenious legislator.[118] As Allan Ramsay remarked in one of the century's numerous echoes of Montesquieu, "Laws do not take shape *a priori* from general principles drawn from human nature. Everywhere laws have arisen from the particular needs and circumstances of individual societies."[119] Lord Kames fully understood the point, observing in a close paraphrase of Montesquieu, "The law of a country is in perfection when it corresponds to the manners of the people, their circumstances, their government."[120] Very different was Montesquieu's stress on general causes explaining the spirit of a given system of laws from treatments of laws as "instituted to meet passing needs like remedies applied fortuitously, which have cured one patient and kill others."[121] And quite different, as well, was Montesquieu's approach from the natural jurisprudence of Adam Smith, who sought to combine, for

an explanation of what laws are appropriate, emphasis on "natural sentiments of justice" with those "outward circumstances" that affect how those
natural sentiments are expressed, so that Smith was concerned with what
he termed in his *Lectures on Jurisprudence* (1762–1763) those "general principles which ought to run through and be the foundation of the laws of all
nations."[122]

What Montesquieu provided was a formulaic anticipation of the mode
of "sociological" exploration that was to prove immensely popular among
such Scots conjectural historians as Sir John Dalrymple of Cranstoun,
Kames, Smith, and Millar. These Scots gave him full credit—some say too
much credit—for sweeping away social contract and putting in its place
the four stages theory of society that linked law and justice to mode of subsistence. Whereas writers prior to Montesquieu had attributed laws to "particular legislators, or to accidental circumstances," Dugald Stewart noted,
"Montesquieu, on the contrary considered laws as originating chiefly from
the circumstances of society; and attempted to account, from the changes
in the condition of mankind, which take place in the different stages of
their progress, for the corresponding alterations which their institutions
undergo."[123]

This historical approach to the study of law was considered so important that Kames asserted in his *Historical Law Tracts* (1758) that law becomes "only a rational study when it is traced historically, from its first
rudiments . . . to its highest improvements in civil society."[124] This evolutionary perspective gave the Scots theorists an organizational device that
Montesquieu's more amorphous treatise lacked. But like the Scots after
him, Montesquieu focused on the presence of property as the key defining point of any legal system. The existence of property in the second,
"herding" stage, Montesquieu had observed, functioned as the chief influence on the development of a code of laws. Where there is no division of
property, a people needs only manners—not laws (XVIII, 13). Property
brings with it, however, a host of changes, including not only laws to protect such property but also changes in marriage customs, in the status of
elders, and in governmental forms (XVIII, 13). The enormous influence
of Montesquieu's stress on mode of subsistence on the Scots was widely
recognized by contemporary theorists. Having heard Adam Smith's lectures in Glasgow, for example, John Millar suggested that Smith had actually "followed the plan that seems to be suggested by Montesquieu; endeavoring to trace the gradual progress of jurisprudence, both public and
private, from the rudest to the most refined ages, and to point out the
effects of those arts which contribute to subsistence, and to the accumulation of property, in producing correspondent improvements, or alterations in law and government."[125] This influence of Montesquieu on the
Scots is hardly surprising since Montesquieu had sent his treatise on laws

to Hume, who was closely associated in Edinburgh with a group gathered around Kames that also included Smith and Millar.[126]

In actual fact, no one developed the essential core of Montesquieu's insight concerning the historicized nature of human character, beliefs, and volition better than Millar himself. In his *The Origin of the Distinction of Ranks* (1779), a remarkable work deserving an important position in the eighteenth-century science of society, Millar observed that each "stage" on the path of human "progress from ignorance to knowledge . . . and from rude to civilized manners" has been "accompanied with peculiar laws and customs." The natural steps in this progression may have varied in their duration owing to "accidental causes," but Millar had no doubt of the uniformity of the progression, or the fact that each socioeconomic stage of development was accompanied by laws, customs, manners, tastes, and sentiments peculiar to it. More than Kames, Smith, or Ferguson, he leaned toward materialist explanations. Hence he concluded that the underlying economic conditions present in a given society will cause individuals to possess the same "ideas and feelings" as other individuals living in societies that have reached the same stage of economic development. Since they will face the same needs and engage in the same activities when they experience the same mode of subsistence, "the character and genius of a nation" will be "nearly the same with that of every other in similar circumstances," just as "in a multitude of dice thrown together at random, the result, at different times, will be nearly equal."[127]

Millar was convinced that even standards of morality will depend upon the particular mode of subsistence a given society has attained. Borrowing a point from Montesquieu, he suggested that the more advanced the level of commerce and manufacturing, the more useful the strict observation of rules of justice and fairness will seem. Hence commercial societies will display a much more highly developed sense of justice than rude and barbarous nations. Consciously rejecting Rousseau's eulogies of man's natural state, Millar asserted that primitive peoples "have seldom any regard to their promise, and are commonly addicted to theft and rapine." He found this readily demonstrable both from such contemporary sources of information as Captain Cook's journals of his voyages and from ancient writings that displayed the character of the ancient Egyptians as well as the early tribes in Gaul.[128]

Millar was not the only Scots theorist to dabble in materialist explanations for social phenomena. Adam Ferguson, for example, suggested that where modes of occupation and climate are the same, men, too, will be the same. Neither the early German nor the early Briton, he suggested, were any different "in the habits of his mind or his body, in his manners or apprehensions, from our American, who, like him, with his bow and his dart, is left to traverse the forest; and in a like severe or variable climate, is obliged to subsist by the chase."[129] William Robertson completely agreed. "In every inquiry concerning the operations of men when united together in society," he asserted, "the first object of attention should be their mode of subsistence. Accordingly as that varies, their laws and policy must be different." Hence Robertson concluded that a distinct set of beliefs, ideas, institutions, customs, manners, and morals will correspond to each of the four socioeconomic stages through which human societies pass: hunting, pasturage, agriculture, and commerce.[130] We clearly see, then, in the works of various eighteenth-century writers, intriguing anticipations of the stress Marx would place on the shaping influence of the economic substructure of a society on the thoughts, inclinations, morality, and conduct of those who reside within a given society. As J. G. A. Pocock has said, "The Scottish theorists were not far removed—though the distances may need stressing—from the hypothesis that men create themselves in history through their mode of production." The Scots arrived at what Pocock termed a "historical and transactional vision of *homo faber et mercator*, shaping himself through the stages of history by means of the division and specialization of labour, to diversification and refinement of the passions."[131] Without question (*pace* Foucault and Skinner), these Enlightenment theories, which we would now consider part of the sociology of knowledge, are readily distinguishable in both content and tone from anything Marx ever wrote. It is also without question, however, that Montesquieu and the Scots he influenced nourished Marx's own thoughts, as is revealed in Marx's own footnotes to *Das Kapital*. Hence this Enlightenment attention to the material as well as the moral substrata of laws, along with the other themes explored in this essay, certainly deserves to be regarded as among the key "sociological" insights developed as part of what is most appropriately labeled "the Enlightenment science of society."

NOTES

1. David Hume, *A Treatise of Human Nature*, ed. L. A. Selby-Bigge (1888; reprint, Oxford: Clarendon Press, 1975), xv–xvi.

2. See, e.g., Emile Durkheim, *Quid Secundatus politicae scientiae instituendae contulerit* (1892), translated as *Montesquieu's Contribution to the Rise of Social Science*, in *Montesquieu and Rousseau: Forerunners of Sociology*, ed. and trans. A. Cuvillier (Ann Arbor: University of Michigan Press, 1960); Albion Small, *Adam Smith and Modern Sociology* (Chicago: University of Chicago Press, 1907); René Hubert, *Les sciences sociales dans L'Encyclopédie* (Paris: Alcan, 1923); W. Sombart, "Die Anfange der Soziologie," in *Hauptprobleme der Soziologie, Erinnerungsgabe für Max Weber*, 2 vols., ed. M. Palyi (Munich and Leipzig: Duncker und Humblot, 1923), 5–19; W. C. Lehmann, *Adam Ferguson and the Beginnings of Modern Sociology* (New York: Columbia University Press, 1930); Robinet de Clery, "Montesquieu sociologue," *Revue*

internationale de sociologie 47 (1939): 221–232; Sergio Cotta, *Montesquieu e la scienza della società* (Turin: Ramella, 1953); H. H. Jogland, *Ursprünge und Grundlagen der Soziologie bei Adam Ferguson* (Berlin: Duncker und Humblot, 1959); W. C. Lehmann, *John Millar of Glasgow, 1735–1801: His Life and Thought and His Contributions to Sociological Analysis* (Cambridge: At the University Press, 1960); Werner Stark, *Montesquieu: Pioneer of the Sociology of Knowledge* (Toronto: University of Toronto Press, 1961); Alan Swingewood, "Origins of Sociology: The Case of the Scottish Enlightenment," *British Journal of Sociology* 21 (1970): 164–180; Georges Gusdorf, *Les sciences humaines et la pensée occidentale*, Vol. 6: *L'Avénement des sciences de l'homme au siècle des lumières* (Paris: Payot, 1973); Ronald Meek, ed., *Turgot on Progress, Sociology, and Economics* (Cambridge: At the University Press, 1973); David A. Reisman, *Adam Smith's Sociological Economics* (London: Croom Helm, 1976); Robert Bierstet, "Sociological Thought in the Eighteenth Century," in *A History of Sociological Analysis*, ed. Tom Bottomore and Robert Nisbet (New York: Basic Books, 1978), 3–38; Sergio Moravia, *La scienza dell'uomo nel settecento* (Rome: Bari, 1978); A. J. Skinner, *A System of Social Science: Papers Relating to Adam Smith* (Oxford: Clarendon Press, 1979); J. G. A. Pocock, "The Mobility of Property and the Rise of Eighteenth Century Sociology," in *Theories of Property: Aristotle to the Present*, ed. A. Parel and T. Flanagan (Waterloo, Ont.: Wilfrid Laurier University Press, 1979).

3. Keith M. Baker, "The Early History of the Term 'Social Science,'" *Annals of Science* 20 (1964): 211–226; Brian W. Head, "The Origins of 'La Science Sociale' in France, 1770–1800," *Australian Journal of French Studies* 19 (1982): 115–132. Earlier, the most common phrases were *sciences morales* and *sciences morales et politiques*. The Société de 1789 was a discussion group founded in the spring of 1790 consisting mainly of moderates interested in stabilizing the political and economic situation in France through the creation of a rational social order. See Baker, "Early History," 215–218.

4. Peter Gay, *The Enlightenment: An Interpretation*, Vol. II: *The Science of Freedom* (New York: Knopf, 1969), 323; italics added.

5. Arthur O. Lovejoy, *The Great Chain of Being* (Cambridge, Mass.: Harvard University Press, 1936), 3–4.

6. Michael Foucault, *The Archaeology of Knowledge* (New York: Pantheon Books, 1972), 12–13.

7. See also Quentin Skinner's seminal article "Meaning and Understanding in the History of Ideas," *History and Theory* 8 (1969): 3–53, for strong emphasis on context and author's intent negating continuity, anticipations, and perennial problems in philosophy. Skinner's methodology is thoroughly debated in *Meaning and Context: Quentin Skinner and His Critics*, ed. James Tully (Princeton, N.J.: Princeton University Press, 1988).

8. See *The Order of Things: An Archaeology of the Human Sciences* (New York: Pantheon Books, 1970), 345, for Michel Foucault's positing of an epistemic chasm at the epoch of the French Revolution. For the importance of the French Revolutionary epoch, see also Keith M. Baker, "Closing the French Revolution: Saint-Simon and Comte," in *The French Revolution and the Creation of Modern Political Culture* (Oxford: Pergamon Press, 1989), 3:323–339; Robert Wokler, "Saint-Simon and the Passage from Political to Social Science," in *The Languages of Political*

Theory in Early-Modern Europe, ed. Anthony Pagden (Cambridge: Cambridge University Press, 1987), 325–338; and W. Jay Reedy, "The Historical Imaginary of Social Science in Post-Revolutionary France: Bonald, Saint-Simon, Comte," *History of the Human Sciences* 7 (1994): 1–26.

9. Foucault, *Archaeology of Knowledge,* 5.

10. See Roy Pascal, "Property and Society: The Scottish Contribution of the Eighteenth Century," *Modern Quarterly* 1 (1938): 167–179; R. L. Meek, "The Scottish Contribution to Marxist Sociology," in *Economics and Ideology and Other Essays: Studies in the Development of Economic Thought* (London, 1967), 34–50; idem, "Smith, Turgot, and the 'Four Stages' Theory," *History of Political Economy* 3 (1971): 9–27; idem, *Social Science and the Ignoble Savage* (Cambridge: Cambridge University Press, 1976).

11. Foucault, *Order of Things,* 370–371.

12. Head, "Origins of 'La Science Sociale,'" 127.

13. Consider, for example, the following summary of Enlightenment philosophy: "This framework, as is well known, conceived man in abstract fashion; that is, individuals were emancipated by logical abstraction from their historic connections and from every social necessity; the concept of society was reduced to its atomic constituents, to the sum of the individuals composing it. Abstract categories of individual psychology, it was thought, sufficed for the explanation of all human facts." (Joseph V. Femia, "An Historicist Critique of 'Revisionist' Methods for Studying the History of Ideas," in *Meaning and Context,* ed. Tully, 166). Femia's essay is a valuable discussion of Skinner's methodology, but his summary of the Enlightenment mentality overlooks the strong holism and historicizing tendencies within the movement.

14. Ferguson, *An Essay on the History of Civil Society,* ed. Duncan Forbes (1767; Edinburgh: Edinburgh University Press, 1966), 220.

15. For "sociological" discussions of "societies and particular groups" within the larger entity "nations," see Jean d'Alembert's *Encyclopédie* article "Character" in *Encyclopedia: Selections,* trans. and ed. Nelly S. Hoyt and Thomas Cassirer (Indianapolis: Bobbs-Merrill Co., 1965), 32–35, and Adam Smith, *The Theory of Moral Sentiments,* ed. D. D. Raphael and A. L. Macfie (Oxford: Oxford University Press, 1976), 230–231. Ample evidence exists that Enlightenment-era figures distinguished the realm of society from the realm of politics. Many would have agreed, for example, with Vico's statement, "political science . . . is nothing other than the science of commanding and obeying in states" (*The New Science of Giambattista Vico,* trans. Thomas G. Bergin and Max H. Fisch [Ithaca, N.Y.: Cornell University Press, 1948], 189).

16. See Hume, *Treatise of Human Nature,* ed. Selby-Bigge, xv–xvi; Ferguson, *Principles of Moral and Political Science,* 2 vols. (1792; reprint, New York: AMS Press, 1973), 1:5–7, 9–10, 63–64; Johann Gottfried von Herder, *Outlines of a Philosophy of the History of Man,* trans. T. Churchill (1784; reprint, New York: Bergman Publishers, n.d.; orig. ed., London, 1800), 103, 162.

17. Meek, *Ignoble Savage,* 1.

18. Durkheim, *Montesquieu's Contribution,* 21. Also relevant is Roger Smith's conclusion in this volume that "as social and historical accounts of human life

acquired prominence, so human nature as a topic in its own right declined in significance" (p. 104).

19. Duncan Forbes, "Scientific Whiggism: Adam Smith and John Millar," *Cambridge Journal* 7 (1954): 649–651. Lovejoy applied the phrase "sociological evolutionism" to Rousseau's perspective in his *Discourse on Inequality*. See Lovejoy, "Monboddo and Rousseau," *Modern Philology* 30 (1933): 275–296; reprinted in Arthur Lovejoy, *Essays in the History of Ideas* (Baltimore: Johns Hopkins University Press, 1948), 38–61. For an early version of this evolutionary perspective not discussed in this essay, see Part II of B. Mandeville's *Fable of the Bees* (1729), ed. F. B. Kaye (Oxford: Oxford University Press, 1924).

20. David Lieberman, "The Legal Needs of a Commercial Society: The Jurisprudence of Lord Kames," in *Wealth and Virtue: The Shaping of Political Economy in the Scottish Enlightenment,* ed. Istvan Hont and Michael Ignatieff (Cambridge: Cambridge University Press, 1983), 222; Forbes, "Scientific Whiggism," 649; Frank Manuel, *The Prophets of Paris: Turgot, Condorcet, Saint-Simon, Fourier, and Comte* (Cambridge, Mass.: Harvard University Press, 1962), 6.

21. Giambattista Vico, *The New Science,* ed. T. Bergin and Max Frisch (Ithaca, N.Y.: Cornell University Press, 1948), 52–53.

22. See Peter Stein, *Legal Evolution: The Story of an Idea* (Cambridge: Cambridge University Press, 1980), 9; and W. Jay Reedy, "History, Authority, and the Ideological Representation of Tradition in Louis de Bonald's Science of Society," *Studies on Voltaire and the Eighteenth Century* 311 (1993): 143–177. Johann Georg Hamann, Johann Gottfried Herder, and Friedrich Heinrich Jacobi all retained a view of history as divinely produced and guided. For strong emphasis on Vico's providential groundings, see Mark Lilla, *G. B. Vico: The Making of an Anti-Modern* (Cambridge, Mass.: Harvard University Press, 1993).

23. Jean-Jacques Rousseau, *The First and Second Discourses,* trans. and ed. Roger D. Masters (New York: St. Martin's Press, 1964), 103.

24. Jean d'Alembert, *Preliminary Discourse,* in Denis Diderot's *The Encyclopedia: Selections,* trans. and ed. Stephen J. Gendzier (New York: Harper and Row, 1967), passim; Voltaire, *Essai sur les moeurs et l'esprit des nations et sur les principaux faits de l'histoire depuis Charlemagne jusqu'à Louis XIII,* ed. René Pomeau, 2 vols. (Paris: Garnier Frères, 1963); Denis Diderot, "Homme," in *Encyclopédie ou Dictionnaire raisonné des sciences, des arts et des métiers, par une société de gens de lettres,* 17 vols. (Paris: 1751–1772; reprinted in 3 vols., Oxford: Pergamon Press, 1969), 2:344–350; David Hume, letter to Hutcheson (September, 1739), quoted by Duncan Forbes, *Hume's Philosophical Politics* (Cambridge: Cambridge University Press), 59.

25. David Hume, "Whether the British Government inclines more to Absolute Monarchy or to a Republic," cited in Forbes, *Hume's Philosophical Politics,* 61, 65.

26. Not surprisingly, this new perspective challenged orthodoxy and brought religious censure. For a list of passages in Montesquieu's chief work censured by religious authorities, see Montesquieu, *The Spirit of Laws: A Compendium of the First English Edition together with an English Translation of An Essay on Causes Affecting Minds and Characters* (1736–1743), ed. David Wallace Carrithers (Berkeley, Los Angeles, London: University of California Press, 1977), 467–468.

27. Montesquieu, *The Spirit of Laws,* ed. Carrithers, 321, 323 (Book XXIV,

chaps. 1, 4). Hereafter, all references to this edition of *The Spirit of Laws* will be cited by book and chapter number within parentheses inserted in the main body of the text.

28. For discussion of Montesquieu's functionalism, see *The Spirit of Laws*, ed. Carrithers, 23–30; Emile Durkheim, *Montesquieu and Rousseau*, 55–57; and Michael Thompson, Richard Ellis, and Aaron Wildavsky, *Cultural Theory* (Boulder: Westview Press, 1990), 109–113.

29. For Voltaire, see *The Philosophy of History*, ed. Thomas Kiernan (New York: Philosophical Library, 1965), 14–20; for Herder, see *Philosophy of the History of Man*, 98–105. See, in general, Frank E. Manuel, *The Eighteenth Century Confronts the Gods* (Cambridge, Mass.: Harvard University Press, 1959).

30. Ferguson, *Principles*, 1:118.

31. See Leon Pompa, *Vico: A Study of the "New Science"* (Cambridge: Cambridge University Press, 1975), 75ff.

32. *Treatise of Human Nature*, in David Hume's *Philosophical Works*, 4 vols. (Boston, 1854), 4:235, cited in W. C. Lehmann, *Adam Ferguson and the Beginnings of Modern Sociology* (New York: Columbia University Press, 1930), 228; Hume, *Inquiry concerning Human Understanding*, ed. Charles W. Hendel (Indianapolis: Bobbs-Merrill Co., 1955), 57–58.

33. Preface to Francis Hutcheson's *System of Moral Philosophy*, 2 vols. (London, 1755), cited in Stein, *Legal Evolution*, 9. Adam Smith's hermeneutical approach is evident in the distinction he drew between "a knowledge of the causes of events" and "a science no less useful," that being "a knowledge of the motives by which men act" (*Lectures on Rhetoric and Belles Lettres . . . 1762–63*, ed. J. M. Lothian [Edinburgh, 1963], 109, quoted by Donald Winch, "Adam Smith's 'Enduring Particular Result': A Cosmopolitan Perspective," in *Wealth and Virtue*, ed. Hont and Ignatieff, 259). See also Knud Haakonssen, *The Science of a Legislator: The Natural Jurisprudence of David Hume and Adam Smith* (Cambridge: Cambridge University Press, 1981), 186–188. For a debunking of the hermeneutical fetish and the view that explanation and understanding are actually inseparable, see Richard Rorty, "Method, Social Science, and Social Hope," in *Consequences of Pragmatism* (Minneapolis: University of Minnesota Press, 1982), 191–210.

34. Martin Staum, "Individual Rights and Social Control: Political Science in the French Institute," *Journal of the History of Ideas* 47 (1987): 411–430; Head, "Origins of 'La Science Sociale,'" 117, 120.

35. See E. J. Hundert, "A Cognitive Idea and Its Myth: Knowledge as Power in the Lexicon of the Enlightenment," *Social Research* 53 (1986): 133–157.

36. Anonymous, "Observation," in *Encyclopédie*, 2:1073. It would be difficult to exaggerate the Enlightenment conviction that a single scientific method was suited to both the natural sciences and the social sciences. It seemed eminently reasonable to the Marquis de Condorcet, for example, to draft an *Essai sur l'application de l'analyse à la probabilité des décisions rendues à la pluralité des voix* (1785). See *Condorcet: Selected Writings*, trans. and ed. Keith Michael Baker (Indianapolis: Bobbs-Merrill Co., 1976), 33–70.

37. Anonymous, "Observation," 2:1073.

38. Condorcet, *Eloge de Michel de l'Hôpital*, in *Oeuvres de Condorcet*, 12 vols.

(Paris, 1847–49), 3:536–537, cited by Keith Michael Baker, *Condorcet: From Natural Philosophy to Social Mathematics* (Chicago: University of Chicago Press, 1975), 220–221.

39. Anonymous, "Observation," in *Encyclopédie*, 2:1073. Hindsight suggests that Montesquieu was the single most important figure in the Enlightenment for the science of society. No other theorist inspired so much "sociological" investigation and speculation, sometimes to corroborate and sometimes to rebut the diverse materials and contentions within *De l'esprit des lois*.

40. Ibid. (italics in original).

41. Jean d'Alembert, "Eléments de Philosophie," in *Mélanges de Littérature, d'Histoire, et de Philosophie*, nouvelle édition, 6 vols. (Amsterdam, 1759), 4:16, cited in Ernst Cassirer, *The Philosophy of the Enlightenment*, trans. Fritz C. A. Koelln and James P. Pettegrove (Princeton, N.J.: Princeton University Press, 1951), 225.

42. David Hume, *Enquiries concerning Human Understanding and concerning the Principles of Morals*, ed. L. A. Selby-Bigge, 3d ed. (Oxford: Clarendon Press, 1975), 83–84.

43. Ibid.

44. Ferguson, *Principles*, 1:97, quoted in Robert Brown, *The Nature of Social Laws: Machiavelli to Mill* (Cambridge: Cambridge University Press, 1984), 117.

45. Diderot, *The Encyclopedia*, ed. Gendzier, 134.

46. Giambattista Vico, *La Scienza Nuova*, quoted by Leon Pompa in *Vico: A Study of the 'New Science,'* 31.

47. Frederick Teggert, *Theory and Processes of History* (Berkeley and Los Angeles: University of California Press, 1960), 94.

48. Ibid.; Stein, *Legal Evolution*, 18.

49. Meek, *Ignoble Savage*, 139.

50. Montesquieu, *The Spirit of Laws*, books 2–8. See Durkheim, *Montesquieu and Rousseau*, 24–35, for a depiction of Montesquieu's typology of governmental forms as a description of societal types. A full description of Montesquieu as a political sociologist would necessarily include his correlations between liberty, form of government, and climate, topography, and soil as well as his population theory and his discussions of the relation between forms of government and volume of territory.

51. Johann Gottfried Herder, *On the Reciprocal Influence of the Government and the Sciences*, in Johann Gottfried Herder, *J. G. Herder on Social and Political Culture*, trans. and ed. F. M. Barnard (Cambridge: At the University Press), 46–47.

52. For a discussion of French sociology as "a generalizing science" seeking laws in contrast to German sociology not seen as advancing the same theoretical claims, see Raymond Aron, *German Sociology*, trans. Mary and Thomas Bottomore (Glencoe, Ill.: Free Press, 1964), 109ff.

53. Pompa, *Vico*, 22–23.

54. *Pensée* 410, in Montesquieu, *Œuvres complètes*, ed. Roger Caillois, 2 vols. (Paris: Editions Gallimard, 1949–51), 2:1111.

55. *Considerations on the Causes of the Greatness of the Romans and Their Decline*, trans. David Lowenthal (1739; Ithaca, N.Y.: Cornell University Press, 1968), 169.

56. Raymond Aron, *Main Currents in Sociological Thought*, 2 vols. (Garden City,

N.Y.: Anchor Books, 1970), 1:15. For a more complete discussion, see David Carrithers, "Montesquieu's Philosophy of History," *Journal of the History of Ideas* 47 (1986): 61–80.

57. See, for example, the clear statement to this effect in Montesquieu's *Essay on Causes Affecting Minds and Characters* (1736–43): "Moral causes shape the general character of a nation and determine the quality of its mind more than do physical causes." (Montesquieu, *The Spirit of Laws*, ed. Carrithers, 443.)

58. Hume, *Enquiry concerning Human Understanding*, in *Enquiries*, ed. Selby-Bigge, 86–88.

59. Ibid., 88–90.

60. "Of the Rise and Progress of the Arts and Sciences," in David Hume's *Essays Moral, Political, and Literary*, ed. Eugene F. Miller (Indianapolis: Liberty Classics, 1985), 112–113.

61. Montesquieu, *The Spirit of Laws*, ed. Carrithers, 417.

62. Immanuel Kant, *Idea for a Universal History from a Cosmopolitan Point of View* (1784), in *Kant on History*, ed. Lewis White Beck (Indianapolis: Bobbs-Merrill Co., 1963), 11.

63. François Quesnay, "Observations sur le droit naturel des hommes réunis en société" (1765; reissued the same year as *Le Droit Naturel*), in *The Economics of Physiocracy: Essays and Translations*, trans. and ed. Ronald L. Meek (Cambridge, Mass.: Harvard University Press, 1963), 54.

64. Ibid., 54–55.

65. François Quesnay, *Philosophie rurale, ou Economie générale et politique de l'agriculture, Réduite a l'ordre immuable des lois physiques & morales, qui assurent la prospérité des empires* (1763), in *Economics of Physiocracy*, trans. and ed. Meek, 69–70.

66. Claude-Adrien Helvétius, *De l'esprit* (Paris: 1758), preface, ii, quoted by Charles Vereker in *Eighteenth-Century Optimism: A Study of the Interrelations of Moral and Social Theory in English and French Thought between 1689 and 1789* (Liverpool: Liverpool University Press, 1967), 186.

67. Anne-Robert-Jacques Turgot, "Etymologie," in *Œuvres complètes*, ed. Gustave Schelle, 5 vols. (Paris, 1913–22), 1:495, cited in Manuel, *Prophets of Paris*, 34.

68. Lord Kames, *Historical Law Tracts*, 2 vols. (Edinburgh, 1758), 1:37 quoted in Peter Stein, "Law and Society in Eighteenth-Century Scottish Thought," in *Scotland in the Age of Improvement: Essays in Scottish History in the Eighteenth Century*, ed. N. T. Phillipson and Rosalind Mitchison (Edinburgh: Edinburgh University Press, 1970), 158.

69. Vico, *Scienza Nuova* (par. 915), cited in Pompa, *Vico*, 112.

70. Meek, *Ignoble Savage*; Ronald Hamowy, *The Scottish Enlightenment and the Theory of Spontaneous Order* (Carbondale: Southern Illinois University Press, 1987); Forbes, "Scientific Whiggism."

71. Vico, *Scienza Nuova* (par. 1108), quoted by Forbes, "Scientific Whiggism," 658.

72. Ferguson, *Civil Society*, 337.

73. Herder, *Travel Diary* (1769), quoted in Herder, *J. G. Herder on Social and Political Culture*, trans. and ed. Barnard, 45 (italics added).

74. Cf. Duncan Forbes's comment in his "Natural Law and the Scottish

Enlightenment," in *The Origins and Nature of the Scottish Enlightenment*, ed. R. H. Campbell and Andrew S. Skinner (Edinburgh: Donald, 1982), 187: "[N]atural law in the Scottish Enlightenment was in dry dock, and . . . the preliminary and auxiliary sciences—psychology, history, 'sociology,' the 'economic interpretation of history'—came to upstage the project itself, so that the latter [natural law] tended to disappear from sight." See also Steven Seidman, *Liberalism and the Origins of European Social Theory* (Berkeley, Los Angeles, London: University of California Press, 1983), 25–28. For a contrary view emphasizing the pervasiveness of social contract theory and trivializing the objections of Hume and Ferguson to such theory, see Otto Gierke, *Natural Law and the Theory of Society: 1500 to 1800*, trans. Ernest Barker (Boston: Beacon Press, 1957), passim and 305. For an authoritative discussion of natural law theory in Hume and Smith, see Knud Haakonssen, "What Might Properly Be Called Natural Jurisprudence," in *Origins and Nature of the Scottish Enlightenment*, ed. Campbell and Skinner, 205–221. For a reminder that the doctrine of natural law is not dependent on a corresponding belief in a state of nature, or an original contract, see Mark H. Waddicor, *Montesquieu and the Philosophy of Natural Law* (The Hague: Nijhoff, 1970), 134.

75. Pierre Bayle, *Nouvelles Lettres à l'occasion de la critique générale du Calvinisme de Maimbourg*, Lettre 17, section 2, cited by James Moore and Michael Silverthorne, "Gershom Carmichael and Natural Jurisprudence," in *Wealth and Virtue*, ed. Hont and Ignatieff, 84.

76. Shaftesbury, *Characteristicks of Men, Manners, Opinions, Times* (1711), quoted by Gladys Bryson in *Man and Society: The Scottish Inquiry of the Eighteenth Century* (Princeton, N.J.: Princeton University Press, 1945), 149.

77. Moore and Silverthorne, "Gershom Carmichael"; Lettre Persane 94, in *Œuvres complètes*, ed. Caillois, 1:269–270; *Treatise of Human Nature*, ed. Selby-Bigge, 493. For important arguments minimizing Montesquieu's rejection of contract and the state of nature, see Waddicor, *Montesquieu and the Philosophy of Natural Law*, 91–99; idem, "Montesquieu et le problème de l'origine des sociétés," *Studi francesi* (1969): 235–246.

78. Hume, "Of the Original Contract," in *Essays Moral, Political, and Literary*, ed. Miller, 474, 487.

79. Ferguson, *Principles*, 1:24.

80. Quoted in *The Scottish Moralists on Human Nature and Society*, ed. Louis Schneider (Chicago: University of Chicago Press, 1967), 84.

81. Kames, *Historical Law Tracts*, 1:36–37, quoted in Stein, *Legal Evolution*, 27; Duncan Forbes's introduction in Ferguson's *Civil Society*, xvi–xvii.

82. As the examples of Locke and Pufendorf reveal, however, it was entirely possible to depict humankind in an original state of nature and still conclude that humans are "naturally sociable." As John Scott has recently emphasized, most theorists who conjured up an original state of nature depicted human beings as living in families and social groups rather than in total independence and isolation. Hence the importance of Rousseau's differing perspective on the "pure state of nature." See John T. Scott, "The Theodicy of the *Second Discourse*: The 'Pure State of Nature' and Rousseau's Political Thought," *American Political Science Review* 86, no. 3 (September, 1992): 701. For appreciation of the same point by David Hume, see

Duncan Forbes, *Hume's Philosophical Politics* (Cambridge: Cambridge University Press, 1975), 71–74. See also, for the stages in Rousseau's state of nature, Arthur Lovejoy's "The Supposed Primitivism of Rousseau's *Discourse on Inequality*," *Modern Philology* 21 (1923), 165–186, reprinted in Lovejoy's *Essays in the History of Ideas*, 14–37.

83. Ferguson, *Civil Society*, 26.

84. Francis Hutcheson, *An Inquiry into the Original of Our Ideas of Beauty and Virtue*, 2 vols. (Dublin, 1725), 1:198–199, cited in Garry Wills, *Inventing America: Jefferson's Declaration of Independence* (New York: Vintage Books, 1979), 287, 290.

85. Montesquieu, *De la politique*, in *Œuvres complètes*, 1:114.

86. For Hegel's reading of Montesquieu, see Michael A. Mosher, "The Particulars of a Universal Politics: Hegel's Adaptation of Montesquieu's Typology," *American Political Science Review* (1984): 179–188; Guy Planty-Bonjour, "L'esprit général d'une nation selon Montesquieu et le Volksgeist hégélienne," in *Hegel et le siècle des lumières*, ed. Jacques d'Hondt (Paris: Presses Universitaires de France, 1974), 7–24; and Steven B. Smith, *Hegel's Critique of Liberalism* (Chicago: University of Chicago Press, 1989). For other Enlightenment discussions of national character, see Immanuel Kant, *Anthropology from a Pragmatic Point of View* (1798), trans. Victor L. Dowdell (Carbondale: Southern Illinois University Press, 1978); Jean d'Alembert, "Character," in *Encyclopedia*, trans. Hoyt and Cassirer, 32–35; David Hume, "Of National Characters," in *Essays*, ed. Miller, 197–215; Smith, *Theory of Moral Sentiments*, 75–76, 204; Ferguson, *Civil Society*, 190.

87. Hume, *Treatise of Human Nature*, quoted by James Moore in "The Social Background of Hume's Science of Human Nature," in *McGill Hume Studies*, ed. David Fate Norton, Nicholas Capaldi, and Wade L. Robison (San Diego: Austin Hill, 1979), 39.

88. Hume, *Essays Moral, Political, and Literary*, ed. Miller, 255–256.

89. Jean-Jacques Rousseau, *The First and Second Discourses*, trans. and ed. Masters, 138.

90. Ibid., 178–179.

91. Ibid., 179.

92. Ibid., 178.

93. Ibid., 180.

94. Herder, *Philosophy of the History of Man*, 164.

95. Quoted in Herder, *J. G. Herder on Social and Political Culture*, trans. Barnard, 35.

96. Herder, *Philosophy of the History of Man*, 194, 197.

97. Lester G. Crocker, *An Age of Crisis: Man and World in Eighteenth-Century French Thought* (Baltimore: Johns Hopkins University Press, 1957), 118.

98. P.-H.-T. d'Holbach, *Système de la nature* (1770), quoted in Vereker, *Eighteenth-Century Optimism*, 190.

99. Robert Nisbet, "Conservatism," in *A History of Sociological Analysis*, ed. Bottomore and Nisbet, 98.

100. Denis Diderot, "Société," in *Œuvres complètes*, ed. J. Assézat and M. Tourneux, 20 vols. (Paris: Garnier, 1875–77), 17:134. See also the article "Société, (Morale)," which includes the sentence: "From the principle of sociability flow, as

from their source, all the laws of *society*, and all our duties towards other men, both general and particular. Such is the foundation of all human wisdom, the source of all the purely natural virtues, and the general principle of all ethics [*la morale*] and of all civil *society*." (*Encyclopédie, ou dictionnaire raisonné*, 3:560; italics in original.)

101. Smith, *Theory of Moral Sentiments*, 22. Michael Ignatieff, in his "John Millar and Individualism," in *Wealth and Virtue*, ed. Hont and Ignatieff, 319–320, glosses the text in question by asserting that "Smith was scathing about this 'natural psychology' of Hutcheson, objecting that the 'force of blood,' or the 'natural connection' exist nowhere but in tragedies and romances."

102. Forbes, "Scientific Whiggism," 670.

103. For other examples of Montesquieu's functionalist emphasis on the delicate equilibrium among a society's diverse component elements, see *Pensées* 413 and 414 in *Œuvres complètes*, 2:1111–1112.

104. Voltaire, *Essai sur les mœurs*, chap. 197, quoted in Cassirer, *Philosophy of the Enlightenment*, 219.

105. Smith, *Theory of Moral Sentiments*, 194; idem, *An Inquiry into the Nature and Causes of the Wealth of Nations*, ed. R. H. Campbell and A. S. Skinner, 2 vols. (Oxford: Clarendon Press, 1976), 1:28–29. The literature on Smith's social psychology is voluminous. An interesting survey of the subject is Robert Heilbroner, "Socialization in Adam Smith," *History of Political Economy* 14 (1982): 427–439.

106. David Lieberman, "The Jurisprudence of Lord Kames," in *Wealth and Virtue*, ed. Hont and Ignatieff, 223.

107. Voltaire, "Climat," in *Dictionnaire philosophique, Œuvres de Voltaire*, ed. A.-J.-Q. Beuchot, 72 vols. (Paris: Didot frères, 1829–1840), 28, 116; Condillac, *Essai sur l'origine des connoissances humaines* (1746), in *Œuvres philosophiques*, ed. Georges Le Roy, 3 vols. (Paris: Presses Universitaires de France, 1947–51), 1:98, cited by Henry Vyverberg, *Human Nature, Cultural Diversity, and the French Enlightenment* (New York: Oxford University Press, 1989), 73.

108. Denis Diderot, *Observations sur le Nakaz*, in *Diderot: Political Writings*, trans. and ed. John Hope Mason and Robert Wokler (Cambridge: Cambridge University Press, 1992), 102.

109. Abbé Raynal, *Histoire philosophique et politique des établissements et du commerce des Européens dans les deux Indes*, 4 vols. (Geneva, 1780), 4:190, quoted by Vereker, *Eighteenth-Century Optimism*, 190.

110. Diderot, *Observations sur le Nakaz*, 89.

111. D'Alembert, "Character," in *Encyclopedia*, trans. Hoyt and Cassirer, 33.

112. Quoted in Herder, *J. G. Herder on Social and Political Philosophy*, trans. Barnard, 38.

113. Whereas nearly all commentators stress the forward-looking, "sociological" direction of this perspective, see Donald J. Kelley, *The Human Measure: Social Thought in the Western Legal Tradition* (Cambridge, Mass.: Harvard University Press, 1990), 219–222, for an important opposing view suggesting Montesquieu was following a path as ancient as that traveled by Ulpian, the Roman jurist of the late second and early third century A.D.

114. See Stein, *Legal Evolution*, 4, 17; John Millar, "The Progress of Science relating to Law and Government," in *An Historical View of the English Government*, 4th

ed., 4 vols. (London, 1812), 4:284–285, quoted by Lieberman, "The Jurisprudence of Lord Kames," 204.

115. J. G. A. Pocock, "Cambridge Paradigms and Scotch Philosophers: A Study of the Relations between the Civic Humanist and the Civil Jurisprudential Interpretation of Eighteenth-Century Social Thought," in *Wealth and Virtue*, ed. Hont and Ignatieff, 245–252.

116. Haakonssen, *Science as a Legislator*, 178–189; Andrew Skinner, "A Scottish Contribution to Marxist Sociology?" in *Classical and Marxian Political Economy: Essays in Honor of Ronald L. Meek*, ed. Ian Bradley and Michael Howard (New York: St. Martin's Press, 1982), 79–114; Donald Winch, *Adam Smith's Politics: An Essay in Historiographic Revision* (Cambridge: Cambridge University Press, 1978), 56–65.

117. Durkheim, *Montesquieu and Rousseau*, 20.

118. For Ferguson on the same point, see *Essay*, 123. For Montesquieu as a sociologist of law, see Eugen Ehrlich, "Montesquieu and Sociological Jurisprudence," *Harvard Law Review* 29 (1916): 582–600; Georges Gürvitch, "La sociologie juridique de Montesquieu," *Revue de métaphysique et de morale* 46 (1939): 611–626; Huntington Cairns, *Law and the Social Sciences* (New York, 1935), 36–37; Stark, *Montesquieu*; and Nicholas S. Timasheff, *An Introduction to the Sociology of Law* (Cambridge, Mass.: Harvard University Press, 1939).

119. From a letter to Diderot in which Allan Ramsay included "some Reflections on the treatise of Crimes and Punishments which you and Suard mentioned at the Baron d'Holbach's during my stay in Paris," quoted by Franco Venturi, "Scottish Echoes in Eighteenth-Century Italy," in *Wealth and Virtue*, ed. Hont and Ignatieff, 346.

120. Lieberman, "Jurisprudence of Lord Kames," 209.

121. Voltaire, *Essay on the Manners and Mind of Nations* (1756), quoted by J. B. Bury, *The Idea of Progress: An Inquiry into Its Growth and Origin* (New York: Dover Publications, 1955), 152. In the passage quoted, Voltaire was lamenting that this is too often the approach taken to the study of laws.

122. Haakonssen, *Science of a Legislator*, 187, 225; Winch, "Adam Smith's 'Enduring Particular Result,'" 261. For Smith's lectures, see Adam Smith, *Lectures on Jurisprudence*, ed. R. L. Meek, D. D. Raphael, P. G. Stein (Oxford: Clarendon Press, 1978).

123. Quoted by Meek, in *Ignoble Savage*, 233–234. Montesquieu announced the four stages—hunting, herding, agriculture, and commerce—in 18:8 of his *De l'esprit des lois*. For Montesquieu's influence on the Scots, see not only the work of Pascal and Meek cited in note 10 above, but also Richard B. Sher, "From Troglodytes to Americans: Montesquieu and the Scottish Enlightenment on Liberty, Virtue, and Commerce," in *Republicanism, Liberty, and Commercial Society, 1649–1776*, ed. David Wootton (Stanford: Stanford University Press, 1994), 368–402. The full text of Dugald Stewart's "Account of the Life and Writings of Adam Smith, L.L.D." is available in Adam Smith, *Essays on Philosophical Subjects*, ed. W. P. D. Wightman and J. C. Bryce (Oxford: Clarendon Press, 1980), 269–332.

124. Kames, *Historical Law Tracts*, 1:v, quoted by Lieberman, "Jurisprudence of Lord Kames," 206.

125. John Millar, "some particulars about Dr. Smith," in Dugald Stewart,

"Account of the Life and Writings of Adam Smith," in Smith, *Essays on Philosophical Subjects,* 265, 273–275. See also Meek, *Ignoble Savage,* 107–109.

126. Stein, *Legal Evolution,* 23.

127. John Millar, *Origin of Ranks,* in Lehmann, *John Millar of Glasgow,* 176–177. Millar's text was originally published in 1771 under the title *Observations concerning the Distinctions of Ranks in Society.*

128. Ibid., 384–385.

129. Ferguson, *Civil Society,* 134; Meek, *Ignoble Savage,* 152.

130. Meek, *Ignoble Savage,* 2.

131. Pocock, "Cambridge Paradigms," 242–243.

NINE

The Non-Normal Sciences

Survivals of Renaissance Thought
in the Eighteenth Century

Gloria Flaherty

Sometimes the non-normal sciences[1] represented a revolt against the excesses of Newtonianism,[2] but mostly they were various kinds of survivals from earlier ages that had retained some of the old symbolism[3] and outer trappings while attempting to gain legitimacy with selection of methods as well as problems from science, that is, normal science. As the scientific community closed ranks and developed into a highly professional subgroup that talked to itself, it began to think of such activities as pseudo-sciences or non-sciences, thus pushing them off to the margins. Polemicists, like Voltaire, supported the cause by producing quotable remarks debunking their otherworldliness, magic, somnambulism, or faith-healing.[4] He zeroed in on revealed religion, especially the Roman Catholic Church, which he blamed for sustaining the belief in magic by allowing for the commerce with devils rather than excommunicating sorcerers as madmen.[5]

The rest of the population might have been excluded from this whole discussion, but they did not suddenly disappear from the scene. They simply continued to view such non-normal sciences as time-honored means of potentially gaining useful information or power.[6] No specialized training was needed for comprehension, but mediators were readily available. Consequently, people went on buying their almanacs, consulting their local herbalists or healers, drinking elixirs bought from boastful mountebanks, and judging neighbors according to the shape of their ears, the lines in their foreheads, their moles, and the other characteristics comprising their physiognomies.[7] Since the boundaries between science and magic were so blurred in the eighteenth-century popular mind, all kinds of new hoaxes could be perpetrated as well. As Roger Hahn has pointed out,

Fads in science were not confined to disciplines still in a fact-gathering stage of development. The imagination of the educated populace was equally receptive to the scientific demonstrations of itinerant lecturers, to inventors of new mechanical devices, and to discoveries of panaceas for man's persistent ailments. The "enlightened" century had its share of the superstitious who unwittingly welcomed magic and quackery in the guise of science.[8]

In some instances, the devotion to superstitions strengthened proportionately to the intensity of the rational scientific assault. This happened with great regularity among the Germans and the Russians.[9] And, according to Constantin Bila's excellent dissertation of 1925, the French were no different. Magical interests became more vigorous throughout all classes of society in the course of the eighteenth century.[10] As Robert Darnton later put it, many Frenchmen preferred to bury Voltaire in order to flock to the likes of Franz Anton Mesmer.[11]

Even those intellectuals and sovereigns who were wont to condemn such activities oftentimes themselves engaged in them either directly or indirectly without comprehending any contradiction, or, like Frederick the Great, without admitting one. If Harvard was still producing alchemical dissertations in the 1770s, and if it took until the 1780s for the Royal Society to discredit once and for all the transmutation of base metals into gold, what could the average person have been expected to understand?[12]

When that person consulted the dictionaries and other standard reference works, which were the repositories of conventional thought, he or she found science defined as any system of knowledge based on self-evident principles. In the early eighteenth century, it could be equated with magic as well as with art and erudition, or with the seven liberal arts, or, as in the *Encyclopédie*, also with the intuitive perception of God or the sublime study of enigmas.[13] Although the Germans became notorious for rejecting Newtonianism as yet another kind of mystification with its own priesthood, rituals, and secret language, their reference works were at least distinguishing science from art by the end of the eighteenth century.[14] But such distinctions did not help facilitate public comprehension of fields, like medicine, that were combinations of art and science. They were the hardest to divorce from magic in the public mind.

The simultaneous success of, on one hand, what we know as modern science, and, on the other, activities that were perpetrated in the name of science, has always posed one of the greatest puzzles for scholars.[15] Starting with the *philosophes,* there have been queries about how one could possibly live in an age of enlightenment, but not in an enlightened age. In this chapter, I should like to discuss a possible solution to the puzzle. That solution is the common denominator shared by all the non-normal scientific activities of the eighteenth century. Attempting to reduce such a superabundance of activities to a common denominator might itself seem as foolish as searching for the philosopher's stone. Nevertheless, it has been suggested for the colonial America by Herbert Leventhal, and, judging from what I have thus far uncovered, seems to apply to the West in general. I should like to look at eighteenth-century alchemy, astrology, animal magnetism, physiognomy, phrenology, and homeopathy as survivals of the same kind of Renaissance thinking that once helped stimulate the major breakthroughs of Western science.[16] Their original context was long, long gone. Nevertheless, they seemed to fill some kind of need during the Enlightenment before they submerged into folklore or became what the nineteenth century then perpetrated as "the Occult." Throughout this whole process, the non-normal sciences helped create a climate, or what might be termed a counterculture, that was conducive to considering alternative problems and methods. This would seem to indicate that there was some similarity between the way alchemy, magic, and the cabala contributed to the emergence of science during the Renaissance and the way their survivals, the non-normal sciences, contributed to the invention of the human sciences in the eighteenth century.

One way the Enlightenment learned about Renaissance thought was from the increasingly popular encyclopedias. Whether English, French, or German, they gave considerable attention to the non-normal sciences and their heritage. These reference works generally agreed with Ephraim Chambers that alchemy, for example, was "a higher more refined kind of chymistry, employ'd in the more mysterious Researches of the Art."[17] In addition to naming the most famous writers on the subject, these works had constant cross-references to chemistry, which they explained as "the Art of separating the several Substances whereof mix'd Bodies are compos'd, by means of Fire; and of composing new Bodies in the Fire, by the Mixture of different Substances or Ingredients."[18]

One listed chemistry, alchemy, the spagyric art, the Paracelsian art, the hermetic art, and pyrosophy as synonyms, while another reported that alchemy was known as poetry in the most ancient writings.[19] Hermes Trismegistus was seriously credited with the invention of that science which explained "all the Phenomena of Nature, from the three Chymical Principles, Salt, Sulphur, and Mercury."[20] In the *Encyclopédie*, hermeticism was described as the science, the system of principles, the theory of the art, and the dogmas of alchemy.[21] Only Samuel Johnson provided the simple listing, "*Hermes* or *Mercury*, the imagined inventer of Chymistry."[22] Some reference works pointed out the difference between true and false alchemy. In the *Encyclopédie* we read that it was unjust to consider it a science of visionaries and frauds when the many who actually practiced it considered it a real science.[23] Genuine alchemists had true philosophical knowledge. They were hermeticists.[24]

Similar coverage was given to astrology, which was also considered both a science and an art. The judicial branch that predicted human affairs from the heavenly book in which God wrote the history of the world got as much space as the natural branch, which was a kind of proto-meteorology.[25] It was said to have been invented by the Chaldeans, perfected by the Egyptians, and transmitted by the Arabs. The French Encyclopedists certainly took up sizable space to provide their readers with detailed information about judicial astrology, all the while disclaiming it as a superstition fashionable among the ruling elite. Moreover, the cross-references were much more extensive than merely to the horoscope or the zodiac.[26]

So great was the volume of publications dealing with the Renaissance magi that bibliographies began to appear so as to create some order for the readership. While some were merely listings of what one given collector had in his library, others used organizational principles involving the alphabet, chronology, or topics.[27] Nicolas Lenglet-Dufresnoy (1674–1755), who contributed to the *Encyclopédie*, was one of the many enlightened Frenchmen who openly pursued studies into all varieties of the paranormal while upholding the conventional rhetorical paradigm. He wrote on apparitions, visions, and revelations as well as dreams and nightmares. His classification of kinds is a kind of nosology of the weird. Like those involved in shamanic researches, he was concerned about the soul's ability to depart the body.[28] He contended that European females along with Easterners and Africans of both sexes had the greatest susceptibility to such experiences because of their vivid imaginations. Climate also played a role, which, he added, explained why the males of middle Europe, especially France and Germany, were able to retain so much level-headed, rational control.[29]

In addition to his treatises, there were his collections of writings that dealt with visions and hearing voices. Bibliographies accompanied most of his publications. The most far ranging was the one that formed volume 3 of his history of hermetic philosophy, which he termed a science. In addition to mentioning collectors and libraries in Paris, London, Leiden, and Vienna, he provided an annotated list. His comments involve a given publication's value among what he differentiated as the collectors, the connoisseurs, and the amateurs, which would seem to indicate that the following the market created had already begun to break down into distinct subgroups according to the sets of problems they identified and addressed, somewhat like the way scientific communities were forming.[30]

Such bibliographies were themselves sometimes the object of satire. The one by Laurent Bordelon (1653–1730) was originally written in French but published in English translation in 1711. Its chatty title told all: *A History of the Ridiculous Extravagances of Monsieur Oufle; Occasion'd by his reading Books treating of Magick, the Black-Arts, Daemoniacks, Conjurers, Witches, Hobgoblins, Incubus's, Succubus's, and the Diabolical-Sabbath; of Elves,*

Fairies, Wanton Spirits, Genius's, Spectres and Ghosts; of Dreams, the Philosopher's Stone, Judicial Astrology, Horoscopes, Talismans, Lucky and Unlucky Days, Eclipses, Comets, and all sorts of Apparitions, Divinations, Charms, Enchantments, and other Superstitious Practices, With Notes containing a multitude of Quotations out of those Books, which have either Caused such Extravagant Imaginations, or may serve to Cure them. The second chapter of this short work comprises six pages tightly listing all the titles in Oufle's magic library. Works by Agrippa led the list, which also included Pico della Mirandola, Johannes Trithemius, Paracelsus, Robert Fludd, and various physiognomical works.[31]

Whatever the debunkers or satirists might have written, the non-normal sciences persisted throughout the eighteenth century in various stages of stagnation, degeneration, recrudescence, or invention. Some, like astrology, were losing intellectual standing so fast that the defenders who came forth had little effect. Ebenezer Sibly (1751–1800) blamed "the stupid prejudices of the times against the real and venerable science of astrology" in his *A Complete Illustration of the Celestial Science of Astrology; Or, The Art of Foretelling Future Events and Contingencies.*[32] It was first published in London in 1790 and became so popular that twelve editions appeared by 1817. Sibly freely mixed Newton with Paracelsus and Hermes Trismegistus because he believed modern science was somehow incomplete without the vitalism of the magical tradition.[33]

Theatrical tendencies became more prominent with the development of what we know as the classic image of the astrologer in a long robe with a high-peaked hat punctuated with images of the stars he was noted for gazing at.[34] Talismans and other such trinkets purportedly affecting astral influences were sold at weekly markets and fairs. Even almanacs were no longer what they once were. Bernard Capp's studies have shown English ones to be a blend of amusement and instruction about tides, myths, recipes, and even normal science.[35]

Alchemy was not faring much better, although for different reasons. Despite much serious work and the corpus of publications, its image was being marred by some of the sincerest of people as well as by some of the grandest charlatans in the history of the West. Johann Salomon Semler, a theology professor in Halle, was the kind of believer who kept the market supplied with books on demonic possession, hermetic medicine, and the Rosicrucians. The alchemical experiments he conducted in his garden house were so successful that he notified the Berlin academy of his ingredients and procedures. When their attempts to duplicate his efforts failed, he was totally nonplussed until he discovered that the homeless soldier whom he had taken in was so grateful that he tried to help his benefactor by regularly adding a little gold leaf. When duty called the soldier away, his wife substituted for him—but she added real gold. This anecdote became so widely known that an otherwise productive scholar was ruined. The history of alchemy published by Karl Christoph Schmieder (1778–1850) reported this unfortunate incident, explaining that alchemical study had by no means ceased at the turn of the century. Hermetic societies were flourishing all over. Their members, however, spared themselves all humiliation by remaining underground out of public sight and by keeping the results of their researches to themselves.[36]

Casanova himself was quite fluent in the alchemical jargon, as we see from the section of his memoirs about Madame d'Urfé. Paracelsus was her favorite among all the magical books and manuscripts she kept in her fully outfitted laboratory where she purportedly transmuted gold. When she did so, however, she followed Agrippa. Casanova also shared her knowledge of Rosicrucianism, with its pledge to silence, its oath, and its aim to heal fellow human beings at no cost. The kind of sexual healing Casanova wanted to do would not, however, have been without its rewards.

Equally, if not more ambitious was Franz Anton Mesmer (1734–1815), who redirected the world's attention to the Paracelsian tradition of magnetic medicine.[37] As a child of the times, he was closely attuned to his contemporaries' wants and aspirations. The *Sturm und Drang* encouraged the quest for originality by self-proclaimed geniuses whose purported purpose was improving human existence in all ways possible. Mesmer succeeded in drawing attention to himself because he recognized the popular desire for adding the aura and glamor of the new science to age-old practices. And he knew how to satisfy that desire. Like the young Wolfgang Mozart, whose patron he briefly was, he had the ability to invent and reinvent himself in order to adapt to certain potentially adverse situations.

Mesmer was trained in South German Jesuit institutions where the Paracelsian tradition remained very much alive and at a time when the number of exorcisms was reaching an all-time high.[38] Information about suggestion, fascination or entrancement, and faith healing came not only through the orthodox channels of the church but also from the prolific literature of travel that everyone was discussing. Again and again, there were descriptions of the seemingly magical cures of aboriginal peoples in foreign lands. After receiving a doctorate in philosophy in 1759, Mesmer registered at the University of Vienna, where he studied law and then medicine. He was granted the medical doctorate in 1766, with the dissertation *Physical-Medical Treatise on the Influence of the Planets*. Unlike the judicial astrologers, he wished to show that celestial bodies acted on earth and that all things acted in turn on celestial bodies. Citing Newton's theory of tides, which was fashionable, rather than Paracelsus on signatures, which was not considered "enlightened," Mesmer concluded that "a tide takes place also in the human body, thanks to the same forces which cause the expansion of the sea and also the atmosphere."[39] The force that was the foundation of all corporal properties he called "animal gravity."

By marrying a wealthy widow, Mesmer was able to establish himself as a physician among the Viennese upper classes. Artists as well as socially notable people frequented his estate and, as word spread, his practice flourished. Sensational success came when he cured a hysterical young woman with a magnet in 1774. He justified his procedures, as he was wont to do throughout his career, with a public letter to a colleague about the medicinal uses of magnets. Taking up the notion of tides, he explained that they penetrated to all constituent parts of the human body and acted on the nerves in such a way as to excite a real magnetism. He called the property that made the body sensitive to universal gravitation "animal gravity" or, adumbrating his earlier dissertation, "animal magnetism" (25). The cure came from establishing in the patient's body, he wrote, "a kind of artificial tide by means of the magnet," which he viewed as the universal panacea similar to what the alchemists thought of as the philosopher's stone (26). He went on to write that he restored menstrual periods and hemorrhoids to their normal condition and was proceeding against "epilepsy, melancholia, mania, and intermittent fever" (28). When the priest supplying him with the magnets began to circulate word that it was the size of the magnets that was crucial, Mesmer quickly dispensed with them, explaining that his hands alone could control the magnetic fluid.

Mesmer's fame had already spread so widely in the southern German-speaking region that he was called in as an unfriendly witness by the Elector of Bavaria in the case of Father Johann Joseph Gassner (1727–1779), who was causing embarrassment as one of the most sought after exorcists of the day. Recognizing the opportunity to juxtapose himself as a man of science and enlightenment, Mesmer did everything Gassner did. However, he gave so-called empirically determined reasons based on his theory. Whereas Gassner produced convulsions in sinful subjects whose demons he was exorcising, Mesmer provoked crises caused by tidal disharmony, which he cured through touching and stroking.[40] This stunning performance won him coveted membership in the Bavarian Academy of Sciences. Other such august bodies in the Holy Roman Empire, however, either quietly distanced themselves from him or carefully pointed out his alchemical antecedents together with his self-promotional activities. The medical men of Vienna who thought they had evidence that what he purveyed was less than scientific hastened his departure from their city, where he was declared a public menace. He was ordered to leave within twenty-four hours.[41]

Shortly thereafter, Mesmer set up practice in Paris, where there was enormous enthusiasm for anything that could be passed off as science.[42] The huge clientele he attracted could not compensate for his lack of acceptance by the scientific establishment so he tried to gain professional stature through publications. In 1779, *Dissertation on the Discovery of Animal*

Magnetism appeared. Reminding his readers that the accomplishments of the past could not be ignored, he confidently announced the discovery of the long-sought panacea, the "universal means of healing and preserving man" (44). Mesmer explained the procedures that cured the hysterical young woman in Vienna a few years earlier. The magnets he applied to her stomach and legs after having her drink a preparation of salts of iron made her feel certain sensations that helped restore her to health. Then Mesmer tried to clarify the background of the turmoil surrounding his departure from Vienna. He also elaborated on his triumph over Gassner, who nevertheless, he conceded, had to be "a tool of nature" (57). When the officials asked Mesmer to account for supposed miracles, he, the man of science, had easily been able to do so.

After explaining away such matters from his past, Mesmer set out the twenty-seven propositions underlying his theory. The tenth one defined animal magnetism as "the property of the animal body which brings it under the influence of heavenly bodies, and the reciprocal action occurring among those who are surrounded by it" (68). Fifteen held that "it is intensified and reflected by mirrors, just like light," and sixteen continued, "it is communicated, propagated and intensified by sound" (68). Furthermore, seventeen maintained, it "may be stored up, concentrated and transported" (68). All such knowledge, Mesmer contended, would enable the physician to determine a patient's state of health and safeguard him against maladies. The conclusion came in proposition twenty-seven: "the art of healing will thus reach its final state of perfection" (70). Mesmer appealed to his enlightened readers to bear with him during his search for hard evidence to dispel the notion that his propositions contained as much illusion as truth (70).

In 1784, a year that turned out to be momentous for him, Mesmer published his "Catechism on Animal Magnetism," an instruction in the secrets of his methods for his adepts. It explained how the power of magnetism could be augmented by establishing direct interconnections among several people. One way was to form a chain by holding hands. Another was the *baquet*, something else he appropriated from current research and claimed as his own invention. In his words,

> It is a vat about six to seven feet, more or less, in diameter by eighteen inches in height. There is a double bottom in the interior of this vat, in which fragments of broken bottles, gravel, stones, and sticks of pounded sulfur and iron filings are placed. All of this is filled with water and covered up with a floor nailed to the vat. On the surface of the lid, six inches in from the rim, one makes various holes in order to allow the passage of iron rods which are arranged so that one end penetrates the bottom of the vat and the other is directed, by means of a curve, over the pit of the stomach of the patient or other affected parts of the body. (83)

Such interconnections, Mesmer continued, existed among plants and trees as well, so that patients could derive benefits by being attached to them. Self-magnetization was also possible. Allegedly even those unable to pay would thus be able to partake of the curing.

As Mesmer's fame spread, he turned more and more to the kind of showmanship that not only revealed the origins of his thought but also competed with other scientific shows. The musical, mystical atmosphere of his Parisian clinic served to put patients in the right frame of mind before the doctor made his grand entrance dressed in sumptuous robes and carrying a magic, that is, magnetized iron wand.[43] The seances also became ritualized in other ways adapted from shamanic curing sessions. The result was that Mesmer was often referred to as a juggler, the eighteenth-century word the French used for shaman.[44]

To supplement this lucrative business, Mesmer created the Society of Universal Harmony, an umbrella-type organization promoting the cause of magnetic healing. It allowed Mesmer to conduct lectures for a subscription fee and had the same purported goal as other such secret societies.[45] It was to reawaken a golden age in which human beings lived in harmony with nature and one another. The striking number of hopeful persons who subscribed in Paris, Strasbourg, Lyon, and Dijon ensured Mesmer's personal fortune, most of which he managed to collect after the French Revolution so that he could retire comfortably.[46] Trouble began, however, when some of the subscribers accused him of perpetrating a grand hoax by failing to give them the secrets of nature that alchemists and philosophers had also long sought. Others worried about the moral peril threatening the French women who allowed themselves to be so touched and tickled that they emitted very strange noises.[47] Still others were concerned that liberal political sympathies were suggested by the neglect of class distinctions among the paying customers.[48] As a result, the government intervened. The royal commission that was appointed concluded that there was no empirical evidence backing Mesmer's theories. Imagination, delusion, imitativeness, and suggestibility were the only reasons they could come up with. The commission also issued a confidential report about the moral implications of Mesmer's procedures stating that there was excessive physical contact and emotional bonding. The Royal Society of Medicine seconded these results.[49] Such outright rejection coupled with public ridicule and scorn drove Mesmer out of Paris.

Like so many predecessors involved in the non-normal sciences and the secret societies connected to them, Mesmer concluded his life trying to shape a particular historical reality after the fact. The culmination of his attempts came in the 1799 *Dissertation by F. A. Mesmer, Doctor of Medicine, on His Discoveries.* He presented himself as seminal thinker who shed new light on the phenomena of the state that had come to be known as somnambulism.

Unlike establishment colleagues who gave authority to their publications
with long erudite discourses about what had transpired in the past, Mesmer wrote without acknowledging the copious preceding or intervening
research on his subject.[50] All over the world and throughout European
medical history, he began, the somnambulistic state brought forth "marvelous apparitions, trances, and inexplicable visions" that were misinter-
preted because of ignorance or because of religious or political prejudices
(90). He viewed them as "nothing but unknown and degenerated conditions" that his procedures could easily in all but a few cases prevent or
cure (90).

Mesmer recounted his difficulties as the lone fighter combatting an entrenched conservative scientific establishment that rejected his very delineation of the problem as quickly as his hypothesized solution. In other
words, he believed his opponents supported the prevalent Newtonian paradigm, refusing to allow him even to apply it to age-old vitalism in a way
that might recombine the two and make sense of otherwise incomprehensible matters that were termed occult.[51] Continuing to claim that he saw
what no one else saw before him, he wrote that scientists classified his early
discovery of such phenomena as chimeras, but later on, when forced to
recognize those phenomena due to increasing awareness of them, those
scientists chose to deny him his originality by making comparisons to instances from antiquity where the words "'universal fluid,' 'magnetism,'
'influence'" had been used (110).

Such phenomena, Mesmer continued, were as old as the infirmities of
man, and for just as long, they misled as well as astonished the human
mind, which tended to attribute them to supernatural causes or to spirits.
These phenomena were characterized as either good or bad depending
on whether they pleased or distressed and included "the oracles, inspira-
tions, the sibyls, prophesies, divinations, witchcraft, magic, the demonology of the ancients; and in our day, the opinions on convulsives and being
possessed" (113). In turn, Mesmer wrote, "superstitious and ignorant beliefs were represented as being either sacred or criminal, depending upon
whether they induced either hope or dread" (113). They provoked frequent revolutions, he added, and led to the rise of political as well as religious charlatanism. Confident of his method, he contended, "I am able to
prove today that whatever has been true in such phenomena, we should
attribute to the same cause, and they should be considered only as variations of the condition called 'somnambulism'" (113).

The reason, he maintained, the establishment produced such uncertain opinions about his work was simple:

> It is because my assertions regarding the processes and the visible effects of
> animal magnetism seem to remind people of ancient beliefs, of ancient prac-
> tices justly regarded for a long time as being errors of trickery. The majority

of men dedicated to science and to the art of healing have only considered my discovery from this point of view: carried away by their first impressions, they have neglected examining it more thoroughly. Others, prompted by personal motives, by professional interest, only wished to regard me as an adversary whom they had to destroy. (128–129)

From the vantage point of comfortable retirement, Mesmer insisted he had risen above the obstacles and carried the banner through the fray, all for the sake of science. Though made to suffer many personal and professional assaults, he wrote, "it is sufficient for me to have the glory of having opened a vast field to the reckoning of science, and of having, to some extent, outlined the route of this new course" (129). Like so many involved in the non-normal sciences who were constantly reinventing themselves, Mesmer managed not only to promulgate his historical ambitions but also to find a following to make them eventually come true.[52]

The concern for health and youth which was inherent in the thinking of the Renaissance magi did not merely produce charlatans and men who were determined to make history. There were medicos who attempted to adapt such thought to current circumstances so as to benefit their contemporaries without much thought to themselves. Samuel Hahnemann (1755–1843) was an example. His university training brought him a medical degree in 1779, but his passion was the non-normal sciences. Having learned English, Italian, and Spanish, he also studied Greek, Latin, Syriac, Hebrew, Arabic, and some Chaldaic. The familiarity with languages ancient and modern enabled him to support himself as a librarian and translator when fellow physicians made trouble for him.[53] And they often did. Hahnemann's criticism of their practices, especially the complex combinations they prescribed for patients, was not welcomed. As a result, many of his appointments were canceled or not renewed. When he began criticizing apothecaries as well, they refused to cooperate with him.

Hahnemann then began dispensing his own medications put together according to the principles of Paracelsus, whom he greatly admired and hoped to emulate. During health, Hahnemann contended, a spiritual power or vital force animated the organism and kept it in harmonious order.[54] Without this animating power, the harmony disappeared, and the organism died. Symptoms of its decline always appeared first, so all the physician needed to do was to recognize them and remove them. Knowledge of the morbid symptoms could be gained, he argued, from observing the effect of medicines on healthy bodies. Through experiments on himself, Hahnemann concluded that what produced disease was also able to cure that disease. It was an idea that he presented as the homeopathic principle of similars. The other basic principle involved the signature of drugs, which meant that a root or herb shaped like an organ should be used in curing diseases of that organ.[55]

In the process of solidifying these principles, Hahnemann developed homeopathy as a system of medicine distinct from allopathy and antipathy, which were what all the other physicians purveyed. Their error lay not only in the kind of medication they prescribed but in their practice of increasing doses. The homeopath was to prescribe only one single, simple medicine at a time and in the smallest amount possible so as to encourage the patient's spiritual power or vital force to restore the balance of health itself. In other words, the smaller the dose, the greater would be the effect.[56]

Continuing to follow in the tradition of Paracelsus, Agrippa, Fludd, and Jacob Böhme, Hahnemann explored animal magnetism as the curative power that influenced the body through touch. This laying on of hands, he maintained, "acts homoeopathically by exciting symptoms analogous to those of the malady." More important, he continued, it imparted "a uniform degree of vital power to the organism when there is an excess of it at one point and a deficiency at another."[57] Hahnemann even went on to attribute to animal magnetism the long list of miraculous cures recorded in the past. He wrote, for example, "To this class belong certain apparent cures that have, in all ages, been performed by magnetisers who were endowed with great natural strength. But the most brilliant results of the communication of magnetism to the entire organism is where it recalls to life persons who have remained in a state of apparent death during a long interval of time, by the resolute and fixed determination of a man in the full vigour of life—a species of resurrection of which history records many examples."[58]

Animal magnetism became scientific enough to serve as a legitimate explanation for a host of matters that had heretofore been considered magical. Joseph Ennemoser (1787–1854), for example, explained at the turn of the nineteenth century in his history of magic:

> magnetism gives us information about the existence and action of the life of dreams, and the power of creation, and in general about the sports and whims of fancy. It is also the best means of breaking the seal which closes the mysteries of antiquity, rich in fancy, whilst it discloses the similarity and depth of man's capacity, and shows an accordance of phenomena which formerly in magic was attributed to enchantment and to deceit, or to those supernatural wonders for which the philosophers could not account, and which an external religion and an inherited faith found not in their Catechism. In fine, Magnetism is able to give the meaning of the symbolic enigmas of ancient mysteries, which were considered quite insoluble, or which appeared matter for the most varied explanations. In the same manner, the manifold declarations of ecstatic seers and mystic philosophers, which are treasured up by persons initiated into the mysteries, will now become more intelligible by means of magnetism.[59]

Its discoverer, Ennemoser wrote, was none other than Paracelsus, who first used the word as it is currently understood. Recognizing the attraction and repulsion of the magnet, which he called the back and the belly, Paracelsus not only related that power to the mutual relationship of the macrocosm and the microcosm, but he also developed his sympathetic cure for disease around it. As part of that cure, there was, among other things, a tincture extracted from the magnet. Ennemoser thereupon reviewed the Renaissance magi and those who had become their adherents, pointing out all the magnetic connections involved in their work.

Other serious figures of this generation, like the eminent chemist Carl Reichenbach (1788–1869), took all of this a step further and proclaimed having found yet another force that was operable throughout the universe. He named it after the Germanic divinity Odin so as to connote all-pervading power. His experiments had shown that "this hitherto unknown force stands midway between magnetism, electricity and caloric."[60] They could easily be duplicated and validated by other scientists, he explained, as long as sensitivities were used. Only those with a peculiar nervous sensibility would be able to perceive the manifestations of od. Mesmerism, Reichenbach contended, was just one specific application of this force in therapeutics.

Another figure, Franz Joseph Gall (1758–1828), was responsible for inventing organology, or what was subsequently dubbed phrenology. Having received his medical degree from Vienna in 1785, he set up what became a very successful practice there that enabled him to pursue his investigations of the human brain. As far as he was concerned, "the brain is exclusively the organ of the soul."[61] Gall held that the brain determined a person's character by its functionings, which could be read from the contours of the skull (fig. 9.1). Those contours or bumps were the external manifestations of the thirty-seven internal, phrenological organs that corresponded, first, to propensities, like love, local attachment, and combativeness, second, to sentiments, like fear, pride, and hope, and third, to intellectual qualities, like form, color, time, wit, and language. Except for idiots, all persons possessed all thirty-seven.[62] Gall strove to prove that mental alienations, suicides, and murders were due to diseases of the brain, which was not fixed at birth but continued to grow and change throughout life's experiences: "The brain of most men hardly acquires its ultimate development till the age of thirty, often even not till forty."[63] He claimed this was inductively determined, repeatedly insisting that "craniology and organology [phrenology] are experimental sciences."[64] Again and again he offered statistical analyses of his dissections.

Phrenology, as John D. Davies has pointed out, was an esoteric science and social philosophy not only in Europe but in America, where it became a popular movement. By the middle of the nineteenth century practical

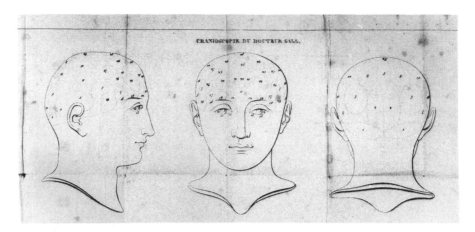

Fig. 9.1. From Franz Josef Gall's *Précis analytique du système du docteur Gall, sur les facultés de l'homme et les fonctions du cerveau nommé vulgairement Cranioscopie,* 3d ed. (Brussels, 1828). Courtesy of the University of Chicago Library

phrenologists were giving individual character readings at so much per head, sometimes performing blindfolded in public, other times conducting private consultations.[65] The profile of the phrenological head partitioned with rectangles and squares was usually prominently displayed by such reader-advisers to attract clients.

Yet another serious man whose work had wide-ranging repercussions was the Swiss pastor Johann Caspar Lavater (1741–1801).[66] They even reached his own home. He reported supporting mesmerism so staunchly that he even practiced magnetic therapy on his own wife.[67] Lavater's most noteworthy contributions came in the 1770s, when he authored fragments on physiognomy, a poorly conceived, rambling work that strove to share with the public his own uncanny ability to judge the character of others from their external appearances. His chatty, confessional style belied his real aim, which was to validate physiognomy as a discipline far above suspicions of charlatanry. Again and again throughout the four large folio volumes, he recalled its illustrious history reaching from the ancient Egyptians and Chaldeans to the Renaissance Italians and on up to the eighteenth century.

Like so many of his contemporaries smitten by the secret sciences, he was in total command of the bibliography. Some of his colleagues even commented about the propriety of such extensive reading in that field for a man of the cloth. Among Lavater's many favorites was della Porta, whose work on natural magic as well as physiognomy he seemed to have read.[68] Lavater also liked the illustrations in della Porta. He printed in the fragments a version of the one comparing human heads and faces to certain animals.

So closely associated with the arcana of the Renaissance magi was physiognomy considered to be in some pastoral circles that Lavater feared being accused of sorcery and of wanting to teach people how to read the deepest secrets of their neighbors' souls so that they could dissemble for profit or gain. The prospect of public ridicule and disgrace stimulated Lavater to do something only few of his fellow travelers did. He became confrontational. He tried to save his reputation and that of physiognomy by explaining that it represented a new kind of science, one "as good as all the other unmathematical sciences."[69] Lavater's explanation—perhaps, one of the reasons why his work enjoyed such astonishing success—comprised a consensus of popular opinion on the subject of science. Physiognomy was, he explained, a human science, like medicine, theology, and the beautiful sciences (*die schönen Wissenschaften*), all of which could be organized according to their very own rules. They were supposed to be different from the mathematical sciences. Just because they dealt with the many ambiguities and uncertainties of existence did not mean that they should be excluded from the company of other scientific disciplines. Like them, physiognomy had practical applications that could help human beings learn to deal with each other and thus create a better world. Furthermore, as many skills were required of the physiognomist as of any other scientist. He had to be able to concentrate; he had to have a good visual memory; he had to be competent in anatomy and drawing; and he had to be a keen observer of human nature as well as the workings of society. As in any other discipline, aptitude was a primary requirement before training could begin. To exemplify this, Lavater wrote that everyone could sing, but only one in a thousand became great doing so.

Lavater was a stickler for supplying his fragments with appropriate drawings to illustrate his points (fig. 9.2). In addition to his own, he solicited some from Johann Wolfgang von Goethe (1749–1832) and many from his best friend since childhood, Johann Heinrich Füssli (1741–1825), who because of his expatriation to England became known as Henry Fuseli. He became involved in Lavater's project early on, but because of his own considerable reading in the literature, disputed his application of physiognomic theories to the fine arts. Fuseli made his case in a series of letters in which he pushed for greater individualization of gestures and passions.[70] The two old friends must have resolved their differences, for Fuseli not only produced illustrations, he also arranged for the translation of the fragments into English. In addition, he helped prepare British audiences for Lavater's ideas by publishing a collection of his aphorisms in 1789. It was so well received that it went through several editions in just a few years. One reader was so taken by this work that he jotted down copious

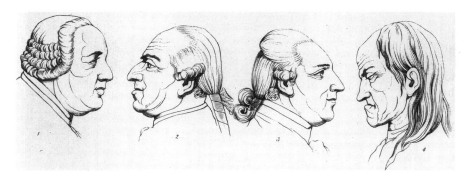

Fig. 9.2. "Four Male Profiles," in Johann Caspar Lavater's *Essays on Physiognomy, designed to promote the knowledge and the love of mankind,* ed. T. Holloway, trans. H. Hunter (London, 1789–98). Courtesy of the Newberry Library, Chicago

notes into his copy.[71] That was Fuseli's other good friend, William Blake (1757–1827), who then, in turn, did some of the illustrations for the English edition of Lavater.

The legacy of physiognomy and other non-normal sciences was actually quite far-reaching. Most obvious was their contribution to "the Occult" and the spiritualism of the nineteenth century. Less obvious was their profound contribution to the invention of the human sciences. They disavowed the mechanization of nature. They kept the individual with all his foibles at the center of attention. They refused to surrender imagination to reason. They stressed the importance of understanding man's effect on man. They upheld the idea of a scientific counterculture. And they believed that joint efforts would contribute to reestablishing world harmony.

NOTES

1. The excellent study that encouraged me to continue exploring "the other side" of the scientific revolution is Herbert Leventhal's *In the Shadow of the Enlightenment: Occultism and Renaissance Science in Eighteenth-Century America* (New York: New York University Press, 1976). Leventhal correctly complained, "There is an almost total neglect of the continuation of ideas and concepts first articulated centuries earlier," p. 1. He was, however, primarily interested in the perpetuation of the Elizabethan worldview in Enlightenment America.

2. Robert Galbreath, in his otherwise valuable "The History of Modern Occultism: A Bibliographical Survey," *Journal of Popular Culture* 5 (Winter 1971): 726, mistakenly assumes the Enlightenment of the late seventeenth century extirpated Neoplatonism, astrology, mysticism, and Near Eastern esotericism, etc., only so that the Romantics could revive them one hundred years later. He is, I believe, correct in writing, "From the late eighteenth century until the present, in varying degrees of popularity, faddishness, and intellectual respectability, the occult has remained

a nearly ubiquitous factor in Western cultural life." James Webb attributes what he considers the occult revival to the crisis experienced in the nineteenth century, in *The Occult Underground* (La Salle, Ill.: Open Court, 1974), 7 and 114. See also the companion volume, which concentrates on the twentieth century, *The Occult Establishment* (La Salle, Ill.: Open Court, 1976).

3. Mircea Eliade, *Occultism, Witchcraft, and Cultural Fashions: Essays in Comparative Religions* (Chicago and London: University of Chicago Press, 1976), 49–52.

4. Margaret Sherwood Libby, *The Attitude of Voltaire to Magic and the Sciences*, Studies in History, Economics, and Public Law, no. 408 (New York: Columbia University Press, 1935), 269–270.

5. Ibid., 215.

6. Compare Judith Devlin's careful study of the lasting effects of this in France: *The Superstitious Mind: French Peasants and the Supernatural in the Nineteenth Century* (New Haven, Conn., and London, 1987).

7. The work I found very helpful in defining the various kinds of physiognomy, divination, etc. was by Jacques Albin Simon Collin de Plancy, *Dictionnaire infernal, ou Répertoire universel des êtres, des personages, des livres, des faits et des choses qui tiennent aux apparitions, aux divinations, à la magie, au commerce de l'enfer, aux démons, aux sorciers, aux sciences occultes, aux grimoires, a la cabale, aux esprits élémentaires, au grand œuvre, aux prodiges, aux erreurs et aux préjugés, aux impostures, aux arts des bohémiens, aux superstitions diverses, aux contes populaires, aux prognostics, et généralement a toutes les fausses croyances, merveilleuses, surprenantes, mystérieuses ou surnaturelles* (Paris, 1844).

8. Roger Hahn, *The Anatomy of a Scientific Institution: The Paris Academy of Sciences, 1666–1803* (Berkeley, Los Angeles, and London: University of California Press, 1971), 91.

9. Valerie A. Tumins, "Enlightenment and Mysticism in Eighteenth-Century Russia," *Studies on Voltaire and the Eighteenth Century* 58 (1967): 1683.

10. Constantin Bila, *La Croyance a la Magie au XVIIIe Siècle en France dans les Contes, Romans & Traités* (Paris, 1925), 6. I am indebted to Bila for many leads.

11. Robert Darnton, *Mesmerism and the End of the Enlightenment in France* (Cambridge, Mass.: Harvard University Press, 1968), 165.

12. Compare, for example, Anton de Haen (1704–1776), who helped create the great medical school in Vienna, yet still defended demonology in the 1770s; Oskar Diethelm, "The Medical Teaching of Demonology in the seventeenth and eighteenth Centuries," *Journal of the History of the Behavioral Sciences* 6 (January 1970): 14.

13. Respectively, Ephraim Chambers, *Cyclopaedia: Or, An Universal Dictionary of Arts and Sciences: Containing The Definitions of the Terms, And Accounts of The Things signify'd thereby, In the several Arts, Both Liberal and Mechanical, And the several Sciences, Human and Divine*, 2 vols. (London, 1728), 2:32; Johann Hübner, *Neu-vermehrtes und verbessertes Reales Staats- Zeitung und Conversations-Lexicon* (Regensburg, 1748), 1025; and *Encyclopédie, ou Dictionnaire Raisonné des Sciences, des Arts et des Métiers* (Neuchâtel, 1765), 14:787–789.

14. Johann Christoph Adelung, *Grammatisch-kritisches Wörterbuch der Hochdeutschen Mundart mit beständiger Vergleichung der übrigen Mundarten, besonders aber der Oberdeutschen*, 4 vols. (Leipzig, 1793–1801), vol. 4: col. 1582. For background, see Henry Guerlac, "Newton's Changing Reputation in the Eighteenth Century," *Carl*

Becker's Heavenly City Revisited, ed. Raymond O. Rockwood (Ithaca, N.Y.: Cornell University Press, 1958), 24–25.

15. Grete de Francesco, *The Power of the Charlatan,* translated from German by Miriam Beard (New Haven, Conn.: Yale University Press, 1939), 164.

16. Peter Gay repeatedly compares the Renaissance and the Enlightenment. He argues that pagan values were tempered by science in both periods, which the *philosophes* saw as two acts in "the great drama of disenchantment of the European mind"; *The Enlightenment: An Interpretation,* 2 vols. (New York: Alfred A. Knopf, 1967), 1:179. He also mentions, without pursuing it further, "that there were poets and scholars steeped in Renaissance conceptions of the world, in correspondences and hierarchies and microcosms, who were troubled by the new science," 1:314.

17. Chambers, *Cyclopaedia,* 1:57.

18. Ibid., 1:217.

19. Respectively, *Deutsche Encyclopädie oder Allgemeines Real-Wörterbuch aller Künste und Wissenschaften von einer Gesellschaften Gelehrten,* 23 vols. (Frankfurt, 1778–1804), 5:499–501; Chambers, *Cyclopaedia,* 1:57.

20. Chambers, *Cyclopaedia,* 1:242.

21. *Encyclopédie,* 8:170.

22. Samuel Johnson, *A Dictionary of the English Language,* 2 vols. (London, 1755).

23. *Encyclopédie,* 1:248–249.

24. Ibid., 8:170.

25. Chambers, *Cyclopaedia,* 1:162–163.

26. *Encyclopédie,* 1:780–783.

27. See, for example, Friedrich Roth-Scholtz, *Catalogus rariorum liborum et manuscriptorum magico- cabbalistico- chymicorum* (Herrenstadt, 1732).

28. Gloria Flaherty, *Shamanism and the Eighteenth Century* (Princeton, N.J.: Princeton University Press, 1992), passim, reviews the history of the reception of shamanism in the early modern period.

29. Nicolas Lenglet-Dufresnoy, *Traité historique et dogmatique sur Les Apparitions, les Visions & Les Révélations particulières, Avec Des Observations sur les Dissertations du R.P. Dom Calmet, Abbé de Sénones, sur les Apparitions & les Revenans* (Avignon, 1761), 246–249.

30. Nicolas Lenglet-Dufresnoy, *Histoire de la Philosophie Hermetique, Accompagnée d'un Catalogue raisonné des Ecrivains de cette Science,* 3 vols. (La Haye, 1752), 3:161, 185, 245, 259, 271, 314.

31. Laurent Bordelon, *A History of the Ridiculous Extravagances of Monsieur Oufle; Occasion'd by his reading Books treating of Magick, the Black-Arts, Daemoniacks, Conjurers, Witches, Hobgoblins, Incubus's, Succubus's, and the Diabolical-Sabbath; of Elves, Fairies, Wanton Spirits, Genius's, Spectres and Ghosts; of Dreams, the Philosopher's Stone, Judicial Astrology, Horoscopes, Talismans, Lucky and Unlucky Days, Eclipses, Comets, and all sorts of Apparitions, Divinations, Charms, Enchantments, and other Superstitious Practices, With Notes containing a multitude of Quotations out of those Books, which have either Caused such Extravagant Imaginations, or may serve to Cure them* (London, 1711), 8, and also 62 and 101.

32. As quoted in Serge Hutin, *History of Astrology: Science or Superstition?* (New York: Pyramid Communications, 1970), 117.

33. Patrick Curry, *Prophecy and Power: Astrology in Early Modern England* (Princeton, N.J.: Princeton University Press, 1989), 135.

34. Hutin, *History of Astrology*, 117.

35. B. S. Capp, *English Almanacs, 1500–1800: Astrology and the Popular Press* (Ithaca, N.Y.: Cornell University Press 1979), 277. See also Leventhal, *Shadow*, 13–65.

36. Karl Christoph Schmieder, *Geschichte der Alchemie* (Halle, 1832; reprint, 1928; reprint, Ulm-Donau, 1959), 596 and 602.

37. Johanna Geyer-Kordesch, "Die Nachtseite der Naturwissenschaft: Die 'okkulte' Vorgeschichte zu Franz Anton Mesmer," *Franz Anton Mesmer und die Geschichte des Mesmerismus: Beiträge zum Internationalen Wissenschaftlichen Symposion anlässlich des 250. Geburtstages von Mesmer, 10. bis 13. Mai 1984 in Meersburg*, ed. Heinz Schott (Stuttgart: F. Steiner, 1985), 20–28 provides illuminating information about Georg Ernst Stahl (1659–1734) and Johann Conrad Dippel (1673–1734), Mesmer's immediate predecessors.

38. Hans Grassl, *Aufbruch zur Romantik: Bayerns Beitrag zur deutschen Geistesgeschichte 1765–1785* (Munich: Beck, 1968), 8–11, 140. Compare seventeenth-century Britain, A. Bryan Laver, "Miracles No Wonder! The Mesmeric Phenomena and Organic Cures of Valentine Greatrakes," *Journal of the History of Medicine and Allied Sciences* 33 (January 1978): 35, 45.

39. *Mesmerism: A Translation of the Original Scientific and Medical Writings of F. A. Mesmer*, trans. George Bloch, intro. Ernest R. Hilgard (Los Altos, Calif.: W. Kaufman, 1980), 15. Page numbers cited in the text refer to this translation. D. M. Walmsley, *Anton Mesmer* (London, 1967), 21, like so many scholars, mentions Paracelsus but gives no specifics.

40. De Francesco, *Power of the Charlatan*, 171, contends that Mesmer's involvement actually brought even more renown to Gassner.

41. Howard W. Haggard, *Devils, Drugs, and Doctors: The Story of the Science of Healing from Medicine-Man to Doctor* (New York and London: Harper and Brothers, 1929), 77.

42. Darnton, *Mesmerism*, 29.

43. Maria M. Tatar, *Spellbound: Studies on Mesmerism and Literature* (Princeton, N.J.: Princeton University Press, 1978), 15. Tatar's summation of Mesmer's biography has been especially helpful.

44. Gloria Flaherty, *Shamanism and the Eighteenth Century* (Princeton, N.J.: Princeton University Press, 1992).

45. Klaus Doerner, *Madmen and the Bourgeoisie: A Social History of Insanity and Psychiatry*, trans. Joachim Neugroschel and Jean Steinberg (Oxford: Basil Blackwell Publisher, 1981), 112–113.

46. Tatar, *Spellbound*, 19.

47. Ibid., 20. Mary Wollstonecraft was later to denounce London magnetizers in *Vindication of the Rights of Woman* (1792) as "lurking leeches" who exploited the credulity of ignorant women; Roger Cooter, "The History of Mesmerism in Britain: Poverty and Promise," in *Franz Anton Mesmer*, ed. Schott, 154.

48. Darnton, *Mesmerism*, 62.

49. Dietrich von Engelhardt, "Mesmer in der Naturforschung und Medizin der Romantik," in *Franz Anton Mesmer*, ed. Schott, 89–91, interestingly charts the

rejection of Mesmer by German men of science, some of whom were themselves involved in shamanic researches.

50. For the development of medical electricity, see Simon Schaffer, "Natural Philosophy and Public Spectacle in the Eighteenth Century," *History of Science: A Review of Literature and Research in the History of Science, Medicine, and Technology in Its Intellectual and Social Context* 21 (1983): 31.

51. Geoffrey Sutton, "Electric Medicine and Mesmerism," *Isis: An International Review Devoted to the History of Science and Its Cultural Influences* 72 (1981): 375–392, compares Mesmer to others who were less threatening to the establishment and its paradigm.

52. Roy Porter, "'Under the Influence': Mesmerism in England," *History Today* 35 (September 1985): 23–25.

53. Lester S. King, *The Medical World of the Eighteenth Century* (Chicago, University of Chicago Press: 1958), 159.

54. Samuel Hahnemann, *The Healing Art of Homoeopathy: The Organon of Samuel Hahnemann,* ed. Edward C. Hamlyn (New Canaan, Conn.: 1979), 15.

55. Haggard, *Devils, Drugs, and Doctors,* 351.

56. *Healing Art,* ed. Hamlyn, 31.

57. Samuel Hahnemann, *The Homoeopathic Medical Doctrine, or, "Organon of the Healing Art"; A New System of Physic,* tr. Charles H. Devrient (Dublin, 1833), 303.

58. Ibid., 304.

59. Joseph Ennemoser, *The History of Magic,* translated from German by William Howitt, 2 vols. (London, 1854), 1:viii.

60. Carl Reichenbach, *Odic-Magnetic Letters,* translated from German by John S. Hittell (New York, 1860), 25.

61. Franz Joseph Gall, *Organology; or, An Exposition of the Instincts, Propensities, Sentiments, and Talents, or of the Moral Qualities, and the Fundamental Intellectual Faculties in Man and Animals, and the Seat of their Organs,* translated from French by Winslow Lewis, 6 vols. (Boston, 1835), 5:263.

62. Franz Joseph Gall, "Sketch of the New Anatomy and Physiology of the Brain and Nervous System of Drs. Gall and Spurzheim, Considered as Comprehending A Complete System of Phrenology, with Observations on Its Tendency to the Improvement of Education, of Punishments, and of the Treatment of Insanity," *The Pamphleteer, Respectfully Dedicated to Both Houses of Parliament* 5 (February, 1815): 233.

63. Franz Joseph Gall, *The Influence of the Brain on the Form of the Head: The Difficulties and Means of Determining the Fundamental Qualities and Faculties, and of Discovering the Seat of Their Organs,* translated from French by Winslow Lewis, 6 vols. (Boston, 1835), 3:19.

64. Gall, *Influence,* 3:27.

65. John D. Davies, *Phrenology, Fad and Science: A Nineteenth-Century American Crusade* (New Haven, Conn.: Yale University Press, 1955), 20 and 31–34.

66. Graeme Tytler, *Physiognomy in the European Novel: Faces and Fortunes* (Princeton, N.J.: Princeton University Press, 1982), 6, writes, "European culture in general appears to have been dominated by what may be aptly described as the Lavaterian physiognomical climate." The second chapter of his book is devoted to Lavater, 35–81.

67. Engelhardt, "Mesmer in der Naturforschung," 91.

68. Tytler seems to agree, 40.

69. Johann Caspar Lavater, *Physiognomische Fragmente, zur Beförderung der Menschenkenntniss und Menschenliebe,* 4 vols. (Leipzig and Wintherthur, 1775–78), 1:52.

70. Marcia Allentuck, "Fuseli and Lavater: Physiognomical Theory and the Enlightenment," *Studies on Voltaire and the Eighteenth Century* 55 (1967): 93–94. I am generally indebted to Allentuck for my discussion of Fuseli and Lavater.

71. Allentuck, "Fuseli and Lavater," 97–98.

TEN

Political Economy

The Desire and Needs of Present and Future Generations

Sylvana Tomaselli

Nothing is more usual and more natural for those, who pretend to discover any thing new to the world in philosophy and the sciences, than to insinuate the praises of their own systems, by decrying all those, which have been advanced before them.
—DAVID HUME, A Treatise of Human Nature

In a Country not furnished with Mines there are but two ways of growing Rich, either Conquest, or Commerce. By the first the Romans made themselves Masters of the Riches of the world; but I think that in our present circumstances, no Body is vain enough to entertain a Thought of our reaping the Profits of the World with our Swords, and making the Spoil and Tribute of Vanquished Nations, the Fund for the supply of the Charges of the Government, with an overplus for the wants, and equally craving Luxury, and fashionable Vanity of the People.
  Commerce therefore is the only way left to us, either for Riches or Subsistence.
—JOHN LOCKE, Some Considerations of the Consequences of the Lowering of Interest and the Raising the Value of Money

When we think of the human sciences in the eighteenth century and more particularly of the contribution of the period to the systematization of knowledge about men and women as creatures of desires and needs, we most readily think of developments in political economy and the enduring achievements of men such as Adam Smith (1723–1790) and Thomas Robert Malthus (1766–1834). Like most other Enlightenment figures, including the great critic of the civilizing process, Jean-Jacques Rousseau (1712–1778), they considered the nature of human needs and desires within a historical perspective, one which revealed the development of civilization to follow the course of the proliferation of needs and which showed society to be propelled by insatiable desires, if not for possessions in and of themselves, then for the admiration and deference bestowed on the wealthy. Tracing the course of political economy has led to a wealth of textual analyses, not only of Smith and Malthus's works but also of that of their fellow theorists on both sides of the Channel.[1] Besides the texts themselves, the circumstances surrounding the creation of university chairs and the manner in which the subject was taught have also been examined, as have the extent of translations of seminal texts, the webs of intellectual influences, the diffusion of the principles of political economy, more generally speaking, and their relationship to economic practice. We are thus rich in knowledge of the history of political economy. And the question here is this: Have we the history of an invention? Or, if in anticipation of the fragmentation of knowledge under which we labor in the twentieth century we take economics and demography as if they were separable intellectual domains (and here I must own that flying in the face of one of my own conclusions, I treat the disciplines as if they were distinct), the question might be phrased in the plural form: Have we the history of two inventions, of two epistemic watersheds?

If one considers Enlightenment writings on such subjects as the history of woman[2] or anthropology,[3] the idea of discovery or of the birth of a discipline or approach seems not entirely inappropriate. In the case of the history of woman, a new subject matter was created in the eighteenth century as the conjectural history of woman examined her condition as well as her nature in a manner hitherto unknown. Historians of woman, like Antoine-Léonard Thomas (1735–1785) or the Vicomte de Ségur (1756–1805), were self-conscious about the novelty of their approach and chose it precisely because it seemed to afford them a true understanding, a science, of woman, one that mirrored and completed the science of man as well as challenged some of its central tenets. To be sure, the Enlightenment excelled at blowing its own trumpet, and the register of innovation was very much in vogue throughout the century. Even among the more self-conscious authors and those who refrained from describing their work in such terms, there emanates a sense of novelty. Think of philosophy, the eighteenth-century science of human nature, and, more specifically, David Hume's (1711–1776) masterpiece *A Treatise of Human Nature: Being an Attempt to introduce the experimental Method of Reasoning into Moral Subjects* (1739–1740), whose opening sentence provides this chapter's epigraph.[4] While he acknowledged that John Locke (1632–1704), Lord Shaftesbury (1671–1713), Bernard Mandeville (1670–1733), Francis Hutcheson (1660–1739), and Joseph Butler (1692–1752) had "begun to put the science of man on a new footing,"[5] Hume nevertheless thought of himself as having done rather more than merely bringing the finishing touches to an epistemological project that forerunners had left incomplete. For all his recognition of his predecessors' achievements and his awareness of the ease with which philosophers and scientists dismissed the work of others and claimed originality (disclosed, for instance, in the passage quoted above), he considered his *Treatise* to have transformed the knowledge of man. Amid his disclaimers, an undeniable boldness emerges:

> For my part, my only hope is, that I may contribute a little to the advancement of knowledge, by giving some particulars a different turn to the speculations

of philosophers, and pointing out to them more distinctly those subjects, where alone they can expect assurance and conviction. Human Nature is the only science of man; and yet has been hitherto the most neglected. 'Twill be sufficient for me, if I can bring it a little more into fashion.[6]

If he was not the only one to bring the science of man "a little more into fashion," Hume did nonetheless have cause to think well of his work. It was, after all, to have the merit of waking no less a figure than Immanuel Kant (1724–1804) from his "dogmatic slumbers,"[7] and while we might seek to resist the rhetorical lure of Hume's opening pages as well as need to qualify the extent to which he thought of the study of man as being on a par with the study of nature by physics, something remains, something like the sense of trepidation, excitement, or originality, some, if not all, of the feelings associated with invention or discovery remains.[8]

That a spirit of innovation and its attendant exhilaration were by no means foreign to political economy is most easily illustrated by the remark that the Marquis de Mirabeau (1715–1789) made apropos of the seminal work of the founder of the physiocratic school of economy, François Quesnay's (1694–1774) *Le Tableau économique* (1758). Adam Smith quoted the comment in *An Inquiry into the Nature and Causes of the Wealth of Nations* (1776) to show the reverence in which Quesnay was held by his disciples and to exemplify that, as Smith put it, "[t]he admiration of this whole sect for their master, who was himself a man of the greatest modesty and simplicity, is not inferior to that of any of the antient philosophers for the founders of their respective systems."[9] Smith reported "a very diligent and respectable author, the Marquis de Mirabeau" to have claimed, "There have been, since the world began,"

> three great inventions which have principally given stability to political societies, independent of many other inventions which have enriched and adorned them. The first, is the invention of writing, which alone gives human nature the power of transmitting, without alteration, its laws, its contracts, its annals, and its discoveries. The second, is the invention of money, which binds together all the relations between civilized societies. The third, is the Oeconomical Table, the result of the other two, which completes them both by perfecting their object: the great discovery of our age, but of which our posterity will reap the benefit.[10]

Quesnay himself was not without sharing some of his admirers' enthusiasm for what Mirabeau saw as the great discovery of physiocracy. Writing to François Véron de Forbonnais (1722–1800), then inspector of commerce, Quesnay explained that, in seeing the true source of a nation's wealth as he suggested it ought to be perceived, that is, as "le produit de la Nature . . . et non le produit de l'art," and reforming taxation accordingly, one would embark on a road which, though unknown to anyone thus far, was none other than the sole path to truth.[11] Nor were attributions of originality and discovery confined to members of the physiocratic sect. Commentators of all kinds have presented the author of the *Tableau Oeconomique* in this light.[12] Adam Smith spoke of physiocracy as a system that,

> with all its imperfections is, perhaps, the nearest approximation to the truth that has yet been published upon the subject of political economy, and is upon that account well worth the consideration of every man who wishes to examine with attention the principles of that very important science.[13]

Thus while physiocracy was not without virulent critics, not least among whom was the abbé Galiani (1728–1787), Mirabeau's enthusiasm was by no means incomprehensible to those outside the sect.

And yet, it is best not to let ourselves be seduced by Mirabeau's talk of discovery. This, in fact, applies not only to physiocracy, but to any eighteenth-century school of political economy. The reason it is preferable not to think along those lines does not lie in the failure of the physiocrats, nor of any other theorists, to deliver anything new, or of import, to economic thought. Nor is it only a matter of arguing that the true founders of political economy are to be found earlier, in the preceding century and the persons of Sir William Petty (1623–1687) in England, or Pierre Le Pesant Seigneur de Boisguilbert (1646–1714) in France.[14] For though there is no doubt that much of what was said on money, bullion, the nature of nations' wealth, manufacturing, the balance of trade, agriculture, consumption, population, the cost and effects of war, taxation, tariff barriers, and levies of all kinds had already been uttered in one form or other in the seventeenth century, and while it is unquestionable that the field of influences is enormous and extends far beyond the parameters of economic writings,[15] the question is not simply one of pushing back the quest for origins by a hundred years or more. Recent scholarship has been far too persuasive in its arguments stressing the continuities between the seventeenth and eighteenth centuries, and between these periods and the Renaissance, for anyone to even contemplate challenging such claims now.[16] Besides this, and all the warnings proffered in different ways by Franco Venturi,[17] Jacques Lacan,[18] or Michel Foucault[19] about the pitfalls of the quest for origins, there is another, though by no means unrelated, as well as very simple, reason why it is preferable to refrain from using the imagery of invention in connection with political economy, namely, that it is likely to distort our understanding of the nature of the subject at hand and of the very real issues of the day, issues which have in fact remained on the political agenda, and which, because of their intrinsic character are likely to continue to be central to political theory as well as practice. Though various histories of the creation of political economy could be, and indeed have been written, tracing the emergence of various concepts such as that of use and exchange value, Quesnay's *produit net*, Smith's division of labor, and so forth, such endeavors have, along with many merits, the tendency to obscure both the character and scope of political economy during the eighteenth century.[20] Rather than regarding Enlightenment, or earlier political economists, as discovering a *terra nova* or inventing new concepts, it is more appropriate, at least in the first instance, simply to consider them as continuing to ponder over the nature of good government and arguing among themselves about what was in the domain of the possible and whose interests government should be conceived of as serving.[21]

Antoine de Montchrétien (ca. 1575–1621), who is generally thought to have coined the term *political economy* when he entitled his treatise *Traicté de l'oeconomie politique* (1615), Boisguilbert, Quesnay, Smith—all were giving advice on how best to govern. Their advice differed, but the science of the legislator was what they were engaged in, and there was little new about the idea of men within or outside courts and government circles proffering advice, be it from motives of self- or public interest, on how to maintain a state. Whether we trace back such endeavors to the mirror of the princes genre and its most famous practitioner, Niccolò Machiavelli (1469–1527), or further still to Thomas Aquinas (1225–1274) or even to Aristotle (384–322 B.C.), the point remains that political economists saw themselves explaining what ought or ought not to be done by rulers to ensure the preservation of the societies they governed within a world of competing and warring nations. Such prescriptions had always entailed delineating the domain of politics and urging heads of states to understand the shape of the landscape and the nature of the objects within it. To use the imagery familiar to political economists of the period, the then age-old language of politics, that of the body, princes were encouraged to learn the physiological intricacies of the body politic.

In his influential *Traicté de l'Oeconomie politique dédié en 1615 au Roy et à la Reine Mère du Roy*, Montchrétien took the most important regal duty to know every detail of this body and one of its most prominent features to be the market economy.[22] Like Machiavelli before him and, as we shall see further on, many other authors subsequently, Montchrétien feared the harmful consequences of the natural indolence of sovereigns.[23] Reiterating the Platonic view that each subject had a natural place and function within the polity, he argued that the wealth of a nation consisted not only in its geographical size and in the number of its inhabitants

> but in ensuring that the land is cultivated and wisely allocating everyone to his task. In any administration there is nothing more pernicious than to neglect to know those one rules, nor anything more dangerous than the indolence which leads one to fail to establish the task they are naturally best suited to perform.[24]

From this he went on to draw a parallel, one which was to be considered nonsensical by the middle of the following century, not least by Rousseau, who argued to this effect in the *Encyclopédie* entry "Economie politique,"[25] namely, that between the family and the state:

> All this comes down to this: that in a state no less than a family it is a blessing mixed with very great profit to rule men in such a way as to follow their particular inclination. As for the relation they bear to one another, utility along with other reasons which would be too long to deduce, one is perfectly entitled to think, *pace* Aristotle and Xenophon, that one cannot separate the economy from government without tearing the principal part from the whole, and that what they called the art of acquiring of wealth, is common to republics as well as to families.[26]

There followed Montchrétien's surprise that such an obvious truth as the centrality of economics to politics had been neglected by the Ancients, whom he clearly admired: "For my part, I cannot but be astonished that political treatises, otherwise so meticulously well written, have forgotten this menagerie to which the duties and necessities of the state oblige one to give the greatest consideration."[27] Sound political administration was for Montchrétien "a universal health of the whole body of the State, and consequently the well-being of each particular member."[28] This entailed a knowledge of the vilest as well as the noblest parts of the body and hence required neglecting neither the activity of the meanest laborers, the liver and blood of the country, nor that of the meanest artisans, the heart and heat of the body, nor that of the meanest merchants, the brain and nervous system of civil society.[29] This said, Montchrétien discussed the regulation of manufactures, the principles of economic activity, the pursuit of self-interest, how self- and public interest were reconciled in civil society, agriculture, commerce, transport, money, and navigation, and, in the final part of the *Traicté*, the nature of princely virtues. As Théodore Funck-Brentano remarked, those who accused Montchrétien of failing to present his thought in a scientifically rigorous manner were blind to the fact that his aim was to address the king and queen in the rhetorically most effective manner to interest them in the economic prosperity of the nation.[30] Political economy was, for him, an art or practice that princes had to be taught by theorists for whom it constituted a science; the former were physicians to the body politic, the latter, their professors of medicine.[31]

That kings and queens had to be economists gradually became a given of political treatises. How they should think of wealth and money and what were the true sources of national affluence were issues that a multitude of writers throughout Europe were to debate. Yet, even in the 1740s, Hume still spoke of this as a radical departure. In the essay "Of Civil Liberty" (1741), he wrote:

> Trade was never esteemed an affair of state till the last century; and there scarcely is any ancient writer on politics, who has made mention of it. Even the ITALIANS have kept a profound silence with regard to it, though it has now engaged the chief attention, as well of the ministers of state, as of speculative reasoners. The great opulence, grandeur, and military atchievements of the two maritime powers seem first to have instructed mankind in the importance of an extensive commerce.[32]

The two maritime powers Hume had in mind were Holland and England. It was his visits to both these countries which had alerted the dramatist Montchrétien to the importance of commerce and the need for France not to be left outdone by these her rivals. The two countries, taken together or separately, were to provide important models of thriving modern commercial societies for Scottish, Irish, French, and other European writers.[33] They were to occupy the place that Germany, Japan, and arguably also Sweden have held in the political imagination of the last third of the twentieth century. Whether conceived as a history of an invention or not, any account of the nature of political economy in the seventeenth and eighteenth centuries must reap the benefit of Hume's hint. Trade became an affair of state as princely advisers and writers exploited the desire of the rulers of poor or economically lagging nations to emulate, and indeed, surpass rich ones.[34] And this, by seeking to pinpoint the source, or sources, of nations' wealth, the generation of surplus, and by holding out policies conducive to maximizing it, like so many sticks whose carrots bore the Machiavellian inscription of glory or, drawing from languages that were to gain in currency during the Enlightenment, the idea of public interest or of the happiness of the country, an idea very much at the heart of the population debate.

When Adam Smith wrote *The Wealth of Nations* (1776), he prefaced his summary of the various schools of economic thought with the following definition:

> Political oeconomy, considered as a branch of the science of a statesman or legislator, proposes two distinct objects; first, to provide a plentiful revenue or subsistence for the people, or more properly to enable them to provide such a revenue or subsistence for themselves; and secondly, to supply the state or commonwealth with a revenue sufficient for the publick services. It proposes to enrich both the people and the sovereign.[35]

Thus the art or practice of rulers which Montchrétien had presented as the application of the theoretical wisdom of political economists was brought together in Smith's account of political economy as an integral part of the science of the legislator. Surveying the field, Smith argued that there were essentially two systems of political economy, the system of commerce, mercantilism, and that of agriculture, physiocracy. However influential these systems were to prove to be, the divergence in opinions on the true nature of wealth arose out of differing economic experiences, in his view:

> Nations tolerably well advanced as to skill, dexterity, and judgment, in the application of labour, have followed very different plans in the general conduct or direction of it; and those plans have not all been equally favourable to the greatness of its produce. The policy of some nations has given extraordinary encouragements to the industry of the country; that of others to the industry of towns. Scarce any nation has dealt equally and impartially with every sort of industry. Since the downfal of the Roman Empire, the policy of Europe has been more favourable to arts, manufactures, and commerce, the industry of towns; than that of agriculture, the industry of the country.
>
> Though those different plans were, perhaps, first introduced by the private interests and prejudices of particular orders of men, without any regard to, or foresight of, their consequences upon the general welfare of the society; yet they have given occasion to very different theories of political oeconomy; of which some magnify the importance of that industry which is carried on in towns, others of that which is carried on in the country. Those theories have had a considerable influence, not only upon the opinions of men of learning, but upon the public conduct of princes and sovereign states.[36]

Of the two systems, it was the mercantile that had been most influential, and hence the mercantile received the best part of Smith's attention. He described how on this popular conception the wealth of nations was conceived in similar terms as that of individuals: "A rich country, in the same manner as a rich man, is supposed to be a country abounding in money; and to heap up gold and silver in any country is supposed to be the readiest way to enrich it."[37] Smith went on to explain how such a view had resulted in attempts to prevent the export of bullion and how "[w]hen those countries become commercial, the merchants found this prohibition, upon many occasions, extremely inconvenient."[38] They had argued that the purchase of foreign goods with bullion was not in itself nefarious to the wealth of the state, when these commodities were exported again to other countries. What mattered was the overall balance of trade.

Among the many authors who had contributed to this school, Smith had more especially in mind Thomas Mun (1571–1641), author of *A Discourse of Trade, from England unto the East Indies* (1621) and *England's Treasure by Forraign Trade* (1664), and Joshua Gee (fl. 1725–1750), author of *The Trade and Navigation of Great Britain Considered* (1729). "In speculation," Smith wrote in an early draft of the *Wealth of Nations*, the thesis that national opulence consisted in the quantity of money "has given occasion to the systems of Mun and Gee, of Mandeville who built upon them, and of Mr. Hume who endeavoured to refute them."[39] Smith also referred to Locke, whom he considered to have given the mercantile system "somewhat more of a philosophicall air and the appearance of probability by some amendments."[40] While Locke had "allowed that some commodities as corn, cloth and cattle were part of the wealth of a nation, but affirmed at the same time that they make but a small or at least an insignificant part of it as being perishable," Smith argued that "it is evident on the slightest attention that the perishable quality of all other commodities is so far from making them inferior to gold and silver, which can not be consumed, that the very thing which [?makes] them to be of greater real worth is their consumptib[il]ity."[41]

Mercantilism, far from presenting an accurate view of the good of the nation, was but the expression of the interest of the merchants, according to Smith. Its arguments "were addressed by merchants to parliaments, and to the councils of princes, to nobles and to country gentlemen; by those who were supposed to understand trade, to those who were conscious to themselves that they knew nothing about the matter."[42] Governments, having been hitherto watchful only of the export of bullion, now concentrated solely on the balance of trade. "The title of Mun's book, England's Treasure in Foreign Trade," Smith noted, "became a fundamental maxim in political oeconomy, not of England only, but of all other commercial countries."[43] This had resulted, among other things, in the neglect of the domestic market, which Smith deemed the most important because it generated the greatest employment.

To disabuse the audience that mercantilism had held captive for far too long, Smith sought to demonstrate that money, gold, and silver were very much like other commodities and that it was not "always necessary to accumulate gold and silver, in order to enable a country to carry on foreign wars, and to maintain fleets and armies in distant countries." For as he pointed out,

> Fleets and armies are maintained, not with gold and silver, but with consumable goods. The nation which, from the annual produce of its domestick industry, from the annual revenue arising of its lands, labour, and consumable stock, has wherewithal to purchase those consumable goods in distant countries, can maintain foreign wars there.[44]

The enormous expenses of the latest wars had been paid by the export of commodities to distant countries to secure either the pay or provision of armies, and the best commodities for this purpose were "the finer and more improved manufactures; such as contain a great value in a small bulk, and can, therefore, be exported to a great distance at little expence." "A country," he continued, whose industry produces a great annual surplus of such manufactures, which are usually exported to foreign countries, may carry on for many years a very expensive foreign war, without either exporting any considerable quantity of gold and silver, or even having any such quantity to export.[45]

Taking up the argument Hume had made in his *History of England* (1754–62), Smith further remarked that what had prevented the "ancient Kings" from engaging in protracted wars was not the lack of money, "but of the finer and more improved manufactures."[46]

Persistent in his critique of the predominant view of wealth and money, he conceded the truth of the popular notion that the discovery of America had resulted in the enrichment of Europe, but this, he contended, was not due to the import of gold and silver which had followed it. Instead, he argued that

[b]y opening a new and inexhaustible market to all the commodities of Europe, it gave occasion to new divisions of labour and improvements of art, which, in the narrow circle of the antient commerce, could never have taken place for want of a market to take off the greater part of their produce. The productive powers of labour were improved, and its produce increased in all the different countries of Europe, and together with it the real revenue and wealth of the inhabitants.[47]

Smith's diatribe next led him to examine how the conflation of the idea of a nation's wealth with that of money had led to trade restrictions and how these were either futile, as, say, the prohibition on the export of wool and the heavy penalties attached to it were well known not to have been effective in deterring large exports of wool,[48] or detrimental to large segments of the population as when cheap imports were prohibited. In the latter case, the mistake was "to consider production, and not consumption, as the ultimate end and object of all industry and commerce."[49] To this, Smith added what was partly but a reiteration of a point we have seen him make already:

It cannot be very difficult to determine who have been the contrivers of this whole mercantile system; not the consumers, we may believe, whose interest has been entirely neglected; but the producers whose interest has been so carefully attended to; and among this latter class our merchants and manufacturers have been by far the principal architects.[50]

In fact, the effect of trade restrictions was to pit one set of manufacturers against another, Smith noted, having a few pages earlier reminded his readership that: "To hurt in any degree the interest of any one order of citizens, for no other purpose but to promote that of some other, is evidently contrary to that justice and equality of treatment which the sovereign owes to all the different orders of his subjects."[51] Thus mercantilism was not only fundamentally unsound in its conception of the true nature of wealth, but also unjust and iniquitous, according to Smith. The tone of his pronouncements on the physiocratic system was to be altogether more benign.

The reason for this was less because he was more partial to the physiocratic view of the market than because "[i]t would not, surely, be worth while to examine at great length the errors of a system which never has done, and probably never will do any harm in any part of the world."[52] Drawing more of a contrast than it was in fact fair to either of the two parties to establish, Smith presented physiocracy as the system that saw land as the sole source of wealth and revenue of every country. Describing the division of society into three classes, the first being that of landed proprietors, the second that of agricultural workers, and the third grouping together artisans, merchants, and manufacturers, Smith went on to argue that the physiocrats erred when they considered the last class "the barren or unproductive class." He explained how this class was very important to the other two, by securing better and cheaper goods, whether foreign or domestic, than they would otherwise have. The industry of merchants, artificers, and manufacturers enabled those who cultivated the land to devote themselves fully to their task and hence contributed to increased productivity: "the plough goes frequently the easier and the better by means of the labour of the man whose business is most remote from the plough."[53] It could only be of benefit to the landed proprietors and the cultivators that the industry of the towns be granted the fullest liberty, for this would ensure the lowest prices for manufactured goods thanks to the increased competition greater liberty would bring. "The establishment of perfect justice, of perfect liberty, and of perfect equality, is the very simple secret which most effectually secures the highest degree of prosperity to all the three classes."[54] Smith contended, and he went on to apply this reasoning to the international market. Just as it was not in the interest, rightly conceived, of the agrarian classes to oppress the manufacturing or mercantile one, so it could never be an advantage to what Smith called "landed nations"

> to discourage or distress the industry of such mercantile states, by imposing high duties upon their trade, or upon the commodities which they furnish. Such duties, by rendering those commodities dearer, could serve only to sink the real value of the surplus produce of their own land, with which, or, what comes to the same thing, with the price of which those commodities are purchased. Such duties could serve only to discourage the increase of that surplus produce, and consequently the improvement and cultivation of their own land. The most effectual expedient, on the contrary, for raising the value of that surplus produce, for encouraging its increase, and consequently the improvement and cultivation of their own land, would be to allow the most perfect freedom of the trade of all such mercantile nations.[55]

In the course of his discussion of mercantilism, Smith had already argued for the removal, albeit gradual, of trading restrictions imposed by metropolises on their respective colonies.[56] Opening the colonies to the trade of all nations would *in the long run* prove most beneficial to those nations which it might initially seem to hurt most. Yet, if Smith's vision was that of a system of perfect liberty, justice, and equality prevailing among nations and if his perspective was always that of an international market, characterized, like his view of domestic ones within modern commercial societies, by an increased division of labor, one must nonetheless not lose sight of the fact that he thought one of the gravest mistakes the physiocrats labored under as a result of their narrow focus on agriculture was their failure to recognize that "the most important branch of commerce of every nation . . . is that which is carried on between the inhabitants of the town and those of the country."[57]

Having exposed the errors of the two predominant schools of political economy, Smith was free to reassert the broad tenets of his political economy: "All systems either of preference or of restraint, therefore, being thus completely taken away, the obvious and simple system of natural liberty establishes itself of its own accord."[58] Under this system, "[e]very man, as long as he does not violate the laws of justice, is left perfectly free to pursue his own interest his own way, and to bring both his industry and capital into competition with those of an other man, or order of men."[59] The implications of this were momentous for politics. For, ironically, the system of natural liberty relieved the sovereign of the very office which Montchrétien and others had so assiduously sought princes to take up, namely, as physicians to the body politic. And this, because a hundred years or so of science of political economy, a science that had evolved precisely to inform a princely practice, was coming to the conclusion that such an office was proving too complex for any individual to assume:

> The sovereign is completely discharged from a duty, in the attempting to perform which he must always be exposed to innumerable delusions, and for the performance of which no human wisdom or knowledge could ever be sufficient; the duty of superintending the industry of private people, and of directing it towards the employments most suitable to the interest of the society.[60]

To superintend as Montchrétien prescribed but in a manner that would have avoided the partiality of mercantilists and physiocrats and succeeded where they failed in securing the aims of political economy would have required a godlike mastery of the workings of the market as constituted by the network of interactions of all the individuals within it. Impossible, such a mastery was also unnecessary. Smith believed in the body's own cures, as he made clear when discussing physiocratic responses to mercantilist economic policies:

Some speculative physicians seem to have imagined that the health of the human body could be preserved only by a certain precise regimen of diet and exercise, of which every, the smallest, violation necessarily occasioned some degree of disease or disorder proportioned to the degree of violation. Experience, however, would seem to show that the human body frequently preserves, to all appearance at least, the most perfect state of health under a vast variety of different regimens; even under some which are generally believed to be very far from being perfectly wholesome. But the healthful state of the human body, it would seem, contains in itself some unknown principle of preservation, capable either of preventing or of correcting, in many respects, the bad effects even of a very faulty regimen.[61]

Smith went on to assert that the market would *in the long run* recover from even mercantile practices, and there was, on this occasion, a particular relish in using a physiological metaphor in view of Quesnay's profession:

Mr. Quesnai, who was himself a physician, and a very speculative physician, seems to have entertained a notion of the same kind concerning the political body, and to have imagined that it would thrive and prosper only under a certain precise regimen, the exact regimen of perfect liberty and perfect justice. He seems not to have considered that in the political body, the natural effort which every man is continually making to better his own condition, is a principle of preservation capable of preventing and correcting, in many respects, the bad effects of a political oeconomy, in some degree, both partial and oppressive. Such a political oeconomy, though it no doubt retards more or less, is not always capable of stopping altogether the natural progress of a nation towards wealth and prosperity, and still less of making it go backwards.[62]

As he had already explained, but with a different imagery, in *The Theory of Moral Sentiments* (1759) as well as earlier in Book IV of the *Wealth of Nations,* it was as if an "invisible hand" operated within the marketplace. Describing how the imagination presented the pleasures of wealth and greatness "as something grand and beautiful and noble, of which the attainment is well worth all the toil and anxiety which we are so apt to bestow on it,"[63] Smith assured his readers that "it is well that nature imposes upon us in this manner."[64] This was the cause of industriousness and of the surplus that resulted from it, given the efficacy of the division of labor prevalent in modern commercial nations. It meant that in spite of the great inequality that characterized such countries, even the needs of their poorest laborers were provided for:

The rich only select from the heap what is most precious and agreeable. They consume little more than the poor, and in spite of their natural selfishness and rapacity, though they mean only their own conveniency, though the sole end which they propose from the labours of all the thousands whom they employ, be the gratification of their own vain and insatiable desires, they divide with the poor the produce of all their improvements. They are led by an invisible hand to make nearly the same distribution of the necessaries of life, which would have been made, had the earth been divided into equal portions among all its inhabitants, and thus without intending it, without knowing it, advance the interest of the society, and afford means to the multiplication of the species.[65]

Was Smith asking princes to be mere witnesses to the spectacle of nature in this the seemingly most artificial of artifices, commercial society? They did appear only to be expected to marvel at the wonders that the invisible hand produced, the promotion of the good of society as the unintended consequence of the pursuit of individual self-interest. Had they just been awakened to the importance of trade to be told that neither they nor any one else could, nor needed to, preoccupy themselves with it?

In his *Account of the Life and Writings of Adam Smith, L.L.D.* (1793), Dugald Stewart (1753–1828), whose admiration for his subject, though perhaps less effusive, was nevertheless a match for that in which Mirabeau held Quesnay, described the process by which politics was gaining the status of a science:

It is fortunate that upon this, as upon many other occasions, the difficulties which had long baffled the efforts of solitary genius begin to appear less formidable to the united exertions of the race; and that in proportion as the experience and the reasonings of different individuals are brought to bear upon the same objects, and are combined in such a manner as to illustrate and to limit each other, the science of politics assumes more and more that systematical form which encourages and aids the labours of future inquirers.[66]

This was an entirely modern project, as ancient philosophers had "confined their attention to a comparison of the different forms of government, and to an examination of the provisions they made for perpetuating their own existence, and for extending the glory of the state."[67] "It was reserved for modern times," he continued, "to investigate those universal principles of justice and of expediency, which ought, under every form of government, to regulate the social order; and of which the object is, to make as equitable a distribution as possible, among all the different members of a community, of the advantages arising from the political union."[68] The science had made sufficient progress to show that rather than political participation, it was in the "equity and expedience of the laws" that the happiness of the people resided. This made ascertaining the principles of jurisprudence or, following Stewart's use of the Smithian formula, "the general principles which ought to run through and be the foundation of the laws of nations," the most important branch of political science. Along with men like Quesnay, A.-R.-J. Turgot (1727–1781), and Cesare Beccaria

(1738–1794), Smith belonged to the modern brand of political philosophers, who rather than working for the improvement of society by "delineating plans of new constitutions," sought to do so by "enlightening the policy of actual legislators." Smith's contribution to this movement was outstanding:

> To direct the policy of nations with respect to one most important class of its laws, those which form its system of political economy, is the great aim of Mr. Smith's *Inquiry*. And he has unquestionably had the merit of presenting to the world, the most comprehensive and perfect work that has yet appeared, on the general principles of any branch of legislation.[69]

Smith's writings belonged, in Stewart's view, to the science of legislation as described by Francis Bacon (1561–1626) in *The Advancement of Science* (1605) and highlighted the difference between ancient and modern attitudes toward wealth, since modern philosophers, in complete contrast to ancient ones, favored economic growth and the system of luxury, and sought ways of enhancing it. Just as Smith had argued that the tenets of different schools of political economy were grounded in different political experiences, rather than the other way round, so Stewart attributed the causes of this change in attitude to a change in actual political practice. Drawing on Hume's "Essay on Commerce" (1754), Stewart perceived the difference between ancient and modern politics to reside essentially in the fact that the latter

> aimed too much at modifying, by the force of positive institutions, the order of society, according to some preconceived idea of expediency; without trusting sufficiently to those principles of the human constitution, which, wherever they are allowed free scope, not only conduct mankind to happiness, but lay the foundation of a progressive improvement in their condition and in their character.[70]

Modern policies, on the contrary, tended to conform "to an order of things recommended by nature." It had been Smith's aim

> to illustrate the provision made by nature in the principles of the human mind, and in the circumstances of man's external situation, for a gradual and progressive augmentation in the means of national wealth; and to demonstrate, that the most effectual plan for advancing a people to greatness, is to maintain that order of things which nature has pointed out; by allowing every man, as long as he observes the rules of justice, to pursue his own interest in his own way, and to bring both his industry and his capital into the freest competition with those of his fellow-citizens.[71]

Summarizing Smith's critique of mercantilism, Stewart effectively raised the same issue that the preceding and all too sketchy account of his system had led us to consider, namely, whether Smith's political economy amounted to a recommendation to sovereigns to let go of the market and to be as neglectful and lazy about it as Montchrétien had admonished them not to remain. What Stewart feared in particular was that Smith's argument for the freedom of trade might "by flattering the indolence of the statesman, . . . suggest to those who are invested with absolute power, the idea of carrying it into immediate execution."[72] Stewart then went on to cite, somewhat surprisingly, the *Éloge de J.-B. Colbert,* which had earned Jacques Necker (1732–1804) a prize from the Académie française in 1773.[73] Necker, who was a firm believer in the need for rulers to intervene in the market, had argued, in the words of what may be presumed to be Stewart's own translation:

> Nothing is more adverse to the tranquility of a statesman than a spirit of moderation; because it condemns him to perpetual observation, shews him every moment the insufficiency of his wisdom, and leaves him the melancholy sense of his own imperfection; while, under the shelter of a few general principles, a systematical politician enjoys a perpetual calm. By the help of one alone, that of perfect liberty of trade, he would govern the world, and would leave human affairs to arrange themselves at pleasure, under the operation of the prejudices and the self-interests of individuals. If these run counter to each other, he gives himself no anxiety about the consequence; he insists that the result cannot be judged of till after a century or two shall have elapsed. If his contemporaries, in consequence of the disorder into which he has thrown public affairs, are scrupulous about submitting quietly to the experiment, he accuses them of impatience. They alone, and not he, are to blame for what they have suffered; and the principle continues to be inculcated with the same zeal and the same confidence as before.[74]

To clear Smith of the charge of exonerating princes from their moral duty to attend to the question of distributive justice and of enabling them to shrug off the responsibility they had to ensure the equity and efficiency of market operations, Stewart stressed the extent to which Smith had urged the utmost caution in implementing his system. Referring to the last edition of the *Theory of Moral Sentiments* (1776), Stewart drew attention to the remarks added by Smith that the public-spirited man "[w]hen he cannot establish the right, . . . will not disdain to ameliorate wrong; but, like Solon, when he cannot establish the best system of laws, he will endeavour to establish the best that the people can bear."[75]

Read in the light of Stewart's commentary, it would seem that modern sovereigns found themselves in the rather unenviable position of knowing that both the considerations of justice and expediency dictated that they do not favor particular interests by intervening in the market and protecting one sector or other of the economy, while being nevertheless morally responsible for the consequences that their disengagement from the economy would bring about. Gradualism was, of course, *de rigueur* in this context.

But Stewart went somewhat further than this. He noted that the practical difficulties that faced the legislator who tried to apply them did not

> detract in the least from the value of those political theories which attempt to delineate the principles of a perfect legislation. Such theories . . . ought to be considered merely as descriptions of the *ultimate* objects at which the statesman ought to aim. The tranquility of his administration, and the immediate success of his measures, depend on his good sense and his practical skill; and his theoretical principles only enable him to direct his measures steadily and wisely, to promote the improvement and happiness of mankind, and prevent him from being ever led astray from the important ends, by more limited views of temporary expedience.

This could prove of only meager consolation to princes given that the most systematic of political economists had just shown that for interventionism not to subvert its aims, an all-knowing mind had to be behind the implementation of its policies. Thus politics seemed to be condemned to remain much as it had always been, a matter of exercising the shrewdest practical judgment about the affairs of men in the world as it is, rather than how it ought to be. Moreover, if the science of political economy consisted in building ideal models that princes could at best only hope to approximate, than this modern enterprise proved not as different from ancient political theory as Stewart suggested. True, there was what Hume saw as the novelty of alerting rulers to the importance of commerce. But if Smith and Stewart and others were at all correct in their analyses, this was an instance in which theory had in fact lagged behind practice. Princes were awake to the significance of commerce. In any event, to speak in these terms is to invite a false dichotomy, for even at the very heart of the theoretical exposition of the Smithian system of political economy the question of practice never left the page.

Not unlike the last part of Montchrétien's *Traicté,* titled "De l'Exemple et des Soins Principaux du Prince," the last book of the *Wealth of Nations* is devoted to the duties of the sovereign as well as to the revenues necessary to discharge them. In contrast to what might falsely have been deemed the duty to encourage or discourage certain economic activities for the sake of the whole of society, pursuing the remaining princely duties did not require impossible feats of ordinary human intellects:

> According to the system of natural liberty, the sovereign has only three duties to attend to; three duties of great importance, indeed, but plain and intelligible to common understandings: first, the duty of protecting the society from the violence and invasion of other independent societies; secondly, the duty of protecting, as far as possible, every member of the society from the injustice or oppression of every other member of it, or the duty of establishing an exact administration of justice; and, thirdly, the duty of erecting and

maintaining certain publick works and certain publick institutions, which it can never be for the interest of any individual, or small number of individuals, to erect and maintain; because the profit could never repay the expence to any individual or small number of individuals, though it may frequently do much more than repay it to a great society.[76]

Smith's discussion of the attention that should be paid to "the publick works and institutions for facilitating the commerce of the society" makes it clear that he had not defined political economy as a branch of the science of the legislator only to demonstrate that no legislator could ever aspire to practice it. Nothing short of a full understanding of what Smith had sought to demonstrate through his description of the operation of the natural system of political economy was required of sovereigns for them to resist the calls of various segments of society to be privileged in one way or other and to appreciate how nefarious such policies had been and would continue to be. Only a true comprehension of the natural system could provide the perspective from which to gauge in what manner the commerce of society could be facilitated; only a thorough knowledge of the condition of work in highly specialized occupations would lead one to realize the need for public provisions for the education of the common people, provisions all the more necessary given that "[i]n free countries, where the safety of government depends very much upon the favourable judgment which the people may form of its conduct, it must surely be of the highest importance that they should not be disposed to judge rashly or capriciously concerning it."[77] Rather than particular instances in which Smith thought the sovereign ought to provide where individuals might be reluctant to do so, such as roads or education, it is the spirit of these chapters which best reveals the extent to which Smith remained true to the nature of the science which Montchrétien had been engaged in. This was a science that sought to encourage their royal or noble pupils to examine the workings of society as they would a body, to see for themselves how each part contributed to the life and well-being of the whole, and to learn how best to attend to any of its ills or foresee its weaknesses. Smith, as we saw, placed a considerable trust in the natural means of recovery and was more than skeptical of what he called "speculative physicians." But this did not make the science of political economy a fanciful and optional subject of princely studies. On the contrary, only as best an understanding of market economies as any human being could muster could persuade one to refrain from administering baneful physics to them; only such an understanding would morally entitle one to prescribe anything to them. Even in the best possible world, sovereigns would have to continue to assess the performance of the market. Stewart's fear that Smith's advocacy of total freedom of trade might provide the excuse Stewart thought "indolent" statesmen would seize on in order to wash their hands of the economy was groundless even in conditions ideal for the implementation of Smith's model.

That rulers were duty bound to acquire all the knowledge necessary to distinguish good from evil and for the proper exercise of their office is the oldest theme of political theory. It is debatable whether Hume was right in claiming that trade was a relatively novel subject in regal curricula. Even so, the notion of innovation seems somewhat out of place in the context of political economy. To maintain the opposite would require a great many qualifications, too many for the advantages such an interpretation would yield. Nearly every aspect of the science, its languages and imagery, including such a concept as that of the invisible hand, have long, if complex, antecedents in ancient and Christian thought. This is not to detract from the genius of the political theorists, least of all the undeniable genius of Adam Smith. On the contrary, to ask whether he invented political economy, or contributed to its invention, is in some way to lessen his real achievement. This is not because he should be seen instead as the author of *The Theory of Moral Sentiments,* one of the best contributions to moral philosophy in Western history, but because the brilliant exercise in political economy he was engaged in would not have been possible but for the existence of a much larger, and effectively more ambitious, set of questions than even that of the nature and causes of the wealth of nations, a set of questions which he and all his fellow intellectuals sought to tackle. To put the matter in another way, to deliver what he did in the *Wealth of Nations* with any degree of intellectual confidence, Smith had to think through substantial moral, political, historical, theological, psychological, and epistemic issues of his day. The certain way to fail to comprehend his political economy and his contribution to that science is to seek to sever it from the other intellectual endeavors, the subjects of the other chapters of this volume, which constitute what we think of as the Enlightenment.

Thus the brief sketch of Smith's pronouncements on the wealth of nations in the preceding pages is inadequate, not only because it skims the surface of what is in any case but part of the argument made in *Wealth of Nations,* nor even because it brings under two single headings, mercantilism and physiocracy, numerous, complex, and often not entirely opposite views, and, what is more, because it does so solely from Smith's never entirely unprejudiced position, but because it isolates in its approach a subject matter from all that gave it importance and meaning. Even a detailed analysis of all the works that considered the topic of national economies up to and including those of the eighteenth century,[78] one which would consider, among other things, the relation between Sir William Petty and his fellow political arithmeticians and what is considered classical political economy, would not do the subject sufficient justice.

To capture the nature of political economy one must cast one's nets further, at least as far as the political economists themselves cast them.[79] Placed in their proper context, their writings must be seen as part and parcel of the wide-ranging debate about the nature and merit of commercial society, its origins, and its future. This debate enticed figures such as Rousseau, the Encyclopédists, and the Scottish and Italian[80] political economists to examine the history of civilization from its infancy to the rise of the system of commerce and luxury.[81] It led them to ponder whether economic growth was limited and, in any event, whether it was morally desirable. Woven into their discourses was the issue of population growth and decline. The then prevalent fear of population decline fueled investigations about the relationship between sexual licence, contraception, mores, luxury, sumptuary laws, sexual inequality, climate, and religion.[82] And these discussions were in their turn but part of an overall quest for an understanding of the causal connections and interconnections between any one aspect of human existence and all the others. These included the issue Hume was addressing when he remarked on the importance that trade had been assuming in political theory since the mid–sixteenth century, namely, the question of the relation between commerce and different types of government. "It has become an established opinion," he wrote, "that commerce can never flourish but in a free government."[83] Though he owned that history seemed to support what he took as a commonplace of his time, Hume was unconvinced:

> If we trace commerce in its progress through TYRE, ATHENS, SYRACUSE, CARTHAGE, VENICE, FLORENCE, GENOA, ANTWERP, HOLLAND AND ENGLAND, &c. we shall always find it to have fixed its seat in free governments. The three greatest trading towns now in Europe, are LONDON, AMSTERDAM, and HAMBURGH; all free cities, and protestant cities; that is, enjoying a double liberty. It must, however, be observed that the great jealousy entertained of late, with regard to the commerce of FRANCE, seems to prove, that this maxim is no more certain and infallible than the foregoing, and that the subjects of an absolute prince may become our rivals in commerce, as well as in learning.[84]

The issue of the relationship between political freedom and economic performance, which has returned time and again on the political agenda, remained an important one throughout the eighteenth century, especially on the Continent. The argument that monarchs who wished to enjoy the benefits of a flourishing trade had to liberalize their regimes was most notably made in the pages of the Baron de Montesquieu's (1689–1755) *De l'esprit des lois* (1748). It never left the political stage. It was also presented the other way round, that is, as a warning that changing the laws regulating prices was likely to cost sovereigns their thrones. The abbé Galiani, one of the *économistes'* best-informed and strongest critics, was indefatigable in his reminders to the *philosophes* of the responsibility they took in advising European sovereigns on economic policies. What Stewart saw as the ancient subject matter of political theory, the typology of governments, was far from irrelevant to such discourses. Writing to Madame d'Épinay (1726–1783), Galiani contended:

> In every government, the legislation pertaining to corn takes on the character of the spirit of the government. Under a despote, the freedom to export is impossible; the tyrant is too afraid of the cries of his starving slaves. In a democracy, the freedom to export is natural and infallible; the governors and the governed being the same people, confidence is unlimited. In a mixed and moderate government, that freedom can only ever be qualified and moderate.[85]

Before turning to the corollaries with which Galiani followed the above passage, it is well to remind ourselves that the science of political economy was a moral science. The *Encyclopédie*'s tree of knowledge shows "COMMERCE INTERIEUR, EXTERIEUR, DE TERRE, DE MER" to require the combined sciences of politics and economy; the latter constituted, along with the science of natural law, the "SCIENCE DES LOIX, OU JURISPRUDENCE"; this science was, in its turn, one of the two branches of moral science, namely, that of its particular application or "MORALE PARTICULIERE" (the other being "MORALE GENERALE," i.e., the "SCIENCE DU BIEN ET DU MAL EN GENERAL. DES DEVOIRS EN GENERAL. DE LA VERTU. DE LA NECESSITE D'ESTRE VERTUEUX, &c"); moral science was itself one of the two branches of the "SCIENCE DE L'HOMME" (the other being "LOGIQUE"). Though the detail of the arrangements may have differed somewhat, there is no doubt that the Scottish political economists saw the science of political economy similarly related to the science of politics, jurisprudence, and ethics. Like his Scottish counterparts, Galiani saw legislators engaged in a moral practice that the right kind of science of political economy could enlighten but that never lessened their moral burden. What legislators were faced with in the eighteenth century was a clear and simple, though awesome, choice. They had to chose between the legitimate claims of present and future generations, between their subjects and their subjects' descendants. Having witnessed the terrible famine in Naples in 1764, Galiani did not hesitate in offering his opinion of the morally acceptable option for rulers when faced with the issue of the lifting of grain prices. His letter to Madame d'Épinay continued thus:

> Corrolaries: If you tamper with the administration of corn in France too much, and succeed in so doing, you will thereby alter the form and constitution of the government; either because this change acts as the cause or becomes the consequence of the liberty to export. But changing the constitution is a wonderful thing once done, not so when it remains to be done. It

dearly troubles two or three entire generations, and benefits only posterity. Posterity is a possible being, we are real ones. Must the real inconvenience themselves for the sake of the possible to the point of being unhappy? No. Therefore keep your government and your corn.[86]

Civilization, Rousseau claimed, began the first time man gave a thought to his tomorrow. By the eighteenth century, this process had become a science, the science of political economy, which sought to speak about tomorrows, the long-term consequences of the endeavor to satisfy today's desires. This science, however informative, did not transform the art of politics, much less simplify it. The choice between present and future generations very much remained; in fact political economy spelled it out with unprecedented clarity.[87]

This choice presented itself not only in the shape of a dilemma about removing or maintaining restrictions on the freedom of trade, about endangering the happiness and the satisfaction of the needs of "real" beings for the sake of seeking to ensure those of their "possible" progeny, but also in the form of a debate about the restrictions governing sexual reproduction itself. Then as now there existed the fear that a society that encouraged or simply allowed human desires to develop unbridled would in fact be courting disaster, whatever benefits it seemed to reap in terms of industriousness and production to meet the needs of existing people. Among these desires, sexual desire received as much attention in various eighteenth-century discourses as did acquisitiveness. Indeed, many a writer argued them to be one.[88] Malthus's warning about the limits to growth may seem to us to have been the loudest in the period, but they were in fact part of a general and very important controversy about the extent to which and the manner in which population growth or decline were subject to human control.[89] This dispute was ubiquitous, and its study, like that of the discussion about the nature of wealth, leads not only to the heart of the economic writings of the period, but to works about such varied topics as toleration, slavery, primogeniture, climate, suicide, duelling, torture, prostitution, celibacy, monasticism, luxury, and the consequences of the development of the arts and sciences. In other words, both subjects impinge on nearly every important aspect of the Enlightenment's evaluation of the morality, manners, and mores of the ancien régime and of modern commercial society more generally speaking. Nothing short of integrating any set of views or pronouncements on population within the overall assessment of the merit or demerit of the progress of civilization and of the comparative worth of ancient and modern civilizations will go toward placing these beliefs in their proper context, and nothing less than this contextualization will enable one to understand their true nature and content.

The notion of invention and the quest for founding fathers is a potentially hazardous intellectual activity. It favors the search for discontinuities and can lead to distortions about the context in which particular schools of thought emerged before being institutionalized as disciplines or becoming formalized discourses about certain topics, such as the economy or population. Neither in the case of political economy nor in that of demography is the notion of invention entirely fruitful. These are human sciences not only because their subjects are people, people's happiness, but because they are and always were about the need and duty of those in power to study the complexity of human societies in their entirety and hence to come to learn the precise limits of human agency. Neither belittled the immense difficulty of choosing between the needs and desires of real and possible beings. Both contributed to our awareness that the choice cannot be evaded.

NOTES

1. Important among the more recent studies are those contained in Istvan Hont and Michael Ignatieff, eds., *Wealth and Virtue: The Shaping of Political Economy in the Scottish Enlightenment* (Cambridge: Cambridge University Press, 1983); Istvan Hont, ed., *Political Economy and the Enlightenment* (London: Routledge, forthcoming); idem, "The Political Economy of the 'Unnatural and Retrograde' Order: Adam Smith and Natural Liberty," in *Französische Revolution und Politische Okonomie* (Trier: Karl Marx House, 1989); idem, "The Rhapsody of the Public Debt: David Hume and Voluntary State Bankruptcy," in *Political Discourses in Early Modern Britain*, ed. N. Phillipson and Q. Skinner (Cambridge: Cambridge University Press, 1992); Albert O. Hirschman, *The Passions and the Interests* (Princeton, N.J.: Princeton University Press, 1977); K. Haakonssen, *The Science of the Legislator: The Natural Jurisprudence of David Hume and Adam Smith* (Cambridge: Cambridge University Press, 1980); Donald Winch, *Adam Smith's Politics: An Essay in Historiographic Revision* (Cambridge: Cambridge University Press, 1978); idem, "Science and the Legislator: Adam Smith and After," *The Economic Journal* 93 (1983): 501–529; R. F. Teichgraeber, *"Free Trade" and Moral Philosophy: Rethinking the Sources of Adam Smith* (Durham, N.C.: Duke University, 1986); Jacob H. Hollander, "The Dawn of a Science," in *Adam Smith, 1776–1926*, ed. J. M. Clark (Chicago: University of Chicago Press, 1928; reprint, New York: A. M. Kelley, 1966), 1–21; Patricia James, *Population Malthus: His Life and Times* (London and Boston: Routledge and Kegan Paul, 1979); Donald Winch, *Malthus* (Oxford: Oxford University Press, 1987); E. A. Wrigley, "The Limits to Growth: Malthus and the Classical Economists," in *Population and Resources in Western Intellectual Traditions*, ed. Michael S. Teitelbaum and Jay M. Winter (Cambridge: Cambridge University Press, 1989), 30–48. For a brief survey of the eighteenth-century population debate, see Frederick G. Whelan, "Population and ideology in the Enlightenment," *History of Political Thought* 7, no. 1 (Spring, 1991): 35–72. Other relevant studies are listed below.

2. See my "Reflections on the History of the Science of Woman." *History of Science* 29 (June, 1991): 185–205.

3. See Robert Wokler's chapter on anthropology (chap. 2) in this book.

4. It is the first sentence of the introduction of David Hume's *A Treatise of Human Nature*, ed. L. A. Selby-Bigge, 2d ed., revised by P. H. Nidditch (Oxford: Clarendon Press, 1987), xiii.

5. Ibid., xvii.

6. Ibid., I.VII.273.

7. Immanuel Kant, *Prolegomena to any Future Metaphysics*, trans. P. G. Lucas (Manchester: Manchester University Press, 1953), 9. For a brief but insightful analysis of Kant's response to Hume, see Roger Scruton, *Kant* (Oxford: Oxford University Press, 1982).

8. For an insightful study of Hume's philosophy, see, for instance, John P. Wright's *The Sceptical Realism of David Hume* (Manchester: Manchester University Press, 1982).

9. Adam Smith, *An Inquiry into the Nature and Causes of the Wealth of Nations*, ed. R. H. Campbell, A. S. Skinner, and W. B. Todd, 2 vols. (Oxford: Clarendon Press, 1976), IV.ix.38, 679. Henceforth this work will be referred to as *WN*.

10. Ibid. The passage Smith cited is from Victor de Mirabeau, *Philosophie Rurale ou économie générale et politique de l'agriculture, pour servir de suite à l'Ami des Hommes* (Amsterdam, 1766), 1:52–53.

11. See François Quesnay, *François Quesnay et la Physiocratie*, 2 vols. (Paris: Institut National d'Études Démographiques, 1958), 1:299, cited in Marguerite Kuczynski, "Quelques points de Comparaison entre Boisguilbert et Quesnay," in *Boisguilbert Parmi Nous, Actes du Colloque international de Rouen* (22–23 mai 1975), ed. Jacqueline Hecht (Paris: Institut National d'Études Démographiques, 1989), 284. The passage in the letter reads:

> Vous fournirez alors une carrière nouvelle dans laquelle personne n'est encore entré et qui est cependant la seule route de la recherche de la vérité qui consiste en ces divers points que les richesses usuelles ne sont qu'un flux de denrées commerciales, toujours détruites par la consommation et toujours renouvellées par la production; que ce qui est revenu ou gain pour une partie des sujets et dépense ou retranchement pour les autres, n'est point revenu pour l'État; mais seulement distribution de revenus, et qu'il n'a de revenus pour l'État que les production naturelles commerciales, et le profit net du commerce avec l'étranger.

The letter ends with these words: "C'est un bel ouvrage inconnu aux humains jusqu'à présent. On verra tous les mouvements utiles et inutiles de la circulation de l'argent et tous les préjugé ridicules des nations sur ces matières." Quesnay, *François Quesnay*, 1:300.

> You will then open a new path no one has yet followed and which is nevertheless the only road for the quest for truth which consists in the following points: that ordinary riches are nothing other than the movement of commercial goods, that what is revenue or gain for some subjects and expense or loss for others is not a State revenue, but only distribution of revenues and that State revenues consist only in natural commercial production and the net profit of foreign exports . . . It is a marvellous work unknown to man until now which will enable him to learn all the useful as well as useless flows of money and all the ridiculous prejudices which nations entertain on these subjects.

12. Dugald Stewart described Quesnay as "the profound and original author of the Economical Table," *Account of the Life and Writings of Adam Smith, LL.D.,* in Adam Smith, *Essays on Philosophical Subjects,* ed. W. P. D. Wightman, J. C. Bryce, and I. S. Ross (Oxford: Clarendon Press, 1980), III.12, 304. See also, for instance, Eric Roll, *A History of Economic Thought* (London: Faber and Faber, 1938), 129. According to Georges Weulersse, the originality of the physiocrats resides in having laid the first principles of modern capitalism; see his "De l'Application de la méthode historique à l'histoire des doctrines économiques, à propos des physiocrates," *Bulletin de la Société d'histoire moderne* (June 1908): 33–36; idem, *Le Mouvement physiocratique en France de 1756 à 1770* (Paris: F. Alcan, 1910); idem, *La Physiocratie sous les ministères de Turgot et de Necker (1774–1781)* (Paris: Presses Universitaires de France, 1950).

13. *WN,* IV.ix.38, 678.

14. Petty is often referred to as the founder of political economy. In *A Contribution to the Critique of Political Economy* (London: Lawrence and Wishart, 1971), 52, Karl Marx describes "classical political economy" as "beginning with William Petty in Britain and Boisguilbert in France, and ending with Ricardo in Britain and Sismondi in France." Frederick Engels follows suit in *Anti-Dühring* (Peking: Foreign Languages Press, 1976), 290. See also, for instance, Eric Roll, *The History of Economic Thought* (London: Faber, 1938), 66. For a collection on the relation between the Seigneur de Boisguilbert, the physiocrats, and various political economists, see *Boisguilbert Parmi Nous, Actes du Colloque international de Rouen (22–23 mai 1975)* (Paris: Institut National D'Études Démographiques, 1989). Quesnay praised Boisguilbert, and Forbonnais said that the latter's views on the grain trade anticipated by eighty years all that was said about it in the eighteenth century (*Principes et observations économiques,* 2 vols. [1767], 1:167), cited by Georges Weulersse, *Le Mouvement physiocratique en France de 1756 à 1770,* 2 vols. (Paris: Mouton, 1910; reprint, Paris: Mouton, 1968), 1:4. *Precursors of Adam Smith,* ed. Ronald L. Meek (London: Dent, 1973), is a useful anthology with notes that highlight the degree to which various writers foreshadowed Smithian political economy. It is not entirely uninteresting, though admittedly somewhat petty, to note that even Michel Foucault seems to have found the language of invention, albeit in quotation marks, difficult to resist: "La 'loi quantitative' n'a pas été 'inventée' par Locke. Bodin et Davanzatti savaient bien au XVIe siècle déjà que l'accroissement des masses métalliques en circulation faisait monter le prix des marchandises; mais ce mécanisme apparaissait lié à une dévalorisation intrinsèque du métal." *Les Mots et les Choses: Une archéologie des sciences humaines* (Paris: Gallimard, 1966), 196. Despite his critique of the methods of the history of ideas and his warnings about teleological readings of history (see note 19 below), his own prose shows the extent to which these practices are embedded in our culture.

15. See, for instance, Akiteru Kubota, "Quesnay, disciple de Malebranche," in Quesnay, *François Quesnay* (note 11 above); 169–196.

16. See in particular the important work in this respect and others of J. G. A. Pocock, e.g., *The Machiavellian Moment: Florentine Political Thought and the Atlantic Republican Tradition* (Princeton, N.J.: Princeton University Press, 1975); idem, *Politics, Language, and Time: Essays on Political Thought and History* (London: Methuen, 1971); and idem, *Virtue, Commerce, and History* (Cambridge: Cambridge University

Press, 1985). Also the publications of Istvan Hont, e.g., his and Michael Ignatieff's "Needs and Justice in the *Wealth of Nations*: An Introductory Essay," in *Wealth and Virtue*, ed. Hont and Ignatieff (see note 1 above); Hont's "Free Trade and the Economic Limits to National Politics: Neo-Machiavellian Political Economy Reconsidered," in *The Economic Limits of Modern Politics*, ed. John Dunn (Cambridge: Cambridge University Press, 1990), 41–120. See also the introduction and essays in *The Languages of Political Theory in Early-Modern Europe*, ed. Anthony Pagden (Cambridge: Cambridge University Press, 1987), especially M. M. Goldsmith's "Liberty, Luxury, and the Pursuit of Happiness," 225–251, and Istvan Hont's "The Language of Sociability and Commerce: Samuel Pufendorf and the Theoretical Foundations of the 'Four Stages Theory,'" 253–276.

17. Franco Venturi, *Utopia and Reform in the Enlightenment* (Cambridge: Cambridge University Press, 1971), 3; his point was taken up more recently by Nannerl O. Keohane in the context of her discussion of Boisguilbert, *Philosophy and the State in France: The Renaissance to the Enlightenment* (Princeton, N.J.: Princeton University Press, 1980), 352.

18. See Jacques Lacan's *The Seminar of Jacques Lacan, Book II: The Ego in Freud's Theory and in the Technique of Psychoanalysis*, ed. Jacques-Alain Miller, trans. S. Tomaselli, notes by J. Forrester (Cambridge: Cambridge University Press, 1988), 5; see also S. Tomaselli, "The First Person: Descartes, Locke, and Mind-Body Dualism," *History of Science* 22 (1984):188ff.

19. "Il faut donc éviter," writes Foucault,

une lecture rétrospective qui ne préterait à l'analyse classique des richesses que l'unité ultérieure d'une économie politique en train de se constituer à tâtons. C'est sur ce mode, pourtant, que les historiens des idées ont coutume de restituer la naissance énigmatique de ce savoir qui, dans la pensée occidentale, aurait surgit tout armé et déjà périlleux à l'époque de Ricardo et de J.-B. Say. (*Les Mots et les Choses*, 177–178)

See also pp. 214–224. Foucault's point bears reiteration. For further comments on his views on the advent of modern political economy, see note 87 below.

20. See, for instance, Eric Roll, *A History of Economic Thought* (London: Faber, 1966).

21. Here I lay myself open to being charged as unimaginative by those who like Eric Roll think that "one would have to be peculiarly unimaginative, indeed, insensitive, not to see the last quarter of the eighteenth century as one of the great watersheds in the evolution of human society." For his argument that from Adam Smith onward "economics becomes recognizable as an independent discipline, indeed as a science, self-conscious and self-consistent; and while its affiliation to social philosophy is still clearly visible, it has now come of age and is ready to lead a life of its own," see "*The Wealth of Nations* 1776–1976," in his *The Uses and Abuses of Economics and Other Essays* (London and Boston: Faber and Faber, 1978).

22. Antoine de Montchrétien, *Traicté de l'Oeconomie politique dédié en 1615 au Roy et la Reine Mère du Roy*, ed. Théodore Funck-Brentano (Paris: Marcel Rivière, 1889). Funck-Brentano's introduction to this now relatively neglected text is useful. On Montchrétien's life, see Richard Griffiths, *The Dramatic Technique of Antoine de Montchretien* (Oxford: Clarendon Press, 1970). His *Traicté* is discussed in Keohane's *Philosophy* (note 17 above), 163–169.

23. See also the discussion relating to Stewart and Necker, below.

24. Montchrétien, *Traicté*, 31. The original text reads:

mais de n'y laisser nulle terre vague et disposer avecques jugement un chacun à son office. En toute administration il n'y a poinct de negligence plus pernicieuse que de ne connoitre pas ceux à qui l'on commande, de paresse plus prejudiciable que de ne sonder pas à quoy plus naturellement ils sont applicables.

25. It should be noted, however, that Rousseau had Sir Robert Filmer (1590–1653) rather than Montchrétien in mind: *Encyclopédie, ou Dictionnaire Raisonné des Sciences, des Arts et des Métiers, par une Société de Gens de Lettres, Mis en ordre et publié par M. Diderot . . . et quant à la partie mathématique par M. d'Alembert*, 17 vols. (1751–65), vol. 5 (1755), pp. 337–349.

26. Montchrétien, *Traicté*, 31. The original text reads:

Tout cela revient à ce poinct: qu'en Estat aussi bien qu'en famille c'est un heur meslé de grandissme profit de mesnager bien les hommes selon leur particulière et propre inclination. Et sur la consideration de ce rapport qu'ils ont ensemble, en ce qui concerne le poinct de l'utilité, joint avec plusieurs autre raisons que seroient longues à déduire, on peut fort à propos maintenir, contre l'opinion d'Aristote et de Xenophon, que l'on ne sçauroit diviser l'oeconomie de la police sans demembrer la partie principale de son Tout, et que la science d'acquerir des biens, qu'ils nomment ainsi, est commune aux républiques aussi bien qu'aux familles.

27. Ibid., 31–32. The original text reads: "De ma part, je ne puis que m'estonne comme en traitez politiques, d'ailleurs si dilligemment escrits, ils ont oublié ceste mesnagerie publique, à quoy les necessités et charges de l'Estat obligent d'avoir principalement égard."

28. Ibid., 18. The original text reads: "une santé universelle de tout le corps de l'Estat, et par conséquent une entière disposition de chaque membre particulier."

29. Ibid., 32.

30. Ibid., 7.

31. Ibid., xxiv–xxv. The analogy implicit in the text is made salient by Funck-Brentano.

32. David Hume, "Of Civil Liberty," in his *Essays: Moral, Political, and Literary*, ed. Eugene Miller (Indianapolis: Liberty Press, 1985), 88–89. The essay was first titled "Of Liberty and Despotism"; it became "Of Civil Liberty" in the 1758 edition of the *Essays*, then called *Essays and Treatises*. There is a sizable literature on Hume's political economy; see, e.g., Eugene Rotwein's introduction to Hume's *Essays: Moral, Political, and Literary* (Oxford: Oxford University Press, 1963); idem, *David Hume: Writings on Economics* (Madison: University of Wisconsin Press, 1955); Marcus Arkin, "The Economic Writings of David Hume—A Reassessment," in *Essays in Economic Thought: Aristotle to Marshall*, ed. Joseph J. Spengler and William R. Allen (Chicago: Rand McNally, 1960), 141–160; Robert Lyon, "Hume's Philosophy of Political Economy" and E. J. Hundert, "The Achievement Motive in Hume's Political Economy," both reprinted in *Hume as Philosopher of Society, Politics, and History*, ed. Donald Livingston and Marie Martin (Rochester, N.Y.: University of Rochester Press, 1991), 35–39, 40–44.

33. One illustration of this is provided by the *Encyclopédie* entry "Politique arithmétique," vol. 12 (1765), which mostly summarized the arguments of Petty, Charles Davenant (1656–1714), and others about the relative wealth of Holland and England in contrast to that of France. For a detailed analysis of the Irish perspective on this debate, see Hont's "Free Trade" (see note 16 above).

34. See on this subject Istvan Hont's "The 'Rich Country–Poor Country' Debate in Scottish Classical Political Economy," in Hont and Ignatieff's *Wealth and Virtue* (see note 16 above), 271–315.

35. *WN*, IV.Introduction 1, 428.

36. Ibid., Introduction and Plan of the work 7, 11.

37. Ibid., IV.i.1, 429.

38. Ibid., IV.i.6, 431.

39. Adam Smith, early draft of *The Wealth of Nations*, in *Lectures on Jurisprudence*, ed. R. L. Meek, D. D. Raphael, and P. G. Stein (Oxford: Clarendon Press), 576. See also *WN*, IV.i.7–8, 431–432.

40. *Lectures on Jurisprudence, Report of 1762–63*, vi.135, 381. For an analysis of Locke's economic views and the manner in which he was generally misunderstood by eighteenth-century economists, see Patrick Hyde Kelly's introduction to his edition of John Locke, *Locke on Money*, 2 vols. (Oxford: Clarendon Press, 1991), 1:1–109.

41. Smith, *Lectures*, vi. 136, 381.

42. *WN*, IV.i.10, 434; see also IV.viii.54, 661.

43. Ibid., IV.i.10, 434–435.

44. Ibid., IV.i.20, 440–441.

45. Ibid., IV.i.29, 444.

46. Ibid., IV.i.30, 445.

47. Ibid., IV.i.32, 448.

48. Ibid., IV.viii.32, 654.

49. Ibid., IV.viii.49, 660.

50. Ibid., IV.viii.54, 661.

51. Ibid., IV.viii.30, 654.

52. Ibid., IV.ix.2, 663.

53. Ibid., IV.ix.15, 669.

54. Ibid., IV.ix.17, 669.

55. Ibid., IV.ix.20, 670.

56. Ibid., IV.ix.44, 606.

57. Ibid., IV.ix.48, 686.

58. Ibid., IV.ix. 50, 687.

59. Ibid.

60. Ibid.

61. Ibid., IV.ix.28, 674.

62. Ibid.

63. Adam Smith, *The Theory of Moral Sentiments*, ed. D. D. Raphael and A. L. Macfie (Oxford: Clarendon Press, 1976), IV.i.9, 183.

64. Ibid., IV.i.10, 183.

65. Ibid., IV.i.10, 184. The invisible hand is also mentioned once in *WN*, IV.ii.9, 456. For a detailed account of Smith's use of this idea and the manner in which he thought the price/wages mechanism to operate, see Hont and Ignatieff, "Needs and Justice," 1–44.

66. Stewart, *Writings of Adam Smith*, in *Essays on Philosophical Subjects* (see note 12 above), IV.1, 309.

67. Ibid., IV.2, 309.

68. Ibid., IV.2, 309–310.
69. Ibid., IV.7, 311.
70. Ibid., IV.11, 314.
71. Ibid. IV.14, 315.
72. Ibid., IV.19, 318.
73. Ibid., IV.20, 318–319. The date is wrongly given as 1763 in the text.
74. Ibid.
75. Ibid., IV.19, 318.
76. *WN*, IV.ix.51, 687–688.
77. Ibid., V.i.f.61, 788.
78. For a very successful approach to the question of the shape of premodern economics, see J. G. A. Pocock, "The Political Limits to Premodern Economics," in Dunn's *Economic Limits of Modern Politics* (see note 16 above), 121–141.
79. This issue was the subject of the King's College Research Centre study on "Political Economy and Society, 1750–1850," part of the findings of which were published in Hont and Ignatieff, *Wealth and Virtue* (see note 1 above).
80. See Franco Venturi's *Italy and the Enlightenment, Studies in a Cosmopolitan Century*, ed. Stuart Woolf, trans. Susan Corsi (London: Longman, 1972); idem, *Utopia* (see note 17 above), and idem, "Scottish Echoes in Eighteenth-Century Italy," in Hont and Ignatieff, *Wealth and Virtue*, 345–362; Richard Bellamy, " 'Da metafisico a mercatante'—Antonio Genovesi and the Development of a New Language of Commerce in Eighteenth-Century Naples," in *Languages of Political Theory* (see note 16 above), 277–299.
81. I have argued the same point about eighteenth-century pronouncements on population growth and decline in "Moral Philosophy and Population Questions in Eighteenth-Century Europe," in *Population and Resources* (see note 1 above), 7–29.
82. Stewart, *Writings of Adam Smith* (see note 12 above), IV.2, 309.
83. Hume, "Of Civil Liberty" (see note 32 above), 92.
84. Ibid.
85. Abbé Galiani, *Lettres de l'Abbé Galiani à Madame d'Epinay, Voltaire, Diderot, Grimm, le Baron D'Holbach, Morellet, Suard, D'Alembert, Marmontel, La Vicomtesse de Belsunce, etc.*, ed. Eugène Asse, 2 vols. (Paris: Charpentier, 1881), 1:138. The original text reads:

> Dans tout gouvernement, la législation des blés prend le ton de l'esprit du gouvernement. Sous un despote, la libre exportation est impossible; le tyran a trop peur des cris des ces esclaves affamés. Dans la démocratie, la liberté d'exportation est naturelle et infaillible: les gouvernants et les gouvernés étant les mêmes personnes, la confiance est infinie. Dans un gouvernement mixte et tempérée, la liberté ne saurait être que modifiée et tempérée.

For a study of this correspondence, see Francis Steegmuller, *A Woman, a Man, and Two Kingdoms: The Story of Madame d'Épinay and the Abbé Galiani* (London: Secker and Warburg, 1992).

86. Ibid., 1:138–139. The original text reads:

> Corrolaires: Si vous touchez trop à l'administration des blés en France, si vous réussissez, vous altérez la forme et la constitution du gouvernement; soit que ce changement soit la cause ou qu'il soit l'effet de la libertée entière d'exportation. Or le changement

de la constitution est une belle chose lorsqu'elle est faite, mais fort vilaine à faire. Elle tracasse rudement deux ou trois générations entières, et n'accommode que la postérité. La postérité est un être possible, et nous sommes des êtres réels. Faut-il que les réels se gênent tant pour les possibles, jusqu'à en être malheureux? Non. Gardez donc votre gouvernement et vos blés.

87. It will be apparent from the foregoing that I do not endorse Foucault's view of the advent of political economy as described in his *Les Mots et les Choses* (see note 14 above) and which he summarizes as follows:

Quant à la mutation que s'est produite vers la fin du XVIIIᵉ siècle dans toute l'*épistémè* occidentale, il est possible dès maintenant de la caractériser de loin en disant qu'un moment scientifiquement fort s'est constitué là où l'*épistémè* classique connaissait un temps métaphysiquement fort; et qu'en revanche un espace philosophique s'est dégagé là où le calssisme avait établi ses serrures épistémologiques les plus solides. En effet, l'analyse de la production, comme project nouveau de la nouvelle "économie politique" a essentiellement pour rôle d'analyser le rapport entre la valeur et les prix; les concepts d'organismes et d'organisation, les méthodes de l'anatomie comparée, bref tous les thèmes de la "biologie" naissante expliquent comment des structures observables sur des individus peuvent valoir à titre de caractères généraux pour des genres, des familles, des embranchements; enfin pour unifier les dispositions formelles d'un langage (sa capacité à constituer des propositions) et le sens qui appartient à ses mots, la "philologie" étudira non plus les fonctions représentatives du discours, mais un ensemble de constantes morphologiques soumises à une histoire. Philologie, biologie et économie politique se consitutent non pas à la place de la *Grammaire générale*, de l'*Histoire naturelle* et de l'*Analyse des richesses*, mais là où ces savoirs n'existaient pas, dans l'espace qu'ils laissaient blanc, dans la profoundeur du sillon qui séparait leurs grands segments théoriques et que remplissait la rumeur du continu ontologique. L'objet du savoir au XIXᵉ se forme là même où vient de se taire la plénitude classique de l'être. (219–220)

There is no doubt that Foucault's analysis is very insightful. His comparison of philology, biology, and political economy is but one of the very fruitful themes he explores in this context. Another is the manner in which he underlines how seeing and sight become the privileged mode of knowing. What is absent in his account is the pragmatic component, the prescriptive intent of political economy (and for that matter also that of the two other disciplines). Insofar as Foucault addresses the issue of the descriptive content of these disciplines, his account is impressive. Much is to be gained from heeding his advice about how we should think about representative schemes. Knowledge, myths, and language in general do not just fulfill the need human beings have to represent the world to themselves and organize their experiences in a meaningful way. We are not just archivists. We are actors. Foucault wrote as if modern philosophy only addresses ontological and epistemological questions: What is there? What do I know? How do I know it? However many philosophical problems attend the question "What can or ought I do?," it remains the fundamental human issue. Its history cannot be ignored even by those who are indifferent to ethical considerations, because that history shapes the history of ontology and epistemology as much as it is shaped by it in its turn. Each is an integral part of the other's structure. Political economy was shaped by its prescriptive and critical intent, one which it always had, whether one thinks of it as originating in the sixteenth, seventeenth, eighteenth, or nineteenth century and whatever one's conception of modernity.

88. This included very different writers, such as Denis Diderot (e.g., his posthumous *Supplément au Voyage de Bougainville*, in *Oeuvres*, ed. André Billy [Paris: Gallimard, 1951]) and Claude Adrien Helvétius (1715–1771; e.g., *De l'Esprit* [1758]).

89. For a discussion of the demographic debate in its own right, see Tomaselli's "Moral Philosophy and Population Questions in Eighteenth-Century Europe," in *Population and Resources* (see note 1 above). To render justice to the wealth of reflections from which Malthus's thought evolved, it is necessary to consider the work of many other prominent writers (see James, *Population Malthus*, note 1 above). Not least among them are Johann Peter Süssmilch (see *"L'Ordre divin": Aux origines de la démographie,* original translation with critical studies and commentaries, ed. Jacqueline Hecht, 3 vols. [Paris: Institut National d'Etudes Démographiques]); Victor Mirabeau (1715–1789; see Joseph Spengler, *French Predecessors of Malthus: A Study in Eighteenth-Century Wage and Population Theory* [Durham, N.C.: Duke University, 1942]); Diderot (see Arthur Wilson, *Diderot* [London and New York: Oxford University Press, 1972]); John Millar (1735–1801; see Michael Ignatieff's "John Millar and Individualism," in *Wealth and Virtue,* ed. Hont and Ignatieff, 317–343); Adam Ferguson (1723–1816; see *An Essay on the History of Civil Society 1767,* ed. Duncan Forbes [Edinburgh: Edinburgh University Press, 1966]); J.-A.-N. Condorcet (1743–1794; see Alexandre Koyré, "Condorcet," in *Études d'Histoire de la Pensée Philosophique* [Paris: A. Collin, 1961], 95–115); W. Godwin (1756–1836; see *Enquiry Concerning Political Justice,* ed. Isaac Kramnick [Harmondsworth: Penguin Books, 1976]); and the Encyclopedists (see Agnes Raymond, "Le problème de la population chez les Encyclopédistes," *Studies on Voltaire* 26, 1963: 1379–1388, and Anita Fage, "Les doctrines de la population des Encyclopédistes," *Population* 6 [1951]: 609–624).

ELEVEN

The Enlightenment Science
of Politics

Robert Wokler

Political science was manifestly not invented in the Enlightenment and may in fact be the oldest of all the human sciences. Indeed, so striking are the pioneering contributions to it of Plato's *Republic* and Aristotle's *Politics* that commentators have often wondered whether its apparent lack of progress since antiquity just indicates that politics is unamenable to scientific study. Such doubts about even its prospects of development are no doubt partly attributable to its own history—to the loss of that sense of community and the identification of human nature with political fulfillment, which had initially inspired it, leaving medieval Christian thinkers to devise principles appropriate merely to the earthly passage of sinful creatures, and modern secular writers to address the selfish relations of persons, divorced from the ideals by which they ought to live. At any rate, for much of its career since classical Greece, the science of politics has apparently sifted the base metal of human nature rather than refined the ore that at its birth gave it a special lustre.

Of course the discipline was at least reinvented by its modern exponents, for many of its now-familiar features may be traced to the Renaissance and Reformation, when the state and the network of its officers and subjects came to be identified within a framework of public law, rights, and sovereignty which we understand, above all, through the doctrines of Jean Bodin, Thomas Hobbes, Samuel Pufendorf, and their disciples.[1] Enlightenment political science crafted many of its principles and much of its terminology out of material inherited from these sixteenth- and seventeenth-century sources, and the manner in which it articulated and implemented this debt to earlier doctrines forms one of its chief features. In seeking both the patronage of rulers and the approbation of the public, its practitioners in the eighteenth century showed an overarching interest in the ways that their ideas, original and borrowed alike, could be broadcast and disseminated. Their campaigns drew philosophy and kingship together in a fashion that Plato and his humanist followers had often dreamt was necessary but hardly thought possible. Political thinkers of the Enlightenment served as ministers in the courts of Maria Theresa, Joseph II, Leopold II, George III, Gustav III, Frederik VI, Louis XVI, and other European rulers. Sometimes, as in the case of the abbé de Condillac and the Duke of Parma, they tutored their sons. Kings, in turn, corresponded with philosophers, sought their company and solicited their advice. Intellectuals presided over scientific and literary academies, penned treatises and occasional essays in defence of political science, and, through F. M. von Grimm's *Correspondance littéraire* and other journals, subscribed to a news service provided by luminaries of the great republic of letters to keep them informed of the latest fashion of ideas circulating in the cosmopolitan capitals of their day. Never before in human history had there been so many readers of books, journals, and periodicals. Encyclopedias, moral weeklies, and even daily newspapers became vehicles for the diffusion of all the human sciences, including politics. Literacy made the spread of enlightenment possible, promoting both doctrines and the reputations of their authors, granting to experts in all subjects a political presence and power in society they had not earlier enjoyed. Perhaps more than anything else, their command of publicity gave the Enlightenment projects of political scientists their most compelling force.[2]

Yet their doctrines also bore striking innovations of substance, in addition to mapping out new avenues of circulation. As the prestige of the Crown and its circles grew in countries such as England, it declined in others like France; each inspired novel defenses of its virtues and fresh critiques of its decay. Imperial power spread across the South Pacific, where it gave rise to perhaps the fiercest attack against colonialism on the part of enlightened thinkers. Out of the New World of America was born the first republic of the modern era, with a federal constitution that articulated the most progressive political science of the day, enshrining civil rights and liberties along lines to which other states would soon aspire, while at the same time granting authority and impetus to an institution of slavery already largely defunct in the Old World. From the violent overthrow of both monarchy and aristocracy in France would be shaped doctrines of popular democracy and the rights of man which, to their detractors, seemed to replace one form of absolutism with another that was worse still. Insofar as they were embraced in the collapse of the ancien régime and in the outbreak of the French Revolution, the eighteenth-century sciences of politics mark the beginning of a new epoch in human history and not just a reflection of the earlier rise of the modern state. Much of the terminology of political life, as well as of the human sciences, was invented then—*perfectibility, ideology, social science, democrat, aristocrat,* and *revolutionary,* for instance, in addition, of course, to *human science* itself.[3] Older expressions, such as the *general will,* acquired a new currency and significance. By the early nineteenth century, emanating from the struggles bred by the French Revolution, would appear *liberalism, socialism,* and their cognates, together with the movements whose aspirations these newly invented words evoked. Prior to the Enlightenment and its apparent repercussions, the theory and practice of politics had never been so closely linked.

Two main lines of enquiry, largely distinct but occasionally connected even within the same works, were pursued by eighteenth-century political scientists—on the one hand, the theoretical study of the principles of legislation, authority, and the structure of government; on the other, the analysis of political behavior and development, including the forces that drive individuals to personal domination or collective action, and societies to historical change. This crude dichotomy might appear designed to differentiate normative from descriptive doctrines, but that is not my purpose, since such contrasts, although expressed by Rousseau, Kant, and others, and associated perhaps above all with Hume's account of the unwarranted derivations of "ought" from "is,"[4] are not the most conspicuous feature of Enlightenment political thought. When the framers of the American Declaration of Independence proclaimed that all political connection between them and Great Britain "is and ought to be dissolved" because British tyranny had abused the inalienable rights of men who were created equal, they did not pause to wonder at the logic of their derivation of what should be from what actually was the case. The point I have in mind is the difference not so much between a science of values and a science of facts as between an overarching political science of rulers and ruling, on the one hand, and an underlying science of the motivations of the ruled, on the other. From the first category have emerged the public policy studies and comparative analysis of government which today lie at the heart of the discipline of political science as it has come to be understood and practiced. From the second have arisen the subjects of political sociology and the politics of development. These comments need to be elaborated, illustrated, and explained.

If the mainly seventeenth-century revolution in science helped to produce Europe's transformation of commerce and industry a century later, its political admirers never intended to emulate its successful overthrow of scholasticism by toppling the state. On the contrary, throughout much of the eighteenth century, and particularly from the early 1750s, they invoked principles of justice and legitimacy in the name of a political science that they hoped might help to bring order out of chaos and avert political upheavals generated by the profligacy and corruption of contemporary regimes. In his impassioned account of the demise of the age of chivalry, Burke was later to decry the Encyclopedists and other political men of letters for igniting the spark of sedition which had enflamed and then laid waste the whole of France. His *Reflections* on the French Revolution of 1790, completed more than two years before the outbreak of the Terror, would thus come to appear a prescient diagnosis of how the sublime abstractions of Enlightenment political science had uncoiled to produce the deadly desecration of that gentle society. But if this work was to prove one of the most significant of all interpretations of the connection between theory and practice, it did injustice to the political doctrines of the Enlightenment. As early as 1762, in a passage of *Emile*, Rousseau—whom Burke was to denounce as the "insane Socrates of the National Assembly"—had remarked upon the impending disaster. "We are approaching a state of crisis and a century of revolutions," he had claimed. "The great monarchies of Europe will not survive much longer."[5] Many other commentators of this period, among them d'Alembert and Voltaire, and later Arthur Young, were to make much the same point. Despite Burke's wholesale condemnation, the diverse policies put forward by eighteenth-century political theorists had been designed to stave off rather than promote revolution, to safeguard and not subvert authority, or, rather, through drastic reform to thwart an uprising that would otherwise explode the governments of their day. Not one of the major political thinkers of the Enlightenment advocated revolution before 1789, whatever debt their more incendiary disciplines later professed to owe to them, and whatever might in fact have been the practical implications of their doctrines.[6] In addressing themselves, as did Hume, to the science of human nature, and in proffering treatments of the subject with such titles as the Marquis de Mirabeau's *La Science ou les droits et les devoirs de l'homme*, or Adam Ferguson's *Principles of Moral and Political Science*, or Gaetano Filangieri's *La scienza della legislazione*, they meant no more nor less than to devise a set of rules for the proper management of human affairs in the light of the known tendencies of human nature, and they subscribed to doctrines of the correspondence of one to the other which seemed to them conducive to the maintenance of political and social harmony.

Among such eighteenth-century doctrines, the one which would eventually come to exercise the widest and most durable influence was utilitarianism, whose leading exponents in the period were Claude Adrien Helvétius, Cesare Beccaria, Jeremy Bentham, and, in many respects, Francis Hutcheson, Voltaire, and Hume. Utilitarians argued that pain and pleasure constituted the sole measure of what was right and wrong for each individual, and that governments should encourage the largest possible amount of happiness and least pain among their subjects—in the phrase, "the greatest happiness of the greatest number," probably inspired by

Leibniz, first employed in English by Hutcheson in his *Inquiry into the original of our ideas of beauty and virtue* of 1725 and later brought to Bentham's notice by way of Beccaria's *Dei delitti e delle pene* of 1764—thus promoting public welfare and utility overall. Because of their hostility to institutions and practices that thwarted the realization of their programs, most utilitarians were thus opposed to those estates, privileged classes and clerical orders, or customary laws and precedents that abounded in Christian and feudal Europe. In the Enlightenment, it was mainly the defects of criminal justice that attracted their notice, including arbitrary arrest or *lettres de cachet*, torture, and civil retribution for moral crime, condemned in each case on what might be termed the negative principle of utility, prescribing that government was most efficient when it merely deterred harm and caused least harm itself. Voltaire's lifelong attack upon religious bigotry and his defence of toleration exercised perhaps their greatest impact upon contemporary public opinion in just this field. But the rhetoric and substance of the utilitarians' campaigns for rational, uniform, and impartial codes of law were also to bear fruit in the civil and constitutional programs of reform instituted by a number of European monarchs in the late eighteenth century and by the French revolutionaries, even before their still greater triumphs of the nineteenth century.[7]

A similar attempt to fuse the theory and practice of politics in a science of legislation for the public welfare inspired the physiocratic philosophy of such figures as François Quesnay, the Marquis de Mirabeau, P.-P. Le Mercier de la Rivière, and P.-S. Dupont de Nemours, of whom the first, a surgeon by training and later physician to Louis XV, was mentor to the others. Like the utilitarians, the physiocrats held that political administration should be founded on scientific principles, which they believed could elucidate the natural laws of social relations, and they also regarded Christian dogma and its pastors as uniquely unsuited to the secular management of public affairs. In their focus upon the rational organization of policy, however, they dealt more with commerce, trade, and economics in general than with criminal law. They promoted the public instruction of every social class, including the peasantry, which often resisted their programs of a free market in grain. They advocated currency reform, the elimination of tariff barriers to trade and industry, and, almost above all else, the rational planning of agricultural production. While hostile to the militarist politics of some European regimes, they were generally well disposed to monarchy, provided its rule was made efficient. They believed constitutional principles were of less consequence than the manner in which laws were administered, and Le Mercier de la Rivière even endorsed what he termed "legal despotism" to encapsulate their concern with actual policy and their disregard for the mere form of government.[8]

In Austria and Germany, J. von Sonnenfels, J. H. G. von Justi, J. J. Moser,

and other publicists of the doctrine of cameralism pressed for more benevolent statesmanship by monarchs well-informed of the needs of their
subjects and by ministers able to implement standardized policies throughout their kingdoms or domains, whose political systems they defined in
terms of the modern territorial state. They adhered, as Sonnenfels remarked, to the principle that the chief foundation of government was "the
promotion of general happiness," and they did much to encourage the
growth of bureaucracy in late eighteenth-century Europe. Less liberal and
more paternalist than the utilitarians or physiocrats, cameralists nonetheless exercised a greater influence in their own day upon those regimes in
which they occasionally held office. In central European universities they
established the predominant form and syllabus of the political sciences—
the *Staatswissenschaften*—as instructed in the German-speaking world for
much of the eighteenth century, although partly on account of the absence
of contemporary translations of their writings, they had scant influence in
France, Italy, or Great Britain. In the nineteenth century, however, through
the diffusion of their principles in other countries, they helped foster the
growing belief of radical reformers, above all Saint-Simon and then later
Marx, that in an enlightened age all varieties of oppressive political control over men and women would be supplanted by the rational administration or supervision of things.[9]

The links between each of these three doctrines and the actual practice
of politics, and especially monarchical rule, in the eighteenth century are,
of course, indirect, complex, and obscure. But in the great ideological
brew that Diderot himself termed "enlightened despotism" in one of his
commentaries on Russia, and which would come to bear that generic name
in the course of the next century, such theoretical potions were important
constituents. The policies of Frederick II of Prussia, Catherine II of Russia,
and Joseph II of Austria were no doubt at least as much the offspring of
the centralizing autocratic regimes that preceded them in each case as of
philosophical principles borrowed from Enlightenment political science.
Most of the leading thinkers of the age characteristically believed "despotism" to mean absolute and arbitrary rule, as the chevalier de Jaucourt defined it in his article on the subject in the *Encyclopédie*, and few were de-
luded by the unholy alliances formed between Voltaire and Frederick, or
between Diderot and Catherine, into supposing they had witnessed any
real marriage of theory and practice. Nevertheless, Frederick's prohibition
of torture, Joseph's abolition of serfdom, and Catherine's zealous commitment to the improvement of Russian culture on a Western pattern, coupled
with the constitutional reforms and legal codes introduced by these and
other rulers, were distilled through and impregnated with the flavor of utilitarianism, physiocracy, and cameralism.[10] After the French Revolution, simi-

lar doctrines were to be embraced once more, and to take new shape, in the ideologies and movements of both Philosophic Radicalism and Saint-Simonian socialism.

Eighteenth-century proponents of such ideas generally believed that monarchy was the most rational and potentially enlightened form of government because it was the least likely to pursue any exclusive and sectarian ambitions as if they formed the public interest. But there were other political thinkers of the period who, even while they endorsed the supreme moral authority of kings, were more concerned to establish the legitimate foundations of monarchy out of the consent of the governed, that is, citizens who willingly made themselves subject to it. The great defenders of royal absolutism by divine right, who had come to the rescue of beleaguered monarchies in the Reformation and Counter-Reformation of the late–sixteenth century, found their services much less in demand in the age of Enlightenment. By the eighteenth century, it had become intellectually fashionable to see royal power as accountable to the will of the people, at least through their delegates. This doctrine, perhaps associated above all with Locke's notion of consent, had after all triumphed in England's Glorious Revolution of 1688, which apparently led to Parliament's designation of a new king and queen of England upon their throne. It had lain at the very heart of social contract theory, moreover, before Rousseau appropriated it for a different purpose. Grotius, Hobbes, Pufendorf, and Locke, together with their disciples, each in different ways drew monarchical conclusions out of a popular compact of association. They all found royal and even hereditary power legitimate only insofar as it was created by collective choice.

No great leap from such assumptions was required for still other political thinkers of the Enlightenment to assert that the beneficiaries of wise legislation should do rather more than just authorize it by their consent, either express or tacit; they should also, it was claimed, be its agents. Diderot, the Baron d'Holbach, and Kant, among others, argued that for the state to serve the needs of its subjects it must not only act on their behalf but ensure that their voices be heard, largely through representative assemblies. Occasionally, such figures invoked a property qualification to differentiate fully active from merely passive citizenship—a thesis that, elaborated by the abbé Sieyès and promulgated in the French Constitution of 1791, came to form a doctrinal barrier to the political self-expression of the *sans-culottes* during the Revolution. Yet the distinction between active and passive citizenship was more generally upheld in the Enlightenment for precisely the opposite reason: not in order to exclude the masses from state control but to ensure that legislators had earned sufficient means to be the masters of their own wills, so that ownership of land or other property might be a measure of independence and public spirit. Eighteenth-century defences of representative government were essentially doctrines in favor of the political exercise of liberty against paternalist rule, as supported by the advocates of enlightened despotism. Kant in particular stressed the importance of this view of liberty. "No one can compel me to be happy in accordance with his conception of the welfare of others," he insisted in an essay on the subject of theory and practice, and he extended his account of representation for the purpose of protecting individual freedom to international assemblies designed to preserve the independence of states, thereby pursuing an approach to world peace which had already been anticipated earlier in the eighteenth century in the *Projet pour rendre la paix perpétuelle en Europe*, dating from 1713, of the abbé de Saint-Pierre.[11]

The leading Enlightenment advocate of popular participation, however, was Rousseau, and his view of liberty, though it greatly influenced Kant's perspective, precluded legislative representation altogether. Rousseau insisted that the only legitimate form of sovereignty was self-rule, or what might be termed direct democracy, and he differed from most other thinkers of his day in condemning English parliamentary practice, whereby electors did not so much depute their authority as relinquish their freedom. Citizens must serve the state by their actual participation in its affairs and not with their purses, he contended, and in adopting a proposition put forward earlier by Locke and Jean Barbeyrac, he decried Grotius's, Hobbes's, and Pufendorf's accounts of the voluntary subjection of a people to their king. The idea of representation was a corrupt modern fabrication, he argued in his *Contrat social* of 1762, unknown before the establishment of feudal government and incompatible with freedom. Inspired by images of ancient Sparta and the Roman Republic, he believed, like Machiavelli, Harrington, and their disciples in Italy, England, and later America, that citizens should exercise vigilance to protect their liberty from appropriation by their own public officials, since sovereign authority could never be legitimately transferred. From a mainly seventeenth-century tradition of theological discourse, in which it had denoted the spiritual bond of a community of believers, he adopted the expression "general will" to mean the concerted voice of independent citizens, thereby granting it a new significance in political science, which has also come to differentiate his doctrine from the ideas of most liberal thinkers after him. As the measure of a state's solidarity, the general will must be distinguished from the will of all, which was Rousseau's phrase for the sum of the interests of particular factions, so that the true freedom or autonomy of citizens—their moral and political liberty—was to be understood only in terms of shared goals and joint action.[12]

Still other Enlightenment thinkers stressed the importance of economic equality rather than political liberty as the fundamental goal to which states should aspire. Rousseau had asserted that there was an unbreakable bond between the two, and he attributed the lack of liberty in most states to the inegalitarian distribution of property which had marked their origin and whose preservation remained the dominant function of their government now. But he also recognized that some policies might encourage equality to the detriment of liberty, and he believed that legislation should seek to remedy only those inequalities of wealth which tended to make the majority of individuals dependent on the will of the few. Nowhere did he encourage a uniform distribution for all persons, and nowhere did he advocate the collective ownership of property as a matter of public interest. Enlightenment socialists such as Dom L.-M. Deschamps, Morelly, and G. B. de Mably, however, characteristically argued that the state should regulate property so as to ensure that no one enjoyed more than the necessities of life. They contended that, in order to overcome the vices of avarice and indolence, there must be public authorities to organize the allocation of goods and services, to enforce strict sumptuary laws, and, in some cases—so as to foster the right frame of mind in the young—to control education. Morelly in particular anticipated the famous dictum of Marx, "From each according to his ability, to each according to his needs," and in the course of the French Revolution such figures as Gracchus Babeuf and Sylvain Maréchal proclaimed that true equality could only be achieved if the iniquitous institution of private property were abolished altogether.[13]

Other thinkers stressed the importance of liberty at the expense of equality, along lines almost diametrically opposed to those pursued by such early socialists. Turgot maintained that the unequal distribution of property everywhere was as desirable as it was inevitable, since otherwise there would be no incentive for enterprising individuals to cultivate the surplus yield from their land, upon which the creation of wealth ultimately depended. The Italians Antonio Genovesi and Giuseppe Palmieri each maintained that the fundamental task of the state was not to impose the heavy hand of equality upon all subjects, but rather to lay the delicate foundations for the exercise of individual liberty and initiative, which alone could give their country a prospect of development out of its state of economic backwardness and stagnation. In England and Scotland, Bernard Mandeville, Joseph Addison, and Adam Smith asserted that the public interest was best achieved by encouraging each individual to pursue his own separate gain in competition with others. This, they believed, would naturally result in common benefit for all, whereas conversely there was little to be expected, and much to be feared, from a concentration of powers designed to promote the general welfare. Smith in particular argued that governments should be "discharged from . . . the duty of superintending the industry of private people," since with the elimination of tariffs, entails, duties, and monopolies, persons would exercise their liberty to their own best advantage, which, in turn, would lead to the production of commodities and distribution of resources most needed by everyone. He thus agreed with those physiocrats who had proclaimed *Laissez faire, laissez aller,* and, although Smith himself expressed doubts about the social implications of such policies, it was ideas of this sort that gave rise to the principles of free market enterprise so central to nineteenth- and twentieth-century liberalism. Where a commitment to solidarity informs Rousseau's vision of the state, a principle of noninterference may be said to lie at the heart of Smith's. Throughout his ethics and philosophy of law, no less than in his political thought, he adopted the stance of an impartial spectator whose task was not to prescribe rules but to test the plausibility of already prevalent moral judgments. His natural jurisprudence was, roughly speaking, the science of such human conduct as could be approved by all persons, if they were properly informed.[14]

Yet quite another distinct and centrally important perspective in Enlightenment political science was the so-called doctrine of the separation or division of powers elaborated by Montesquieu. Like Smith and other liberals, Montesquieu opposed the institution of absolute power, even for the sake of facilitating egalitarian ends. In place of it he put the case for political liberty, which he identified far more closely than natural liberty with responsibility, obligation, and law. For Montesquieu, as he explained in the eleventh book of his *De l'esprit des lois* of 1748, it was a triumph of the English constitution that it had promoted such liberty more than any other nation, through its differentiation of legislative from executive power, with the additional distinct influence of another factor, which he called the power of judgment. His emphasis upon the role of this third power was novel, significantly different from the views of Aristotle, Locke, or Viscount Bolingbroke, to which his doctrine of the separation of powers is often compared, but, having introduced it, Montesquieu in fact elaborated his account of the strength of English government rather more in terms of its mixed or balanced constitution, embracing elements of monarchy, aristocracy, and democracy, as well as two distinct chambers in its parliament, each possessing the power to reject legislation, while connected to an executive power in such a way that all the branches of government were required to act together. Such claims about England's constitution were in fact less original than his brief comments about the distinctive power of judgment, for they recapitulated arguments that could indeed be traced to Aristotle and, with respect to England, had been frequently made before, not least by Hume in his essay "That politics may be reduced to a science" of 1742, in which he too praised "an hereditary prince, a nobility without vassals, and a people voting by their representatives." Hume, that is, shared, and indeed had conceived independently, the same respect for the rule of law and the excellence of an English constitution whose mixed and balanced nature protected liberty best. But it was Montesquieu's ideas about legislative, executive, and judicial powers which were to exercise the greatest influence upon the formation of the Constitution of the United States of America of 1787, and its defense by Alexander Hamilton and James Madison in their *Federalist Papers*.[15] A revolution originally fought in the name of English liberty and not against it was to give institutional prominence to a fleeting idea of the separation of powers, which the Founding Fathers of America plucked from a Frenchman's fulsome tribute to the merits of an English system of government they otherwise deemed inappropriate to their needs.[16]

Montesquieu was, in his day, regarded as the most important of all eighteenth-century political and social thinkers, and his European admirers drew much inspiration from further aspects of his doctrine—his theory of the influence of climate upon human character, for instance, and his general account of the spirit of the laws. But these and other features of his philosophy form part of the science of political behavior, that is, of the underlying motivations and conduct of people in pursuit of power and as subjects of government, to which I turn next. My remarks in the preceding paragraphs have been addressed to what I earlier called the overarching political science of rulers and ruling. That science of legislation for the public welfare took multifarious forms throughout the period, and almost all the leading ideologies of the post French Revolutionary era, together with many of the themes of public policy studies in the contemporary world, may be traced to these varieties of political theory and practice in the Enlightenment.

In rejecting both the classical conception of man's political nature and the Christian idea of original sin, some of the principal theorists of the eighteenth century subscribed instead to the view that civil society had been manufactured by those persons who had entered into it to suit their aims. The state was thus neither natural to man nor imposed by God; it was artificial and of human design alone. Various images of the social contract were elaborated by proponents of this view, for this notion expressed it in perhaps its most richly developed form, stipulating as it did that governments were originally established by acts of will—by the consent of persons who, before there were any governments, must have lived in a mere state of nature. That, indeed, is essentially what is meant by the expression "state of nature" in most of its permutations; it is the condition of uncivilized, masterless men and women. But this idea of a social contract as framed by individuals in a pre-political state, as well as winning many adherents in the Enlightenment, also attracted objections and criticism. Rousseau, who passionately subscribed to it himself, nevertheless challenged to all its earlier constructions with which he was familiar, since they required that persons in their original condition should already possess the attributes that only membership of civil society could bring to them. His state of nature, unlike the mainly seventeenth-century versions of Grotius, Hobbes, Pufendorf, and Locke which he condemned, was a primitive and unreflective, almost animal, state of savagery, unpopulated by makers of promises and covenants. Hume, Smith, Burke, Bentham, and others rejected outright all ideas of the state of nature and the social contract, partly on the grounds that consent and the willful alienation of liberty formed an implausible foundation for the establishment of governments and the maintenance of authority within them, and partly because they thought it absurd that political philosophers should have imagined that there could ever have been a time when mankind lived in a state of solitude and license. Even if politics is not self-evidently natural to the human race, they claimed, society must be. It would be more sensible to contend that government had originally been established by force, later tempered by long obedience; more realistic to suppose that habit and utility made persons compliant to law, than consent.[17] By the end of the eighteenth century, the elaboration of such objections put speculative social contract theory under a strain from which it never really recovered—at least not until very recent times, when it has been resuscitated, mainly in America, in a new form and for different purposes.[18]

But if its supposition of the rational creation of authority by way of a transfer of natural rights came to seem flawed, it contained at least one feature that carried greater conviction, even among critics whose doctrines were couched in different terms. It embraced, that is, a theory of the promptings of human nature which explained why persons might be motivated to obey the rule of law. Political thinkers of all denominations in the Enlightenment, and not just advocates of the social contract, were anxious to identify those attributes of mankind's character which made the maintenance of civil society possible. Was it, as Locke contended, because our species was marked by a spirit of goodwill and mutual assistance? Was it, as Smith believed, because of our propensity to truck and barter? Was it, as Burke suggested, because man is fundamentally a religious animal? One of the major achievements of social contract theory was to put forward a case for communal relations based upon the pursuit of self-interest alone. In the absence of both the ancient Greek notion of man's political nature and the Christian idea of divinely appointed government, most eighteenth-century commentators could not perceive any communal spirit among individuals which might express either their own nature or the will of God. Enlightenment theorists of the social contract seemed to offer an explanation of how bonds of association might be accepted by persons who were not originally inclined toward collective action or social solidarity. Egoism and selfishness alone, they argued, could account for political union. Although unimpressed by much of the vocabulary of social contract theory and its concomitant state of nature, other political scientists of the period found themselves equally drawn to the idea of self-interest as the mainspring of government. The establishment of community relations out of need or interest rather than desire or inclination forms one of the central and most widespread themes of eighteenth-century political theory in all its denominations.[19]

Enlightenment conceptions of natural selfishness owe an extraordinary debt to the philosophy of Hobbes, whose social compact doctrine had been built round propositions about the native fears and appetites of human beings. The agreement of persons to live in peace with one another under an absolute sovereign, he had asserted, was largely inspired by their fear of violent death and their desire for commodious living, since, as he put it, they found no pleasure but only grief in keeping company. Most seventeenth- and eighteenth-century thinkers who came after him were outspokenly critical of Hobbes's conception of the state of nature as a state of war, but many were persuaded by Pufendorf's essentially reformulated version of the same doctrine in his *De jure naturae et gentium* of 1672. Mankind's natural selfishness was not so much conducive to aggression as to timidity, claimed Pufendorf. In their original state, our ancestors would have been weak and apprehensive, at risk from attack both from other persons and other creatures. In order to overcome their feebleness they would have had to join together, their prospects of survival enhanced by cooperation. This was, as has been noted in another chapter,[20] the doctrine of natural sociability or *socialitas*, by which Pufendorf drew a positive conclusion—that is, community—from a negative source, selfishness. Accepting with Hobbes that human appetites were infinite, Pufendorf believed that as certain needs and desires were satisfied, their fulfillment generated further needs and desires, which could only be met by new forms of social organization and communal life. Whereas Hobbes had portrayed the passage from the state of nature to the commonwealth as one great constitutional leap of the imagination, Pufendorf, by contrast, proceeding from similar premises, concluded that civil society must have passed through different stages of growing complexity and refinement. In his doctrine of that more gradual transformation of mankind from its initial barbarism lies the seeds of the Enlightenment's conjectural history of the evolutionary stages of civilization. In the hands of Turgot, Smith, and others, it was to become a predominantly economic theory of social development, in which each successive epoch could be understood as shaped round a particular mode of sustenance—hunting, shepherding, agriculture, and commerce, in turn—through which the increasing population of the world progressively matured. Yet we should be mistaken to regard this doctrine as a theory of economic or material forces. The philosophy of Pufendorf and his disciples remained one of human design and

manufacture, and even the causes of the wealth of nations—which Smith
investigated in what was subsequently to prove perhaps the most influential of all Enlightenment contributions to human science—did not operate independently of men's wills. It was a theory of how scattered individuals might have elected to cooperate, each for his or her particular gain,
thereby producing mutual benefit for all. In the sense that this still remained a theory of the way in which the binding agreements that form
civil society might have been pursued, it formed a part of its authors'
wider political doctrines, the underpinning and scaffolding of their science of legislation.[21]

By adopting a Hobbesian perspective on human nature as modified by
Pufendorf, it was thus possible for Enlightenment proponents of this doctrine to speculate upon civilization's development toward commercial society, which in the next century would be described as the age of capitalism. If the Enlightenment's most formidable proponent of that doctrine
was Smith, its fiercest critic was Rousseau, who perceived much the same
scenario as humanity's long day's journey into night. Within civil society,
men and women live, as it were, outside themselves, he argued in his *Discours sur l'inégalité* of 1755, and to that extent their nature has been deformed and debased. In seeking their fulfillment in commerce, they become enthralled by passions of which savages are free. The term *finance,*
no less than the word *representation,* is a modern invention, Rousseau claims
in the *Contrat social.*[22] In the ancient world, public revenue was made up
not of currency but produce, with services rendered in person rather than
through money, and with citizens flying to the assemblies, drawn by an attachment to the common good more absorbing than the pursuit of private gain. Such assertions about mankind's progressive loss of freedom in
the course of civilization lie at the heart of Rousseau's political philosophy,
even though it too was often couched in the language of social contract
theory, including a pre-political natural state. The compact that gave force
to civil society, as he conceived it, was a fraud, perpetrated by the rich
against the poor, who were traduced into accepting the ostensibly impartial rule of law, which then armed those whom it benefited against those
they had dispossessed. Civilization was a yoke of despotism, wrapped round
its victims like a mantle of justice, authorized by their own consent.

This inversion of the predominant Enlightenment conception of the
social contract as the measure of mankind's rise was at least partly inspired
by Rousseau's rejection of the central premise of that tradition—in effect,
that civil society was the rational product of its members' wills. It was wrong
to suppose that man makes the state, for, on the contrary, it is the state
which makes man, he observed—persons everywhere assuming the form
cast upon them by their governments. So far from men's moral principles
determining their politics, it was their political institutions which shaped

their morality—a proposition to which Plato and Aristotle could also have subscribed, except that Rousseau's main point was to uncover the sinister source of mankind's corruption rather than the uplifting goal of its moral destiny. With respect to uncultivated human nature, he was adamant that it possessed none of the traits and tendencies that earlier social contract thinkers had imagined necessary for the establishment of political association. Savage men and women, he thought, were closer to animals than to civilized persons, differing from other creatures by virtue not of attributes they could only have acquired in society, but of their capacities—their freedom to respond to the promptings of nature in a variety of ways, and their *perfectibility*, a term Rousseau invented in his *Discours sur l'inégalité*, meaning something like moral plasticity or educability, such as had enabled our forebears to make cumulative changes from one generation to the next, thereby facilitating their passage out of the state of nature into society.[23]

This conception of perfectibility may seem akin to Hobbes's and Pufendorf's idea of the infinitude of human appetites, but it was put forward for a different purpose, to show that our desires within and for civil society had not been naturally generated, and that in the continual effort to satisfy them our condition had in fact worsened. Joined to the notion that human nature is shaped by politics, moreover, perfectibility might also mean that rightly constituted government could promote virtue, just as pernicious government had encouraged vice. Although Rousseau himself looked only with nostalgia to the partly mythical past of mainly Sparta and Rome, some of his followers after the outbreak of the Revolution adopted the idea to justify a comprehensive reconstruction of the French state, which they were convinced would give rise to new patterns of truly communitarian behavior. Even before 1789, a number of utopian thinkers—Deschamps in his *Vrai système* and L. S. Mercier in his *L'An 2440* among them—had drawn blueprints of imaginary and exotic worlds, dedicated to the spirit of fraternity. Later, during and following the campaigns for national regeneration leading to the establishment of the First French Republic, E.-L. Boullée, F.-L. Aubry, and others mapped out the blueprint of a visionary new city named Liberty, with its monuments to the Revolution and temples of Equality.[24] The frequently remodeled architecture of Paris in particular—that most publicly oriented of all modern capitals—has often borne the stamp of changing fashions in political philosophy. But it was above all Rousseau's own uncompromising commitment to popular sovereignty which fired the imagination of utopian thinkers and politicians alike, both under the Jacobins and for a time even after their overthrow. No figure of the Enlightenment was then more venerated and eulogized than "le bon Jean-Jacques." Through their attachment to a new simplicity of manners, dress, and speech, through their civic enthusiasm kindled as a substitute for priestly theology, in their hymns, festivals, and Cult of the Supreme Being, above all as manifested in the political career of the Incorruptible Robespierre, champion of the poorer classes and herald and guardian of the Republic of Virtue, Rousseau's worshipful admirers endowed his doctrines with the force and trappings of a popular doctrine whose moment of historical realization had arrived. It was largely because of such associations that the real legacy of Rousseauism was later held to be the sour fruit propagated by the policies of the Committee of Public Safety and the Reign of Terror under its dictatorship.[25]

In their attachment to the perfectibility of mankind, Enlightenment political thinkers did not always imagine such rapid and comprehensive metamorphosis. Some commentators warmed instead to the more gradual but perhaps also more durable prospects of reform that might be achieved by a public-spirited system of education. In elaborating an empiricist psychology to the effect that the mind alters with each new impression and each change in its environment, Helvétius contended that every person is no more than the product of his or her own upbringing. As distinct from Rousseau, who in *Emile* had propounded a system of negative education designed to free children from their dependence on others so that they might learn by their own experience, he put the case, especially in his posthumously published *De l'homme* of 1773, for a program of rigorous instruction, so as to enlighten pupils in the ways of social utility and fire their enthusiasm for the community's interest, through which their self-love would be best fulfilled. "L'éducation peut tout," he declared, postulating that human nature could be utterly reshaped and retrained. Such notions were not likely to endear his philosophy to orthodox Christians, who indeed believed human nature to be more bleak and virtue more divine in inspiration than were allowed by his mundane optimism. Helvétius's chief work, *De l'esprit*, published in 1758, had already provoked consternation in theological circles, for although his doctrines were not predominantly addressed to questions of Christian dogma, they were rightly understood by his interpreters, Jansenists foremost among them, to be materialist denials of the spirituality of the soul and of the central place of religious teaching as the foundation of morality. No other work of the Enlightenment was to suffer greater censure from ecclesiastical and civil authorities alike than *De l'esprit*. His near contemporary, the Baron d'Holbach, himself a materialist convinced that human conduct could be modified by manipulating its external causes, attacked Christianity more directly for the ignorance and mental torpor that it fostered and upon which it fed, allowing just the same that religious belief had also often excited strong feelings—that is, of prejudice, bigotry, intolerance, and persecution.[26]

The supposed conflict between progressive education and backward theology of course lies at the heart of the Enlightenment's crusade against the forces of darkness in general, insofar as its whole campaign was dedicated to lifting men's and women's veil of ignorance, superstition, and irrationalism shrouded by their religious doctrines. It was in reason's light that eighteenth-century political thinkers sought to dispel the shadows in which their adversaries lurked. Voltaire, d'Alembert, Condorcet, and many others joined Helvétius and d'Holbach in their perception of human history as one great struggle between the friends and enemies of enlightenment—between nefarious tyrants, priests, and barbarians, on the one hand, and civilized, educated, and thus liberated men of science and letters, on the other. In promoting their multifarious schemes of popular instruction, they sought to overcome mankind's credulous enthrallment to the presbyters of supernatural powers which prevented congregations of the faithfully blind from acquiring a worldly knowledge of the good and a desire to practise it.[27] Such anticlericalism manifestly fanned hostility to the church, culminating, in the course of the Revolution, in the confiscation of its property and the civil constitution of the clergy.

But the champions of Enlightenment were not always so intolerant of religious faith. Many agreed with Voltaire that so long as minorities and dissenters were protected, governments could usefully disregard their archaic canons and eccentric rituals. Better still, there should be numerous religions, all of them minorities. And while this idea of toleration may perhaps have been the leading principle of progressive thinkers throughout the period as a whole, it was embraced by others who also perceived certain positive aspects in religious zealotry. Foremost among such figures was Rousseau, who in the *Contrat social* and elsewhere elaborated the tenets of a civil religion which would unite devotion to God with political service, though he rejected the Christianity of the Gospels as an otherworldly religion, which made the state susceptible to tyranny. In that conception of a fraternal rather than intolerant faith, Rousseau showed his never less than ardent admiration for the *Discourses* of Machiavelli.

Montesquieu sometimes adopted a similar perspective, but more often he commented on the appropriateness of different religions to diverse circumstances—Islam being more suited to Asians, he supposed, and Christianity to Europeans, while, within Europe, Catholicism was better disposed to monarchy, and the Protestant faith to republicanism. Assertions of this sort about the correspondence between moral beliefs and political institutions form the most important and influential feature of his whole social philosophy. More than any other Enlightenment thinker, Montesquieu turned his attention to the underlying sources and internal causes that produced particular forms of government and constrained legislative programs within them. In his account of Rome's rise and fall in his *Considérations sur les causes du grandeur des romains* of 1734, and even more in his subsequent *De l'esprit des lois*, he approached his subject in the manner he believed characteristic of the nonhuman sciences of his day—that is, by seeking to identify the causes, trends, and forces that gave men's and women's conduct its momentum and direction. Laws, he claimed, were the necessary relations that derive from the nature of things, controlling the affairs of persons, much as other laws accounted for the revolution of the planets or the growth of organic matter. No major eighteenth-century theorist was less interested in the distinction between empirical facts and moral values;[28] on the contrary, Montesquieu was mainly concerned to explain values by reference to facts, connecting physical causes, such as climate, to moral causes, such as religion and manners, and then moral causes in turn to government and legislation. Thus each type of government, he remarked, has its underlying principle—for republics, virtue; for monarchy, honor; and for despotism, fear—with the corruption of government always arising from the corruption of its principle. Every society is rooted in the dispositions of the people who comprise it, their *esprit général* or general spirit setting limits to what may be enacted as law, which their rulers forget at their peril.[29]

Such propositions were to exercise the profoundest influence on Enlightenment political and social thought in the late eighteenth century. Adam Ferguson, John Millar, and many other philosophers of the Scottish Enlightenment were captivated by Montesquieu's conception of the spirit of the laws and the need to accommodate particular forms of government to suit the established customs, manners, and mores of distinct peoples. Rousseau devoted the third book of his *Contrat social* to similar ideas, which in the Revolution were to inspire conservative readings of his doctrines that were no less authoritative than the Jacobin tributes to his utopian radicalism. Under the Directory and then the Consulate, following the fall of Robespierre, a science of society such as Montesquieu had articulated was expounded in more physiological terminology, now concerned with the hygiene and metabolism of the body politic, perceived as having been upset by the frenzy of political activity that had marked the early Revolutionary period.[30] But this language was just Montesquieu's approach—his focus on regulative mechanisms and the *esprit général* of a society—in a new idiom. In the light of what was deemed their failure under the First Republic and the Jacobins, the politically ambitious eighteenth-century sciences of government and legislation began to succumb to a differently conceived, more preservative, deep structural, social science of administration.[31]

NOTES

1. Particularly notable treatments of these themes in early modern political thought can be found in J. H. Burns and Mark Goldie, eds., *The Cambridge History of Political Thought: 1450–1700* (Cambridge: Cambridge University Press, 1991);

Nannerl Keohane, *Philosophy and the State in France: The Renaissance to the Enlightenment* (Princeton, N.J.: Princeton University Press, 1980); and Quentin Skinner, *The Foundations of Modern Political Thought*, 2 vols. (Cambridge: Cambridge University Press, 1978).

2. See Matthew S. Anderson, *Europe in the Eighteenth Century, 1713–1783*, 3d ed. (London: Longman, 1987); Roger Chartier, *Lectures et lecteurs dans la France d'Ancien Régime* (Paris: Editions du Seuil, 1987); Maurice Cranston, *Philosophers and Pamphleteers: Political Theorists of the Enlightenment* (Oxford: Oxford University Press, 1986); Robert Darnton, *The Literary Underground of the Old Regime* (Cambridge, Mass.: Harvard University Press, 1982); and Harry C. Payne, *The Philosophes and the People* (New Haven, Conn.: Yale University Press, 1976).

3. It is one of the central propositions of Michel Foucault's *Les Mots et les choses* (Paris: Gallimard, 1966) that man as a subject of science was invented around the end of the eighteenth century (see especially chaps. 8 and 10). His account of an epistemic transformation of the structure and categories of the human sciences at the close of the Enlightenment has much to commend it, but not the suggestion that the sciences of man first arose then, which this essay and indeed the whole of this collection seek to contradict.

4. In Book III, part 1, section 1 of David Hume's *Treatise of Human Nature*, dating from 1739–40. For diverse interpretations of the sense of that distinction, see W. D. Hudson, ed., *The Is-Ought Question* (London: Macmillan and Co., 1969). Modern critiques of ethical naturalism have often been traced to this passage in Hume. For other commentaries on the putative disjunction of facts from values in eighteenth-century moral philosophy, see Arthur Prior, *Logic and the Basis of Ethics* (Oxford: Clarendon Press, 1949), and David Raphael, *The Moral Sense* (London: Oxford University Press, 1947).

5. Jean-Jacques Rousseau, *Emile*, livre 3, in his *Œuvres complètes*, ed. Bernard Gagnebin and Marcel Raymond et al. (Paris: Gallimard, 1959–), vol. 4, p. 468; Edmund Burke, *A Letter to a Member of the National Assembly* (1791), in his *Writings and Speeches*, vol. 8: *The French Revolution, 1790–94*, ed. L. G. Mitchell (Oxford: Clarendon Press, 1989), 312–314.

6. Daniel Mornet's *Origines intellectuelles de la Révolution française, 1715–1787* (Paris: Armand Colin, 1933) is still perhaps the best known, if now rather dated, treatment of the Revolution's Enlightenment seeds. W. F. Church, ed., *The Influence of the Enlightenment on the French Revolution: Creative, Disastrous, or Non-existent?* (Boston: Heath, 1964), offers selections from prominent commentaries mainly of the nineteenth and twentieth centuries. Important recent contributions to the subject include K. M. Baker, ed., *The Political Culture of the Old Regime*, vol. 1 of *The French Revolution and the Creation of Modern Political Culture* (Oxford and New York: Pergamon Press, 1987); idem, *Inventing the French Revolution* (Cambridge: Cambridge University Press, 1990); Roger Chartier, *Les origines culturelles de la Révolution française* (Paris: Seuil, 1990); André Delaporte, *L'idée d'égalité en France au XVIIIe siècle* (Paris: Presses Universitaires de France, 1987); François Furet and Mona Ozouf, eds., *Dictionnaire critique de la Révolution française* (Paris: Flammarion, 1988); and Emmet Kennedy, *A Cultural History of the French Revolution* (New Haven, Conn.: Yale University Press, 1989).

7. See Vincent Hope, *Virtue by Consensus: The Moral Philosophy of Hutcheson, Hume, and Adam Smith* (Oxford: Clarendon Press, 1989); Marcello Maestro, *Cesare*

Beccaria and the Origins of Penal Reform (Philadelphia: Temple University Press, 1973); Giuseppe Zarone, *Etica e politica nell'utilitarismo di Cesare Beccaria* (Naples: Ist. Italiano Studi Storico, 1971); Peter Gay, *Voltaire's Politics: The Poet as Realist* (Princeton, N.J.: Princeton University Press, 1959); David Miller, *Philosophy and Ideology in Hume's Political Thought* (Oxford: Clarendon Press, 1981); Ross Harrison, (London: Routledge and Kegan Paul, 1983); and Shirley Letwin, *The Pursuit of Certainty* (Cambridge: Cambridge University Press, 1965).

8. See Elizabeth Fox-Genovese, *The Origins of Physiocracy: Economic Revolution and Social Order in Eighteenth-Century France* (Ithaca, N.Y.: Cornell University Press, 1976); Steven L. Kaplan, *Bread, Politics, and Political Economy in the Reign of Louis XV,* 2 vols. (The Hague: Martinus Nijhoff, 1976); and Georges Weulersse, *Le mouvement physiocratique en France, de 1756 a 1770* (1910; reprint, Paris: Alcan, 1968); idem, *La physiocratie à la fin du règne de Louis XV (1770–1774)* (Paris: Presses Universitaires de France, 1959); idem, *La physiocratie sous les ministères de Turgot et de Necker (1774–1781)* (Paris: Presses Universitaires de France, 1950).

9. See Pierangelo Schiera, *Il cameralismo e l'assolutismo tedesco: Dall'arte di governo alle scienza dello stato* (Milan: Giuffrè, 1968); Albion Small, *The Cameralists, the Pioneers of German Social Policy* (1909; reprint, New York: Burt Franklin, 1962); and Keith Tribe, *Governing Economy: The Reformation of German Economic Discourse, 1750– 1840* (Cambridge: Cambridge University Press, 1988).

10. For Diderot's use of the expression "despotisme éclairé," see his *Mémoires pour Catherine II,* in his *Oeuvres politiques,* ed. Paul Vernière (Paris: Garnier, 1963), 116, and John Hope Mason and Robert Wokler, eds., *Diderot's Political Writings* (Cambridge: Cambridge University Press, 1992), 207–208. On the theory and practice of enlightened despotism in the eighteenth century, see Matthew S. Anderson, *Historians and Eighteenth-Century Europe, 1715–1789* (Oxford: Clarendon Press, 1979); Stuart Andrews, *Enlightened Despotism* (London: Longman, 1967); Derek Beales, *Joseph II,* vol. 1: *In the Shadow of Maria Theresa* (Cambridge: Cambridge University Press, 1987); François Bluche, *Le Despotisme éclairé* (Paris: Fayard, 1968); Klaus Epstein, *The Genesis of German Conservatism* (Princeton, N.J.: Princeton University Press, 1966); Franklin Kopitzch, ed., *Aufklärung, Absolutismus und Bürgertum in Deutschland* (Munich: Nymphenburger Verlagshandlung, 1976); Leonard Krieger, *Kings and Philosophers, 1689–1789* (New York: W. Norton, 1980); Isabel de Madariaga, *Russia in the Age of Catherine the Great* (London: Weidenfeld and Nicolson, 1981); Wolfgang Neugebauer, *Absolutischer Staat und Schulwirklichkeit in Brandenburg-Preussen* (Berlin: de Gruyter, 1985); Gerhard Ritter, *Frederick the Great: An Historical Profile* (1936, in German; reprint, Berkeley and Los Angeles: University of California Press, 1968); and H. M. Scott, ed., *Enlightened Absolutism: Reform and Reformers in Later Eighteenth-Century Europe* (Basingstoke: Macmillan, 1990).

11. See Mason and Wokler, *Diderot's Political Writings,* introduction, and "Articles from the *Encyclopédie*"; Anthony Strugnell, *Diderot's Politics: A Study of the Evolution, of Diderot's Political Thought after the 'Encyclopédie'* (The Hague: Nijhoff, 1973); Immanuel Kant, "On the Common Saying: 'This May be True in Theory, but it does not apply in Practice,'" in *Kant's Political Writings,* ed. Hans Reiss (Cambridge: Cambridge University Press, 1970); Hans Saner, *Kant's Political Thought: Its Origins and Development* (1967, in German; reprint, Chicago: University of Chicago Press, 1973); and Murray Forsyth, *Reason and Revolution: The Political Thought of the Abbé Sieyes* (Leicester: Leicester University Press, 1987).

12. See especially Jean-Jacques Rousseau's *Contrat social*, II.ii–iii and III.xv; Richard Fralin, *Rousseau and Representation* (New York: Columbia University Press, 1978); Roger D. Masters, *The Political Philosophy of Rousseau* (Princeton, N.J.: Princeton University Press, 1968); Judith N. Shklar, *Men and Citizens: A Study of Rousseau's Social Theory*, 2d ed. (Cambridge: Cambridge University Press, 1985); and Paule-Monique Vernes, *La ville, la fête, la démocratie: Rousseau et les illusions de la communauté* (Paris: Payot, 1978). The most notable study of Rousseau's political theory in its historical context is still Robert Derathé's *Jean-Jacques Rousseau et la science politique de son temps* (1950; reprint, Paris: J. Vrin, 1970). On Rousseau's conception of the general will and its antecedents, see Patrick Riley, *The General Will before Rousseau: The Transformation of the Divine into the Civic* (Princeton, N.J.: Princeton University Press, 1986).

13. On utopian socialism in the Enlightenment, see especially Bronislaw Baczko, *Utopian Lights: The Evolution of the Idea of Social Progress* (1978, in French; reprint, New York: Paragon House, 1989); Walter Bernardi, *Morelly e Dom Deschamps: Utopia e ideologia nel secolo dei lumi* (Florence: Olschki, 1979); Brigitte Coste, *Mably: Pour une utopie du bon sens* (Paris: Klincksieck, 1975); Robert B. Rose, *Gracchus Babeuf, the first revolutionary Communist* (Stanford: Stanford University Press, 1978); Hans Ulrich Thamer, *Revolution und Reaktion in der französischen Sozialkritik des 18.Jahrhunderts* (Frankfurt: Akademische Verlagsgesellschaft, 1973); and Franco Venturi, *Utopia and Reform in the Enlightenment* (Cambridge: Cambridge University Press, 1971).

14. On liberal political economy and the science of legislation in the period, see Maurice M. Goldsmith, *Private Vices, Public Benefits: Bernard Mandeville's Social and Political Thought* (Cambridge: Cambridge University Press, 1985); Knud Haakonssen, *The Science of a Legislator: The Natural Jurisprudence of David Hume and Adam Smith* (Cambridge: Cambridge University Press, 1981); Oscar Nuccio, *Economisti italiani del XVIII secolo* (Rome: Bizzarri, 1974); Richard F. Teichgraeber III, *"Free Trade" and Moral Philosophy: Rethinking the Sources of Adam Smith's 'Wealth of Nations'* (Durham, N.C.: Duke University Press, 1986); Franco Venturi, *Italy and the Enlightenment: Studies in a Cosmopolitan Century* (London: Longman, 1972); and Donald Winch, *Adam Smith's Politics: An Essay in Historiographic Revision* (Cambridge: Cambridge University Press, 1978).

15. See Montesquieu's *De l'esprit des lois*, Book XI, and David Hume's "That Politics may be Reduced to a Science," in his *Essays: Moral, Political, and Literary*. For commentaries on Montesquieu and Hume, see especially F. T. H. Fletcher, *Montesquieu and English Politics (1750–1800)* (London: Edward Arnold, 1939); Henry J. Merry, *Montesquieu's System of Natural Government* (West Lafayette, Ind.: Purdue University Studies, 1970); Melvin Richter, *The Political Theory of Montesquieu* (Cambridge: Cambridge University Press, 1977); Robert Shackleton, *Montesquieu: A Critical Biography* (1961; reprint, Oxford: Oxford University Press, 1970); Duncan Forbes, *Hume's Philosophical Politics* (Cambridge: Cambridge University Press, 1975); Knud Haakonssen, ed. *Hume's Political Essays* (Cambridge: Cambridge University Press, 1994); Jonathan Harrison, *Hume's Theory of Justice* (Oxford: Oxford University Press, 1981); David Miller, *Philosophy and Ideology in Hume's Political Thought* (Oxford: Clarendon Press, 1981); and Ernest Mossner, *The Life of David Hume* (1954; reprint, London: Clarendon Press, 1970).

16. On the Enlightenment and American revolutionary political thought, see

especially R. R. Palmer, *The Age of the Democratic Revolution*, 2 vols. (Princeton, N.J.:
Princeton University Press, 1959–64); John R. Pole, *Political Representation in En-
gland and the Origins of the American Republic* (London: Macmillan, 1966); Garry
Wills, *Inventing America: Jefferson's Declaration of Independence* (Garden City, N.Y.:
Doubleday, 1978); idem, *Cincinnatus: George Washington and the Enlightenment* (Gar-
den City, N.Y.: Doubleday, 1984); and Gordon S. Wood, *The Creation of the American
Republic, 1776–1787* (Chapel Hill, N.C.: University of North Carolina Press, 1969).

17. On social contract theory, see J. W. Gough, *The Social Contract: A Critical
Study of Its Development*, 2d ed. (Oxford: Clarendon Press, 1957); David Gauthier,
Morals by Agreement (Oxford: Clarendon Press, 1986); Michael Lessnoff, *Social
Contract* (London: Macmillan, 1986); Michael Levin, "The Social Contract," in
Dictionary of the History of Ideas, ed. Philip Wiener (New York: Scribner, 1973–74),
4:251–263; and Riley, *Will and Political Legitimacy: A Critical Exposition of Social
Contract Theory in Hobbes, Locke, Rousseau, Kant, and Hegel* (Cambridge, Mass.: Har-
vard University Press, 1982).

18. I have in mind especially John Rawls's *A Theory of Justice* (Cambridge, Mass.:
Belknap Press, 1971). See also Norman Daniels, ed., *Reading Rawls: Critical Studies
in Rawls' "A Theory of Justice"* (Oxford: Basil Blackwell, 1975).

19. See especially Albert O. Hirschman, *The Passions and the Interests: Political
Arguments for Capitalism before its Triumph* (Princeton: Princeton University Press,
1977), and Ronald Meek, *Social Science and the Ignoble Savage* (Cambridge: Cambridge University Press, 1976).

20. See my "Anthropology and Conjectural History in the Enlightenment,"
chapter 2, page 37, in this book.

21. See Samuel Pufendorf's *De jure naturaé et gentium*, II.i.6, II.iii.15, II.iii.20,
and IV.iv.2. If some of my points here about the place of certain theories of human
nature in Enlightenment political science appear to recapitulate my remarks in
the earlier chapter, that is because social contract theory in the period so often
formed a part of its conjectural histories of man's development. See also Istvan
Hont, "The Language of Sociability and Commerce," in *The Languages of Political
Theory in Early-Modern Europe*, ed. Anthony Pagden (Cambridge: Cambridge University Press, 1987), 253–276; Fiammetta Palladini, *Discussioni seicentesche su Samuel
Pufendorf* (Bologna: Il Mulino, 1978); idem, *Samuel Pufendorf discepolo di Hobbes*
(Bologna: Il Mulino, 1990); and Haakonssen, *The Science of a Legislator.*

22. See Rousseau's *Contrat social*, III.xv, in his *Oeuvres complètes*, 3:429–430.

23. For fuller treatments of the themes of Rousseau's political thought covered
in the last two paragraphs, see my "Perfectible Apes in Decadent Cultures: Rousseau's Anthropology Revisited," *Daedalus* (Summer 1978): 107–134; idem, "Rousseau's Two Concepts of Liberty," in *Lives, Liberties, and the Public Good: New Essays in
Political Theory for Maurice Cranston*, ed. George Feaver and Fred Rosen (London:
Macmillan, 1987), 61–100; and idem., "Rousseau's Pufendorf: Natural Law and
the Foundations of Commercial Society," in *History of Political Thought* 15 (1994):
373–402.

24. See Baczko, *Utopian Lights*, 217–310.

25. The most substantial treatment of Rousseau's influence upon the course of
the French Revolution is to be found in the notes and commentaries of the last
nine volumes (XLI–XLIX) of R. A. Leigh's magisterial edition of the *Correspondance complète de Rousseau* (Geneva, Banbury, and Oxford: The Voltaire Founda-

tion, 1965–). See also Roger Barny, *Rousseau dans la Révolution: Le personnage de Jean-Jacques et les débuts du culte révolutionnaire, Studies on Voltaire and the Eighteenth Century*, vol. 246 (1986); idem, *L'éclatement révolutionnaire du rousseauisme* (Paris: Belles Lettres, 1988); Carol Blum, *Rousseau and the Republic of Virtue* (Ithaca, N.Y.: Cornell University Press, 1986); Norman Hampson, *Will and Circumstance: Montesquieu, Rousseau, and the French Revolution* (London: Duckworth, 1983); Joan McDonald, *Rousseau and the French Revolution: 1762–1791* (London: Athlone Press, 1965); and James Miller, *Rousseau: Dreamer of Democracy* (New Haven, Conn.: Yale University Press, 1984).

26. On the philosophy of Helvétius and its reception, see especially D. W. Smith, *Helvétius: A Study in Persecution* (Oxford: Oxford University Press, 1965). On d'Holbach, see William H. Wickwar, *Baron d'Holbach: A Prelude to the French Revolution* (London: Allen and Unwin, 1935).

27. On the hostility to Christianity of Enlightenment philosophies of history, see especially K. M. Baker, *Condorcet: From Natural Philosophy to Social Mathematics* (Chicago: University of Chicago Press, 1975); Peter Gay, *The Party of Humanity: Essays in the French Enlightenment* (London: Weidenfeld and Nicolson, 1964); idem, *The Enlightenment: An Interpretation*, 2 vols. (London: Weidenfeld and Nicolson, 1967–70), vol. 1: *The Rise of Modern Paganism*; Frank E. Manuel, *The Eighteenth Century Confronts the Gods* (Cambridge, Mass.: Harvard University Press, 1959); John McManners, *The French Revolution and the Church* (London: S.P.C.K., 1969); and R. R. Palmer, *Catholics and Unbelievers in Eighteenth-Century France*, 2d ed. (New York: Cooper Square Publishers, 1961).

28. A point pursued by Rousseau himself, in *Emile*, Livre V, where he remarks that Montesquieu failed to distinguish between political right and the positive law of established governments (see his *Œuvres complètes*, 4:836). Montesquieu's claim about the nature of laws introduces the first chapter of Book I of the *De l'esprit des lois*.

29. See especially Montesquieu's *De l'esprit des lois*, Book XIX.

30. On the passage from a science of politics to a science of society in the course of and soon after the French Revolution, see especially K. M. Baker, "Closing the Revolution: Saint-Simon and Comte," in *The Transformation of Political Culture, 1789–1848*, ed. François Furet and Mona Ozouf, vol. 3 of *The French Revolution and the Creation of Modern Political Culture* (Oxford and New York: Pergamon Press, 1989), 323–338; Brian Head, *Ideology and Social Science: Destutt de Tracy and French Liberalism* (Dordrecht: Nijhoff, 1985); Georges Gusdorf, *La conscience révolutionnaire: Les idéologues*, vol. 8 of his *Sciences humaines et la pensée occidentale* (Paris: Payot, 1978); Sergio Moravia, *Il pensiero degli idéologues: Scienza e filosofia in Francia (1780–1815)* (Florence: La Nuova Italia, 1974); and R. Wokler, "Saint-Simon and the Passage from Political to Social Science," in *Languages of Political Theory in Early-Modern Europe*, ed. Pagden, 325–338.

31. A few paragraphs of this essay are developed from material in my essay "The Enlightenment," in M. A. Riff, ed., *Dictionary of Modern Political Ideologies* (Manchester: Manchester University Press, 1987), 74–86. For correcting at least one dreadful oversight, or for extending a helpful hand in a fleeting moment, I am grateful to Istvan Hont, Geraint Parry, Maurizio Passerin d'Entrèves, and David Raphael.

INDEX

Designer: U.C. Press Staff
Compositor: Prestige Typography
Text: 10/12 Baskerville
Display: Baskerville
Printer: Maple-Vail Book Manufacturing
Binder: Maple-Vail Book Manufacturing